Microsoft®
Flight Simulator 98

OFFICIAL

Strategies & Secrets™

Ben Chiu

with Bruce Williams

and Bill Hoscheit

SYBEX®

San Francisco • Paris • Düsseldorf • Soest • London

ASSOCIATE PUBLISHER: **Roger Stewart**

CONTRACTS AND LICENSING MANAGER: **Kristine O'Callaghan**

ACQUISITIONS AND PUBLICATIONS MANAGER: **Dan Brodnitz**

ASSOCIATE MANAGING EDITOR GAME BOOKS: **Kari Brooks**

EDITORS: **Barbara Brodnitz and Sam Mills**

PRODUCTION EDITOR: **Nina Kreiden**

PROOFREADER: **Bill Weintraub**

BOOK DESIGN AND PRODUCTION: **Van Winkle Design Group**

ILLUSTRATOR: **Tony Jonick**

COVER DESIGN: **Calyx Design**

Library of Congress Card Number: 99-67009

ISBN: 0-7821-2634-0

Manufactured in the United States of America

10 9 8 7 6 5 4 3 2 1

To friendships—

Friends are our copilots in life. What makes a friend so special is they're not tied to us by blood—one must make conscious efforts to make and keep them. So when you're squawking 7700 on life's transponder and true friends come to your aid, a man can truly count himself blessed. Many thanks to my friends—I have basked in the warmth of your friendship and am deeply humbled.

—Ben Chiu

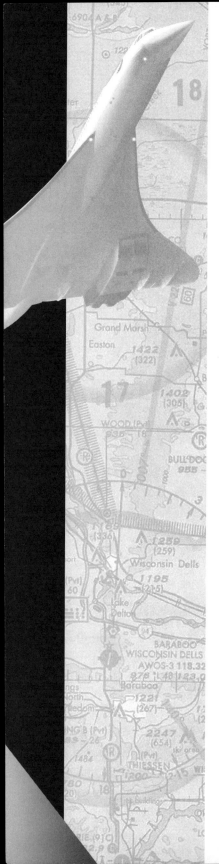

Acknowledgments

Just as a movie director tends to get the most credit for creating a film, the author often receives all the credit for a book. In both cases, it's really a group effort. I'd like to thank the following people for their tireless efforts and contributions to the production of this book.

Carlos Bea (ATP, CFII, Learjet Captain)

Daniel Brodnitz (Sybex)

Kari Brooks (Sybex)

Joseph Favors (Pratt and Whitney, ret.)

Bill Hoscheit (Microsoft MVP)

Nina Kreiden (Sybex)

Robert Lock (PC Press)

Rod Machado (ATP, CFII)

Tory McLearn (Sybex)

Mike Singer (S&T Onsite)

Michael Slingluff (Mooney Aircraft Corporation)

Diana Van Winkle (Book Production and Design)

Kit Warfield (Microsoft UA Lead)

Bill Weintraub (Proofreader)

Rhonda West (Private Pilot, 1999 Amelia Earhart Ninety-Nine's Aviation Scholarship Recipient)

Bruce Williams (CFII, Microsoft Flight Simulator Product Planner)

Charles G. Wiswell (ATP, Founder, Swift Airline, now known as Wings West)

Alan K. Yecny (FAA-Designated Pilot Examiner, Air San Luis)

Table of Contents

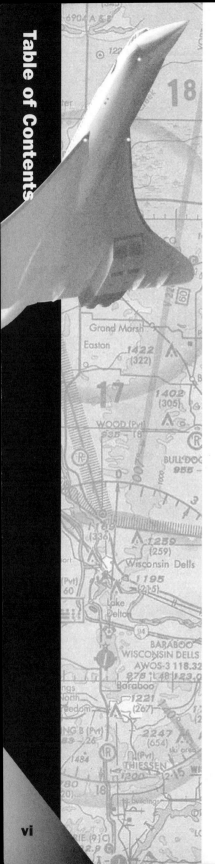

CHAPTER 7:
Taking the Long Way Around 179

CHAPTER 8:
Expanding Flight Simulator 2000's Horizons 229

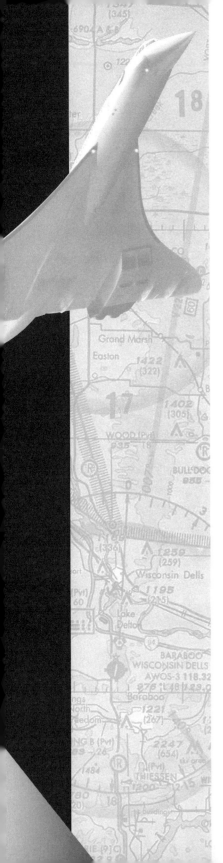

Foreword

Rod Machado

Ben Chiu loves aviation. You can see it in his eyes, hear it in his voice, and feel it in his writing. He's one of the fortunate few who find their passion early in life. Our good fortune is that Ben loves to communicate, and when it comes to writing, he's a real pro! Having written several books and a plethora of magazine articles on flight simulations, he's earned his place in this field as a respectable authority.

Ben's capabilities as an aviation educator, however, go beyond this deep understanding of simulations. As a licensed commercial pilot, he knows what makes airplanes fly and how to fly them. As a certified flight instructor, he knows how to talk about airplanes—both real and simulated—in terms everyone can understand.

So tighten your seatbelt, put your hands on the controls, and throttle up: Ben's about to take you to a higher level of aviation understanding. You'll learn how to navigate airplanes ranging in size from four place trainers to aerodynamically svelte Mach-busters equipped with sophisticated cockpit instrumentation. And you'll learn to do it like a real pilot flying a real airplane. Prepare for a unique thrill the first time you navigate to a distant airport, shoot an instrument approach, and land with reduced visibility. The moment those wheels kiss the runway you'll feel that special pride that comes from learning and applying professional flight skills successfully.

This is what makes aviation a passionate enterprise. It's exciting, it's challenging, and it attracts talented people like Ben. Therefore, I congratulate you for finding such an excellent educator. You're in the hands of a very capable flight instructor.

—*Rod Machado*

Flight instructor, author, educator, humorist

http://www.rodmachado.com

Preface

Welcome to the *Microsoft Flight Simulator 2000 Official Strategies & Secrets* guide from Sybex! Meeting the new millennium head-on, *Microsoft Flight Simulator 2000* is the latest incarnation of the most popular computer entertainment title of all time, and the most well-rounded civilian flight simulation out there today. It's hard to believe, but *Flight Simulator* has been around for 17 years and it's going stronger than ever.

One of the things that many new pilots observe early on is that aviation is a huge subject. It almost seems like the more you learn, the less you know. As flight simulations become more and more realistic, the complexities of real-world aviation become integral to the experience. When I designed the Inside Moves series of *Flight Simulator* books for Microsoft Press a couple of years ago, I knew I couldn't possibly relate everything there is to know about the subject in a single book. That's why I planned the original series around distinct levels of knowledge.

The first book, *Microsoft Flight Simulator 98: Inside Moves* (Microsoft Press, 1997; note that this is *not Flight Simulator 2000: Inside Moves*), covers basic *Flight Simulator* configuration and usage essentials, from aviation conventions to basic flight maneuvers and instrumentation. *Instrument Flight Techniques with Flight Simulator 98* (also Microsoft Press, 1998; written with Rod Machado, creator of the flight lessons in *Flight Simulator 2000* and the *Flight Simulator 2000 Pilot's Handbook*), goes over the finer points of aircraft handling technique. It also covers aviation theory, including chart-reading and instrument procedures. If, after reading the manual and this book, you need more information on any of these topics, I highly recommend the foregoing titles (and not just because I wrote them). Although they were originally written for the previous version of *Flight Simulator*, the concepts, flight procedures, and conventions remain valid.

This guide picks up where those books left off. To get as much new information as possible into this book, I've made every attempt not to repeat information you can find in the *Flight Simulator 2000* package or my earlier books. I won't rehash emergency procedures, aerobatics, or anything else those sources cover. In this book you'll learn how to get where you want to go. It introduces aircraft flight procedures, systems, and simulation features new in *Flight Simulator 2000* and *Flight Simulator 2000 Professional Edition*. The information in these pages takes you to the next level of aviation knowledge and ties in with the knowledge you acquire from reading and completing Rod's lessons, and/or from earlier Inside Moves books.

Whether you're a new virtual VFR (Visual Flight Rules) student pilot, an IFR (Instrument Flight Rules) student, or a *Flight Simulator* veteran making the transition to the newest aircraft in the *Flight Simulator 2000* hangar, *Microsoft Flight Simulator 2000 Official Strategies & Secrets* is the comprehensive guide you seek. Please keep in mind that this guide is intended for use with *Microsoft Flight Simulator 2000* and cannot replace actual flight training from a Certified Flight Instructor.

Clear skies. Smooth landings. And welcome to the world of *Microsoft Flight Simulator* in the 21st century!

—*Ben Chiu*

http://www.benchiu.com

How to Use This Book

This book is divided into 10 chapters that contain 6 tutorials. When relying solely on printed media and dealing with complex tasks such as flight operations, tutorials have proven to be the best method of introducing pilots to new aircraft, systems, and procedures.

Each chapter in this book presents a new method of navigation or new navigation system and related aircraft procedures. The tutorial chapters range from simple to complex in technical theory and cockpit workload. Each new tutorial builds on skills and knowledge acquired from the one before. Thus, it's best to tackle each chapter in order.

Flight plans developed by notable real-world private pilots, certified flight instructors, and airline transport pilots lie at the heart of each tutorial. You'll learn how things are done and, perhaps more important, *when* to do them.

Finally, this guide focuses especially on the new aircraft *Flight Simulator 2000* introduces. For more detailed information about specific aircraft carried over from previous versions, refer to the titles I recommended in the introductory paragraphs.

Features

Again, in the following chapters you'll acquaint yourself first with simple concepts, and then move on to more complex ones. Because we cover two versions of *Flight Simulator 2000* here, Chapters 6 and 7 feature aircraft exclusive to *Flight Simulator 2000 Professional Edition*, the Mooney Bravo and Raytheon (Beechcraft) King Air 350. Even though these chapters feature aircraft your version may not include, the navigation concepts and features apply to most other aircraft. You can and should fly the tutorials in these chapters with one of the other aircraft.

Flight Simulator 2000 Professional Edition includes 6 additional cities, as well: Boston, Washington, D.C., Seattle, Berlin, Rome, and Tokyo. Although some tutorials fly into or out of a couple of cities included only in *Flight Simulator 2000 Professional Edition*, there's enough detail in *Flight Simulator 2000*'s standard version to complete those flights accurately.

I've arranged the chapters as follows:

+ Chapter 1, "Check Before Flight," covers software configuration essentials and supplemental hardware tips and recommendations to help make your virtual flight experiences as productive and enjoyable as possible. We'll also cover some of the important details about *Flight Simulator 2000*'s interface and important terminology we'll be using throughout the book.

✝ Chapter 2, "Getting from Point A to Point B," provides the simplest answer to that nagging question, "How do I get to where I want to go?" I'll introduce pilotage and the most fundamental aspects of aviation navigation. Then you'll take the Sopwith Camel up for a VFR flight from Santa Monica to Chino, California.

✝ Chapter 3, "Asking for Directions and Arriving on Schedule," offers a step-by-step tour of how VFR radio navigation increases flight accuracy. You'll fly from America's busiest municipal airport— Van Nuys—through Los Angeles International's busy Class B airspace and a quick landing at Torrance/Zamperini Field in the Cessna 182RG.

✝ Chapter 4, "Computers in the Cockpit," ties the segments of IFR flight into a complete flight plan to show you how it all fits together. I introduce the Boeing 777-300's advanced features and you'll fly this technological wonder from New York's John F. Kennedy International Airport to an ILS (Instrument Landing System) Category III approach into Chicago's O'Hare International Airport.

✝ In Chapter 5, "Supersonic Flight," we discuss the technical hurdles and characteristics of supersonic aviation. You'll take the fabulous Concorde on a supersonic flight from London's Heathrow International Airport into New York's John F. Kennedy International Airport.

✝ Chapter 6, "In Through the Out Door: Flying a LOC BC," details the intricacies of flying the world's fastest production piston single, the Mooney Bravo, on a flight from Los Angeles International to a localizer back course approach into Santa Maria Public Airport (also in California).

✝ In Chapter 7, "Taking the Long Way Around," you'll fly the turboprop King Air 350 on a flight from Seattle–Tacoma International Airport down to Victorville–Southern California International Airport. This flight culminates with the oft-misunderstood (and feared!) DME arc approach.

✝ In Chapter 8, "Expanding *Flight Simulator 2000*'s Horizons," Microsoft MVP Bill Hoscheit examines *Flight Simulator 2000*'s nearly limitless expansion potential for incorporating aftermarket aircraft, scenery, and utilities.

✝ In Chapter 9, "*Flight Simulator* as a Training Aid," Microsoft Flight Simulator Product Planner and CFII Bruce Williams discusses the finer points of how the skills you acquire during your time with *Flight Simulator 2000* can augment real-world flight training.

✝ Chapter 10, "You're Never Alone…When You're Flying on the Zone," introduces multiplayer *Flight Simulator 2000* flight and online resources.

✝ Finally, the book's three appendices provide selected VFR Terminal and IFR Terminal Procedure charts and plates, as well as a handy keyboard command reference.

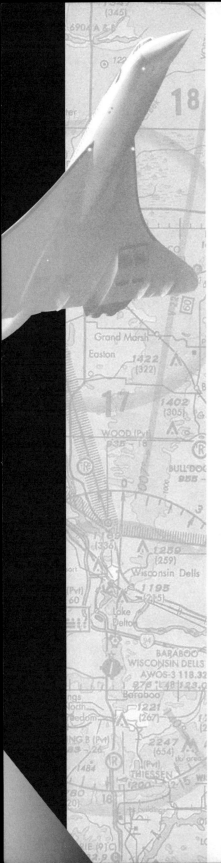

A Letter from the Publisher

Dear Reader,

At Sybex, our goal is to bring you the best game strategy guides money can buy. We hire the best authors in the business, and we bring our love of games to the look and feel of the books. We hope you see all of that reflected in the strategy guide you're holding in your hands right now.

The important question is: How well do YOU think we're doing?

Are we providing you with the kind of in-depth, hardcore gaming content you crave? Is the material presented in a way you find both useful and attractive? Are there other approaches and/or types of information you'd like to see but just aren't getting? Or, are our books so perfect that you're considering nominating them for a Pulitzer this year?

Your comments and suggestions are always valuable. We want to encourage even more feedback from our readers and make it even easier for you to get in touch with us. To that end, we've created an e-mailbox for your feedback. We invite you to send your comments, criticism, praise, and suggestions to gamesfeedback@sybex.com and let us know what you think.

We can't guarantee we'll respond to every message; but we can promise we'll read them all, take them to heart, and then print them out and use the hard copy to make festive hats for everyone in the building.

Most of all, we'll use your feedback to continuously improve the quality of our books. So please, let us hear from you!

Roger Stewart
Associate Publisher

Check
Before Flight

Chapter 1

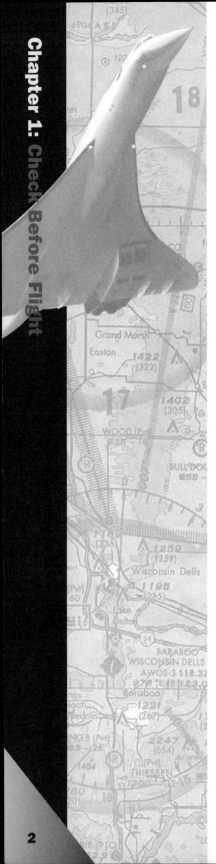

*J*ust as any good pilot determines that an aircraft is airworthy before taking off, a virtual pilot should do the same. Although there are no risks to your person or your computer if you just jump into Flight Simulator 2000 *and take off, a little time spent setting up correctly for your intended flight can head off needless frustrations and make your overall virtual flight experience much more enjoyable.*

In this chapter, we'll discuss several Flight Simulator 2000 *configuration setups and controller recommendations. We'll also seek to familiarize you with a couple of the features and concepts you'll encounter often throughout the rest of the book. So if you're ready, let's get started so that we can get up in the air as quickly as possible.*

Recommended Configurations

Flight Simulator 2000's Display, Sound, Realism, Instrument, and Controller setting options affect how your aircraft behaves within the simulation. The ideal configuration for your flights depends on your hardware and the type of flying you intend to do. We'll specify critical configuration settings within each tutorial, but the following basic guidelines will get you started.

Display Settings

Ever since the earliest computer games, unless you owned the fastest computer on the planet (and that was never a guaranty either), we have been forced to choose between eye-pleasing graphics and smooth graphics performance. In the last couple of years, hardware technology has made gains on processor-hungry simulation software, but the software still leads. If you're not up to date with the latest and greatest hardware (join the club), you'll have to make some compromises.

The term *frame rate* refers to how many times per second the screen graphics are updated. Don't confuse this with your monitor's or graphic card's refresh rates. Frame rates dictate how smoothly an image moves on your screen; refresh rates control how often your screen is redrawn. For example, if your frame rate is too low, an image will move in perceivable steps, rather than in a smooth motion. If your refresh rate is too slow, your screen will appear to flicker, regardless of whether an image is moving.

Refresh rates are strictly hardware (monitor and graphics card) controlled, but other than possibly giving you a headache, they won't much affect how your *Flight Simulator* aircraft moves across your screen. (Some older graphics cards lose frame-rate performance when you set them to high refresh rates.)

Fortunately, frame rates are controlled by a combination of graphics card performance, system speed, and software configurations. The faster your frame rate, the smoother the image motion appears. Smooth frame rates may seem a matter of aesthetics, but there's more to it. Even if your frame rate is slow, your system recognizes control inputs at a closer-to-normal (read "faster") speed.

As frame rates decrease, the gap between what you see and what your computer "sees" widens. Problems occur when this mismatch is so great that your aircraft becomes uncontrollable. By the time the screen reacts to your control input, you may already have overcorrected or overcontrolled the aircraft based on a previous image motion.

Minimum frame-rate tolerances vary, but most people find anything less than 15 frames per second too jerky. Again, what's tolerable or acceptable also depends on the type of flying you do. For example, if you're out sightseeing, you can usually afford to sacrifice a few frames in favor of more detailed graphics, but if you're flying serious IFR you'll favor faster instrument updates over pretty terrain objects (that you're unlikely to see while you're in the clouds anyway).

To bring up the frame rate display, press Shift+Z twice (Figure 1.1). Note that your frame rate decreases as graphics resolution, color depth, objects, number of windows, and window sizes increase. Because so many variables are involved, we'll discuss only how each of *Flight Simulator 2000*'s settings affect your frame rates. From there, you'll have to experiment with what works best for your situation and flight objectives.

> ▶ **Warning**
>
> *There's a lower limit for frame rates. It does little good to keep your graphics detail very high if your frame rates become so low you must constantly rekite your airplane by crashing into the ground.*

```
FRAMES/SEC = 013.8  +1.0 Gs
```

Figure 1.1:
Use the Frame Rate display to determine optimum *Flight Simulator 2000* **configurations.**

Hardware Settings

To reach the Hardware Settings tab (Figure 1.2), from the Options menu select Settings, Display, and then Display Settings. Here are some recommendations and insights into how each setting affects graphics performance.

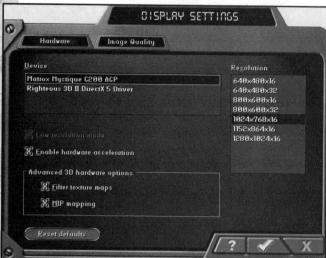

Figure 1.2:
Locate the Hardware
Settings tab in the
Display Settings
window.

Device
Select the fastest graphics device/card you have in your system. Note that you must run some graphics cards based on chipsets such as the 3Dfx Voodoo II in full-screen mode—press Alt+Enter to toggle between full-screen and window modes—to use them in 3D accelerated mode. If you plan on using features that display in a separate 2D window (which won't show up in full-screen mode), select a graphics device that can accelerate graphics in windowed (non–full-screen) mode.

Low Resolution Mode
Use this setting only if your system is close to or at the minimum recommended system specification written on the outside of the *Flight Simulator 2000* box. You can select this mode only if you have a nonaccelerated graphics card.

Enable Hardware Acceleration
If the graphics device you selected is a 3D accelerator, this should apply automatically. If it didn't, enable this box. You must enable this option to select any of the 3D-only accelerators in the Device box.

Filter Texture Maps
This setting is available only if you've enabled the hardware acceleration box. It smoothes textures, removing their blocky appearance. Whether this option affects your frame rate significantly depends on your graphics card.

MIP Mapping
This setting, too, is available only if the hardware acceleration box is enabled. MIP (*multim in parvum,* which means many things in a small place) mapping is the method some graphics cards employ to create an illusion of depth. If your graphics card supports MIP mapping well, enabling this setting may improve *Flight Simulator 2000*'s appearance and frame rate.

Resolution

Select *Flight Simulator 2000*'s screen resolution and color depth here. Generally, the higher the resolution and the color depth, the slower your frame rate. But many of today's 3D accelerator cards allow for higher screen resolutions and color depth with very little penalty. Experiment to see what your card can handle. In any case, higher screen resolutions make it easier to read your instruments. Increased color depth has less immediate visual impact.

▶ **Note**

The Resolution setting works with 2D cards, too.

Image Quality

Tweak *Flight Simulator 2000*'s image quality from the Image Quality tab, also located in the Display Settings window (see Figure 1.3). This is where you gain or lose the most graphics performance.

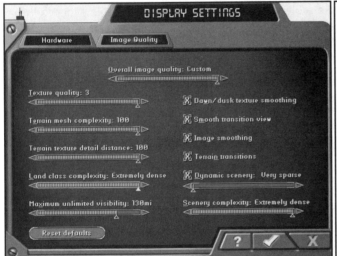

Figure 1.3:
To bring up the Image Quality dialog, click the appropriate tab at the top of the Display Settings window.

Due to the numerous variables involved, we'll only discuss how each of the following Image Quality settings affects your frame rates (if at all). From there you'll have to experiment with what works best for your hardware and flight objectives.

Overall Image Quality

This option affords you six preset levels of image quality (1–6), and a seventh user-configurable custom setting. The presets are a good place to start your quest for frames. Once you get in the ballpark, go ahead and play with the other settings to customize the look and feel.

Texture Quality

Choose from Texture Quality levels 0–3. Higher levels increase the intricacy of surface textures. Textures, of course, are graphic representations that mimic material surfaces. The value of this setting depends on your flight altitude. At higher altitudes you won't notice much visual difference at lower settings. (This setting has no effect if Terrain Texture Detail Distance is set to zero.)

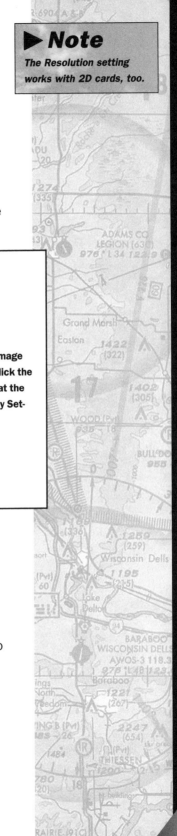

Terrain Mesh Complexity

You may adjust this setting, in 1 percent increments, from 0 to 100 percent. Higher settings increase the detail of the underlying terrain mesh. Terrain mesh basically connects a bunch of elevation points to make a "framework" for hanging textures. The more complex the mesh, the more elevations are recreated.

This setting has a great impact on your frame rate, relative to where you fly. It affects you more if you're flying over complex terrain (mountains for example). Terrain Mesh Complexity set down to the 40 to 60 percent range seems to afford the best performance on most machines.

Terrain Texture Detail Distance

This setting controls how far from your current position terrain textures are created—again, adjustable in 1 percent increments, from 0 to 100 percent. You'll take a bigger frame-rate hit as you move this slider to the right, so try to keep it as low as you can tolerate. At lower settings, you shouldn't miss the terrain textures if you're flying very low, very high, at low visibility, or in the clouds. A range of 40 to 60 percent provides best performance on most machines.

Land Class Complexity

Control the number of displayed terrain texture types using this setting. The seven Land Class Complexity settings are Extremely Sparse, Very Sparse, Sparse, Normal, Dense, Very Dense, and Extremely Dense. High settings provide a greater variety of textures for a more realistic terrain. Lower settings reduce those textures to just a few types; grasslands, for example, will show less variation.

As you'd expect, increasing this setting slows performance. Consider setting it no higher than Dense, and then only on high-end machines: cranking this setting up vastly increases the amount of texture pushed through your system, and the amount of terrain processing required for every frame. Higher settings may make things prettier at high altitudes and from farther away, but most of the time they're unnecessary.

Maximum Unlimited Visibility

This setting, stepped in 10-mile increments from 60 to 150 miles, applies only when you set Visibility to Unlimited in the Weather dialogue. (Refer to Chapter 2 for details on weather settings.) Higher settings reduce the amount of haze visible on the horizon.

Dawn/Dusk Texture Smoothing

This feature provides for gradual, realistic transitions between day and night (sunrises and sunsets). If you have a slower machine, enabling Dawn/Dusk Texture Smoothing may slow performance—but, as with other graphics-specific options, only when you're flying during these transitions.

Smooth Transition View

When enabled, this option inserts cinematic camera-tracking transitions when you switch views (cycled with the S key). This option affects your frame rate only if you switch camera views.

Image Smoothing

This feature is meant to smooth jagged edges (enabling it may decrease performance on slower machines). In reality, you'll find little visual difference between settings.

Terrain Transitions

Enabling this option allows textures to swap smoothly between scenery types. When it's disabled, you'll see generic color patches rather than textures for a period of time when you fly from one type of scenery to another. If you have a slower machine, enabling this option may decrease performance.

Dynamic Scenery Complexity

Dynamic scenery is the animated, computer-driven aircraft and ground vehicles populating certain airport areas.

There are six Dynamic Scenery complexity settings: Very Sparse, Sparse, Normal, Dense, Very Dense, and Extremely Dense. As you'd expect, the more you ask your computer to display, the slower your frame rate becomes. Because these animated objects move about on their own and your interaction with them is basically limited to staying out of their way, you can decide how valuable this feature is to your flight activities.

Scenery Complexity

The six Scenery Complexity settings are Very Sparse, Sparse, Normal, Dense, Very Dense, and Extremely Dense. This setting controls the number of visible ground objects. If you're out sightseeing, set this for Extremely Dense. If you're flying by ground references, set this option at least to Normal, or you'll lose features such as roads and rivers.

The level of frame rate loss you'll experience with this setting depends on the scenic area. For example, higher settings will affect your frame rate less in relatively empty desert scenes than in busier urban areas.

Sound Settings

To access the Sound Settings window (Figure 1.4), click on Sound in the Settings submenu. Whether or not sound settings will affect your frame rate depends on the speed of your system and the type of sound card or computer sound system you own. Some older sound cards rely on CPU (Central Processing Unit) power to operate, as do USB (Universal Serial Bus) sound systems. Of course, any processor cycles required to produce sound are taken away from graphics processing—reducing your frame rate.

▶ Note

Many third-party scenery designers include dynamic scenery within their products.

▶ Warning

You won't experience a frame rate reduction at the highest Dynamic Scenery Complexity setting when you're flying beyond airport areas that support dynamic scenery, so be aware that your frame rate may drop off radically when you enter such areas.

SOUND SETTINGS

☒ Engines

☒ Cockpit

☒ Environment

☒ Navigation

☒ Adventures

Figure 1.4:
Depending on your
sound hardware,
your sound settings
may or may not produce
a frame rate change.

Limiting some of *Flight Simulator 2000*'s sounds may produce a slight increase in frame rate if your sound system is of one of the afore-mentioned types. Sound volume is a matter of personal preference. Nevertheless, here are some guidelines:

Engines: This box toggles engine sounds. Although you may be tempted to turn off the seemingly endless engine drone during long flights, you might be better served by turning the volume slider down so you can hear audible alerts of engine failure (if they're enabled in System Failures).

Cockpit: Cockpit sounds include gear and flap operations, and stall and overspeed warning horns. These can give you an idea of whether your gear and flaps are working (although you still should check the indicators) and can warn you of potential problems. Enabling this option may help reduce cockpit workloads.

Environment: The Environment setting controls wind, wheel roll, and crash sounds. Although an audible alert for when your wheels touch the ground can be useful (given the lack of other sensory feedback), the other sounds are of little practical use.

Navigation: This option toggles navigation aid sounds, including radio station identification codes and ILS marker beacons. Regardless of whether you're flying IFR, you may want to keep this option enabled; it operates only part of the time, and radio station identification is directly under your control via key commands or mouse clicks.

Adventures: If you fly adventures, you must enable this option or lose the ability to hear the adventure's sounds—namely, *voices*. But the importance of voice sounds (such as ATIS—Automated Terminal Information Services) isn't restricted to adventures. If voice messages consume too much processing time you can turn them off and text messages will continue to display across the top of your screen.

▶ **Tip**

Press the Q key at any
time to toggle sounds on
and off.

Realism Settings

Flight Simulator 2000's aircraft realism settings are global settings. In other words, whatever settings you select here will affect every aircraft that you fly until you change them. Select the Aircraft menu option and click on Realism Settings from the drop-down menu to access the Realism Settings window (Figure 1.5).

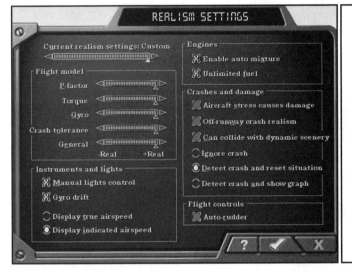

Figure 1.5:
You can select preset Realism Settings or create a custom configuration.

The three preset realism settings are Easy, Medium, and Hard. Table 1.1 shows how they differ. With a couple of exceptions, this book assumes that you'll be flying at the Hard setting. It's recommended that if you're fairly new to all of this, enable Ignore crash. Although it's not very realistic, the benefits should be obvious if you're just beginning.

Table 1.1: Preset Realism Settings

Setting	Easy	Medium	Hard
P-factor	0%	50%	100%
Torque	0%	50%	100%
Gyro	0%	50%	100%
Crash Tolerance	0%	50%	100%
General	0%	50%	100%
Manual Lights Control	—	—	X
Gyro Drift	—	X	X
Display True Airspeed	X	—	—
Display Indicated Airspeed	—	X	X
Enable Auto Mixture	X	X	—
Unlimited Fuel	X	—	—

continued on next page

Setting	Easy	Medium	Hard
Aircraft Stress Causes Damage	—	—	X
Off-runway Crash Realism	—	—	X
Can Collide with Dynamic Scenery	—	X	X
Ignore Crash	—	—	—
Detect Crash and Reset Situation	X	X	X
Detect Crash and Show Graph	—	—	—
Auto-rudder	X	X	—

The other exception is the Auto-rudder feature. If you don't own a rudder controller, you're better off letting *Flight Simulator 2000* handle rudder-control duty. But if you want to fly aerobatics, or practice crosswind landings and slips, you should disable Auto-rudder. Although there are those who can fly perfectly well controlling the rudder from the keyboard, it does make the task harder than it is in real life.

Instrument Settings

Select Instrument from the Settings submenu to reach the Instrument Settings window (Figure 1.6). Three options augment usability; the fourth can affect graphics performance. Here are some recommendations.

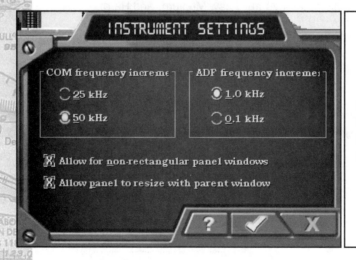

Figure 1.6:
One of these instrument settings can affect your graphics performance.

COM Frequency Increments

This option sets the increments—25 or 50 kHz—for tuning the COM (communications) radio. Because it moves in smaller increments, using the 25 kHz setting requires more key presses to change frequencies if you use keyboard commands rather than mouse clicks. If you fly within the U.S. and at lower altitudes, you can generally do with 50 kHz increments, but 25 kHz narrow-frequency channels are becoming more common. Your choice really depends on where you fly.

ADF Frequency Increments
ADF, of course, stands for Automatic Direction Finder. Options are 1 kHz or .1 kHz increments. As with COM frequency, smaller increments mean more key-pressing. If you fly within the U.S., you generally won't need the smaller increments.

Allow for Nonrectangular Panel Windows
This option allows instrument panels to be rendered in nonrectangular shapes. Not all video cards handle this feature well. All panels are rectangular, but parts of the window/panel that have other shapes (usually the corners) become transparent to create the illusion that they're not. If enabling this feature degrades your machine's performance, you have more to gain (and won't miss much) if you disable it.

Allow Panel to Resize with Parent Window
This option determines whether your instrument panel will resize with the *Flight Simulator 2000* window. If you resize that window often, disabling this option forces the instrument panel to retain its size and shape. This prevents the instrument panel from losing its proportions (round gauges becoming oval, for example) and instrument text from becoming illegible.

Controllers

Controller hardware is perhaps the most underestimated, most misunderstood, and yet most critical component for realistic simulation experiences. Quite simply, the proper controller, set up correctly, makes all the difference in the world. When you consider that these controllers (whether keyboard, mouse, dedicated flight controller, or a combination) provide your sole physical interface with *Flight Simulator 2000*'s virtual world, you'll appreciate their importance.

Controller Recommendations

It should come as no surprise that most people find a joystick or flight yoke easier to use for flying virtual aircraft than using a keyboard and mouse. Base the type of controller you select on the aircraft you intend to fly, personal preference, whether you'll be use it as a dedicated flight simulation controller, and, of course, cost.

In addition to physical layouts (joystick vs. yoke vs. gamepad or other controller), each controller type has its own characteristics to consider. Beyond the usual things (connector type, grip size, features, layout), characteristics such as travel (total movement from stop to stop), type of movement (viscous vs. spring-loaded), whether it's self-centering, and overall feel affect how realistically you'll perceive the experience. To some people, these are minor considerations. For those serious about their sim'ing realism, however, it's everything.

It doesn't feel like flying the real thing!

One of the most common complaint among pilots trying computer flight simulations for the first time is how x doesn't feel like its real-world counterpart. "Feel" is subjective, but if setup (installation and calibration) and physical differences (joysticks vs. yokes) aren't issues, there are other things to consider.

Feel is based on the size and mass of the control, amount and type of resistance, how that resistance is applied (springs, hydraulic pressure, aerodynamic forces that increase with airspeed, and/or artificial feedback), whether it self-centers or not, and total controller travel in relation to control surface movement. For example, if the real-world yoke has 10 inches of movement from full elevator down to full elevator up, and your computer yoke moves only 6 inches, your computer yoke (and virtual aircraft) will feel more sensitive.

Fortunately, Flight Simulator 2000 offers a few adjustments that can help compensate for variations in controller hardware. (Refer to this chapter's "Controls Sensitivities" section for more on this subject.)

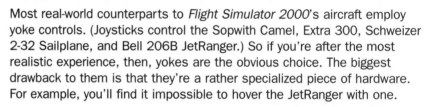

Yokes

Most real-world counterparts to *Flight Simulator 2000*'s aircraft employ yoke controls. (Joysticks control the Sopwith Camel, Extra 300, Schweizer 2-32 Sailplane, and Bell 206B JetRanger.) So if you're after the most realistic experience, then, yokes are the obvious choice. The biggest drawback to them is that they're a rather specialized piece of hardware. For example, you'll find it impossible to hover the JetRanger with one.

Flight yokes are available with a wide range of features (and prices!). CH Products' new Flight Sim Yoke line is the most well rounded example out there. Their yoke action has no center detent for pitch or roll axis movement. This makes for more realistic flight-control action and feel than their predecessors.

The Flight Sim Yoke is available in standard PC gameport and USB models. Features shared by the PC gameport version of its older siblings are an analog throttle lever, a four-way hat switch, and various button functions, including a gear switch, bi-directional flap switch, two two-way rocker switches, and three push buttons. The USB version shown in Figure 1.7 (not the less-capable USB LE) adds prop control and mixture control levers.

These features are valuable in complex simulations such as *Flight Simulator 2000* because the more you can access commands by moving levers or pressing buttons, the less you'll need to peck at a keyboard and memorize complex keystrokes. All things considered, the CH Flight Sim Yoke USB sets the standard in value, functionality, and realism for yoke controllers. Check out CH's Web site, http://www.chproducts.com/fltsimyoke.html, for more information.

Rudder Controllers

If you're into realism, fly with wind, or fly aerobatics, you'll need to control your rudder. Some people can manage rudder control via keyboard alone, but, again, using the keyboard makes this task harder than it is in real life—and makes hovering the helicopter impossible.

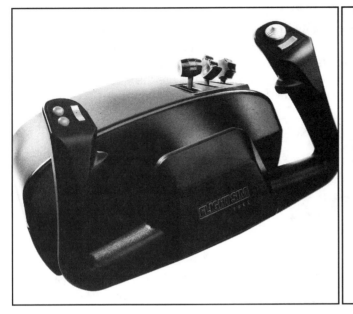

Figure 1.7:
CH Products' Flight Sim
Yoke USB features prop
and mixture levers.

Some joysticks have a built-in twist-action rudder-control function. As unnatural as that may sound, it works well once you get used to it. If you seek realism however, consider getting rudder pedals. The most important considerations here are connector type and compatibility with your other controllers. If you own a USB yoke or joystick, for example, standard gameport rudder pedals won't work with them.

CH Products' Pro Pedals (Figure 1.8) offers many sought-after features: they're available in gameport and USB versions, are small enough to fit comfortably below most desks, are compatible with most other controller systems, have gas-pedal and brake-pedal movement (for driving sims), and—perhaps most important—they're reasonably priced.

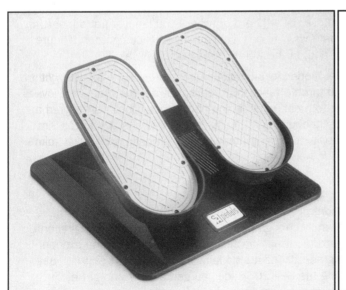

Figure 1.8:
CH Products' Pro
Pedals is available in
gameport and USB
versions.

Joysticks

Joysticks, which work well for simulations and many other types of games, are the most versatile controllers. If you can concede some realism, and play a lot of other games or air-combat sims, a joystick is a great choice. Get a stick with at least one view hat (see Figure 1.9), however, and extra buttons (beyond the standard two found on basic models).

Figure 1.9:
The F-16 Fighterstick from CH Products has one eight-way hat switch, three four-way hat switches, three single-fire buttons, a trigger, trim controls, and a rotary throttle.

The joystick may seem like the most cost-conscious choice, but be aware that joysticks vary in quality. If you buy a really cheap stick from some company you've never heard of (where you'll never get support for it), you'll likely waste your money. Poor-quality joysticks go out of calibration easily, and, in the worst cases, simply break.

Other considerations include additional features, such as twist-action rudder control and throttle functions. Realism aside, they can save you a lot of money—not to mention desk and floor space. Consider programming features, as well. Although *Flight Simulator 2000* allows you to reassign commands, the ability to program multiple key presses and/or key combinations can come in handy.

▶ **Warning**

A stiff joystick—one that strongly resists moving off-center—will hinder your ability to hover helicopters in Flight Simulator 2000.

Throttles

Out of all of the controllers we'll discuss, throttle controllers are the least critical. You'll generally change power settings only once per flight-configuration change (instrument approaches and landings being the exceptions), and if you're flying aerobatics it's usually full-on or full-off. But if you're thinking of hovering the Bell 206B, do yourself a favor and get a dedicated throttle controller (if your joystick doesn't have a throttle function on it already).

Most stand-alone throttle controllers are packed with additional programmable buttons and switches. Some throttles will even allow you to program your joystick, as well. Naturally, if your main controller (joystick or yoke) has a throttle function already, a stand-alone throttle is unnecessary, and may not even work.

Controls Sensitivities

The other critical aspect of controllers is in their setup. Even if you've got the best controllers known to man, if they're installed and/or set up incorrectly they'll ruin your experience by causing unrealistic aircraft responses. *Flight Simulator 2000* allows you to compensate for differences in controller hardware via the Controls Sensitivities window (Figure 1.10), accessed by choosing Sensitivities in the Controls submenu.

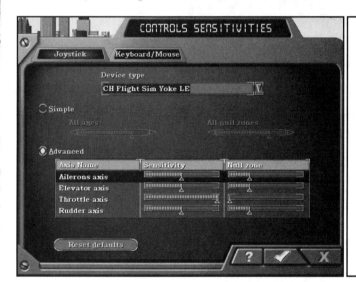

Figure 1.10: Adjust Controls Sensitivities and Null zones here.

Select Simple to adjust all controller axes the same amount; select Advanced to adjust individual axes. Use the Sensitivity option to adjust how much you achieve with a specified controller movement. Null zone— the amount of dead space in the neutral controller positions—can compensate for less-than-ideal controller hardware that produces jumpy control inputs in the neutral position.

Controller variations and combinations are so numerous, it's impossible to recommend exact settings for the most realistic controller setups. However, you can at least get your controllers in the ballpark using these suggested settings:

1. Begin with the C-182S sitting on the runway.

2. Select Views menu, then View Mode, and then Spot Plane.

3. Use the keypad keys (with Num Lock on) to track the camera view to the rear of the aircraft (Figure 1.11).

▶ **Warning**
Your must calibrate your controller(s) properly before you adjust control sensitivities. See Flight Simulator 2000's *Simulator Help section of onscreen help for instructions.*

4. Move your controls as you watch the C-182S's corresponding control surfaces. If they reach the end of their travels before your controller reaches its stops, decrease the Sensitivities adjustment for that axis. You seek a setting where both the control surface and your controller meet maximum deflection at the same time.

5. Repeat Step 4 until you've adjusted all control axes.

Figure 1.11:
If your control surfaces reach maximum deflection before your controller does, adjust the Sensitivities for the offending axis.

Flight Simulator Interface Conventions

We should go into a little more detail about how to operate *Flight Simulator 2000*'s interface. Because *Flight Simulator 2000* is a *Windows* program, all the usual *Windows* conventions—dragging window borders to resize them and right-clicking on objects for a quick menu, for example—are present. You can click on virtually every button and knob on *Flight Simulator 2000*'s aircraft instrument panel to activate or deactivate it. But one interface convention unique to *Flight Simulator* is the way that you set multiple-position instrument selections, such as radio frequencies.

Place your cursor over the knob or control for a moment to change the cursor into a hand. Placing the cursor left of the control generates a minus sign within the hand; placing it to the right generates a plus sign within the hand (Figure 1.12).

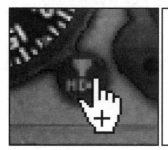

Figure 1.12:
Click on multi-selectable controls when this cursor displays to increase their setting.

Clicking a control with a plus sign in the hand cursor increases the selection; clicking it with a minus sign decreases it.

Icon Buttons

New in *Flight Simulator 2000* are the icon buttons on some instrument panels. You can still access panel views, such as radio stack and magnetic compass, using the familiar key commands Shift+1 through 9. But now you can click icon buttons to access them, as well (Figure 1.13). Because the key combinations for accessing additional panel views vary from aircraft to aircraft, using these icons helps reduce hit-or-miss keyboard fumbles.

Figure 1.13:
These icon buttons access (from left to right) the radio stack, GPS, throttle quadrant, magnetic compass, and fuel panel.

Checklists

As in the real world, checklists play a major part in cockpit procedure. Although you should use checklists during important phases of flight—for example, before takeoffs and landings—there's a danger in trying to memorize every item on the list. We're all human, and so we're bound to make mistakes and miss something. Operating an airplane safely, especially during critical phases of flight like takeoffs and landings, requires you to perform many tasks in the proper sequence. Using a checklist reduces the likelihood that you'll forget to do something important—like extend the landing gear.

We'll be using several checklists throughout this book. You can find shorter onscreen versions in *Flight Simulator 2000*. Press F10 to access *Flight Simulator 2000*'s onscreen checklists (Figure 1.14). To cycle through the kneeboard pages, press F10 again.

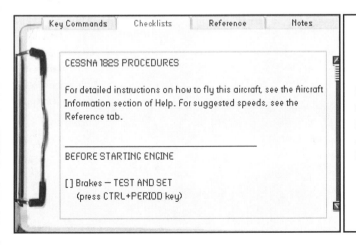

Figure 1.14:
Checklists are now part of the kneeboard. Access them via the F10 key.

Say It Aloud

Although you might feel a little self-conscious at first, I always recommend that student pilots get into the habit of reciting checklist items out loud and to touch each instrument or control called out in the checklist. (Touching your monitor's screen leads to fingerprints and contaminants such as cheesy puff dust, so you can skip that part!) You'll look and sound like you know what you're doing (a comfort for first-time passengers), and, because it slows you down, you'll miss fewer items. It's also good training for when you go for your Commercial Pilot or Certified Flight Instructor license. Reading checklists aloud is the sign of a professional. So when you watch the old movies on TV where the pilot and copilot are busy talking their way through their checklists, know that in at least those instances, Hollywood has recreated fact rather than fantasy.

▶ *Tip*

The kneeboard Notes page can be modified like checklists to contain important text information like the navigation log for your flight. The files you need to modify are *_notes.txt, where * is the name of the aircraft.

Customizing Checklists

If you miss details in the checklists provided here, or if you wish to streamline *Flight Simulator 2000*'s kneeboard versions, you can customize individual aircraft checklists using a simple text editor, such as *Windows 9x*'s Notepad applet (Figure 1.15).

Keep these particulars in mind as you modify checklists or create your own:

⌖ Aircraft checklists are named *_check.txt, where * is the name of the aircraft, and you'll find them in their folders in *Flight Simulator 2000*'s main Aircraft folder.

⌖ Checklists wrap lines that stretch beyond 48 characters. (Spaces count toward this total.)

⌖ Changes won't take effect until you exit and restart *Flight Simulator 2000*.

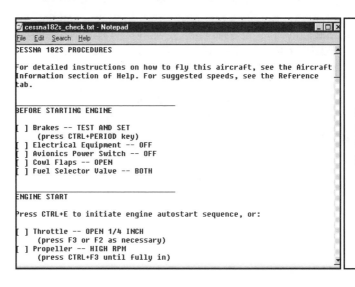

Figure 1.15: Modify individual kneeboard aircraft checklists using the *Windows 9x* Notepad applet.

V Speeds

"V" stands for velocity. Although the term "V speeds" translates to the redundant "velocity speeds," it's the term pilots use to indicate maximum and minimum airspeeds used during takeoffs, landings, and other situations. Determining these airspeeds is critical to operating an aircraft safely.

V Speed	Description
V_1	Take-Off Decision Speed: Speed that would make it impossible to remain on the runway after a rejected takeoff.
V_2	Take-Off Safety Speed: Speed at 35 feet AGL, assuming an engine failure at V_1
V_{35}	Takeoff Safety Speed at 35 AGL with both engines operating, calculated as V_2 + 6 KTS
V_A	Maneuvering Speed: Avoid abrupt control movements above this speed.
V_{FE}	Maximum Flaps Extension/Extended Speed: Don't extend or operate with full flaps above this speed.
V_{LE}	Maximum Landing Gear Extended Speed: Don't exceed this speed with landing gear extended.
V_{LO}	Maximum Landing Gear Operation Speed: Don't extend or retract landing gear above these speeds.
V_{MC}	Minimum Control Speed: Lowest airspeed at which a multiengine airplane is directionally controllable with the critical engine inoperative and the operating engine at takeoff power. For multiengine aircraft with features such as autofeather, V_{MCA} is quoted with one engine inoperative, autofeather armed, and the other engine at takeoff power.
V_{MO}	Maximum Operating Speed: Do not deliberately exceed these speeds in any flight regime. M_{MO} is the same, specified by Mach number.
V_{NE}	Never Exceed Speed
V_{NO}	Maximum Structural Cruising Speed
V_R	Rotation Speed: Speed that the pilot pitches the nose of the aircraft up (lifts the nose) on takeoff
V_{REF}	Landing Reference Speed: Target speed over the runway threshold for landing
$V_{REF + 20}$	Landing Reference Speed plus 20 KTS
V_S	Stalling Speed: Minimum steady flight speed during which the airplane remains controllable
V_{SO}	Stalling Speed Landing Configuration: Stall speed or minimum steady flight speed during which the airplane remains controllable in landing configuration

continued on next page

V Speed	Description
V_{S1}	Stalling Speed Specific Configuration—Stall speed or minimum steady flight speed during which the airplane remains controllable in a specified flight configuration
V_{SSE}	Intentional One-Engine-Inoperative Speed
V_X	Best Angle-of-Climb Speed: gains the most altitude for the least distance covered
V_{XSE}	One-Engine-Inoperative Best Angle of Climb Speed.
V_Y	Best Rate of Climb Speed: Gains the most altitude in the shortest time
V_{YSE}	One-Engine-Inoperative Best Rate of Climb Speed.

Other Important Airspeeds

The following descriptions are for airspeeds not considered V speeds.

Terminology	Description
Emergency Descent	Use this airspeed when making an emergency descent.
Max Range Glide	This airspeed produces maximum horizontal glide distance for a given altitude.
Turbulent Air Penetration	Recommended airspeed for turbulent air penetration, when the aircraft can structurally handle V_A
Maximum Demonstrated Crosswind Component	Velocity of the crosswind component where adequate control during takeoff and landing was demonstrated for aircraft certification. This is a guideline value, not a limit.

Getting From Point A to Point B

Chapter 2

*I*n this chapter we'll begin discussing aviation navigation and flight planning basics. We'll fly Flight Simulator's tried-and-true Sopwith Camel in our tutorial, because of its simplicity and lack of radio navigation instruments. The idea behind this approach is twofold: First, it'll allow you to concentrate on where we are and where we're going (instead of worrying about complex cockpit procedures or being preoccupied with keeping the aircraft in the air). Secondly, it won't tempt anyone into "cheating" by using the radio navigation equipment—because there isn't any!

It was probably someone flying a similar aircraft who coined the expression "flying by the seat of your pants," because it doesn't get any more basic than this. That said, next to flying a sailplane, it's perhaps the purest flight experience you can have. So if you're ready, let's go fly a kite!

Flight-Planning Basics

Don't confuse *flight planning* with a *flight plan*. According to the FARs (Federal Aviation Regulations), a flight plan is "specified information, relating to the intended flight of an aircraft that is filed orally or in writing with air traffic control." The FARs require pilots to file flight plans when operating under IFR. Figure 2.1 shows an FAA (Federal Aviation Administration) flight plan form.

U.S. DEPARTMENT OF TRANSPORTATION FAA **FLIGHT PLAN**	(FAA USE ONLY) • PILOT BRIEFING • STOPOVER • VNR				TIME STARTED	SPECIALIST INITIALS

1. TYPE	2. AIRCRAFT IDENTIFICATION	3. AIRCRAFT TYPE/ SPECIAL EQUIPMENT	4. TRUE AIRSPEED	5. DEPARTURE POINT	6. DEPARTURE TIME		7.CRUISING ALTITUDE
VFR					PROPOSED (Z)	ACTUAL (Z)	
IFR							
DVFR			KTS				

8. ROUTE OF FLIGHT

9. DESTINATION (Name of airport and city)	10. EST. TIME ENROUTE		11.REMARKS
	HOURS	MINUTES	

12. FUEL ON BOARD	13. ALTERNATE AIRPORT(S)	14. PILOT'S NAME, ADDRESS & TELEPHONE NUMBER & AIRCRAFT HOME BASE		15. NUMBER ABOARD
HOURS MINUTES		17. DESTINATION CONTACT/TELEPHONE (OPTIONAL)		
16. COLOR OF AIRCRAFT		CIVIL AIRCRAFT PILOTS. FAR Part 91 requires you file an IFR flight plan to operate under instrument flight rules in controlled airspace. Failure to file could result in a civil penalty not to exceed $1000 for each violation (Section 901 of the Federal Aviation Act of 1958, as amended). Filing of a VFR flight plan is recommended as a good operation practice. See also Part 99 for requirements concerning DVFR flight plans.		

(Copy of) FAA Form 7233-1 (8-82)   **CLOSE VFR FLIGHT PLAN WITH**_____**FSS ON ARRIVAL**
Freq._____

/X — no xpndr   /T — xpndr no mode C   /U — xpndr w/ mode C   /D DME, no xpndr   /B DME, xpnder no C   /A DME, xpndr w/C

ATIS	TIME	WIND	VIS	CEILING	TEMP	DP	ALT	R/W

Figure 2.1: This is a flight plan form. Don't confuse it with the act of flight planning.

Flight planning encompasses the performance, navigational, and operational calculations required to complete a flight safely. To quote the CFRs again, "Each pilot in command shall, before beginning a flight, become familiar with all available information concerning that flight." Although flight planning is required to file a flight plan, flight planning and flight plans aren't the same things.

Interestingly, the only requirements specifically named by the CFRs regarding VFR flight planning in the vicinity of airports are determining runway lengths at airports of intended use and landing and takeoff distance information. To realistically make a flight safely, we need to make sure the weather is acceptable, that we have enough fuel to make it to our point of destination, and that we can refuel there (unless you plan on *pushing* the airplane home!). We'll cover these concepts throughout these navigation discussions and tutorials. For now, let's just keep things simple.

Pilotage

The first navigation method we'll discuss is *pilotage*. Pilotage literally means navigation by visual reference to landmarks. This is the most basic form of aviation navigation and, perhaps not surprisingly, one of the most widely used by *Flight Simulator* enthusiasts.

The way it works is pilots, with or without a map or chart, fly from one recognized visual landmark to the next until they get where they want to go. For short trips, flying without a map isn't a problem, especially if a lot of unique or familiar landmarks lie along your route.

Because pilotage, by definition, requires visual references to landmarks, difficulties may arise when the ground is obscured by weather or when flying over featureless terrain without changing navigation methods. However, there are things that we can do to help us get where we need to go when flying over unfamiliar terrain and/or long distances. Let's discuss that next.

The Navigation Log

To make a long flight using pilotage, you simply need to make a list of landmarks that lie along your route. This list of landmarks, commonly referred to as checkpoints, or *waypoints* (a waypoint, or *fix*, as it's called in instrument flight, is an arbitrary navigation reference point) is known as a *navigation log* or *flight log*. A navigation log can be a very simple list. In the sample (Table 2.1), "Mag. Course" stands for magnetic course, or the desired flight path measured relative to magnetic north; "nm" stands for nautical miles; and "ETE" stands for estimated time en route.

► **Note**

Navigation logs that use radio NAVAIDs (Navigation Aids) would contain another column for NAVAID frequencies.

Table 2.1: Simple VFR (Visual Flight Rules) Navigation Log

Waypoint	Mag. Course	Altitude	Distance	ETE
County Airport	220°	4,500'	13 nm	0:09
Jct. 37	215°	4,500'	12 nm	0:08
Blue Lake	245°	4,500'	23 nm	0:15
Community College	245°	2,500'	10 nm	0:07
City Airport	—	TOTAL	58 nm	0:39

The basic pilotage drill works like this:

1. When you recognize the first landmark on your flight log, fly toward it.

2. Look down at your navigation log for a reminder of what landmark to look for next and how long it should take to get there.

3. Note the time and change course and/or altitude as called for.

4. When you recognize the next landmark, start flying toward that.

5. Go back to Step 2 and repeat until you reach your destination.

▶ *Tip*

You don't need to fly over a landmark if you've already spotted the next one on your flight log. Just fly directly to the next landmark (if doing so won't cause you to fly over or through an area you're trying to avoid).

VFR Charts

If you plan to travel somewhere you've never been, or if your trip is fairly long, the only way you'll be able to make up a navigation log is with a map of some sort. You could use detailed road maps for this purpose, but in the aviation world, pilotage pilots use charts designed for VFR (Visual Flight Rules) flight. The most common ones used in the U.S. are Sectional Charts (Figure 2.2), known as *sectionals*, and VFR Terminal Area Charts (TACs, Figure 2.3), known as *terminal charts*.

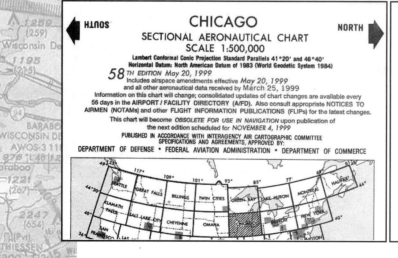

Figure 2.2:
Sectional Aeronautical Chart

VFR TERMINAL AREA CHART
ST LOUIS
SCALE 1:250,000

Lambert Conformal Conic Projection Standard Parallels 33° and 45°
Horizontal Datum: North American Datum of 1983 (World Geodetic System 1984)

52 ND EDITION July 15, 1999
Includes airspace amendments effective July 15, 1999
and all other aeronautical data received by May 20, 1999
Information on this chart will change; consolidated updates of chart changes are available every
56 days in the AIRPORT / FACILITY DIRECTORY (A/FD). Also consult appropriate NOTICES TO
AIRMEN (NOTAMs) and other FLIGHT INFORMATION PUBLICATIONS (FLIPs) for the latest changes.
This chart will become OBSOLETE FOR USE IN NAVIGATION upon publication of
the next edition scheduled for DECEMBER 30, 1999

PUBLISHED IN ACCORDANCE WITH INTERAGENCY AIR CARTOGRAPHIC COMMITTEE
SPECIFICATIONS AND AGREEMENTS, APPROVED BY:
DEPARTMENT OF DEFENSE • FEDERAL AVIATION ADMINISTRATION • DEPARTMENT OF COMMERCE

ST LOUIS CLASS B AIRSPACE

See back of this chart for procedural information
within the St Louis Class B Airspace

EXAMPLES OF CLASS B ALTITUDES
$\frac{70}{}$ --- Ceiling in hundreds of feet MSL
$\frac{30}{}$ --- Floor in hundreds of feet MSL

CONTROL TOWER FREQUENCIES ON ST LOUIS TERMINAL AREA CHART

Figure 2.3:
VFR Terminal
Area Chart

Sectionals are scaled at 1:500,000—that is, 1 inch on the chart represents 6.86 nautical miles. TACs, on the other hand, are scaled a bit lower (1:250,000, where 1 inch represents 2.43 nautical miles) and TACs only depict the airspace designated as Class B. We'll go into what exactly Class B means later in this chapter, but for now (as far as charts go), it means TACs are available only for cities with really big airports, such as Los Angeles International and Chicago O'Hare International. TACs' greater level of detail makes it easier to decode the intricacies of these complex airspaces.

VFR charts for other parts of the world go by a variety of names, but they're otherwise very similar. For example, Canadian airspace sectionals are called Canadian VFR Navigation Charts, or Canadian Pilotage Charts, and are scaled at 1:500,000. Canadian VFR Terminal Charts (1:250,000 scale) are the equivalents of TACs.

Where to Get Charts

The NOAA (National Oceanic and Atmospheric Administration) publishes U.S. sectional and terminal charts. Various agencies, such as the Defense Mapping Agency, and private companies, such as Jeppesen, publish charts for other areas of the world. You can get them from the following sources:

Mail Order—There are scores of mail order pilot supply houses out there, but the largest and arguably the most complete is Sporty's Pilot Shop. Contact them at 1-800-LIFTOFF in the U.S., or 49-611-22042 in Germany.

Retail Pilot Shops—Most small airports have some sort of FBO (Fixed Base Operator) that sells pilot supplies. Check your local phone book. Or, if you're adventurous, take a ride out to your local airfield and ask around. But be forewarned that the aviation bug may bite you!

Jeppesen—SimCharts are available at http://www.jeppesenpcpilot.com

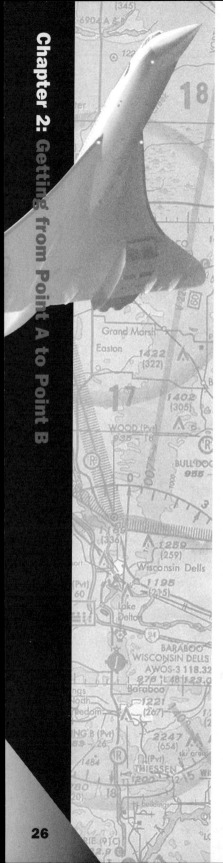

Pilots—Charts are dated to make room for the inevitable changes and updates. To a real pilot, this planned obsolescence means their charts are always expiring, which renders them useless. If you ask nicely (please don't be a pest—especially if the pilot is still flying the airplane!), many pilots will happily give you their expired charts for free (or cheap), if they have any.

On the Web—A couple of places on the Web sell or post real-world charts. Other sites sell charts designed strictly for use in flight simulations. Most major search engines can direct you. One such source is The Mapbase at http://www123.pair.com/mapbase/.

Selecting Waypoints

Again, a waypoint is an arbitrary navigation reference point. In terms of pilotage, waypoints are our visual landmarks. Next to choosing a safe altitude to fly at (to avoid premature "landings"), selecting waypoints is probably the most important part of pilotage flight planning. After all, if you can't find any waypoints listed in your navigation log, you're lost!

Naturally, you'll want to select waypoints that lie along your intended route. But your route may vary due to obstructions, airspace restrictions (more on those later), or lack of landmarks between your starting point and your destination.

Adding Important Waypoints

While all waypoints matter, here's a few you absolutely don't want to overlook: departure and destination waypoints (yes, pilots can forget where they're going!), and those that mark heading and altitude changes.

The following tips can help ensure you don't forget where *you're* going:

✝ Consider adding a brief text description (with a diagram if you're using a written/paper navigation log) to your destination waypoint. Make careful note of the runway layout and/or any unique characteristics about the airport. This will help you recognize it, or more importantly, not to mistake another airport as your destination. (It's always humbling to land at the wrong airport!)

✝ Your next-to-last waypoint should be about 10 miles from your destination, to allow for descent to traffic pattern altitude. If that distance won't allow for a comfortable descent, add waypoints farther from your destination for descending in increments (a step-down approach).

Pitfalls

We could talk about what makes a good waypoint choice, but it's probably simpler to discuss what makes for a *bad* one. Here are some common pitfalls to watch out for when selecting waypoints for your navigation log.

Nonpermanent Landmarks—Make sure you select landmarks that will be there when you need them. A ship, truck, or snowman, for instance, might not be there very long. This is less an issue in *Flight Simulator 2000* than it is in the real world.

Generic Landmarks—Selecting generic landmarks is a fast way to get yourself lost. Unless a building is uniquely colored or shaped, or the only building within 25 miles, it makes a poor choice for a pilotage landmark. On the other hand, a group of buildings might be OK, but if there are groups of similar buildings nearby, you're just asking for in-flight heart palpitations if you don't select other landmarks to rely upon.

Too Few Landmarks—If your landmarks that are too far apart, there's a real danger you'll never see the next landmark, or that you'll lose sight of the last one as you search for the next. Both scenarios can lead to a lot of confusion and sweating in the cockpit. (The kind of sweating that the big propeller up front blowing air on you won't help!)

Landmarks That Lie Too Close Together—If you select landmarks that are too close together, you risk missing the next landmark. You can pass by the second landmark before you spot the first.

Man-made Landmarks That Are Too Small—That is, anything smaller than an airport or stadium. If you're stuck, select a couple of smaller landmarks in the same area to increase the odds you'll spot at least one.

Building a VFR Navigation Log

Let's talk about how to build a basic VFR navigation log. After you've selected your waypoints, take a ruler or better yet a *plotter* (a fancy ruler designed for working with maps and charts), and pencil in a course line that connects them. The completed line represents your route. You'd list NAVAID frequencies along your route, if you were using them.

Next, note your magnetic course for each leg (section between waypoints) of your route. The easiest way to determine magnetic courses is to use the plotter's compass rose, but you can make accurate estimates by referencing a nearby NAVAID compass rose on the chart itself (see Figure 2.4).

To use a chart's compass rose, place a parallel course line (you needn't draw it) over the nearest compass rose center. This shows you the magnetic course.

Now measure the distances between waypoints. Use the scale located on the chart's legend or on your plotter to convert the distances into nautical or English miles, depending on the instrumentation of your aircraft. Armed with these distances you can calculate each leg's ETE (Estimated Time En Route).

▶ *Tip*

Sometimes selecting a generic landmark is unavoidable. One way to differentiate it is to note nearby landmark characteristics. For example, a hill and a road intersection may lie next to your landmark building. Note such characteristics in your navigation log.

▶ *Tip*

Routes that fly to one side of your checkpoints (rather than directly over) make it easier to spot the checkpoints.

▶ **Note**

We use magnetic course headings because magnetic north (where compasses point) isn't located in the same place as the North Pole (true north). However, magnetic north and true north can and do align.

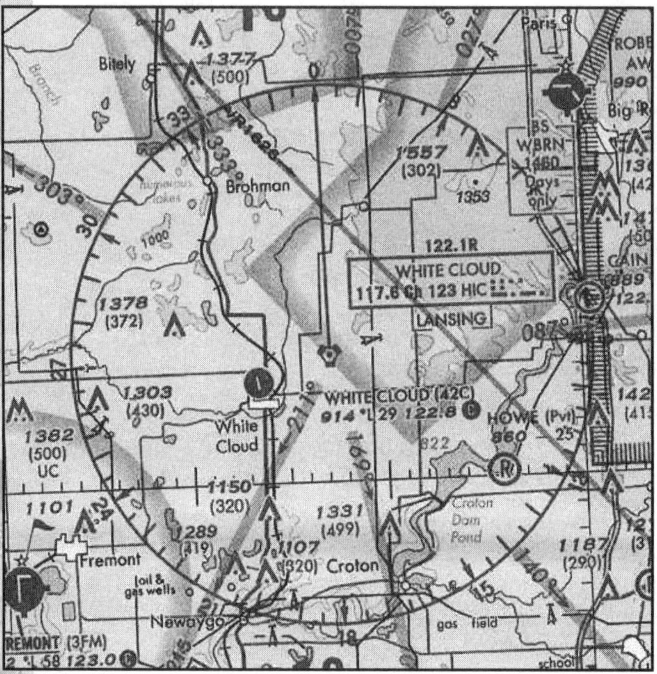

Figure 2.4:
A chart's compass rose can help you determine magnetic course headings when you're not flying from NAVAID to NAVAID.

► **Note**

When calculating ETEs for aircraft built after 1976, measure course legs in nautical miles. TAS in these aircraft are given in knots (nautical miles per hour).

ETE is related to the aircraft's ground speed. As you know, ground speed varies with the wind. An aircraft's true airspeed (TAS) in level flight equals your ground speed when the winds are calm. To keep things simple, let's calculate ETE with no wind (winds calm).

First, divide the Camel's TAS (125 mph at 3,000 feet on a standard day) by 60 (number of minutes in an hour). Now take the leg distance and divide it by the quotient that we just calculated. For example, a 15-mile leg would take 7.2 minutes to fly at 125 mph TAS (15 ÷ 2.08 = 7.2).

Finally, because you're flying in a 3-D world, you must select altitudes for each leg of your flight. You'll choose cruise altitudes based on terrain/obstacles, airspace restrictions, aircraft performance, and/or weather conditions. We'll cover weather first. Terrain and obstacles are easy enough to understand—don't fly into them! We'll discuss aircraft performance and airspace restrictions later in this chapter.

Importing Weather

Other than a structural failure (mechanical failures are rarely fatal in the Camel, because it can land just about anywhere), the only other major hazards you may confront are weather-related. (Getting lost isn't that bad, *if* you can land and ask for directions.)

Flight Simulator 2000 gives you the ability to recreate real-world weather information in your virtual world. To import real-time weather reports into *Flight Simulator 2000*, first log onto the Internet. In the World menu, click on Weather, and then click on the Real World Weather button (Figure 2.5). *Flight Simulator 2000* does the rest.

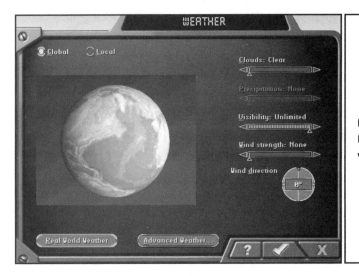

Figure 2.5:
Import real-world
weather from here.

Flight Simulator's Real World Weather feature always creates local weather. But it doesn't affect the Global weather settings at all. Global weather is like the background or canvas on top of which local weather is painted. Local weather will only exist in the area around that station, and will decay over distance to the global weather setting. If another local weather observation exists along your flight path, weather will morph between the two local weather settings.

Real World Weather data comes from a Jeppesen server, which captures METARs (Aviation Routine Weather Reports). Data is updated every fifteen minutes. All current METARs are downloaded at the same time and are used in *Flight Simulator 2000*'s local weather settings. Where you are when you download the weather has no effect on the final result.

Weather is then interpolated from station to station in the mesh unless of course the station has no valid METAR. In these cases weather is interpolated back to the single Global weather setting. The distance that a METAR will be effective is related to the distance to the next nearest METAR reporting stations. This is why weather is represented as an irregular mesh of reporting points.

Winds Aloft

As the name suggests, winds aloft are just that—winds above the surface. Although surface conditions are important for airport operations because you're so close to, or on (or wanting to be back on!), the ground, winds aloft are important to the cruise portion of your flight.

As you know, any crosswind component you encounter in flight will alter your ground track or ground speed (Figure 2.6). You also know that crosswinds require heading changes to correct for wind drift. Correcting ground-track problems caused by crosswinds is simple if you can see the ground or have a NAVAID to track, but calculating changes in ground speed requires a little more effort.

▶ **Tip**

To save a Real World Weather setting, just save the Flight. A .WX file (a compact binary format) will be created along with the .FLT that saves all of the weather information that was downloaded. When you reload the Flight, you'll get the weather.

▶ **Tip**

After you download weather data from the Internet, the Weather window dialog boxes reflect current weather conditions at your location.

Knowing your ground speed is important, because if your ground speed changes, so does your flight time. Arriving at your destination on schedule is less a matter of concern than fuel shortage problems caused by changes in your ETE time. Winds aloft forecasts can help you fine-tune your en route flight times.

There are those who use *Flight Simulator*'s DME (Distance Measuring Equipment) or TAS setting to "calculate" their current ground speed, but problems associated with using those methods can bite you if you're not aware of them. First, DME ground speed is accurate only if you're heading directly toward or away from the transmitting NAVAID. Second, contrary to what some desktop pilots believe (or, rather, what they forget), TAS equals ground speed only in calm air. If you're flying with a wind—well, you get the idea.

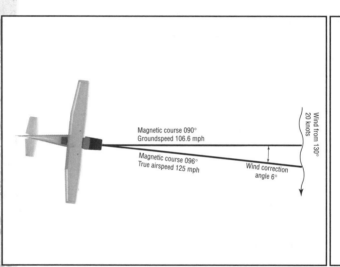

Magnetic course 090°
Groundspeed 106.6 mph

Magnetic course 096°
True airspeed 125 mph

Wind correction angle 6°

Wind from 130°
20 knots

Figure 2.6:
Although you can correct your ground track, winds will always affect ground speeds.

Calculating Your Ground Speed

To get an accurate ground speed estimate (remember, winds aloft are forecasts), use a wind component diagram, such as the one shown in Figure 2.7. By plotting the difference between the winds aloft at your current cruise altitude and your true course and TAS, you can estimate changes in your ground speed.

To give you an example of how a wind component diagram works, let's say your flight plan has you flying a magnetic course of 090 degrees in your Camel, and the winds at your altitude are from 130 in reference to True North at 20 knots. Find the 20-knot circle on the diagram and place your finger where that circle meets the 40-degree radial line. (The difference between your course and wind direction is 40 degrees.) You can read your headwind (or tailwind, in other cases) on the scale to the left. In this example, you face a 16-knot headwind component.

Because you're flying the Camel here (where your cruise TAS is in mph) you must convert knots to mph, and then subtract the headwind component (or add the tailwind component) from your TAS to come up with your ground speed. To save you the trouble of doint the math, the answer is 106.7 mph ground speed—a difference of 18.4 mph. That may not seem like a big deal, but on long flights it can mean the difference between landing safely and a very long walk home.

In an ideal world, you'd naturally try to select an altitude with favorable winds (read *tailwind*) for your direction of flight. There are other factors to consider, however.

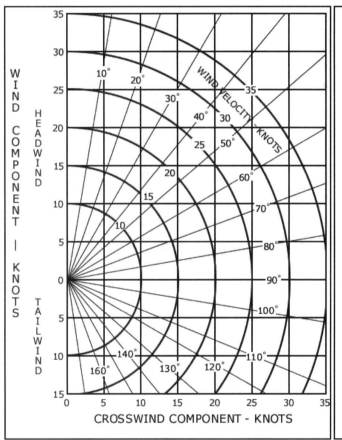

Figure 2.7:
Wind Components

Controlled Airspace

Controlled airspace is a generic term that refers to all classes of airspace defined in accordance with the FAA airspace classification system established in 1995. These parcels of air are considered "controlled" because you must meet specific restrictions and conditions before you may fly within them legally.

It would be inefficient to recite the complete CFR definitions for the whole airspace classification system here, but we'll cover the most relevant details. If you want to read up on them on your own, pick up an FAR/AIM reprint.

Controlled Airspace and *Flight Simulator 2000*

Many Flight Simulator *veterans have been gleefully flying around for years without any concern for controlled airspace—and that's perfectly fine. There's little danger of the guys from Microsoft yanking your pilot's license if you repeatedly violate airspace in* Flight Simulator *as the FAA would if you did the same thing in the real world.*

Many virtual pilots argue that, because Flight Simulator *"doesn't model interactive ATC," they feel justified in flying anywhere they want, anytime they want. Of course, you should be able to fly anywhere, anytime in* Flight Simulator; *it's one of the best parts of virtual flight, if you ask me!*

Controlled airspace in the real world, just as it is in Flight Simulator, *are arbitrary bits of space that are only visually marked on maps. The only way you know you've violated controlled airspace in the real world is from ATC, or, after the fact, the FAA. Those unpleasant aspects of ATC aren't modeled, but the absence of reprimand is hardly a good rationale for ignoring controlled airspace. Ignore airspace if you want, but if you're interested in realism and accuracy, follow the regulations.*

On the other hand, you have no one to request clearance from in order to enter some classes of airspace. In those cases, you can assume you have permission (although this has the net effect of ignoring controlled airspace).

If you're flying IFR, we recommend that you ignore controlled airspace and assume you have got the clearances ATC would provide. If you're flying VFR, follow weather minimums in all classes of airspace and adjust your flights to avoid all Class A through Class D airspace intrusions (except at your departure and destination airports). You'll find your virtual flights far more rewarding if you abide by the rules of the sky.

Airspace Classifications

Before we talk about specific restrictions and weather minimums, we should define what the boundaries of each class of airspace are. Figure 2.8 shows the respective airspace classes.

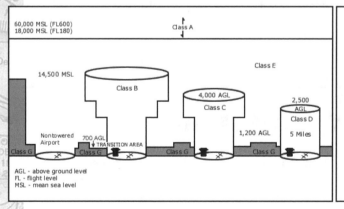

**Figure 2.8:
Airspace Classification**

Class A—Starts at 18,000 feet and extends up to and including flight level 600, including 12 nm beyond the coast of the continental U.S. This airspace isn't marked on charts.

Class B—Begins at the surface and extends up to 10,000 feet. Boundaries are marked with solid blue lines.

Class C—Begins at the surface and typically extends up to 4,000 feet AGL. Boundaries are marked with solid magenta lines.

Class D—Generally circular, with a diameter of about 5 sm (statute miles); a statute mile is 5,280 feet, or 1.609 km, and often includes extensions to accommodate instrument approaches. Begins at the surface and typically extends to 2,500 feet above the airport. Boundaries are marked with dashed blue lines.

Class E—Controlled airspace not designated Class A, B, C, or D; includes low-altitude airways. It begins at either 700 or 1,200 feet above the surface and extends upward to the base of any overlying controlled airspace. Boundaries are marked with dashed magenta lines, or with shaded magenta (700 feet AGL) or shaded blue (1,200 feet AGL) lines.

Class G—All airspace not designated Class A, B, C, D, or E. Typically begins at the surface and extends upward to 700 or 1,200 feet AGL, or 14,500 feet MSL. Boundaries of Class G airspace aren't explicitly marked.

▶ Note

In the U.S. there is no such thing as Class Fairspace.

Airspace Restrictions and Requirements

Table 2.2 shows the most common Airspace restrictions and requirements. All radio and Mode C transponder (a transponder with automatic altitude reporting capability) requirements prevail, unless otherwise authorized by ATC.

Table 2.2: Common Airspace Restrictions and Requirements

Airspace	Clearance	Required Equipment	Pilot Minimums	Other Requirements
Class A	Required prior to entering	Radio and Mode C transponder	Private	IFR only
Class B	Establish 2-way communications prior to entering	Radio and Mode C transponder	Private or special endorsement	Private to takeoff or land at main airport
Class C	Required prior to entering	Radio and Mode C transponder	—	Mode C required to overfly below 10,000'
Class D	Establish 2-way communications prior to entering	Radio	—	—
Class E	Only when weather is below VFR minimums	—	—	—
Class G	—	—	—	—

VFR Weather Minimums

VFR airspace weather minimums are pretty simple. If the weather doesn't meet the minimums listed in Table 2.3, you can't fly VFR.

Table 2.3: VFR Airspace Weather Minimums

Airspace	Flight Visibility	Distance from Clouds
Class A	—	—
Class B	3 sm	Clear of clouds
Class C	3 sm	500' below
		1,000' above
		2,000' horizontal
Class D	3 sm	500' below
		1,000' above
		2,000' horizontal
Class E Below 10,000' MSL	3 sm	500' Below
		1,000' above
		2,000' horizontal
Class E Above 10,000' MSL	5 sm	1,000' below
		1,000' above
		1 sm horizontal
Class G 1,200' or less above the surface		
Day	1 sm	Clear of clouds
Night	3 sm	500' below
		1,000' above
		2,000' horizontal
More than 1,200' above the surface but less than 10,000' MSL	—	—
Day	1 sm	500' below
		1,000' above
		2,000' horizontal
Night	3 sm	500' below
		1,000' above
		2,000' horizontal
More than 1,200' above the surface and at or above 10,000' MSL	5 sm	1,000' below
		1,000' above
		1 sm horizontal

Flying the Sopwith Camel

As mentioned earlier, you'll be flying the Camel because of its simplicity and lack of modern navigation instruments. Like other aircraft of its era, the Camel is constructed of wood and cloth. There's some debate about whether it's construction or performance in the wind that gives such aircraft the nickname "kite."

Aircraft Performance

Performance is a rather relative concept. At one time, the Sopwith Camel was considered one of the world's best-performing fighter aircraft. Although it's still a marvel, it falls short in some areas. Modern fighter pilots have compared its climb rate to that of a pigeon. Its roll rate is sluggish even by WWII standards. But because it's simple (it doesn't even have flaps), can fly so slowly, and can take off from and land just about anywhere, it's one of the most fun aircraft to fly.

V Speeds

You needn't know many V speeds to fly the Camel safely. This is the reason that we chose this simple aircraft for the first tutorial. All the Camel's V speeds are listed as IAS (indicated airspeed).

V_R	60 mph IAS
V_Y	60 mph IAS
V_S	48 mph IAS
V_{NO}	114 mph IAS

Advanced Systems

Advanced systems? Again, like the term "performance," advanced systems are relative. The nifty oil pressure gauge on the left side of the instrument panel (Figure 2.9) gives a visual indication of whether oil is circulating in the engine. That's about it for advanced systems. It's as basic as it gets but in its time the Camel was one of the best fighter aircraft the world had ever seen.

> ▶ **Warning**
>
> *The Sopwith Camel's ASI (Air Speed Indicator) is indexed in mph, not knots.*

Figure 2.9:
The Sopwith Camel's oil pressure gauge is a simple glass tube connected to the engine's oil system.

Flight Plan

Now we've covered some of the basics that you'll need to know to make this flight. In the following sections, we'll get a little more specific about how it all applies, and we'll cover the same components for each tutorial.

Airports

You'll fly from the famous Santa Monica Airport in southern California to Chino Airport—home of the Planes of Fame Museum, a fitting destination for a WWI warbird!

A quick check of your LAX terminal chart reveals that SMO and CNO runways are long enough to take off from and land on. (The longest runways are 5,000 feet and 7,000 feet, respectively. Refer to the chart legend to learn how to extract that information.)

Route

In the following navigation log (see Table 2.4), SMO is the 3-letter identifier for Santa Monica Airport, and CNO is the 3-letter identifier for Chino Airport.

Table 2.4: Navigation Log

Waypoint	Course	Altitude	Distance	ETE
SMO	030°	2,800'	3 m	0:02
Twin High-Rise	048°	2,800'	8 m	0:04
Griffith Park Observatory & Dodger Stadium	048°	2,800'	8 m	0:04
Rose Bowl	108°	3,500'	9 m	0:05
El Monte Airport	095°	3,500'	11 m	0:06
Mt. San Antonio College	095°	Descend to 1,400'	13 m	0:07
CNO	27L	TOTAL	52 m	28 minutes

▶ Note

The LAX terminal chart good for this tutorial flight is reproduced in Appendix A.

You'll take off from SMO and fly the runway heading of 030 degrees until you reach the first waypoint—a couple of high-rise buildings. Then turn right to heading 048 degrees to go northeast toward Griffith Park Observatory (it will lie to your left) and Dodger Stadium (to your right). This roundabout route avoids LAX's Class B airspace to the east and south.

From there, continue on the same heading toward the Rose Bowl stadium and turn right to heading 108 degrees, which leads directly over El Monte Airport. There you'll switch to a heading of 095 degrees. That should take you to your descent waypoint, Mt. Antonio College. Continuing on heading 095 degrees, you should find CNO about 13 miles later. Winds usually favor runways 26L and 26R, so based on your direction of arrival, expect right traffic to runway 26R.

Altitude

What makes this flight so interesting is that you have so many things to avoid. As far as cruising altitudes go, you must:

+ fly high enough to avoid flying into a hillside or building

+ fly high enough above the terrain to buy you the most options should your engine quit

+ fly low enough to avoid entering Burbank's Class C airspace to the north and LAX's Class B airspace directly above

+ fly high enough to avoid entering El Monte's Class D airspace

Typically, when selecting cruise altitudes, you'll consider weather and winds aloft (you've seen to it that you have perfect weather) and aircraft performance, as well. (Optimal performance/fighting altitude for the Camel in WWI was 12,000 feet, and its service ceiling is 19,000 feet.) Finally, your cruising altitudes should coincide with VFR cruising altitude guidelines (Figure 2.10).

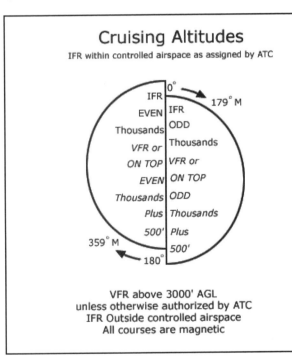

Cruising Altitudes
IFR within controlled airspace as assigned by ATC

IFR
EVEN
Thousands
VFR or
ON TOP
EVEN
Thousands
Plus
500'

0°
179° M

IFR
ODD
Thousands
VFR or
ON TOP
ODD
Thousands
Plus
500'

359° M
180°

VFR above 3000' AGL
unless otherwise authorized by ATC
IFR Outside controlled airspace
All courses are magnetic

**Figure 2.10:
IFR and VFR
Cruising Altitudes
and Flight Levels**

After takeoff, you'll climb to 2,800 feet and stay at that altitude until you fly over the Rose Bowl. This altitude is high enough to avoid all terrain and obstacles along your route, and low enough to keep you below Burbank's Class C outer ring (3,000–4,800 feet) and LAX's Class B airspace (5,000–10,000 feet). Figure 2.11 depicts Class B airspace viewed from the side. You're below the 3,000-foot AGL reference height for VFR cruise altitudes, so you needn't comply with VFR cruising altitude guidelines. As a precaution, however, you won't fly at 2,500 feet while heading eastbound, just in case someone following the guidelines is flying in the opposite direction.

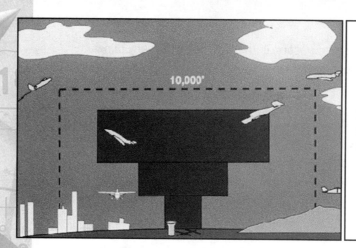

Figure 2.11:
Class B Airspace,
Side View

Beyond the Rose Bowl, and clear of Burbank and LAX, climb to 3,500 feet. This altitude meets VFR cruise guidelines and allows you to clear El Monte's Class D airspace (surface to 2,800 feet, as indicated by the "28" in the angle brackets), yet it's low enough to allow for a comfortable descent into Chino.

The next-to-last waypoint (Mt. San Antonio College) makes a good descent waypoint because it's approximately 10 miles from Chino. This gives you enough time to descend to Chino's pattern altitude of 1,400 feet—your last planned altitude before landing.

Fuel/Performance

Maximum range for the Sopwith Camel is 300 miles. (Its fuel capacity wasn't designed for extended flights; it's a fighter.) Because the Camel lacks a cockpit fuel gauge, you must track your fuel consumption based on flight time. The camel burns about 16 gallons per hour and carries about 40 gallons. That works out to about 2.5 hours at cruise. No matter how you calculate it, you have more than enough fuel to make your 52-mile hop.

Special Considerations

✝ The Sopwith Camel is a tail dragger. The rudder is very sensitive, so make sure you adjust your controller sensitivities properly. Otherwise, you're in for a bumpy ride.

✝ There's no autopilot. You must hand-fly the whole way. There's elevator trim, but you don't have the luxury of rudder or aileron trim. You must maintain a little right rudder and right aileron to compensate for the Camel's (relatively) powerful engine torque.

✝ Among other things, the Camel lacks a radio or transponder. You can take this flight legally without a radio and a Mode C transponder (required when flying within 30 nm of a Class B airspace primary airport). But to do so you must obtain clearances from each agency along your route prior to making the flight. You must let everyone know when to expect you and from which direction. For this flight, assume you've made the proper arrangements.

▶ **Tip**

It's better (read "safer") to descend to pattern altitude before entering the airport traffic pattern than it is to descend inside it. It's very difficult to see what's directly below you as you descend, and you don't want to descend into an aircraft already in the pattern.

▶ **Note**

You can't lean the fuel mixture on the Camel to obtain better fuel economy.

▶ **Warning**

Don't try this flight for real without radio contact, or at least phoning the agency controlling the airspace you wish to enter beforehand to get permission.

Flight Tutorial

At this point you need to set up the Flight in *Flight Simulator*. First, transport yourself to Santa Monica Airport: in the World menu, select Go to Airport. Next, click on the Search Airport IDs radio button and type KSMO in Type Airport ID, or select from the list box, as shown in Figure 2.12.

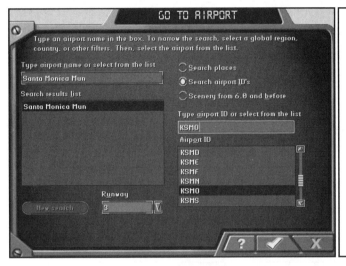

Figure 2.12: Transport yourself to any airport in *Flight Simulator 2000* from the Go to Airport window.

The success of your flight hinges on spotting landmarks, so to keep things simple, don't bother importing real-world weather for now. (In subsequent flights, you're more than welcome to try completing the flight using actual weather conditions.) You'll also want to make this flight during the day, so to change time of day, select Time & Season in the World menu. In the Time of Day box, select Day, as shown in Figure 2.13. Then click the green check box at the bottom of the window, and you're set.

▶ **Warning**

Because you're navigating by pilotage, you can set all Graphics options to minimum (if you are running a very low-end machine). However, scenery complexity must be set to Normal.

Figure 2.13: Change your flight's time of day from this dialogue box.

Before Takeoff

The Camel is one of *Flight Simulator*'s old-timers, so we'll skip detailed checklists and begin right from the runway. The following before-takeoff tips will come in handy in all of your flights.

✛ Titling the view simulates raising and lowering the seat in a real airplane. Press Shift+Enter to raise the seat, and Shift+Backspace to lower (Figures 2.14 and 2.15). Press Ctl+Spacebar to return the view to its default position.

✛ If you have enough system memory, cycling through all your cockpit views (use numpad keys with Num Lock on) reduces the pausing associated with view changes. The first time you switch to a new view, *Flight Simulator* must load what you're seeing, creating a pause. Loading views before you take off can minimize this pausing while you're in flight. Be sure to hold each view long enough for everything to load completely during your initial view cycling, or you'll still experience a longer than necessary pause.

✛ Arrange your cockpit items (charts, navigation log, pencil, and paper) so they're readily available during your flight.

✛ Remember to make use of *Flight Simulator 2000*'s ability to pause the simulation when you press the P key. This is especially useful if you're reading along here as you fly.

Figure 2.14:
Default "Seat" Position

▶ Note

Switching views after adjusting your seat returns the view to its default position.

Takeoff

Check the time on the clock on the right side of the instrument panel (Figure 2.16) and note it in your log. Next, *smoothly* increase throttle to full power by pressing the F3 key several times. You must *gently* apply some right rudder to compensate for the Camel's torque/left-turning tendencies.

Figure 2.15:
Press Shift+Enter to
raise the "seat."

Figure 2.16:
Aviation Timekeeper,
Circa 1914

At 35-40 mph IAS, push slightly forward on the stick until the tail comes up. Don't be too aggressive raising the tail, or you'll just bury the prop in the runway. Rotate at 60 knots and ease the airplane off the runway.

Climb

Adjust pitch attitude to climb at V_Y (60 knots). Fly the runway heading 030 degrees and climb to 2,800 feet. At V_Y, you'll reach your first waypoint (the twin high-rise shown in Figure 2.17) before you reach your cruise altitude.

Once you cross the waypoint, turn right to heading 048 degrees. The Camel's compass, located in the center of the instrument panel (Figure 2.18), rotates like a compass—that is, backward compared to a DG (Directional Gyro). This can surprise you if you're not expecting it. Each short index line represents 5 degrees; the longer index lines represent 10-degree increments. Continue climbing to 2,800 feet.

> ▶ **Tip**
>
> *The Camel's rudder control is very sensitive. Move the rudder slightly, and then hold it for a second to see what it does. Make corrections from there. Constantly chasing the airplane with the rudder leads to overcontrolling, which typically ends your flight prematurely.*

Figure 2.17:
The Twin High-Rise,
your first waypoint, is
at the center. (View is
tilted downward for
clarity.)

Figure 2.18:
Each short index line
represents 5 degrees;
the longer index lines
represent 10-degree
increments.

Cruise

At 2,800 feet, level off and let the airplane accelerate. Reduce power to
2,200 rpm, using the F2 or F3 keys. (The Camel has a fixed-pitch prop, so
any slight climb or descent will alter your rpm.) Adjust your elevator trim
using numpad 7 for nose down and numpad 1 for nose up.

Your next waypoint is the Griffith Park Observatory and Dodger
Stadium. The observatory will pass to your left (Figure 2.19) and
the stadium will pass on your right (Figure 2.20).

Figure 2.19:
Griffith Park Observatory (ground textures have been turned off for clarity.)

Figure 2.20:
Dodger Stadium

Refer to these checkpoints just to make sure you're still on course. Now continue to fly heading 048 degrees until you reach your next waypoint, the Rose Bowl (Figure 2.21).

Cruise Climb

After crossing the Rose Bowl, turn right to heading 108 degrees, increase power to full by (press F4), and climb to 3,500 feet. Recall that you're climbing so you can clear El Monte Airport's airspace (Figure 2.22).

When you're directly over El Monte, turn left to heading 095 degrees, as your navigation log indicates. Maintain 3,500 feet.

▶ *Note*

On your leg from the Twin High-Rise to Griffith Park, you can see the Hollywood sign and the Hollywood Bowl off your port wing, and the Capital Records building off your right wing.

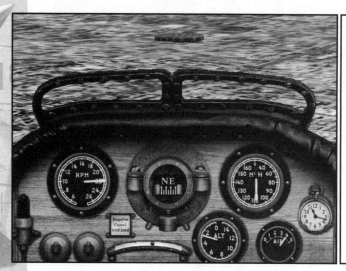

Figure 2.21:
The Rose Bowl

Figure 2.22:
El Monte Airport
(View is tilted down-
ward for clarity.)

Descent

The navigation log shows you'll begin your descent to Chino at Mt. San Antonio College. If you're flying along and keeping track of your flight time (you should be about 21 minutes into the flight), you'll notice *Flight Simulator 2000* doesn't model Mt. San Antonio College. What are you supposed to do now?

You'll do what you would in the real world when you miss a landmark: pick up your chart and start looking for another landmark (hopefully larger) in the same area. In this case, Brackett Airport (Figure 2.23) to the north and the little lake just west of the end of its runways (both on the left of your flight path) fit the bill.

**Figure 2.23:
Brackett Airport—time
to begin your descent
into Chino.**

To descend, use the F2 key to reduce power to about 1,600 rpm. As long as you don't try to maintain altitude with the stick, the airplane will descend by itself. Level off at 1,400 feet and increase power to about 1,800 rpm, using the F3 key. That should slow you to about 90 mph IAS.

Maintain your heading of 095 degrees to stay out of Brackett's Class D airspace. You're looking good! Chino should appear directly off your nose in a few minutes (Figure 2.24).

**Figure 2.24:
Chino!**

Approach

Enter the pattern for runway 26L using right traffic and reduce power to about 1,000 rpm, using F2 or F3 keys, when you're abeam the approach end of the runway. Adjust pitch attitude to maintain about 60 mph IAS during base and final, as shown in Figure 2.25. Smoothly increase or decrease throttle using the F3 and F2 keys to adjust your descent rate.

**Figure 2.25:
Adjust pitch attitude to
maintain about 60 mph
IAS on final.**

Landing

As soon as landing on the runway is assured, smoothly reduce throttle to idle by pressing the F2 key and establish the usual slight nose-up attitude. The Camel has no wheel brakes, so just let it roll to a stop.

Congratulations! If you've followed along, you're sitting on the runway at Chino. If you got lost, the following tips should help:

✛ Don't turn back right away if you think you're lost. Most of the time you're just behind schedule, and haven't crossed your waypoint yet.

✛ Be vigilant and track your progress on your navigation log and on your chart. Holding it turned in the direction you're flying (that is, so your chart's course line is pointed at the front of your airplane) can help you keep track of where you are.

✛ If you've determined you're lost, backtrack to your last known position and try again. But be sure to monitor your fuel. Nothing's worse than being lost and low on fuel.

✛ If all else fails, look for huge landmarks, such as coastlines or mountain ranges, and see if you can match them to anything on your chart. Find any airport and land ASAP.

> ▶ *Tip*
>
> *When landing any taildragger, you should hold full up elevator (back stick) as soon as the tailwheel is on the runway. Hold full up elevator all the way to tiedown.*

Asking for Directions and Arriving on Schedule

Chapter 3

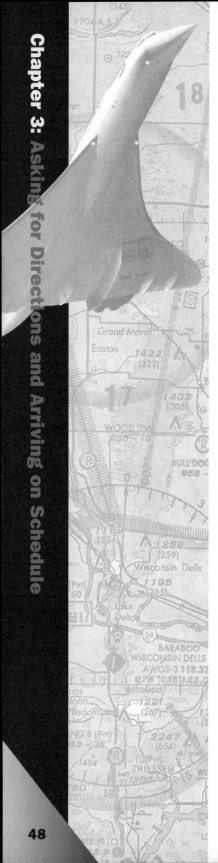
*T*he complex aircraft (aircraft with constant speed props and retractable landing gear) trainer position in the Flight Simulator 2000's flight line is the Cessna 182R RG (occasionally referred to in the simulation as the 182RG).

We'll begin this chapter by relating pilotage to the flight-planning concepts of dead reckoning and VFR radio navigation. We'll also talk about some handy NAVAID tricks you can use when you begin your IFR flights. Then we'll top off the chapter with a hands-on introduction to the 182R RG. We have lots to cover, so let's get started.

Dead Reckoning

As ominous as it may sound, dead reckoning is a navigation technique that sometimes meant the difference between life and death to many pioneer aviators. The term derives from *deduced* reckoning practices (because navigation was based on computations—that is, *deduced* by accounting for airspeed, course, heading, wind conditions, ground speed, and elapsed time). As the story goes, this colorful phrase came about because, in the early days of aviation, if you deduced wrong, you were as good as dead.

Practical VFR

In Chapter 2, you used pilotage to get where you wanted to go. But you also used dead reckoning calculations to build your flight plan to Chino. Technically, the only difference between true dead reckoning and what you accomplished there is that dead reckoning doesn't rely on visual check-points.

You're probably thinking that neither pilotage nor dead reckoning in themselves are very reliable (comforting?) ways to navigate anything but the shortest hops. You're right. That's precisely why pilotage and dead reckoning typically are used together. Even then, however, accuracy requires a lot of work—and, in some cases, luck.

Radio navigation greatly improves accuracy and simplifies flight planning and safety. In the sections that follow, we discuss ways to maintain as much accuracy as possible, regardless of your VFR navigation method.

Magnetic Compass Quirks

Several compass usage/behavioral characteristics affect the magnetic compass in the real world. Fortunately, *Flight Simulator 2000* relieves you from having to deal with them, because some of them aren't modeled.

The magnetic compass errors modeled are:

╋ **Lag and lead errors**—a compass will initially move in the opposite direction when turning from a northerly heading, and will initially lead a turn when turning from a southerly heading.

╋ **Acceleration/deceleration errors**—when accelerating a compass will swing to the north, and when decelerating the compass will swing towards the south when flying an easterly or westerly heading.

Nevertheless, quirks and all, the magnetic compass is a very reliable instrument. To bring up the compass window in the Cessna 182RG (Figure 3.1), press Shift+4 or click Instrument Panel on the Views menu, and then click Compass.

Figure 3.1:
The magnetic compass isn't prone to failure.

Directional Gyro

As a refresher, on a standard instrument cluster, the DG (Directional Gyro, commonly known today as the Heading Indicator, shown in Figure 3.2) is located in the center of the instrument panel, below the Attitude Indicator (AI). Unlike a magnetic compass, the DG hasn't the foggiest idea where north is until you tell (set) it.

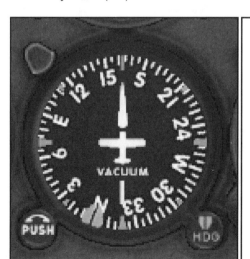

Figure 3.2:
The DG is located just below the AI in a standard instrument cluster.

▶ *Warning*

When setting your DG manually, remember that magnetic compass readings are reliable only when an aircraft is sitting on the ground, or in level, unaccelerated flight.

To set the DG manually (which is more like calibrating it), view your heading on the magnetic compass, and then click on the knob on the lower-left side of the DG to make it agree with the compass. *Flight Simulator 2000* also allows you to automate this task by simply pressing the D key.

The knob to the lower-right of the DG is used to set the autopilot heading bug, discussed in a later chapter. We'll talk about the autopilot a little later, but you adjust it the same way—by clicking on it.

Bracketing

One concept that will greatly improve your NAVAID tracking comes from a technique known as "bracketing." Here's how it works:

⁺ *Once you're established on a radial, pick a heading and hold it there. Most of the time a heading that coincides with your OBS (Omni Bearing Selector) setting is a good place to start.*

⁺ *Watch the CDI (course deviation indicator) needle to see if it moves. If it does, pick a new heading in the direction of the CDI needle movement and turn to it.*

⁺ *If the CDI needle continues to move in the same direction, pick another heading farther in the direction of the deviation, or if the CDI moves in the opposite direction, pick another heading slightly short of your original heading and turn to that.*

⁺ *Continue making smaller and smaller corrections until the CDI needle remains steady.*

⁺ *When you learn this technique, remember that bracketing doesn't require your DG be set to coincide with the magnetic compass once you're on a radial, so there's no need to obsess over keeping them in synch. All you're interested in are reference headings and their relationships to the CDI needle/radial. It makes no difference what the DG numbers say. If you're overly concerned with DG numbers, you may try to track radials with the same heading as your OBS selection, causing you to "chase the needle" excessively.*

Airspeeds Revisited

Aviation involves two types of airspeed—IAS and TAS. It's time to talk about how and when to use each in dead reckoning navigation.

Indicated Airspeed

Recall that IAS is the actual instrument indication for a given flight condition. Factors such as an altitude other than standard sea level, errors in the instrument, and errors due to installation, compressibility, and the like will cause variations between the instrument indication and actual flight speed.

Although IAS is everything when it comes to keeping an aircraft in the air (the airplane only cares about how many air molecules it feels under its wings and in its engines, not how you measure them), in that form it's useless for navigational purposes. For navigation purposes, TAS is what you're after.

True Airspeed

A quick review: TAS is airspeed that considers altitude and air density together, corrected for temperature differences. In simplest terms, TAS removes the environmental condition variables of airspeed (converted to a standardized reference scale, so to speak).

The relevance of TAS to flight-planning and navigation lies in calculating ground speed. Although we're only measuring your speed in an air mass that floats above the ground, as you learned in the last chapter, it's possible to calculate ground speed if you know the direction and speed of that air mass.

DME Ground Speed

Experienced pilots rely on DME (Distance Measuring Equipment) to quickly acquire their ground speed while they're in flight. This really saves on calculations, because you simply read your ground speed off the instrument. Unfortunately, you can't use DME for flight-planning because you're still on the ground. Also important to note is that DME works only with some NAVAIDs (VOR-DMEs, VORTACs, and localizers equipped with DME) and is not available all the time.

Except for the Sopwith Camel and the Schweizer 2-32 Sailplane, every aircraft in *Flight Simulator 2000* is equipped with DME. You'll find their displays in various places on their respective instrument panels (Figure 3.3).

> ▶ **Warning**
>
> *DME ground speeds are accurate only when you're flying more or less directly toward or away from the DME-transmitting NAVAID (e.g., VOR-DMEs, VORTACs, and localizers equipped with DME).*

Figure 3.3: This DME is located on the Cessna 182R RG's instrument panel. Use this switch to select which NAV radio it's slaved to.

In addition, *Flight Simulator 2000*'s single-engine prop planes have additional DME displays on their radio stack windows. (See Figure 3.4.)

Figure 3.4: This is the 182R RG's radio stack. This switch toggles the NAV radio it's slaved to.

NAVAID Trivia and Tips

If you've completed Rod's lessons and/or read the material recommended at the beginning of this book, you have a pretty good understanding of how NAVAIDs work and how to read them. But before moving to the next stage and discussing how to use them, we offer some lesser-known tidbits of information to help you master them.

VOR

VOR (Very high frequency Omnidirectional Range) beacons are the backbone of aviation radio navigation. There are three classes of VORs—High, Low, and Terminal. Table 3.1 shows reception and frequency ranges for each VOR class.

Table 3.1: VOR Range and Frequency Table		
VOR Class	**Reception Range**	**Frequency Range**
HVOR	40 nm (below 18,000') 100 nm (above FL450) 130 nm (18,000'–FL450)	112.00 – 118.00
LVOR	40 nm (below 18,000')	112.00 – 118.00
TVOR	25 nm (below 12,000')	108.00 – 112.00
These are minimum "guaranteed" ranges. Reception ranges are typically greater, but vary with location and obstacles.		

It's important to note that minimum reception ranges only apply if there are no obstructions, because VOR reception is line-of-sight.

Tracking VOR Radials

Use the following tips when tracking radials:

+ Radials are always *from* the VOR.

+ The CDI needle doesn't point to the VOR. It only indicates your position relative to the selected VOR radial.

+ It's easier to fly a specific radial inbound by changing the OBS to read 180 degrees opposite the radial with a *To* flag indication. For example, to fly inbound on the 090 radial, set the OBS to 270 and you'll be able to fly that radial inbound with a To flag.

NDB

NDB (Non-Directional Beacons) are tracked with an ADF (Automatic Direction Finder). As simple as these systems are, pilots tend to have trouble using them because the mental calculations required are pretty high. But there are a couple of ways to minimize some of the mental gymnastics in the cockpit.

Magnetic Bearings and Relative Bearings

These tips will help you find your radials and never lose your bearings:

+ Like VOR radials, NDB bearings are always considered to be *from* the NDB.

+ Although there are no flags on an ADF, the head of the ADF arrow always points to the NDB, so the tail always indicates the bearing. For example, a 90-degree bearing *to* an NDB indicates you're west of the station. Conversely, a 90-degree bearing *from* an NDB indicates you're east of the station.

+ To find the magnetic bearing to an NDB station quickly, mentally superimpose the position of the ADF needle over your DG, as shown in Figure 3.5. The NDB's magnetic bearing will coincide with the mental needle position on the DG.

+ "NDB Relative bearings" are relative to your position and orientation, and always relative to the nose of your aircraft equaling 360 degrees. For example, an NDB at your three o'clock position will have a relative bearing of 90 degrees, and an NDB at your six o'clock position will have a relative bearing of 180 degrees. Using the technique of super-imposing the ADF needle on the DG eliminates the need for relative bearings in the cockpit.

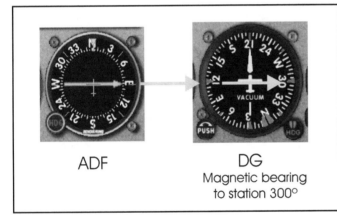

ADF

DG
Magnetic bearing
to station 300°

Figure 3.5: Superimpose the position of the ADF needle over your DG to find the magnetic bearing to station.

Intercepting NDB Bearings

To intercept an NDB bearing, determine the magnetic bearing to station using the aforementioned technique (superimpose the position of the ADF needle over your DG). Then determine the magnetic heading you need to obtain the angle of interception you want (typically 30–45 degrees).

You'll know when you're on course/on the outbound bearing when your ADF needle's tail points at your desired magnetic bearing. Then simply turn to the heading that equals the magnetic bearing of the ADF needle's tail to fly outbound, or turn to the magnetic bearing indicated by the pointy end of the ADF needle to fly inbound.

NAVAID Tricks

Understanding how radio navigation instruments work and how to read them is only as valuable as your ability to answer a basic navigation question: "Where am I?" Here are some useful NAVAID tricks often overlooked by non-instrument-rated pilots.

Identifying NAVAIDs

Always identify every NAVAID before you rely on it. The act of identification ensures that you're receiving a reliable signal and, more important, that you're tracking the right NAVAID. This procedure may sound silly, but you'd be surprised how many times pilots track the wrong VOR by inadvertently tuning in the wrong frequency.

There are two ways to identify NAVAIDs. The first is by using the following commands and listening for the proper three-letter Morse code station identifier.

NAVAID	Keystroke
VOR1	Ctrl+1
VOR2	Ctrl+2
DME1	Ctrl+3
DME2	Ctrl+4
NDB	Ctrl+5

The second method doesn't require you to know Morse code. You can identify VOR and ADF reception by viewing the Radio dialog box shown in Figure 3.6. (To access the Radio WIndow, click Navigation in the Aircraft menu and then click Radios.) The corresponding identifier, name, and position will appear on the right of the window when it's tuned.

Flying Direct

The ability to fly directly to a NAVAID can not only save you a lot of time (by shortening the distance between two points), it can also save your virtual skin should you get lost. The actual procedures are quite simple and as you'll see, these same skills will come in very handy later on.

Direct to VOR

To fly directly to a VOR, first tune in the VOR frequency and identify the NAVAID using one of the aforementioned methods. Next turn the OBS by pressing the V+1 on your keyboard for NAV1's VOR indicator head (press V+2 for NAV2's indicator head) followed by the − (hyphen) and = (equal sign) keys until you center the CDI (Course Deviation Indicator) needle with a To flag. Note the OBS setting (in the top-center of the indicator head) and turn to that heading. That heading will take you directly to the VOR.

▶ **Note**

You can retrieve information about any airport or NAVAID by double clicking the item in the Map View.

▶ **Tip**

To remember which flag you want to see to fly direct to a VOR is to remember that you want to fly To the station.

Direct to NDB

Flying direct to an NDB is extremely simple. Just turn your airplane in the direction of the NDB needle until it centers/points straight up. Recall that the ADF needle always points to an NDB.

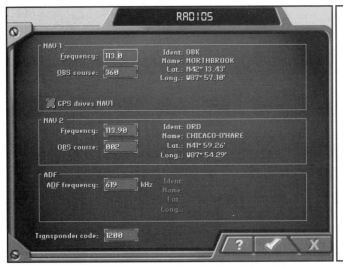

Figure 3.6:
View this window to identify VOR and ADF reception without using Morse code.

DME, ADF, and VOR Intersections

Tracking a radial can get you where you want to go, but it doesn't tell you how far along/where you are on your course. Using intersections can help give you your precise location.

An intersection is where two paths cross. In radio navigation this requires two instrument readings. Note that this doesn't mean two instruments. By triangulating your position between two NAVAIDs (two VORs, two ADFs, or a VOR and an ADF), you can determine your position. But the easiest NAVAID-based method for locating intersections uses DME. Let's talk about that first.

DME will tell you your present distance (minus slant error) from a DME-enabled VOR. Because you know (or can quickly find out) which radial you're on, you can determine your position on that radial (as shown in Figure 3.7).

ADF intersections are simple to find, too. Remember that the tail of the ADF needle always points to the NDB's bearing from. Simple, right? The hard part is figuring out whether you're before or after (flown past) a given intersection/radial. If you remember that ADF needles always move to the rear of your aircraft (the six o'clock position on your ADF), it will be easy to figure out. For example, if the ADF needle's direction is moving away from your intersection's bearing from the NDB, you've passed it. Figure 3.8 illustrates this concept.

Figuring VOR intersections is the most confusing part for pilots, because VORs have To and From flags. To avoid this confusion, always use a To OBS setting—180 degrees from the radial. For example, instead

▶ **Warning**

If a wind is present, flying direct to an NDB with no regard for bearings will cause you to home in rather than track directly to it.

of trying to look for a 090-degree radial with a From setting (remember, all radials are From), set your OBS for a 270-degree To setting. (See Figure 3.9.)

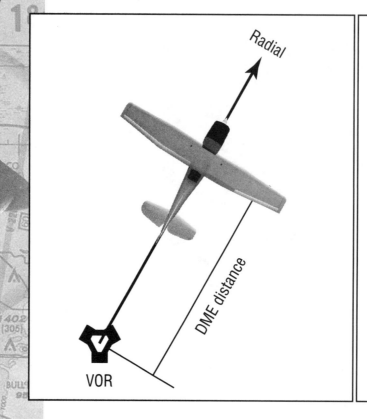

Figure 3.7:
You can define intersections using DME.

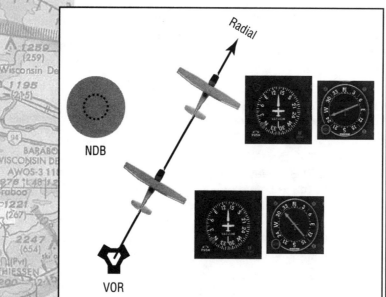

Figure 3.8:
The lower airplane is on the 270-degree NDB radial. The upper aircraft has just passed the 210-degree radial.

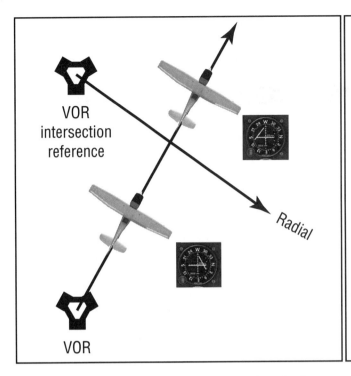

Figure 3.9:
The lower airplane
hasn't crossed the
090-degree radial, and
the upper airplane has.

Now imagine yourself sitting in an airplane in the center of the VOR indicator head; mentally picture the indicator head so the OBS index is rotated toward where the VOR is located. In other words, if the VOR is on the right side of your aircraft, picture the top of the display in the two o'clock position. If the VOR is located to the left of your airplane, picture the top of the display facing the 10 o'clock position. When you do this, it should be clear whether you've crossed the intersection radial.

Flying the Cessna 182RG

Beyond the fact that the 182RG has retractable landing gear and the 182S doesn't, flying the Cessna 182RG is very similar to flying the 182S in many ways. For those of you moving from *Flight Simulator 98*'s 182RG, *Flight Simulator 2000*'s 182RG is basically the same except it that it now sports cowl flaps (as they do in the real world). In any event, all Cessnas modeled in *Flight Simulator* reflect the simplicity and stability found in their real-world counterparts.

Aircraft Performance

For you *Flight Simulator 98* veterans, aside from landing gear capability, the main difference between the familiar 182S and the 182RG is that the 182RG has a carburetor, while the 182S is fuel-injected. Performance differences between the two (besides the 5-hp advantage in favor of the RG) lie mostly in the reduced drag afforded by retractable landing gear.

V Speeds

Like some aircraft built after 1975, all Cessna 182RG V speeds are listed as KIAS (Knots Indicated Air Speed).

V Speed	KIAS
V_R	50
V_Y	88
V_X	59
V_A	—
(3,100#)	112
(2,550#)	101
(2,000#)	89
V_S	41
V_{SO}	39
V_{NE}	181
V_{NO}	159
V_{LE}	140
V_{LO}	140
V_{FE}	—
0° to 10°	140
10° to 20°	120
20° to FULL	95
Approach	—
Flaps UP	70–80
Flaps FULL	65–75
Short Field Flaps FULL	64
Max. Demonstrated Crosswind Component	18 knots
Max Range Glide	—
(3,100#)	80
(2,550#)	72
(2,000#)	64
Emergency Descent	—
(Gear down)	80

Advanced Systems

The Cessna 182RG has four advances over the Sopwith Camel we flew in the last chapter—a constant-speed prop, fuel-mixture control, retractable landing gear, and flaps. Rod discusses flaps in the *Flight Simulator 2000 Pilot's Handbook*, so we'll discuss the others here.

Constant-Speed Propeller As you know, a constant-speed prop is like a transmission for your airplane. It may intimidate you at first, but if you think of it as a gearshift, you won't have any trouble. Simply use it to shift into high gear when you're on the cruise configuration. Press Ctrl+F2 to lower prop rpm and Ctrl+F3 to raise prop rpm. Or simply drag the prop control (the blue knob) with your mouse, but it's difficult to move it precisely that way.

Mixture Control The mixture control leans the fuel-to-air mixture ratio. The leaner (less fuel going in) you can run the engine, the better your fuel economy. Of course, if you run your engine too lean, you can damage it: fuel acts as a coolant, and if you run it too lean you'll starve your engine and it will stop running.

Although you'll generally lean your engine above 3,000 feet, due to the consequences of overleaning, you'll lean your engine for maximum fuel economy only when you're in cruise configuration. Use Ctrl+Shift+F2 to lean the fuel mixture and Ctrl+Shift+F3 to enrich it. You can also use your mouse to adjust your fuel mixture (the red knob), but, as with the prop control, it's difficult to adjust precisely.

Retractable Landing Gear The 182R RG's retractable landing gear is an electric/hydraulic system. An electric pump creates the necessary hydraulic pressure to raise and lower the landing gear. Toggle the landing gear using the G key, or click on the landing gear control lever (Figure 3.10) on the lower-left side of the instrument panel. If you have a landing-gear failure, you can attempt to re-pressurize the system by repeatedly pressing Ctrl+G to pump the gear into the down-and-locked position.

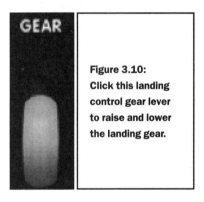

**Figure 3.10:
Click this landing
control gear lever
to raise and lower
the landing gear.**

To help prevent gear-up landings, the 182R RG has a gear warning horn. It sounds if you lower the flaps to 20 degrees or greater without the gear lowered, and when you retard the throttle below 10 inches MP (manifold pressure) with the gear retracted.

Cowl Flaps It's funny how intimidating cowl flaps can be to pilots unfamiliar with them. Cowl flaps are nothing more than cockpit-controlled cooling vents for the engine. The idea is keep the engine in the proper operating temperature range: open them to cool the engine and close them to let the engine warm up.

The cowl-flap control on the 182R RG is located near throttle and carburetor heat control (Figure 3.11). To operate cowl flaps, simply click on the end of the control in the position you desire. Up is open and down is closed. Closingg cowl flaps cuts drag slightly.

Carburetor Heat Carburetor ice can form any time there's moisture in the air, independent of the OAT (Outside Air Temperature). However, carburetor ice is most likely to form when the air is humid and the OAT is below about 70° F. When a fluid (such as aviation gasoline) evaporates, it cools the surrounding air, like a refrigerator. Any moisture in the air can freeze and accumulate in the carburetor throat. If the accumulation is great enough, it can choke the engine.

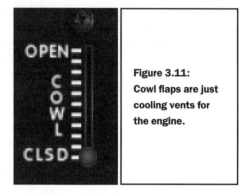

Figure 3.11:
Cowl flaps are just cooling vents for the engine.

To operate carburetor heat, press the H key. You'll generally only apply carburetor heat when the engine is operating outside of the MP green arc range—and, of course, when you suspect carburetor ice. If you experience a drop in MP at a constant setting, suspect carburetor ice. If your suspicions about carburetor ice are correct, you'll experience a slight drop in MP followed by a rise in MP a few minutes later.

Flight Plan

We'll be applying some of the skills we discussed earlier in this chapter for a VFR flight. We'll also be putting to use the radio navigation techniques and aircraft controls we covered.

Airports

We'll be flying from Van Nuys Airport (the busiest municipal airport in the United States) to Torrance, Zamperini Field (TOA). What's unusual about this flight is Los Angeles International Airport (LAX) and its Class B airspace which lies directly in between both airports.

The longest runway at Van Nuys is 8,000 feet. The longest runway at Zamperini is 5,000 feet. Given that the sea level, minimum required hard surface runway lengths at maximum gross weight on a standard day (15°C) are 1,515 feet for takeoff and 1,400 feet for landing in zero wind, we're in good shape.

> ▶ *Tip*
>
> *Icing conditions can be generated from the advanced weather dialog box.*

Route

Here's the navigation log for our trip to Zamperini:

Waypoint	Frequency	Course	Altitude	Distance	ETE
VNY ATIS 118.45	113.1	160°	2,800'	7.5 nm	00:06
Sepulveda Pass 7.5 DME from VNY	110.8	Direct ~160°	3,500'	5 nm	00:02
SMO	110.8	132°	3,500'	3 nm	00:01
LAX SFRA	110.8 xpdr 1201	132°	3,500'	4 nm	00:02
Northrop/ Hawthorne Airport 7.5 DME from SMO	110.8 xpdr 1200	132°	1,100'	4 nm	00:03
Mobile Refinery	111.4 (AVX)	174°	1,100'	2.6 nm	00:02
TOA (26 DME from AVX) ATIS 125.6		TOTAL		26.1 nm	00:16

As mentioned earlier, what makes this flight really interesting is that we'll be navigating through LAX's Class B airspace through its VFR corridor (officially called the Los Angeles Special Flight Rules Area). If the SFRA didn't exist, we'd have to either request clearance to transition through (guess who gets priority—a 747, or our little Cessna?), or we'd have to fly around the outside of LAX Class B airspace, which would double our trip distance.

From Van Nuys Airport, we'll fly outbound on VNY R-160 degrees (160 degrees radial) over the Sepulveda Pass (a ridge of mountains that separates the San Fernando Valley, where Van Nuys is located, and the Los Angeles basin). The significance of the Sepulveda Pass as a waypoint will be discussed in the next section.

We'll then fly direct to SMO VOR and outbound on SMO R-132 degrees. We chose this radial because the LAX SFRA specifies a narrow flight path, which happens to be exactly the same!

We use Northrop/Hawthorn Airport as the next waypoint because its located just beyond LAX's SFRA. It's important to know when we're clear of the SFRA because we need to switch our transponder back to 1,200, and begin our descent to TOA.

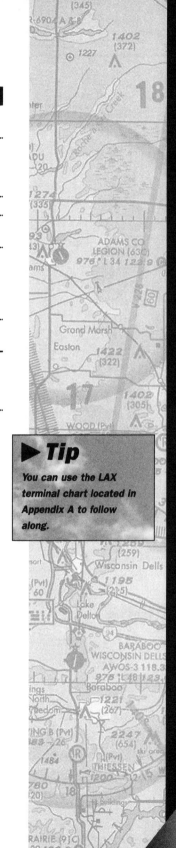

► **Tip**

You can use the LAX terminal chart located in Appendix A to follow along.

We'll continue on SMO R-132 degrees until we reach TOA's northern approach visual reporting point, the Mobile Oil Refinery. Instead of totally relying on this visual landmark that we might not see or recognize (remember what happened to us in Chapter 2 when we were looking for Mt. San Antonio College?), radio navigation allows us to use 11 DME from SMO R-132 degrees to mark this waypoint. As an added benefit, this waypoint is located in the perfect spot—if we turn directly towards TOA at that point it'll deliver us on a downwind 45, pattern entry into TOA. How convenient!

Altitude

After takeoff we'll climb to 2,800 feet. This will keep us below Burbank Airport's Class C airspace floor, which begins at 3,000 feet. Once we're clear of the Burbank's Class C (just on the other side of the Sepulveda Pass—7.5 DME from VNY) we can climb to 3,500 feet. We selected 3,500 feet because it's a proper VFR cruise altitude and the required altitude to fly through the LAX SFRA.

LAX's Class B airspace floor begins at 5,000 feet after exiting the SFRA and rises to 8,000 until about midway in the San Pedro Channel. Since TOA's airspace begins 4 nm from our SFRA exit point, we need to begin our descent to TOA's pattern altitude of 1,100 feet right away. We need to descend 2,400 feet (3,500 feet – 1,100 feet = 2,400 feet) in 4 nm.

Considering a typical descent airspeed of 110 KIAS (which works out to 1.83 miles per minute), we need to descend 2,400 feet in 2.18 minutes/1,101 fpm (4 ÷ 1.83 = 2.18 and 2,400 ÷ 2.2 = 1,100.9). That descent rate is a little steep for this class of aircraft. We can compensate by slowing to and descending at 90 KIAS, and by beginning our descent about as soon as possible after exiting the LAX SFRA.

At 90 KIAS we can descend at 900 FPM and make our target altitude within the flight leg distance. While this is less than ideal, with some deliberate effort we can descend to pattern altitude without sacrificing safety, comfort, or resorting to zig-zagging and/or flying in circles while descending to lose altitude.

Fuel/Performance

We have more than enough fuel to make our 26.1 nm trip. The following pages are cruise performance charts for the Cessna 182RG. These are used for flight planning purposes and to determine optimum cruise performance settings.

Cessna Model R182

CONDITIONS: 3100 lbs., Recommended Lean Mixture, Cowl Flaps Closed

Cruise Performance: Pressure Altitude 2000 Feet

RPM	MP	20°C Below Standard Temp -9°C			Standard Temp 11°C			20°C Above Standard Temp 31°C		
		%BHP	KTAS	GPH	%BHP	KTAS	GPH	%BHP	KTAS	GPH
2400	23				76	148	13.6	73	149	13.2
	22	74	143	13.3	71	145	12.8	69	146	12.4
	21	69	140	12.4	67	141	12.0	64	142	11.6
	20	64	136	11.6	62	137	11.3	60	138	10.9
2300	23	75	145	13.5	72	146	13.1	70	147	12.6
	22	71	141	12.7	68	142	12.3	66	143	11.9
	21	66	137	11.9	64	138	11.5	62	139	11.2
	20	61	134	11.2	59	135	10.8	57	135	10.5
2200	23	72	142	12.9	69	143	12.5	67	144	12.1
	22	67	139	12.1	65	140	11.7	63	141	11.4
	21	63	135	11.4	61	136	11.0	59	137	10.7
	20	59	131	10.7	57	132	10.3	55	133	10.0
2100	23	67	139	12.2	66	140	11.8	63	141	11.5
	22	64	136	11.5	62	137	11.2	60	137	10.8
	21	60	132	10.9	58	133	10.5	56	134	10.2
	20	55	128	10.1	54	129	9.8	52	129	9.5
	19	51	124	94	50	124	9.1	48	125	8.9
	18	47	119	8.7	45	119	8.5	44	120	8.2

Cruise Performance: Pressure Altitude 4000 Feet

RPM	MP	20°C Below Standard Temp -13°C			Standard Temp 7°C			20°C Above Standard Temp 27°C		
		%BHP	KTAS	GPH	%BHP	KTAS	GPH	%BHP	KTAS	GPH
2400	23				78	153	14.0	75	154	13.6
	22	76	148	13.7	73	149	13.2	71	150	12.8
	21	71	144	12.8	69	145	12.4	66	146	12.0
	20	66	140	12.0	64	141	11.6	62	142	11.2
2300	23	77	149	14.0	75	150	13.5	72	151	13.0
	22	73	145	13.1	70	147	12.7	68	148	12.2
	21	68	142	12.3	66	143	11.9	64	144	11.5
	20	64	138	11.5	61	139	11.1	59	140	10.8
2200	23	74	146	13.3	71	148	12.9	69	149	12.4
	22	70	143	12.5	67	144	12.1	65	145	11.7
	21	65	138	11.8	63	140	11.4	61	141	11.0
	20	61	135	11.0	59	136	10.7	57	137	10.3
2100	23	70	134	12.7	64	145	12.2	65	146	11.8
	22	66	140	11.9	64	141	11.5	62	142	11.2
	21	62	136	11.2	60	137	10.9	58	138	10.5
	20	58	132	10.5	55	133	10.1	54	134	9.8
	19	53	128	9.8	51	129	9.5	50	129	9.2
	18	49	123	9.1	47	124	8.8	46	124	8.5

Cruise Performance: Pressure Altitude 6000 Feet

RPM	MP	20°C Below Standard Temp -17°C			Standard Temp 3°C			20°C Above Standard Temp 23°C		
		%BHP	KTAS	GPH	%BHP	KTAS	GPH	%BHP	KTAS	GPH
2400	22				75	154	13.6	73	155	13.1
	21	76	148	13.2	71	150	12.7	68	151	12.3
	20	69	145	12.3	66	146	11.9	64	147	11.5
	19	64	140	11.5	61	141	11.1	59	142	10.8
2300	23				77	155	13.9	74	156	13.4
	22	75	150	13.5	72	151	13.0	70	152	12.6
	21	70	146	12.7	68	147	12.2	66	148	11.8
	20	66	142	11.9	63	143	11.5	61	144	11.1
2200	23	76	151	13.7	74	152	13.3	71	153	12.8
	22	72	147	12.9	69	148	12.5	67	150	12.1
	21	67	144	12.1	65	145	11.7	63	146	11.4
	20	63	140	11.4	61	141	11.0	59	141	10.7
2100	23	72	148	13.1	70	149	12.6	68	150	12.2
	22	68	144	12.3	66	145	11.9	64	146	11.5
	21	64	141	11.6	62	142	11.2	60	142	10.8
	20	60	137	10.9	57	137	10.5	56	138	10.2
	19	55	132	10.1	53	133	9.8	52	133	9.5
	18	51	128	9.4	49	128	9.1	48	128	8.8

Cruise Performance: Pressure Altitude 8000 Feet

RPM	MP	20°C Below Standard Temp -21°C			Standard Temp -1°C			20°C Above Standard Temp 19°C		
		%BHP	KTAS	GPH	%BHP	KTAS	GPH	%BHP	KTAS	GPH
2400	21	76	153	13.6	73	154	13.1	70	155	12.7
	20	71	149	12.7	68	150	12.3	66	151	11.9
	19	66	145	11.9	63	146	11.5	61	147	11.1
	18	61	140	11.1	59	141	10.7	57	142	10.3
2300	21	73	151	13.1	70	152	12.6	68	153	12.2
	20	68	147	12.2	65	148	11.8	63	149	11.4
	19	63	142	11.4	61	143	11.1	59	144	10.7
	18	58	138	10.6	56	138	10.3	54	139	9.9
2200	21	70	148	12.5	67	149	12.1	65	150	11.7
	20	65	144	11.7	63	145	11.3	60	146	11.0
	19	60	140	11.0	58	141	10.6	56	141	10.3
	18	56	135	10.2	54	136	9.9	52	136	9.5
2100	21	66	145	11.9	64	146	11.5	61	147	11.2
	20	62	141	11.2	59	142	10.8	57	142	10.5
	19	57	137	10.5	55	137	10.1	53	138	9.8
	18	53	132	9.7	51	132	9.4	49	133	9.1
	17	49	127	9.0	47	127	8.7	45	127	3.4

Cruise Performance: Pressure Altitude 10,000 Feet

RPM	MP	20°C Below Standard Temp -25°C			Standard Temp -5°C			20°C Above Standard Temp 15°C		
		%BHP	KTAS	GPH	%BHP	KTAS	GPH	%BHP	KTAS	GPH
2400	20	73	154	13.1	70	155	12.6	68	156	12.2
	19	68	149	12.2	65	150	11.8	63	151	11.4
	18	63	145	11.4	60	145	11.0	58	146	10.6
	17	58	140	10.6	56	140	10.2	54	141	9.9
2300	20	70	151	12.6	67	152	12.2	65	153	11.8
	19	65	147	11.8	63	148	11.4	61	149	11.0
	18	60	142	11.0	58	143	10.6	56	143	10.3
	17	56	137	10.2	53	138	9.8	52	138	9.5
2200	20	67	149	12.1	65	150	11.7	62	150	11.3
	19	62	144	11.3	60	145	10.9	58	146	10.6
	18	58	140	10.5	56	140	10.2	54	140	9.9
	17	53	134	9.8	51	135	9.4	49	135	9.1
2100	20	64	146	11.5	61	146	11.2	59	147	10.8
	19	59	141	10.8	57	142	10.4	55	142	10.1
	18	55	136	10.1	53	137	9.7	51	137	9.4
	17	51	131	9.3	49	131	9.0	47	131	8.7
	16	46	125	8.6	44	125	8.3	43	125	8.1

Cruise Performance: Pressure Altitude 12,000 Feet

RPM	MP	20°C Below Standard Temp -29°C			Standard Temp -9°C			20°C Above Standard Temp 11°C		
		%BHP	KTAS	GPH	%BHP	KTAS	GPH	%BHP	KTAS	GPH
2400	18	65	149	11.7	62	150	11.3	60	151	10.9
	17	60	144	10.9	57	145	10.5	55	145	10.1
	16	55	138	10.0	53	139	9.7	51	139	9.4
	15	50	132	9.2	48	132	8.8	46	132	8.6
2300	18	62	147	11.3	60	148	10.9	58	148	10.6
	17	57	142	10.5	55	142	10.1	53	142	9.8
	16	53	136	9.7	51	136	9.3	49	136	9.0
	15	48	130	8.8	46	130	8.5	44	129	8.3
2200	18	60	144	10.9	58	145	10.5	56	145	10.2
	17	55	139	10.1	53	139	9.7	51	139	9.4
	16	50	133	9.3	48	133	9.0	47	133	8.7
2100	18	57	141	10.4	55	141	10.0	53	142	9.7
	17	52	136	9.6	50	136	9.3	49	136	9.0
	16	48	130	8.9	46	130	8.6	44	129	8.3

Cruise Performance: Pressure Altitude 14,000 Feet										
		20°C Below Standard Temp -33°C			Standard Temp -13°C			20°C Above Standard Temp 7°C		
RPM	MP	%BHP	KTAS	GPH	%BHP	KTAS	GPH	%BHP	KTAS	GPH
2400	16	57	143	10.3	54	143	10.0	52	143	96
	15	51	137	9.5	49	137	9.1	48	136	8.8
2300	16	54	141	10.0	52	141	9.6	51	141	9.3
	15	49	134	9.1	48	134	8.8	46	134	8.5
2200	16	52	138	9.6	50	138	9.3	48	138	9.0
	15	47	131	8.8	46	131	8.5	44	131	8.2
2100	16	50	134	9.2	48	134	8.9	46	134	8.6

Special Considerations

Chances are pretty good that if you look up in the sky the next time you hear an airplane fly overhead, it'll be one of the rather ubiquitous high-wing Cessnas. There's very little in the area of special attention that has to be conducted to fly this popular aircraft safely. But one aspect of aviation that affects all powered aircraft is noise abatement.

In an effort to be good virtual neighbors with the people living near our virtual airports, we should follow the noise abatement procedures for Van Nuys. As with most aircraft-generated noise, the further the distance the sound producer is from the observer, the quieter (read: less disturbing) it'll be. But because we're flying straight out (runway heading) and climbing above 1,000 feet AGL, we meet the minimum noise guidelines.

Flight Tutorial

Since we're flying the Cessna 182R RG, select it from the Aircraft menu, Aircraft selection. Next use the World menu's Map View dialogue and move yourself to Latitude N34°12.39', Longitude W118°29.50', Altitude +802, and Heading 342 as shown in Figure 3.12. This will place you at the base of the Van Nuys Airport control tower.

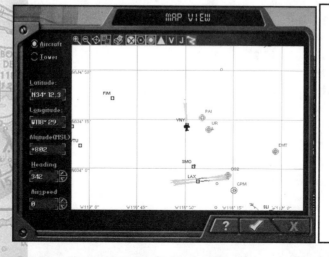

Figure 3.12:
You can move yourself to an exact location using the Map View window.

There are no minimum Display details required for this flight, but the weather must be VFR. If you're taking your first flight, consider making this a day flight to simplify things.

Before Starting Engine

Naturally, because the engine is already started, you'll have to shut it down before we can start it again. This may seem silly, but we'll do this just so we can cover how to start the engine manually.

You can shut the 182R RG's engine down by pressing Ctrl+Shift+F1. This will place the fuel mixture lever in the full lean position.

Action	Response
Preflight Inspection	COMPLETE
Passenger Briefing	COMPLETE
Seats, Belts, Harnesses	ADJUST AND LOCK
Brakes	TEST AND SET

Press Ctrl+"." (period) to set the parking brakes. The PARKING BRAKES message will flash on the screen when it's engaged.

Avionics Power Switch	OFF

The Avionics Power switch (Figure 3.13) is located on the lower center of the instrument panel. Click on it with your mouse to toggle.

Figure 3.13:
The avionics power switch controls all power to your radios.

Electrical Equipment	OFF
Circuit Breakers	CHECK IN
Landing Gear Lever	DOWN
Autopilot	OFF

There is a secondary autopilot master switch located in the upper-left corner of the instrument panel between the combo vacuum and Amp gauge and the clock (see Figure 3.14). When the light is off, the autopilot is disengaged.

▶ *Tip*

If you'd like to fly this flight again with the same conditions, use the Save Flight function by pressing the ";" (semicolon) key.

▶ *Note*

If you want to fly this flight from start to finish begin here. Otherwise you can jump ahead to the Before Takeoff Checklist.

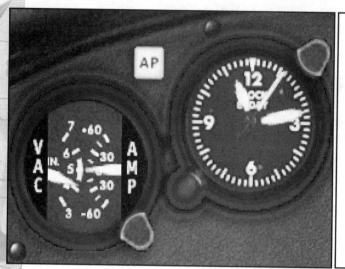

Figure 3.14:
When the "AP" light is off, the autopilot is disengaged. You can click it to toggle it on and off, but it won't operate if the master switch is turned off.

Cowl Flaps	OPEN
Fuel Selector Valve	BOTH

The fuel selector (Figure 3.15) is located just to the left of the carb heat control and its switch is operated by mouse clicks. Just click on the position you desire to set it.

Figure 3.15:
Unless you have a fuel imbalance problem while in level flight, the fuel selector switch remains in the Both setting most of the time.

Starting Engine

You could use the automatic engine start procedure (Ctrl+E) here, but how much fun would that be?

Action	Response
Prime	AS REQUIRED

The primer (Figure 3.16) injects a bit of fuel into the engine to help it start. It's located on the far-left side of the instrument panel. Each mouse click will cause it to send one pump's worth of fuel into the engine. Clicking it three times will simulate what's typically required for starting a cold engine.

Figure 3.16:
Click the primer pump
three times before
starting a cold engine.

Carburetor Heat	**COLD**

When the carburetor heat control is in, it is in the cold position. Press the H key to toggle it.

Throttle	**PUMP once, leave open 1/4"**

Press F4 followed by F1, then F3 about 6–8 times.

Propeller	**HIGH RPM**

The prop should still be at high, but to double-check, press Ctrl+F4 once.

Mixture	**RICH**

Press Ctrl+Shift+F4 to move the mixture control to full rich.

Propeller Area	**CLEAR**

This is a warning to bystanders that you're going to start the engine. Although we don't have any virtual people walking around the flightline, if you feel a bit self-conscious, you don't need to yell "clear prop!" in the middle of the night.

Master Switch	**ON**

The master switch (Figure 3.17) is really a split-switch. The left side connects the airplanes, electrical system to the engine alternator (and doubles as a circuit breaker of sorts), and the right half connects the battery to the system. Make sure you flip both halves on with your mouse.

Auxiliary Fuel Pump	**ON (CHECK FOR PRESSURE) THEN OFF**

Not modeled.

Ignition Switch	**START**

Click and hold the ignition switch shown in Figure 3.18 where it says START until the engine kicks over, or press the M key followed by pressing and holding the = (equals) key until the engine starts.

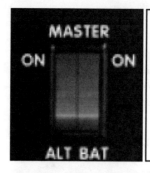

Figure 3.17:
The master switch is a split switch that connects the airplane's electrical system to the alternator and battery.

Figure 3.18:
You have to hold the ignition switch until the engine starts—just like a real engine!

Oil Pressure   CHECK

The oil pressure gauge (Figure 3.19) is located below the fuel gauges on the left side of the instrument panel. What you're looking for is an oil pressure reading. At low RPM/idle, it's normal to have oil pressure readings below the green arc.

Figure 3.19:
The oil pressure gauge is located to the bottom right of the fuel gauges.

Starter	CHECK DISENGAGED

If starter were still engaged, the ammeter would indicate full-scale charge with engine running at 1,000 RPM. Note this because we'll run across this later again when we talk about turbine engines.

Avionics Power Switch	ON
Navigation Lights and Beacon	ON AS REQUIRED

Press the L key to turn on the NAV lights and Beacon.

Radios	ON

The avionics switch controls radio power. Once the engine is started, go ahead and listen to ATIS on 118.45. From here we'd make a call to ground control for clearance to taxi to the runway. To do this, press Shift+2 to bring up the radio stack, then press the C key and the – (hyphen) and = (equals) keys to tune the radio.

We're going to be using runway 16L for our flight today, so go ahead and release the parking brake (the "." [period] key) and taxi straight ahead. Make a right turn at the first intersection and stop facing 160 degrees (in the direction we'll be taking off). We'll perform our engine run-up there.

> ▶ **Note**
>
> *Note that we're taking off from mid-field. Van Nuys runway is long enough to do this.*

Before Takeoff

Action	Response
Parking Brake	SET
Passenger Seat Backs	MOST UPRIGHT POSITION
Seats, Belts, Harnesses	CHECK SECURE
Cabin Doors	CLOSED AND LOCKED
Flight Controls	FREE AND CORRECT
Flight Instruments	CHECK AND SET

One of the tricks of the trade is to develop cockpit flow patterns with your procedures. For example, you want to try and move in a systematic fashion from one side of the instrument panel to the other. So if we start on the left, we'll check the time, double-check our fuel on board, make sure the AI has spun up, set the DG by pressing the D key, set the ALT by pressing the B key, and so on.

At this point, we'll begin entering our NAVAID frequencies and headings. Enter 113.10 into NAV1 by using your mouse or by pressing the N key followed by the – (hyphen) and = (equals) keys. To change the numbers after the decimal, press the N key again.

Next, change the OBS of NAV1 to 160 degrees by clicking on the OBS knob or by pressing the V key and using the – (hyphen) and = (equals) keys again. Finally, the transponder should be set for VFR (1200). Use

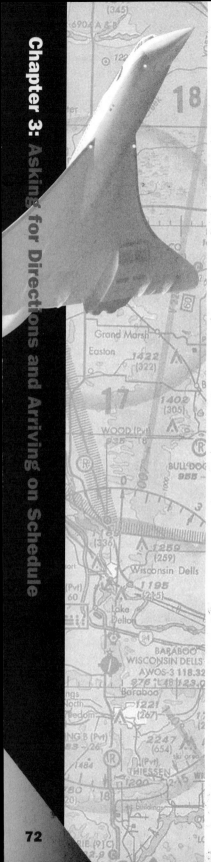

your mouse or press the T key followed by the − and = keys to adjust if necessary.

Manual Primer	LOCKED

This is handled automatically for you.

Auxiliary Fuel Pump	ON (CHECK FOR PRESSURE) THEN OFF

Not modeled.

Mixture	RICH

Press Ctrl+F4 again. If their wait or taxi time is very long, some pilots will lean the engine while still on the ground.

Fuel Quantity	CHECK
Fuel Selector Valve	RECHECK BOTH
Elevator and Rudder Trim	SET FOR TAKEOFF

Takeoff trim is in the center of the indexes.

Throttle	1,700 RPM

Press F3 to increase power to 1,700 RPM.

Magnetos	CHECK

Using your mouse, click on the mag switch/ignition switch from the B position to the L position, back to B then R, then finally back to B. RPM drop should not exceed 175 RPM on either, and 50 RPM differential between the two.

Carburetor Heat	CHECK

Press the H key once and note the RPM drop. Press H once again to turn it off. Note the rise in RPM. This is normal.

Propeller	CYCLE

Cycle the prop by pressing Ctrl+F1 followed by Ctrl+F4 a couple seconds later. The idea here is to stress the prop governors and circulate warm oil through them.

Suction Gauge	CHECK

Not modeled.

Throttle	800-1,000 RPM
Throttle Friction Lock	ADJUST

This is a mechanical device, so it isn't modeled.

Strobe Lights	AS DESIRED

It's considered good form to keep the strobe lights on at all times while the airplane is flying, but as a courtesy to aircraft landing at night, it's best to keep them off until you're cleared onto the runway. Press the O key to toggle the strobe lights on.

Radios and Avionics	SET

We've already taken care of the avionics earlier. This step is to remind you to switch to the tower frequency before calling them. How embarrassing!

Radio Lights Dimmer	FULL COUNTERCLOCKWISE

Not modeled.

Autopilot	OFF
Wing Flaps	SET FOR TAKEOFF

To make life simpler, we'll takeoff with zero flaps—we have plenty of runway.

Cowl Flaps	OPEN
Brakes	RELEASE

Takeoff

After receiving clearance (you're cleared), taxi out to the center of the runway and takeoff. You should be a pro at this by now.

Action	Response
Wing Flaps	0°–20°
Carburetor Heat	COLD
Power	FULL THROTTLE AND 2,400 RPM
Mixture	FULL RICH
Elevator Control	LIFT NOSE AT 50 KIAS
Climb Speed	70 KIAS (FLAPS 20°) 80 KIAS (FLAPS UP)
Brakes	APPLY MOMENTARILY WHEN AIRBORNE

Hit the brakes (the "." [period] key) once before retracting the landing gear. This is to stop the wheels from spinning.

Landing Gear	RETRACT IN CLIMB OUT
Wing Flaps	RETRACT

Climb

Okay, track VNY R-160 degrees outbound. At 500 feet AGL (1,300 feet MSL) reduce power to 23 inches Hg. or full throttle, whichever is less, and 2,400 RPM using the F2 and F3 keys for throttle and Ctrl+F2 and Ctrl+F3 for the prop.

Action	Response
Airspeed	90–100 KIAS
Fuel Selector Valve	BOTH
Mixture	FULL RICH (MAY BE LEANED OVER 3,000')
Cowl Flaps	OPEN AS REQUIRED

Climb to 2,800 feet and level off until reaching 7.5 DME from VNY. At that waypoint continue your climb to 3,500 feet and switch NAV1 to SMO on 110.8 and fly direct to SMO (shown in Figure 3.20) using the technique we covered earlier.

Cruise

Once you climb to 3,500 feet we'll put the airplane into cruise configuration. We can use 23 inches MP and 2,400 RPM, so we'll stick with that.

> ### ▶ Tip
> *Be sure to watch the MP gauges. Your MP setting will slowly decrease as your altitude increases.*

Figure 3.20:
Santa Monica—looks different from the air doesn't it?

Action	Response
Power	15–23 IN. HG. 2,100-2,400 RPM (NO MORE THAN 75% POWER)
Elevator and Rudder Trim	ADJUST
Mixture	LEAN

Use the Ctrl+F2 command to slowly lean the engine until the engine sputters. Then quickly press Ctrl+F3 several times to richen the mixture slightly.

Cowl Flaps	CLOSED

After passing SMO and turning left to track the SMO R-132 degrees outbound into the LAX SFRA, tune the transponder to 1201 as shown in Figure 3.21. (Use the T key and the – (hyphen) and = keys. Press T again to cycle through the transponder's digit placements.)

When we come abeam Northrop/Hawthorne Airport (7 DME from SMO and as shown in Figure 3.22) reset the transponder back to 1200. This is also the waypoint where we begin our descent.

Descent

Once we're clear of LAX's SFRA we need to immediately begin our descent to 1,100 feet—TOA's pattern altitude. This would also be a good time to listen to Zamperini ATIS (125.6). You can perform the Descent Checklist while listening. Nothing's quite like cockpit-multitasking!

▶ Tip

We won't be using a lot of fuel on this trip, but if there's an imbalance between the right and left tanks during a long cruise, switch to the fullest tank to try and even them out.

Figure 3.21: Squawk 1201 on your transponder when you fly over LAX in the SFRA.

Figure 3.22: Northrop/Hawthorne Airport

Action	Response
Fuel Selector Valve	BOTH
Power	AS DESIRED

You don't want to reduce power too quickly or too much (outside of the MP green arc) because this can shock-cool the engine. High performance engines don't take kindly to temperature changes as well as low-power trainer engines. Also remember that MP will creep up on you as you descend.

Because we want to descend fairly quickly, pull the power back to 15 inches MP. Control pitch to maintain altitude and slow to 90 KIAS. To further increase our descent rate without increasing in our airspeed, we'll create some drag by pressing G to drop the landing gear, and adding two notches of flaps (press the F7 key twice).

Mixture	ENRICHEN AS REQUIRED
Carburetor Heat	AS REQUIRED
Cowl Flaps	CLOSED
Wing Flaps	AS DESIRED (0°–10° BELOW 140 KIAS, 10°–20° BELOW 120 KIAS, 20°–FULL BELOW 95 KIAS.)

You should see Zamperini Airport (Figure 3.23) just ahead and to the right of our nose during our descent. Just before reaching 11 DME from SMO turn right and fly directly towards the middle of the airport. This will place us on a 45-degree downwind pattern entry.

Figure 3.23:
Zamperini Airport is
just ahead and to
the right.

Before Landing

Level off at TOA pattern altitude 1,100 feet. Add power and reduce flaps
to 10 degrees by pressing the F6 key once. (We don't need all that drag
anymore.) If you're used to flying airport traffic patterns with zero flaps, go
ahead and retract them all the way.

Action	Response
Passengers Seat Backs	MOST UPRIGHT POSITION
Seats, Belts, Harnesses	SECURE
Fuel Selector Valve	BOTH
Landing Gear	DOWN BELOW 140 KIAS

Remember the landing gear is already down.

Landing Gear	CHECK DOWN
Mixture	RICH
Propeller	HIGH RPM
Carburetor Heat	ON
Autopilot	OFF

> **▶ Tip**
>
> *Landing gear and flaps
> can be extended below
> 140 KIAS to increase rate
> of descent.*

> **▶ Tip**
>
> *Turn on your landing lights
> (even in the daytime)
> whenever you're in the
> vicinity of airports. Just
> like when you're driving a
> car, this makes it easier
> for everyone to see you.*

Approach and Landing

You should be an old pro at landing by now. There's nothing unusual about
landing at Zamperini that should cause you any problems. Since we arrived
from the north, we'll be landing on runway 29R (see Figure 3.24).

**Figure 3.24:
Cleared for landing
runway 29R**

Action	Response
Airspeed	70–80 KIAS (FLAPS UP)
Wing Flaps	AS DESIRED
Airspeed	65–75 KIAS (FLAPS DOWN)
Trim	ADJUST
Touchdown	MAIN WHEELS FIRST
Landing Roll	LOWER NOSE WHEEL GENTLY
Braking	MINIMUM REQUIRED

After Landing

After touchdown, taxi clear of the runway as soon as possible and come to a stop. Perform the After Landing Checklist and, when you're ready, taxi over to the terminal.

Action	Response
Wing Flaps	UP
Carburetor Heat	COLD
Cowl Flaps	OPEN

Securing Airplane

Action	Response
Parking Brake	SET
Throttle	IDLE
Avionics Power Switch	OFF
Mixture	IDLE CUT-OFF
Ignition Switch	OFF
Master Switch	OFF
Control Lock	INSTALL

This is a mechanical pin that's inserted into the control column to keep the flight control surfaces from flopping around and being battered by the wind.

Cowl Flaps	CLOSE
Fuel Selector Valve	RIGHT OR LEFT

This prevents fuel from crossfeeding onto the other tank and exiting the fuel venting system.

    Congratulations! You made it! Due to the precision flying required to make this flight correctly, and the close proximity of the airports (causing a fairly high cockpit workload level) you're obviously ready for some IFR work. Let's move on to the next chapter.

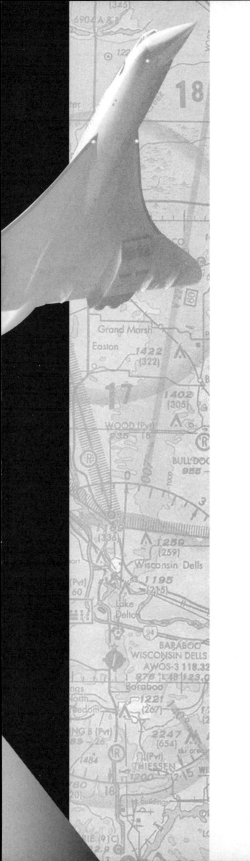

Computers
in the Cockpit

Chapter 4

*O*ne plane making its first appearance in Flight Simulator 2000 *is the Boeing 777-300. The triple* 7 *is the first airliner completely designed on computers, so it shouldn't come as any surprise that the whole airplane is filled with 'em. But since we fly from the front office (the cockpit), we'll only concern ourselves with the cockpit computers.*

In this chapter we discuss IFR flight planning and en route concepts, as well as advanced IFR procedures. Then we'll take the 777 out for a spin to introduce you to its features and put what we've learned to the test. Get ready to step into the newest generation of civil aviation aircraft!

IFR Procedures

Like any flight, an IFR trip includes several parts—departure, en route, arrival, and approach. An IFR flight, however, is strictly controlled, and each segment of the flight is built on a foundation of standard procedures so both pilots and ATC know what to expect.

Selecting the most appropriate procedures for each phase of a flight creates an IFR flight plan. In the pages that follow, we'll introduce and discuss each section not already covered in the lessons. It's probably best if we start at the beginning, with departures.

Terminal Procedures

U.S. terminal procedures, commonly referred to as IFR plates, contain Instrument Departure Procedures (DPs), STARs (Standard Terminal Arrivals), and instrument approach procedures. In the U.S., NOAA publishes these procedures. Jeppesen also publishes them for the U.S. and other parts of the world. You can acquire terminal procedure books in the same places discussed in Chapter 2, where we covered sectionals and terminal charts. Sample Jeppesen Sim Charts are featured in the back of the Pilot's Handbook. They're worthy of your consideration as well.

Instrument Departures

Instrument Departure Procedures (formerly called "SIDS") describe the altitudes, headings, courses, and other information used for taking off and getting on your way under IFR. Not all airports with instrument approaches have specific departure procedures. For those that don't, some sort of departure procedure will typically be found along side the IFR takeoff minimums (weather minimums) section of the instrument approach procedure(s) for the runway you're using.

Note that departure procedures are usually specified for a particular runway; it's important to select the right one if the airport has multiple runways. Some DPs are also aircraft specific (turbojet only, for example). Furthermore, each DP typically has a couple of transitions. *Transitions* are routes that connect the airspace around the airport to the airways that you use for the en route phase. Think of transitions as on-ramps to aerial freeways.

Naturally, you want to select the transition that most closely sends you in the direction of your destination or the entry point to the airway you want to use.

Departure procedures are identified by names and letter-number codes, much like airport and NAVAID identifiers. DPs with transitions are identified by replacing the last three coded characters of the DP with the transition code. For example, the transition code for the FREEHOLD THREE DEPARTURE (FREH3.RBV) would be (FREH3.EWC) for the FREEHOLD THREE DEPARTURE ELWOOD CITY transition.

Vectored DPs

In the aviation world, *vector* refers to radar vectors. You encounter them when ATC uses radar to send you on a specific heading that guides (vectors) you to where they want you to go. Some DPs are vector departures, meaning ATC will guide you out of the area after takeoff.

As you might suspect if you're new to IFR flight, ATC is the glue that holds this whole system together. Although *Flight Simulator 2000* doesn't model real-time ATC, except in scripted adventures, you can still fly vectored DPs by following the departure routes as published and then simply flying the appropriate transition. We'll demonstrate how that works in our tutorial.

IFR En Route Navigation

All typical "by the book" IFR flights begin with a DP and end with an approach. Depending on how large, or rather how busy, the airport you're flying into is, there may be a STAR procedure (we'll get to that in a minute) just before the approach.

The part of the flight between the DP and the approach (or STAR in some cases) is known as the en route portion of the flight. This is the most flexible section of an IFR flight plan, but it still has many restrictions. Let's talk about them next.

IFR En Route Charts

There are two basic types of IFR charts used for en route IFR navigation. They're called IFR En Route High Altitude (Figure 4.1) and IFR En Route

> **▶ Note**
>
> *Some DPs and STARs are in effect at certain times for noise abatement. Read carefully, or you may select the wrong procedure.*

Low Altitude (Figure 4.2) charts. As their names suggest, they're differentiated by which flight altitudes they cover. In the U.S., High Altitude charts cover airways above 18,000 feet MSL (see the back of the poster included with this book for a representation of one), and Low Altitude charts cover airways lower than (and not including) 18,000 feet MSL in the U.S. The transition level is lower in many other countries.

H-6
EAST COAST
PANELS
FGHIJ
1" = 18 NM

H-5
SOUTHCENTRAL
PANELS
ABCDE
1" = 30 NM

UNITED STATES GOVERNMENT
FLIGHT INFORMATION PUBLICATION
IFR ENROUTE HIGH ALTITUDE - U.S.
For use at and above 18,000' MSL

EFFECTIVE 0901Z 15 JUL 1999
TO 0901Z 9 SEP 1999

Consult NOTAMs for latest information
PUBLISHED IN ACCORDANCE WITH INTER-AGENCY AIR CARTOGRAPHIC COMMITTEE
SPECIFICATIONS AND ARRANGEMENTS APPROVED BY
DEPARTMENT OF DEFENSE • FEDERAL AVIATION ADMINISTRATION • DEPARTMENT OF COMMERCE

Figure 4.1:
IFR En Route High Altitude chart

L-4
PANELS
EFGH
1" = 16 NM

L-3
PANELS
ABCD
1" = 30 NM

UNITED STATES GOVERNMENT
FLIGHT INFORMATION PUBLICATION
IFR ENROUTE LOW ALTITUDE - U.S.
For use up to but not including 18,000' MSL
HORIZONTAL DATUM: NORTH AMERICAN DATUM OF 1983

EFFECTIVE 0901Z 15 JUL 1999
TO 0901Z 9 SEP 1999

Consult NOTAMs for latest information
PUBLISHED IN ACCORDANCE WITH INTER-AGENCY AIR CARTOGRAPHIC COMMITTEE
SPECIFICATIONS AND ARRANGEMENTS APPROVED BY
DEPARTMENT OF DEFENSE • FEDERAL AVIATION ADMINISTRATION • DEPARTMENT OF COMMERCE

Figure 4.2:
IFR En Route Low Altitude chart

▶ **Warning**
High- and low-altitude en route charts don't use the same scale and individual high- and low-altitude charts use different scales.

The biggest difference between the two types of charts (besides which altitudes they're designed for) is the level of detail they depict. Aircraft flying at high altitude are assumed to be traveling faster and farther than their lower altitude counterparts. Therefore High Altitude charts are smaller scale and depict less detail (and are relatively less cluttered) than Low Altitude charts. IFR En Route charts can be found at most of the sources (except for the Web) discussed in Chapter 2.

In the U.S., en route charts depict federal airways, which are basically highways in the sky. Low altitude airways are preceded with the letter "V." (The "V" stands for VOR airway, but they're more typically called Victor airways—Victor is the phonetic alphabet name for the letter "V.") The letter "J," which stands for Jet route, precedes high altitude airways.

▶ **Tip**
High and low en route airway routes (minus altitudes, and so on) can be viewed using Flight Simulator 2000's Map View feature (under the World menu).

Minimum En Route Altitudes

Minimum en route IFR altitudes, or MEAs, (see Figure 4.3) are the minimum flight altitudes allowed on that route (between navaids or intersections). MEAs provide standard terrain/obstacle clearance (2,000 feet above the highest obstacle within 4 nautical miles from centerline in mountainous areas, and 1,000 feet above obstacles within 4 nautical miles from centerline in other areas) and assure navigational signal coverage unless otherwise noted. (The term "MEA Gap" points out areas where you may not receive navigation signals at the MEA.)

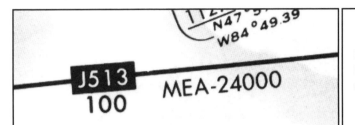

Figure 4.3:
MEAs are displayed
along the route.

IFR Cruise Altitudes

Low altitude IFR cruising altitudes and high altitude IFR cruising altitudes are shown in Figure 4.4. You can fly at any of these altitudes as long as you're above the MEA for your route (provided your aircraft is properly equipped and capable of flight at those altitudes).

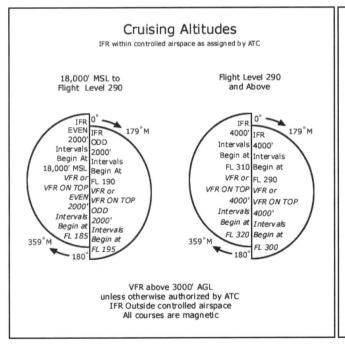

Figure 4.4:
VFR and
IFR cruise
altitudes
depend
on your
magnetic
course.

Standard Terminal Arrivals

STARs generally exist only for larger or higher traffic airports; East Armpit Airport may not have one, whereas LAX has several. As with DPs, the idea here is to select the STAR that most closely matches your arrival

▶ **Tip**

Although you could climb or descend to stay above each of the various MEAs between fixes, you're better off selecting a cruise altitude that will clear all MEAs along your route. Doing so minimizes your cockpit workload by reducing the number of flight configuration changes during your trip.

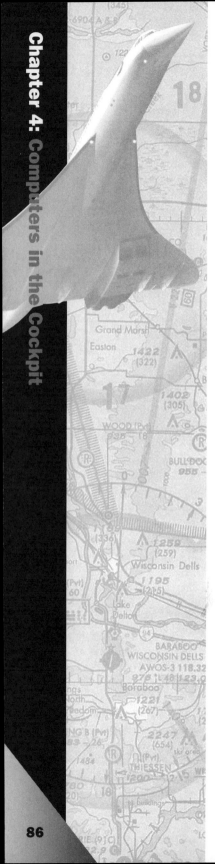
direction. STARs should also be selected based on which approach you intend to use; some STARs are used only for certain approaches, which in turn are exclusive to certain runways.

Replacing the first three characters of the STAR with the transition code identifies the STAR's transition. For example, the transition code for ACTON SIX ARRIVAL (AQN.AQN6) would be (EDNAS.AQN6) for the ACTON SIX ARRIVAL EDNAS transition.

Feeder Routes

Feeder routes are published routes that connect en route airways to instrument approaches (more specifically the IAF—Initial Approach Fix). There can be several feeder routes connecting to multiple IAFs on some of the more elaborate approaches. You'll see feeder routes on the approach plates themselves, if they exist.

Radar Vectors

Many approaches require ATC vectoring to the IAF or approach. Even if you're not running one of the scripted adventures in *Flight Simulator 2000,* you're not totally out of luck. For example, to simulate these vectored approaches fly to one of the NAVAID intersection references and then fly directly to the intersection on the LOC (Localizer) path. We'll illustrate how to do this in our tutorial as well.

Cat III ILS

Category II and Category III ILS approaches are precision approaches with lower weather minimums than the standard Category I procedures you've covered in the *Pilot's Handbook* lessons. This means that if you possess the required special aircrew authorizations and are flying an aircraft with the appropriate certification (the Boeing 777-300 is certified for Cat III operations), you can land at airports with extremely low visibility. The DH (Decision Height) and RVR (Runway Visual Range) minimums for ILS Categories I through III are as follows:

ILS Category	DH Minimums (Feet)	RVR Minimums (Feet)
Category I	200	1,800
Category II	100	1,200
Category IIIa	None, or below 100	700
Category IIIb	None, or below 50	150
Category IIIc	None	0

RVR is measured visibility using a transmissometer (that's the name) projector and receiver. The transmitter and receiver are mounted at 250 or 500 feet apart, and then a known intensity of light is emitted.

Obstructions such as smoke, fog, and so on, cause changes in the intensity of the light seen by the receiver. This number is then weighed against the time of day and is computed into an RVR value. Here's an RVR/visibility conversion table:

RVR (Feet)	Visibility (statute Miles)
1,600	$1/4$
2,000	$3/8$
2,400	$1/2$
3,200	$5/8$
4,000	$3/4$
4,500	$7/8$
5,000	1
6,000	$1 1/4$

You've probably noticed that Category IIIc approaches can be made in zero visibility. This means exactly what you're thinking—you can land without seeing the runway. Isn't technology awesome!

Flying the Boeing 777-300

The Boeing triple 7 is a highly automated, two-pilot, fly-by-wire marvel of technology. One paradox of technology is that the more advanced something becomes, the simpler it is to use. The triple 7 illustrates this concept well. Although it's one of the most technologically complex aircraft in the air, it's perhaps one of the easiest to fly, thanks to a great design and the integration of computers on the flight deck.

Although it may be easy to fly, let's not forget that the triple 7 is a BIG airplane— it can carry up to 479 passengers in two classes. For comparison, a 747-400 typically carries about 416 passengers. Therefore, you still need to plan your maneuvers ahead of time and plan for W-I-D-E turns.

Aircraft Performance

At the heart of the 777's performance and range is its ETOPS (Extended-range Twin-engine OperationS) design. ETOPS qualification is awarded to only the most reliable engine/aircraft combinations, which is why the 777 is certified to fly the most direct routes to nearly anywhere in the world.

V Speeds

Unlike light aircraft, the takeoff and landing V speeds for larger aircraft are determined by the weight of the aircraft as well as the weather conditions. Following are the various 777-300 V speeds for maximum gross aircraft weight on a standard day at sea level:

▶ **Note**

Although it may seem like a big jump going from a Cessna 182 to a Boeing 777, all of its automation makes the triple 7 an easier bird to handle than, say, the LearJet 45.

▶ **Note**

The diameter of a 777 engine is about the same as that of a 737's fuselage!

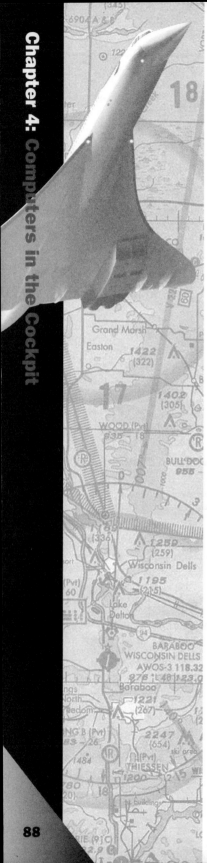
V Speed	KIAS or Mach
V_1	153 KIAS
V_R	156 KIAS
V_2	162 KIAS
V_{2+15}	177 KIAS
V_{2+20}	182 KIAS
M_{MO}	Mach .87
V_{LE}	270 KIAS/ .82 Mach
V_{LO}	270 KIAS/ .82 Mach
V_{FE}	—
1°	255 KIAS
5°	235 KIAS
15°	215 KIAS
20°	200 KIAS
25°	190 KIAS
30°	180 KIAS
V_{REF}	157 KIAS

Advanced Systems

The triple 7 is arguably the most advanced commercial airliner in service. As such, just about everything in this airplane is advanced. Here are a few of its most notable systems and features.

Primary Flight Display

The PFD (Primary Flight Display), shown in Figure 4.5, is the LCD (Liquid Crystal Display) on the left side of the instrument panel. LCDs were selected in the real triple 7 because they are smaller and lighter, produce less heat, have better legibility in sunlight, and are more reliable than standard CRT (Cathode Ray Tube) displays. The PFD is really five instruments in one:

1. On the far left is the ASI. The magenta digits at the very top reflect the autopilot speed setting. KIAS is displayed on the middle ribbon scale. The Mach number is displayed on the bottom. The magenta ASI bug on the ribbon scale reflects the autopilot speed setting for reference.

2. In the center of the PFD is the AI. The magenta colored bars are the Flight Director indicator references. Above the AI are the ILS marker lights (they display only when markers are passed). Along the left and bottom borders of the AI are the glideslope and LOC indexes, respectively, which show up only when an ILS is tuned in.

3. To the right of the AI is the ALT. The magenta digits at the very top reflect the autopilot ALT setting. The magenta ASI bug index on the

ALT ribbon reflects the autopilot target altitude, and the digits along the bottom display the current barometric pressure setting.

4. On the far right is the VSI. It indicates 1,000, 2,000, and 6,000 feet per minute increments. The green index line points to your VSI, and the double magenta-colored index lines reflect the current autopilot VSI setting.

5. Across the bottom is the DG. The HDG bug is in magenta.

Figure 4.5:
The PFD is really five instruments in one.

Auto Brake

Auto brake is like the antilock braking systems found on many newer automobiles today—it prevents the aircraft's wheels from locking up and flat spotting when the brakes are applied. Auto brakes are a very useful feature for pilots flying huge aircraft such as the 777 because the mass of the aircraft and the physical distance between the wheels and cockpit make it extremely difficult to know when your brakes are locked—until suddenly you're skidding instead of braking.

What separates auto brakes from standard automobile antilock brakes is that auto brakes actually apply themselves. You can select any of the following auto brake settings by clicking on the Auto Brake control (Figure 4.6) with your mouse.

Figure 4.6:
The Auto Brake control switch is located to the left of the Landing Gear control lever.

+ **RTO (Rejected Take Off)**—This setting is used for takeoff. In the event of a rejected takeoff, the brakes will be automatically fully applied when the throttle is returned to idle. Braking will remain applied until the pilot disarms the system or the auto brake automatically disarms (see below).

+ **1, 2, 3, MAX**—This sets the auto brake for engagement after landing. Setting 1 is the lowest (least amount of automatic braking), and MAX is the highest (maximum automatic application after landing).

+ **OFF**—This bypasses the auto brake system.

The auto brake can be disengaged by the pilot applying the brake, or by switching the auto brake to the Off position.

Any time the auto brake is armed, you'll see an EICAS (Engine Instrument and Crew Alerting System) message on the Flight Monitoring screen (Figure 4.7.) While we're on the subject, let's talk about the EICAS next.

AUTOBRAKE RTO

Figure 4.7:
The EICAS Flight Monitoring screen will, among other things, indicate which Auto Brake mode you've selected.

EICAS

The LCD panel on the right half of the pilot's station instrument panel is the EICAS (Engine Instrument and Crew Alerting System). *Flight Simulator 2000*'s version combines a couple of displays into a single panel for your convenience. This version has three modes that can be selected by clicking on the switch located at the lower-right center of the panel, as shown in Figure 4.8.

EICAS
ND   EICAS 2

Figure 4.8:
This switch selects the EICAS screen modes.

The first mode is Navigational Display, shown in Figure 4.9. It has three sub-modes in the real triple 7. These have been boiled down into a single, simplified mode for *Flight Simulator 2000*: the VOR mode (known as the HSI (Horizontal Situation Indicator) mode in *Flight Simulator 2000*).

Figure 4.9:
ICAS ND (VOR) mode

You may recall that an HSI is nothing more than a directional gyro with NAV instruments in the center. The white arrow is NAV1, the green arrow is NAV2, and the blue arrow is the ADF needle.

The number between the brackets is the current magnetic heading. The magnetic course selected on the autopilot control panel/OBS appears in the upper-right corner of the display, next to the abbreviation "CRS." The upper-left corner displays the ADF frequency and bearing; the lower-left and right corners show the frequencies and DME settings for NAV1 and NAV2, respectively. Each of these readouts is color-coded to match its respective "arrow."

The second mode is Flight Monitoring, shown in Figure 4.10.

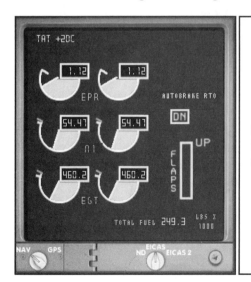

Figure 4.10:
EICAS Flight Monitoring mode

▶ **Tip**

One of the neatest aspects of the triple 7's VOR mode is that it displays the three-letter identifier for each NAVAID, so there's no need to listen to audible (and annoying!) beeps and dashes to identify NAVAIDs.

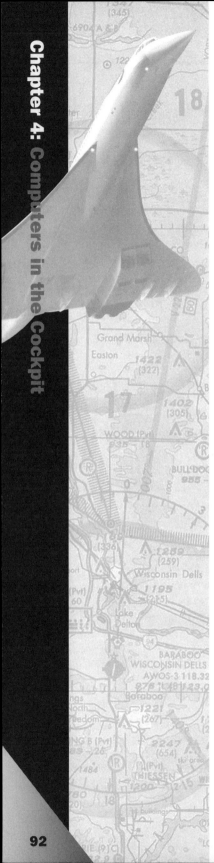

Flight Monitoring displays:

+ **TAT**—total air temperature in degrees Celsius, adjusted for compressibility effects.

+ **EPR**—the engine pressure ratio is the total pressure ratio across the engine (nozzle total pressure to compressor face total pressure). Pilots use EPR as one of the primary indications of engine power.

+ N_1—engine compressor speed.

+ **EGT**—exhaust gas temperature.

+ **Landing Gear indicator**.

+ **Flap Position indicator**.

+ **Total Fuel indicator**—measured in pounds x 1000.

+ **Annunciator section**—displays general conditions, such as auto brake setting. (Equipment operation and caution/warning items are included here on the real 777.)

Each type of caution and warning has visual color-coding cues that may be accompanied by an alert sound:

+ **Red** means warning. An example of a warning item would be disengagement of the autopilot.

+ **Amber** is a cautionary message. A caution item would be the disengagement of the auto-throttle.

+ **Indented** on the warning list indicates an advisory. Advisories are not announced with sound.

The third mode is Engine Detail (Figure 4.11). It displays:

+ N_2—turbine speed.

+ **FF**—fuel flow in kilograms per hour.

+ **Oil Pressure**—works the same way as the analog versions we've seen in the Cessna 182R RG.

+ **Oil Temperature**—same as above.

+ **Oil Quantity**—in gallons.

+ **VIB**—engine vibration.

Wing De-Ice and Engine Anti-Ice

De-ice systems differ from anti-ice systems in that anti-ice prevents ice from forming, and de-ice removes ice that's already accumulated.

Figure 4.11:
EICAS Engine
Detail mode

The triple 7 is equipped with wing de-ice and engine anti-ice systems. As you're aware, icing on the wings is detrimental to aerodynamic efficiency. On the other hand, getting a big enough piece of ice in a turbine engine can destroy it. This is why anti-ice is used in the engine. Activate the triple 7's de-ice and anti-ice systems by using your mouse to click on the De-Ice switch located on the far left of the overhead panel, as shown in Figure 4.12.

Figure 4.12:
This De-Ice switch is located on the far left of the overhead panel.

Autopilot

The autopilot isn't unique to the triple 7. All of the aircraft in *Flight Simulator 2000* have one, except for the Camel, Extra 300, Sailplane, and JetRanger. It's a critical component for a Cat III ILS, however, so we should talk about it now. Like the autopilots found in each of *Flight Simulator 2000*'s aircraft equipped with one, the 777's autopilot is a three-axis unit: pitch, roll, and yaw.

The Boeing 737-400, Boeing 777-300, and Learjet 45 also have autopilot throttle control. In the Boeing jets, this feature is called the auto-throttle. The autothrottle is technically a "cruise control for airplanes" because it controls the throttle setting just as cruise controls do on automobiles. But the autothrottle differs in that it also acts as a maximum power rev limiter when used in conjunction with the TO/GA feature. TO/GA stands for takeoff/go-around throttle control. You can click the TO/GA button located the top of the throttle quadrant (click the airplane icon above the PFD to display) or press Ctrl+Shift+R. When you have the auothrottle armed and engage the TO/GA, the engines will automatically produce the maximum allowable thrust.

One autopilot feature that's new to *Flight Simulator 2000* is the flight director (Figure 4.13). A flight director is essentially the brains of the autopilot without the muscle. The flight director is simple to use and to follow. It works very much like an ILS; as long as you keep the flight director's bars in the center, you'll stay on course. The horizontal bar indicates pitch, and the vertical bar indicates course.

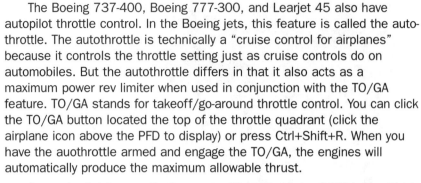

Figure 4.13:
The flight director is a new *Flight Simulator 2000* autopilot feature.

The triple 7's autopilot controls (Figure 4.14) sit on the top of the instrument panel. From left to right, top to bottom, the control, function, and alternate key commands (if any) are shown in Table 4.1.

Figure 4.14:
The autopilot of the 777-300 sits on top of the instrument panel.

▶ **Warning**

"Noisy" is a term used to describe electrical signals that contain random spikes and/or dropouts. If you have a noisy joystick/throttle and/or gameport (if you're not using USB), autothrottle and keyboard throttle commands, such as reversers, may not work at all or won't work properly. This is because the erroneous inputs from the joystick throttle control conflict with Flight Simulator 2000's *commands.*

Table 4.1: Autopilot Control, Function, and Alternate Key Commands

Control	Function	Key Command
F/D On Off	Flight director toggle	—
A/T Arm	Auto-throttle toggle	Shift+R
CRS window	Sets OBS	V (or V+1 or V+2 for more than one NAV)
AP	Autopilot master switch	Z
NAV	NAV1 hold	Ctrl+N
HDG knob	Selects heading	
HDG	Heading hold switch	Ctrl+H
BC	Backcourse mode	Ctrl+B
APR	Approach hold	Ctrl+A
IAS/MCH window	Selects airspeed/Mach	—
IAS	Airspeed hold switch	Ctrl+R*
MCH	Mach speed hold	Ctrl+M*
ALT	Altitude hold	Ctrl+Z
ALT knob	Sets altitude	—
VSI dial	Sets VSI	—
LVL	Wing leveler	Ctrl+V
Y/D	Yaw damper	Ctrl+D

Additional Autopilot Features		
TO/GA	Autothrottle rev-limiter	Ctrl+Shift+R*

* Auto-throttle must be enabled in order to engage or function.

Electronic Checklist

The Boeing 777 has electronic checklists that are displayed on the upper, outer MFDs (Multi-Function Displays) on the center console located between the pilot and copilot. (Yes, there are a few more of these handy units than are found on the instrument panel.) *Flight Simulator 2000*'s kneeboard feature is a good substitute for the additional display because it offers many of the same features inherent to electronic checklists, most notably reduced cockpit clutter and convenience—you won't have to search for it under your seat after flying through some turbulence!

Thrust Compensation System

With a fly-by-wire aircraft, a thrust compensation system is simply a matter of adding some more flight rules to the PFCC software. As reliable as the triple 7's engines are, being a multiengine aircraft, it's still susceptible to the physics of yaw produced when an engine fails. The thrust compensation system in the 777 responds automatically when an engine fails. For example, the system automatically applies rudder to compensate for the yaw. This feature can be simulated in *Flight Simulator 2000* by engaging the autopilot yaw damper.

Flying by Wire

A conventional jet airliner is controlled by a system that takes control inputs from the pilot and sends them to a bunch of hydraulic systems that pull cables attached to the flight control surfaces. Conversely, the triple 7 is a fly-by-wire aircraft. In this type of system, the pilot's control inputs are read by transducers and sent to the aircraft's PFCC (Primary Flight Control Computer). The PFCC then sends its commands (which are typically modified by software "flight rules"—we'll get to those in a minute) to the hydraulics systems, which operate the flight control surfaces.

One of the neat things about fly-by-wire systems is their ability to incorporate flight envelope protection programs. These programs are flight rules that are governed by the PFCC and cause the aircraft to behave the way that the designers want.

In the case of the triple 7, one of the flight envelope protection programs is that bank angles of less than 30 degrees don't require pitch input to remain in level flight; this is handled automatically by the PFCC. But bank angles greater than 30 degrees do require manual pitch input.

Another protection is that in over speed conditions, the pilot loses the ability to further trim the elevator down. As stall conditions arise, the sequence of events begins with a loss of up-elevator trim control followed by a stick-shaker warning, and finally automatic full application of thrust.

> ▶ **Note**
>
> *Terminal procedure charts for this flight have been included in Appendix B.*

Flight Plan

We'll be taking the 777-300 on an IFR flight to apply some of the flight planning concepts covered in this chapter. We'll also be using the autopilot to illustrate how an advanced aircraft can use technology to decrease cockpit workloads.

Airports

We'll be flying from John F. Kennedy International Airport in New York City Airport to Chicago O'Hare International—the busiest airport in the United States. The longest sea-level runways at JFK and ORD (O'Hare) are 14,572 feet and 13,000 feet respectively. The takeoff and landing distances of the triple 7 at maximum gross weight on a standard day is 11,000 feet, so we're within limits.

Because this is an IFR flight, we need to select an alternate airport in case we can't land at our destination. Although we can land in 0/0 weather because we're certified to land with Cat III ILS minimums, we can't discount the possibility of an avionics failure or other emergency that would call for an alternate airport. We can use Detroit Metropolitan Airport or Indianapolis International Airport as alternates because they're in the vicinity and have low minimums and runways long enough to accommodate our aircraft.

Route

Here's the navigation log for your flight to Chicago O'Hare International Airport:

Waypoint	Frequency	Course	Altitude	Distance	ETE
JFK	ATIS* 118.72	—	—	—	—
CRI	112.3	218° To 223° From	2,500' minimum, 5,000' maximum	43 nm	00:10
—>SAX	115.7	311° From	FL350	49 nm	00:06
LHY	110.8	311° To 301° From	FL350	50 nm	00:06
MINEO (50DME) DKK	116.2	294° To 281° From	FL350	130 nm	00:16
J68X (72DME) FNT	116.9	284° To 258° From	FL180	200 nm	00:25
(37 DME) PMM	112.1	252° To 261° From	5,000' minimum	109 nm	00:26
(46 DME) OBK	113.0	256° To 240° From	5,000' minimum	48 nm	00:11
SEXXY 14R (Cat III)	109.75	142° ILS	5,000'	20 nm	00:05
ORD	ATIS 135.4	TOTAL		649 nm	01:45

* Requires .25 kHz radio increment spacing. Go to Options menu, choose Settings, and select Instrument.

   We'll take off from runway 31L using the Kennedy Seven Departure, Breezy Point Climb, COATE transition. This departure is basically a climbing left turn directly to CRI VOR R-039, then outbound on R-223, followed by vectors to SAX VOR.

   From there, we'll take J36 all the way to FNT VOR, where we'll pick up the Pullman Four Arrival Flint transition and take that to OBK VOR. We'll then proceed into ORD using ORD Cat III ILS RWY 14R.

Altitude

You'll find that most IFR flights have many minimum altitude requirements, but there are occasionally MAAs (Maximum Authorized Altitudes) as well. One of the reasons we're flying J36 instead of a more direct route is that J36 doesn't have an MAA that's below our best cruise altitudes, while the more direct J584, which the *Flight Simulator 2000* flight planner will select for you, does.

> ▶ **Note**
>
> **Due to the spacing between VOR stations along J36, we've placed waypoints defined by DME to note the changeovers.**

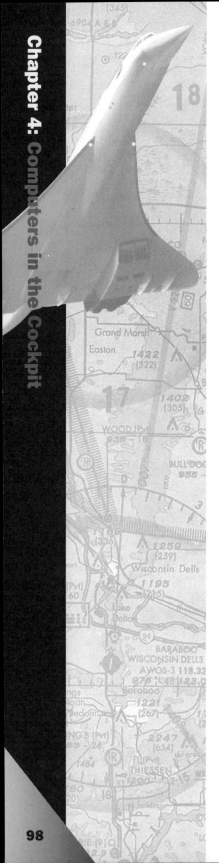

After takeoff we need to cross 2 DME from CRI above 2,500 feet, but be no higher than 5,000 feet at 3 DME from CRI. The MEA on J36 is FL310. MAA between LHY and MINEO is FL370. We'll be flying at FL350 to minimize altitude changes.

From FNT to PMM, the MEA is FL180. Then from PMM to SEXXY inter-section (ever wonder who thinks of these names?), we'll be flying the minimum published altitude of 5,000 feet. From there we'll take the ILS the rest of the way in.

Fuel/Performance

The Boeing 777-300 has three fuel tanks—left main, right main, and center. *Flight Simulator 2000*'s triple 7's main fuel tanks have a capacity of 16,400 gallons each, and the center fuel tank has a capacity of 12,400 usable gallons. To save you the math, the total fuel capacity of the triple 7-300 is 45,200 gallons (135,318 kilograms/298,320 pounds.)

With a full fuel load, the 777-300 has a range of up to 5,600 nautical miles (6,450 statute miles). At maximum gross weight, range is reduced to about 3,700 nm at Mach .84. On a standard day at FL300, the minimum fuel burn at Mach .84 is about 11,985 kilograms (26,400 pounds) per hour, and at maximum gross weight it's 18,115 kilograms (39,936 pounds) per hour.

For flight planning purposes, the minimum basic fuel load (fuel for taxi, takeoff, climb to FL300, descent plus the required 45-minute reserve) is 7,320 gallons (21,914 kilograms/48,312 pounds).

Special Considerations

There are noise abatement restrictions on all jet operations over JFK, 24 hours a day. Fortunately, they have been incorporated into the JFK's DPs. This is why after takeoff from runway 31L we make a fairly tight left turn to take us over the ocean as soon as possible.

Our second special consideration is that because we're capable of flight faster than 250 KIAS, we have speed limits to maintain. Specifically we have to remain under 250 KIAS during all flight below 10,000 feet.

Flight Tutorial

To set up this flight, we need to first switch to the 777-300, if you haven't already done so. Next, use the Map View dialog box to move the aircraft to North 40°38.46', West 73°46.79', Altitude +30, and Heading 320, as shown in Figure 4.15.

Since we're flying IFR and we'll be performing a Cat III ILS, the time and weather at ORD won't make much of a difference to us, other than extremely high winds that would prevent us from landing on runway 14L. However, we do need to meet the required takeoff weather minimums at JFK, which for runways 31L and 31R are a standard 1 statute mile visibility for twin-engine aircraft.

**Figure 4.15:
Move to JFK using the
Map View dialog.**

Before Engine Start

Once again, to perform this flight all the way from startup to shutdown, we have to shut the engines down first. Do so by pressing Ctrl+Shift+F1. Otherwise, just go ahead and skip down to the "Taxi" section below.

Action	Response
Exterior Inspection	COMPLETED
Passenger Signs	ON
Flight Instruments	CHECKED

Press the B key to set your ALT.

Auto Brake	RTO
FMC and ACARS	CHECKED AND SET

The FMC is the Flight Management Computer. In *Flight Simulator 2000,* the GPS (Global Positioning System) will perform many of the same functions, but we'll leave that for another chapter. In the meantime we'll begin using the autopilot, so let's set it up for departure.

Our first waypoint is CRI, so dial in 112.3 on the NAV1 radio, 218 degrees on the autopilot CRS window, 5,000 feet in the autopilot ALT window, and 250 in the IAS/MACH autopilot window. You set the autopilot by clicking on the appropriate knobs and display windows as discussed earlier. Once you've entered the parameters, click the IAS, NAV, ALT, and Y/D Autopilot mode buttons. This will save us some time. Once we're airborne, all that'll be necessary is turning on the autopilot master switch by pressing the Z key.

ACARS stands for Aircraft Communications Addressing and Reporting System. This is a digital data link system for civil and business aviation

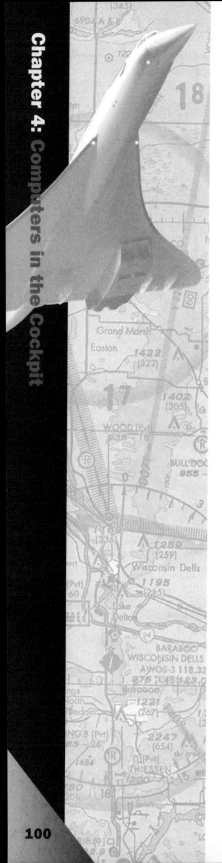

and their companies. At present, ACARS transmissions are sent via VHF radio (although HF is in developmental testing). These coded transmissions are used by major airlines for communications between aircraft and ground facilities. If you've ever wondered how those departure and arrival boards at the airport know when a flight is on time or delayed, well, here's your answer.

Fuel Control switches   CUTOFF

If you shut down the engines as instructed at the start of this section, the fuel control switches should already be at the cut-off setting. The fuel control switches are located just below the throttle quadrant (press Shift+4 to display), as shown in Figure 4.16. The only difference is that instead of being variable, the fuel control switches have only two settings, RUN and CUTOFF.

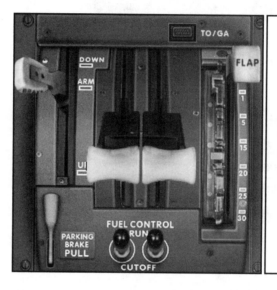

Figure 4.16:
The throttle quadrant window can be called up by pressing Shift+4.

Fuel   KG, CHECK WITH FLIGHT PLAN

This step is used to verify whether the ground crew gave you enough fuel to make the trip. Since we're flying with a full load of fuel, we're in good shape.

Logbook   CHECK

Status   CHECK

The logbook referred to is the aircraft's maintenance logbook. As pilot in command, you're responsible for the airworthiness of the aircraft. You've got the final say on whether you go or don't go. So you're checking that the required maintenance has been performed and that the aircraft status (a report provided by the ground crew) is normal for your flight.

At this point, we'd set our COM radio and listen to JFK ATIS, then obtain ATC clearance to verify our flight plan. When we were sure that we're clear on everything, we'd then obtain clearance for pushback and engine start.

Engine Start

Action	Response
Parking Brake	SET

Press Ctrl+ "." (period) or click on the parking brake handle located on the lower-left side of the throttle quadrant.

FMC Preflight	COMPLETE
Beacon	ON

The navigational beacon and other light switches (see Figure 4.17) are located on the lower-left side of the instrument panel.

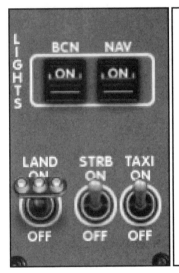

Figure 4.17:
The light switches on the 777-300 are located on the lower-left side of the instrument panel.

Seatbelts	SECURE
Start	R AND L

The startup procedure is very similar to what we're used to with the Cessna in *Flight Simulator 2000*. The only differences are a couple of key commands. First, verify that the engine area is clear. Then set throttles to idle (press F1) and open the fuel control switches (Ctrl+Shift+F4).

Next, switch the EICAS to the Flight Monitoring screen by clicking on the little button on the lower-right corner of the display. Start both engines simultaneously by pressing the J key followed by pressing and holding the = (equals) key until the engines reach 45 percent N_1, or by clicking and holding each engine's starter on the overhead panel individually.

> **▶ Tip**
>
> *To simulate pushback press the Y key to enter Slew mode, then press numpad 5 a couple of times with Num Lock off. Press numpad 2 when you want to stop. Finally press the Y key again to exit Slew mode.*

After Engine Start

Action	Response
APU	OFF

The APU (Auxiliary Power Unit) is an onboard generator that supplies power for air-conditioning and such to the aircraft while the engines are off. Because the engines are now running, we can turn it off. Shutoff is handled automatically for you in *Flight Simulator 2000*.

Action	Response
Engine Anti-ice	AUTO

Engine Anti-ice is controlled by the De-Ice system switch (as is pitot heat) in *Flight Simulator 2000*. Leave the switch in the off position.

Action	Response
Recall	CHECK

Recall refers to checking the EICAS annunciator panel. When the WARN light is extinguished (to the left of the autopilot master control panel), then everything is normal. See Figure 4.18.

Figure 4.18:
A warning light will alert you if you have to look at the annunciator panel.

Action	Response
Controls	CHECK

This check is to make sure that the controls are free and correct. You might want to take the time to verify that your control sensitivities are within acceptable range.

Taxi

Action	Response
Elevator Trim	SET FOR TAKEOFF

The Elevator Trim Position indicator (labeled Pitch Trim) is located to the right of the standby AI. You can adjust the trim setting by using numpad 1 and numpad 7 with Num Lock off, or by clicking on the trim dial just below the indicator shown in Figure 4.19. Takeoff position is anywhere within the green range, but it's best to set it somewhere in the middle.

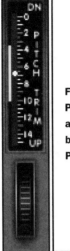

Figure 4.19:
Pitch trim can be adjusted with the dial below the Pitch Trim Position indicator.

Auto Brakes	RTO
Auto-Throttle	ARMED
Pitot Heat	ON
Parking Brake	RELEASE

Release the parking brake by pressing the "." (period) key.

After obtaining taxi clearance, we taxi out to runway 31L. We need to make a left turn and head for the end of the runway. Even with an airport diagram in your hand, it's often difficult to find your way around a big airport. In the real world, ground control can provide directions (you'd request progressive taxi), so to make up for lack of such useful service, let's use a top-down view window.

To create a top-down view window, shown in Figure 4.20, press Shift+]. You can zoom the view in or out using the – (hyphen) and = (equal) keys, and you can resize the window using the standard Windows conventions (drag a corner or side). Also note that the window will rotate as you move, keeping the top of the window always pointed in the same direction you're facing. Finally, to close the map window, press the] key.

▶ *Tip*

When nosewheel steering is insufficient for making really sharp turns while taxiing, use differential braking (applying brakes to only one side of the aircraft). The F11 key individually applies the left brake, and the F12 key applies the right brake by itself.

▶ **Warning**

The 777-300 is a BIG airplane. Make sure you give yourself plenty of clearance when you taxi around.

Figure 4.20:
Creating a map window
can help you figure out
where you are.

Before Takeoff

Action	Response
Flaps	CHECK

Set flaps to 5 degrees by pressing the F7 key twice or clicking on the flap control lever located on the right side of the throttle quadrant. Flap position is displayed on the EICAS Flight Monitoring screen.

Takeoff Data	CHECKED AND SET

Takeoff

If this were a real flight, after receiving takeoff clearance we'd be on our way.

Action	Response
Lights	AS DESIRED

Turn the landing lights and anticollision/strobe lights on.

Transponder	ON

It's always on.

Power	MAXIMUM N_1

We'll be using the autopilot for takeoff. Just hit the TO/GA button (Ctrl+Shift+R) and hang on!

At 80 KIAS make sure your ASI is *alive*. (Crosscheck your indication with your copilot's indication as well.) Rotate at 156 KIAS and ease back on the stick to achieve an initial climb attitude of about 15 degrees pitch. Smoothly adjust pitch attitude to about 10 degrees to accelerate after your climb is established and you cross at least 500 feet AGL.

Landing Gear	UP

Upon achieving a positive rate of climb, retract the landing gear by pressing the G key. Immediately begin a left turn to heading 250 degrees and when you've cleared 500 feet AGL (513 feet MSL), you can engage the autopilot. You're now on course to CRI. Return the EICAS back to VOR Mode to verify your course.

Flaps	RETRACT

You can retract your flaps at any point above 175 KIAS by pressing the F5 key.

Auto Brake	OFF

Climb

Our initial rate of climb should be something like 1,800 feet per minute. After crossing CRI, set the autopilot CRS to 223 degrees; the autopilot will take us outbound on the Breezy Point Climb profile. Upon clearing CRI 3 DME, we'll simulate receiving ATC vectors to SAX. We do this by flying to SAX directly and beginning our climb-to-cruise altitude, and we'll let the autopilot handle this for us.

The first thing on the to-do list is to get our climb going. Click on the autopilot's ALT knob and dial in 35,000 feet. Next enter SAX's frequency into your NAV1 radio (doing so will automatically take the autopilot out of NAV mode). (Press Shift+2 to bring up the radio stack and enter the frequency.) Now rotate the CRS/OBS until you've lined up the CDI (Course Deviation Indicator) with a To reading to SAX. Finish off by re-engaging NAV Mode with Ctrl+N.

From this point on, we'll be flying the autopilot. We'll adjust our autopilot speed as we climb. As we climb above 10,000 feet, we'll switch the autopilot MCH mode and climb/fly at .60 Mach, as shown in Figure 4.21.

After crossing SAX, adjust the autopilot CRS to track 311 degrees. We'll fly that outbound to LHY. Because LHY is so close to SAX and because J36 shares the same radials, once we're established on SAX R-311 degrees, change NAV1's radio to LHY's frequency. Hit the NAV mode button to engage the autopilot NAV again and take us inbound to LHY on R-311 degrees.

Note

If we were taking off manually, you could jam the throttle full forward or pull it back all the way with impunity because the 777 is a fly-by-wire aircraft, so the flight computer will adjust the engines for you.

Tip

If you want to increase your rate of climb, adjust the autopilot's VSI dial.

Above 16,000 feet we'll set the autopilot for .84 Mach and get some speed out of this puppy. Finally, turn the landing lights off after climbing above 18,000 feet.

**Figure 4.21:
Flying directly to
SAX and climbing at
.60 Mach**

► **Note**

*As you fly above FL180,
don't forget to set your
altimeter to 29.92"!*

Cruise

When we reach our cruise altitude, the autopilot will establish level flight. (No need to adjust the elevator trim!) Our airspeed should be .84 Mach (gotta love that autopilot!). You're no doubt now familiar with the routine—the cruise portion of the flight is where we monitor flight progress, engine operation, and fuel management.

Upon crossing LHY, set the CRS to track R-301 degrees. At 50 DME (MINEO) from LHY, switch off NAV Mode, tune in DKK's frequency (116.2) on NAV1, and set 294 degrees in the autopilot CRS window. When you click NAV mode back on, the autopilot will take us to DKK. After crossing DKK, set 281 degrees on the CRS window.

Descent

At 72 DME from DKK, switch to FNT VOR frequency, using the same technique (frequency change, CRS change, NAV Mode on). We'll track R-284 degrees inbound to FNT and begin our descent. The autopilot descent process is very similar to what we've been doing so far, except we now toggle ALT mode instead of NAV mode, and we have to make a MCH adjustment. We'll walk you through it after you complete the descent checklist.

Action	Response
Briefing	COMPLETE/CHECKED
VREF	CALCULATED
Flaps	SET

No flaps are required at this time.

Auto Brake	RTO
Recall and Notes	CHECK

First reduce the autopilot MCH to .65 Mach. This will reduce power and help us descend without exceeding M_{MO}. (It's awfully hard to descend when the airplane wants to climb!) Next set FL180 in the autopilot's ALT window. Our VSI descent rate shouldn't be more than a comfortable 1,800 FPM. If it is, use the VSI dial to set it.

Once we cross FNT, fly outbound on R-258 degrees. 37 DME from FNT, we'll descend further (use 250 KIAS on the IAS setting, and 5,000 feet for ALT on the autopilot) and switch to PMM to fly inbound on R-252 degrees. (Don't forget to hit the NAV button after you switch frequencies!)

After descending below FL180, hit the B key once to set the ALT to local barometric pressure and turn the landing lights on. Then after crossing PMM, fly outbound on R-261 degrees.

Approach

At 46 DME from PMM, switch to OBK VOR and track R-256 degrees inbound. Now tune in ORD ATIS and set your ALT again (press the B key). We also want to set up for the approach. Enter 240 degrees in the autopilot's HDG window. You'll see why in a minute.

After crossing OBK, flip NAV mode off and then hit the HDG mode button. This will place us on an intercept course with ORD 14R ILS. Reduce the autopilot IAS to 190 KIAS and dial in ORD's 14R ILS frequency in NAV1 (109.75). Finally, switch the autopilot to APR mode and complete the approach checklist.

Action	Response
Glide Slope	ON

For your convenience, this is always on in *Flight Simulator 2000*.

Autopilot	OFF

Since we're flying a Cat III approach, we leave the autopilot engaged.

Flight Director	OUT

Out means off. Unfortunately we can't disengage the flight director in *Flight Simulator 2000* without disengaging the autopilot, too—so we'll leave this on.

Flaps	15°

Press the F7 key three times.

> ▶ *Tip*
>
> *As you descend below FL180, you're supposed to set your altimeter to match the setting at destination. Since we're too far away to receive our destination's (ORD) ATIS, and we don't have the luxury of en route ATC to inform us, simply press the B key to set the altimeter to the correct setting.*

Before Landing

Action	Response
Cabin	READY

This refers to the passenger cabin.

Action	Response
Altimeter	SET

Press the B key once again for good measure.

Action	Response
Speedbrake	ARMED

The speedbrake can be set to automatically deploy on touch down by pressing Shift+ /.

Action	Response
Autopilot	CONFIGURED FOR MISSED APPROACH PROCEDURE

We'll be using the autopilot all the way down to touchdown, so this isn't possible on this flight.

Landing

Final approach speed is 150 to 160 KIAS (depending on landing weight). For our flight we can set the IAS in the autopilot to 150 KIAS.

Action	Response
Landing Gear	DOWN

Press the G key and verify that the gear is down in the EICAS.

Action	Response
Flaps	30°

Press F7 three more times.

There's little to do now until touchdown, except enjoy the ride. Your instruments on approach should look like Figure 4.22.

After touchdown, reverse thrusters will engage automatically. To manually engage reverse thrust, press and hold the F2 key (or KP3 with the Num Lock off). Disengage reverse thrust at 80 knots by pressing the F1 once and apply brakes (the"." (period) key). At 60 knots, disengage the auto brake.

▶ **Tip**

When you're all lined up for the approach into ORD, save the Flight so you can watch the 777-300 land itself over and over again.

Figure 4.22:
On final!

After Landing

Exit the runway at 15 knots or less. Before taxiing to parking, complete the after-landing checklist.

Action	Response
Landing and Strobe Lights	OFF
Flaps	UP

Press F5.

Spoilers	DOWN

Press the / key.

Auto Brake Selector	OFF
Autothrottle and Autopilot	OFF

Click the auto-throttle off and press the Z key to disengage the autopilot.

Parking

Action	Response
Parking Brake	SET

Press Ctrl+"." (period).

Fuel Flow	CUT OFF

Press Ctrl+Shift+F1.

Welcome to the windy city! Hope you had pleasant flight. You might wonder why the guys who fly these really advanced aircraft get paid the really big bucks when they're so easy to fly. Well, it's because they know how to fly the thing when everything *doesn't* work properly!

Now that you've seen how an airliner is flown, let's take a look at the pinnacle of civilian transports—the Concorde!

▶ *Tip*

When you feel comfortable, try flying the 777-300 and the other Flight Simulator 2000 *aircraft with the* System Reliability settings *(under the Aircraft menu) set for failures. Just remember that you don't get many second chances in the real world, and you'll come to appreciate what these pilots do.*

Supersonic
Flight

Chapter 5

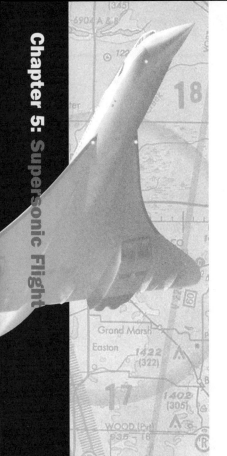
*T*he addition of the Concorde to Flight Simulator's *aircraft hangar was inevitable. The Concorde is arguably the most fascinating civilian aircraft in service today. Although the design is nearly twice as old as Flight Simulator itself, the Concorde's impressive safety and performance records illustrate that this aircraft was clearly years ahead of its time.*

The tutorial in this chapter covers the operations associated with supersonic flight from London's Heathrow Airport to John F. Kennedy Airport in New York. As you'll see, there's a lot more to flying this aircraft than just kicking in the afterburners and holding on for an exhilarating ride. If you're ready to join the Mach 2.0 club, strap yourself in!

Aerodynamics of Supersonic Flight

Since the Wright brothers' first 12-second flight in 1903, the quest for speed has continued relentlessly. By WWI, the fastest aircraft was the French Spad XIII—achieving 138 mph and 21,000 feet of altitude. By the end of WWII, jet engines made possible high-speed flights of faster than 500 mph. Figure 5.1 shows that any speed above 350 mph through Mach 7.0 and beyond is considered high-speed flight.

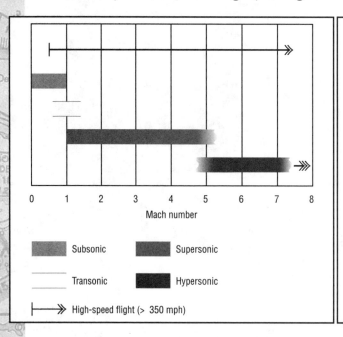

Figure 5.1:
High-speed flight begins at 350 mph (Mach 0.45).

For many years, the idea of exceeding the speed of sound seemed like trying to pass through an impenetrable wall, giving rise to the then popular notion of a *sound barrier*. To many people at the time, exceeding the speed of sound seemed almost as implausible as sending a man to the moon. It wasn't until Chuck Yeager and the Bell X-1 that supersonic flight became a reality. The rest, as they say, is history.

Naturally, as the pilot in command of a supersonic aircraft, it's important to understand some of the dynamics involved with supersonic flight. Let's start by discussing what the speed of sound is.

The Speed of Sound

As the phrase suggests, the speed of sound is the velocity at which sound travels. Obviously, in aviation the speed of sound refers to the velocity at which sound travels through air. The speed of sound in air depends only on the static temperature of the air. This velocity decreases as the temperature lowers and increases as the temperature rises. For example, the speed of sound is 661.48 knots at 59.0°F (15°C), slowing to 602.0 knots at −30.0°F (−34.4°C) and slowing even more to 573.6 knots at −69.7°F (−56.5°C), as illustrated in Table 5.1.

Table 5.1: Standard Altitude Table

Altitude (Ft)	Density Ratio	Pressure Ratio	Temperature (°F)	Temperature Ratio	Speed of Sound (Kn)
0	1.0000	1.0000	59.00	1.0000	661.5
1000	0.9711	0.9644	55.43	0.9931	659.5
2000	0.9428	0.9298	51.87	0.9862	657.2
3000	0.9151	0.8962	48.30	0.9794	654.9
4000	0.8881	0.8637	44.74	0.9725	652.6
5000	0.8617	0.8320	41.17	0.9656	650.3
6000	0.8359	0.8014	37.60	0.9587	647.9
7000	0.8106	0.7716	34.04	0.9519	645.6
8000	0.7860	0.7428	30.47	0.9450	643.3
9000	0.7620	0.7148	26.90	0.9381	640.9
10000	0.7385	0.6877	23.34	0.9312	638.6
15000	0.6292	0.5643	5.51	0.8969	626.7
20000	0.5328	0.4595	-12.32	0.8625	614.6
25000	0.4481	0.3711	-30.15	0.8281	602.2
30000	0.3741	0.2970	-47.98	0.7937	589.5
35000	0.3099	0.2353	-65.82	0.7594	576.6
*36089	0.2971	0.2234	-69.70	0.7519	573.8
40000	0.2462	0.1851	-69.70	0.7519	573.8
45000	0.1936	0.1455	-69.70	0.7519	573.8
50000	0.1522	0.1145	-69.70	0.7519	573.8
55000	0.1197	0.0900	-69.70	0.7519	573.8
60000	0.0941	0.0708	-69.70	0.7519	573.8

* Tropopause (boundary between the troposphere and stratosphere) begins

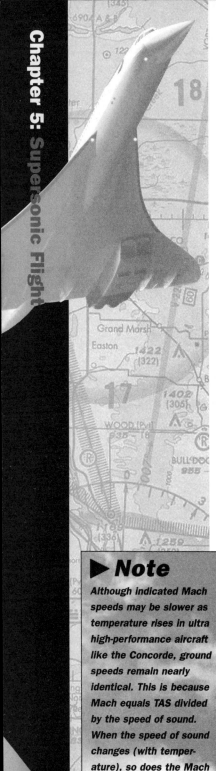

A general gas law defines these variances as the relationship of pressure, temperature, and density (assuming no change of state or heat transfer). This law states that "density varies directly with pressure, inversely with temperature."

Nonstandard Temperatures

Because the speed of sound is so closely tied to temperature, we should mention that variations in temperatures affect the performance of all aircraft. As the temperature rises, performance decreases. These performance variations are due to engine power and aerodynamic losses. You can keep track of important temperatures on the Concorde's Outside Air/Skin Temperature gauge (Figure 5.2), located just above the digital clock in the lower center of the instrument panel. This instrument is a bit unique because it does some calculations for you.

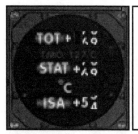

Figure 5.2:
The Concorde's Outside Air/Skin Temperature gauge calculates how many degrees over ISA (International Standard Atmosphere) the current outside air temperature is.

The readout in the center of the gauge labeled STAT (STandard Air Temperature) displays what the current OAT (Outside Air Temperature) would be if it were a standard day outside. The readout below it labeled ISA (International Standard Atmosphere) displays how many degrees variation from ISA temperature the current outside temperature really is. The top display labeled TOT (which stands for TOTal air temperature) shows the skin temperature read by the sensors on the nose of the aircraft. Note that the maximum operation temperature (expressed as T_{MO}) is +127°C.

The "Sound Barrier"

As we mentioned earlier, the difficulties that were encountered by pilots attempting to fly beyond an aircraft's critical Mach number (we'll get to what that is in a minute) and the overall mystique of supersonic flight led to the popular phrase *sound barrier*. In hindsight, most aerodynamicists agree that the biggest problem faced with approaching or exceeding Mach 1.0 was caused by the absence of engines powerful enough to overcome the rapid rise in drag that begins at an aircraft's critical Mach number. But in order to understand the factors that determine an aircraft's critical Mach number, we need to understand the compressible characteristics of air (its *compressibility*).

As an object moves through an air mass, it creates pressure disturbances (changes in velocity and pressure) in the airflow around the object. These pressure disturbances propagate through the air at the speed of sound in waves because air molecules simply flow/push against

> ▶ *Note*
>
> *Although indicated Mach speeds may be slower as temperature rises in ultra high-performance aircraft like the Concorde, ground speeds remain nearly identical. This is because Mach equals TAS divided by the speed of sound. When the speed of sound changes (with temperature), so does the Mach number when TAS remains constant.*

each other—the same way that sound travels. A typical subsonic airflow pattern around an airfoil is shown in Figure 5.3.

When an object moves at or beyond the speed of sound, it's moving faster than air molecules can get out of the way, which causes them to bunch up and come against the object with a "shock." In the simplest terms, instead of the molecules making room and flowing over the object as they do at slow velocities, air molecules are suddenly forced out of the way and must change their pressure and velocity abruptly at sharp angles (see Figure 5.4). A *compression wave* forms at the leading edge of the object when its velocity nears and exceeds the speed of sound.

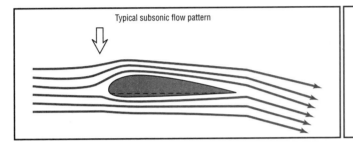

Figure 5.3:
During subsonic flight, there's enough time for the airflow to change (move out of the way) well ahead of the airfoil.

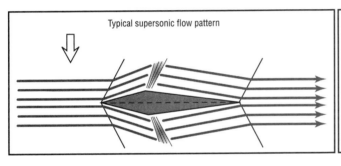

Figure 5.4:
In supersonic flight there's no apparent change in the airflow pattern ahead of an airfoil.

As you may know if you've studied basic aerodynamics, even without compressibility effects, drag increases with the square of the velocity, and the power requirement, which is drag multiplied by velocity, increases with the cube of velocity. In simpler terms, if you double your velocity, the resultant drag is four times as great. And it takes eight times the power to double your velocity! The effect of compressibility on drag (and subsequently power requirements) increases these values even more to astronomically high values. This is why an aircraft's maximum drag is experienced just before reaching Mach 1.0.

Mach Numbers

The designation *Mach* was named after Ernst Mach, a Czech-born Austrian philosopher and physicist who contributed to the study of sound. The speed of sound is known as Mach 1.0. Mach 2.0 is twice the speed of sound and so on. More specifically, a Mach number is the ratio of TAS (True AirSpeed) to the speed of sound.

When an aircraft's TAS is used to calculate a Mach number, it's referred to as the *airplane Mach number*. If a velocity from some point on

> ▶ **Note**
> *The efficiency of a good propeller is about 80 percent at best. This is achieved at speeds of about 250–350 knots. Efficiency drops off rapidly afterwards. This is another reason why the development of other aircraft propulsion methods were required to exceed Mach 1.0.*

an airplane is referenced, the resultant value is referred to as a *local Mach number*. The Concorde cruises at Mach 2.0, which at standard temperatures roughly translates to 23 miles per minute, 1 mile per 2.5 seconds, and 1,900 feet per second. Now that's hauling gas!

Machmeter

A Machmeter is an instrument that measures and indicates speed relative to the speed of sound. We know that the divergence between IAS and TAS becomes greater as air density decreases (typically when altitude is gained or temperature rises). In the simplest term, a Machmeter is essentially a TAS indicator calibrated in Mach increments. It becomes particularly useful at the very high altitudes at which the Concorde flies. The Concorde's Machmeter is located just to the left of the HSI (Horizontal Situation Indicator) on its instrument panel. Figure 5.5 shows what it looks like.

Figure 5.5:

The Concorde's Machmeter is located to the left of its HSI (Horizontal Situation Indicator).

Mach Tuck and Critical Mach Number

As early subsonic aircraft in the 1940s approached the speed of sound (usually in a dive), peculiar things began to happen. Aircraft began to buffet and had a tendency to "tuck under" (nose down) into a steeper dive than the pilot usually intended. (Expletives deleted!) If this tuck-under effect wasn't recognized and corrected by the pilot, the control forces became so strong that recovery became impossible. The airspeed where these potentially fatal effects occurred became known as the aircraft's *critical Mach number*.

Subsequently, critical Mach numbers, which obviously were not to be exceeded, were assigned to all subsonic jet airplanes. The destabilizing effect in pitch comes about when an airplane exceeding its critical Mach number creates supersonic flow shock waves over the wing. As Figure 5.6 and Figure 5.7 illustrate, this situation causes the airplane's center of lift (the center of all aerodynamic forces for nearly all angles of attack) to move rearward in relation to the airplane's CG (Center of Gravity—which is not changed by velocity), and it creates the gradually increasing nose-down pitching movement. The severity of Mach tuck is of course dependent upon the airplane's stability characteristics as well as other factors.

▶ **Note**

An airplane can experience compressibility effects at flight speeds below the speed of sound because subsonic and supersonic flow can exist over different portions of an aircraft. An example of such an area is the upper half of an airfoil. The velocity of the airflow there is typically higher than below it.

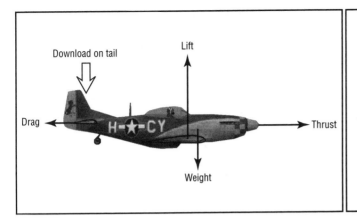

Figure 5.6:
In subsonic flight, stability is easily maintained by the downloaded tail when the center of gravity is ahead of the wing's aerodynamic center.

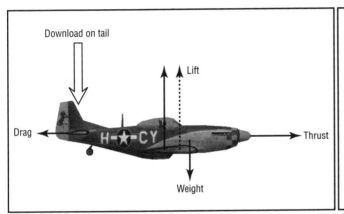

Figure 5.7:
At transonic and supersonic speeds a wing's aerodynamic center shifts rearward and increases the tail download required to counteract the resultant nose-down tendency.

Supersonic Weight and Balance

The concepts of weight and balance are pretty easy to understand. The heavier that something is (an airplane in our case), the more effort (*force* is the proper term) is required to move it. The heavier the airplane, the more lift must be generated by the wings to get it off the ground. And if the airplane is too heavy, you stand the chance of overstressing something. Not only can that cause your ground crew to get really angry, but it can also cause structural failures—and those will pretty much ruin any pilot's day.

The term "balance" refers to the aircraft's CG. (Remember, the Center of Gravity is the point where an object will balance as if it's suspended by an imaginary string.) We've discussed how the relationship of an aircraft's CG to its aerodynamic center affects its pitch stability. So in addition to how much weight an aircraft carries, where it carries this weight is also very important.

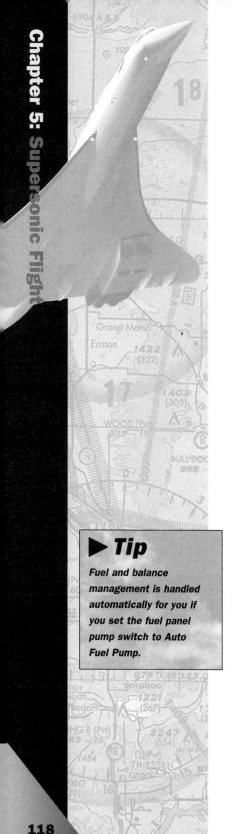

The Concorde suffers from the same weight and balance problem that other aircraft have to deal with—it consumes fuel and fuel has weight—but because it's a supersonic aircraft, it needs to contend with Mach tuck issues as well.

Recall that as the aircraft goes supersonic, the wing's aerodynamic center shifts rearward in relation to the center of gravity, increasing the required elevator power to prevent an uncontrollable dive. To offset the effects of Mach tuck, the Concorde's engineers devised an elaborate weight and balance monitoring and fuel transfer system. By transferring weight (in the form of fuel) rearward as the aerodynamic center moves rearward, the relationship between the CG and aerodynamic center can be maintained so that elevator force requirements can be kept to acceptable levels.

Transferring Fuel

The real Concorde has a total of 13 fuel tanks (tanks 1–11, with two a/b tanks). They are

Left wing collector tank #1	**Center forward fuselage #9**	**Right wing collector tank #4**
Left wing main tank #5	**Center fuselage wing #10**	**Right wing main tank #7**
Left wing tip tank #5a	**Center fuselage rear #11**	**Right wing tip tank #7a**

Tanks #2, #3, #6, and #8 are direct-feed tanks (one per engine).

Because the real Concorde is flown with a mandatory three-person crew, the *Flight Simulator* team designed *Flight Simulator 2000*'s Concorde with fewer tanks to reduce your cockpit workload. Nevertheless, transferring fuel is still a critical job that requires diligence and precision if you choose to manage fuel manually.

When the real Concorde is parked at the gate, its tanks are filled to the levels specified by the crew (levels vary with trip length, headwinds, total load, expected delays, and so on), and the rear tank is left empty. This forward CG configuration facilitates loading the aircraft with passengers and cargo (the largest cargo hold is in the rear of the fuselage). Having a forward CG reduces the risk of the aircraft lifting its nose in the air (causing a tail strike) while it's being loaded.

Although the Concorde's pilot and copilot are responsible for monitoring weight and balance changes throughout the flight, the flight engineer performs the actual transfers. The flight engineer will transfer fuel among the Concorde's 13 tanks at least five times during a typical flight from the CG control at the flight engineer's station. Table 5.2 outlines these transfers.

> ▶ **Tip**
>
> *Fuel and balance management is handled automatically for you if you set the fuel panel pump switch to Auto Fuel Pump.*

Table 5.2: Concorde Fuel Transfers

Flight Configuration	CG	Action
Empty	52.88%	Enter weights and fuel info into CG computer (handled automatically by *Flight Simulator 2000*).
Taxi	53.5% +/−.3	Pump fuel to rear tank to obtain takeoff CG.
Takeoff	53.5% +/−.3	Check takeoff range setting.
Supersonic Cruise Mach 2.0	59%	Adjust fuel as necessary to maintain CG and lateral balance and to keep engines fed.
Deceleration	Around 55% (varies with airspeed)	Pump fuel from rear tank and/or wing tanks to forward tank to maintain proper subsonic CG.
Landing	52.3–53%	Pump fuel from rear tank and/or wings to forward tank to obtain landing CG.
Taxi	Shifting forward	Pump as much fuel to the forward tank as possible to facilitate unloading.

The Concorde's CG control computer calculates the aircraft's weight and CG in real time. As you might imagine, when you have to keep track of some 26,000 Imperial gallons of fuel (95,600 kgs) that's consumed at the rate of 5,638 Imperial gallons (20,500 kgs/22.6 tons!) per hour, it really helps the flight engineer determine which tanks need to be filled or emptied. Your remaining fuel onboard is monitored by the fuel total indicator shown in Figure 5.8, just to the right of the CG indicator on the center of the instrument panel.

Figure 5.8:
Remaining fuel onboard is monitored by the fuel total indicator and is indexed in kg (Kilos).

The acceptable calculated CG ranges are displayed in two areas on the Concorde's instrument panel. Although each of these areas indicates the same information, they're displayed in different forms. The orange Machmeter bugs indicate the acceptable Mach speed range for a current CG. The other area is on the CG indicator shown in Figure 5.9. This area displays the current CG location (white Index indicator) and acceptable CG range in percentages (also indicated by orange bugs).

As complicated as this may all sound, the idea is to keep the needles and indexes in between the CG-range bugs. There are two ways to do this. Since acceptable CG ranges vary with Mach speed, you can either change the CG by transferring fuel in the proper direction, or you can slow down or speed up as conditions warrant. Of course, since your passengers want to get to where they're going ASAP (a pretty safe assumption—they wouldn't be flying the Concorde otherwise), slowing down isn't usually the best option.

Figure 5.9:
Located just above the ALT, the Concorde's CG indicator displays its current CG position in percentages. The red light at the top warns if the CG is out of range.

Fuel is manually transferred in *Flight Simulator 2000*'s Concorde from the Fuel Panel window (Figure 5.10). You can access it by pressing Shift+6. The left side displays the four fuel gauges for the four tanks. The top gauge is the front tank, the bottom is the rear, left is left, and right is right. Moving the fuel pump control switch located on the right half manually transfers fuel fore and aft, and the Xfeed switch in the center of the fuel gauges controls cross-feeding (transferring fuel between the lateral tanks).

Maximizing Fuel Efficiency through Fuel/Weight Transfer

As efficient as Concorde's Olympus engines are, the old auto racing axiom still applies: any force that's not going in the same direction that you want to go is just causing drag and slowing you down. Most people believe that, short of deploying spoilers, losing an engine, or flying with the landing gear extended, uncoordinated flight (flying with excessive or insufficient rudder application) is the only way to produce unwanted excess drag. But excess drag can be created even when flying in coordinated flight—even with the autopilot enabled. Fortunately, the Concorde's weight control/transfer system can minimize these problems.

Most airplanes are designed for pitch stability generated by downward pressure on the horizontal stabilizer. (As airspeed increases, it causes the nose of the aircraft to pitch up.) As we've seen with the factors that cause Mach tuck, the further forward the aircraft's CG is, the more downward pressure is required to keep the nose level. This added downward pressure also produces additional drag. Therefore, minimum drag will be achieved with the most rearward CG (within the specified range limits of course!) because the least amount of downward tail pressure will be required.

The second source of weight-controllable excess drag comes from flying with uneven lateral weights. When one wing is heavier than the other, the opposite aileron application will be required to keep the wings level (regardless of whether the pilot or autopilot is applying the corrective control pressure). This additional control deflection also produces unnecessary additional drag.

> ▶ **Tip**
>
> *If you're ever confused about which direction you need to transfer fuel to accommodate a CG change, just remember to move fuel in the same direction that you need to move the CG position indicator index needle. For example, to move the CG position indicator index needles rearward, you'd transfer fuel to the rear tank and vice versa. Simple!*

Figure 5.10:
Press Shift+6 to access the Concorde's Fuel Panel window.

> ▶ **Warning**
>
> *The Fuel Transfer pumps turn themselves off when the tank that you're transferring to is filled or the fuel tank selector is changed.*

You can detect wing balance problems by watching the Control Positions indicators (Figure 5.11), located on the lower-right side of the Concorde's instrument panel. When you're flying on a constant heading and see uneven elevon positions, you have an imbalance problem. It can be corrected by moving fuel from the wing flying with the elevon down to the wing with the elevon positioned upward.

Reading the Control Position indicators is simple: the Concorde has three elevons per wing (one inboard and two outboard of the engines) and a split two-section rudder. The control position indicators at the top of the display are for the rudder. Elevons are displayed to the sides, shown as if you were looking at each control surface from the rear of the aircraft pointed forward. In other words, an elevon position indication to the top of the display indicates elevons in the up position, and a right indication on the rudder indicator indicates a rudder positioned to the right.

> ▶ **Note**
>
> *These elevons are erroneously identified as spoileron [sic] indicators in* Flight Simulator 2000's Pilot's Handbook. *Actually, the Concorde doesn't have flaps, slats, or spoilers—elevons are a combination elevator and aileron.*

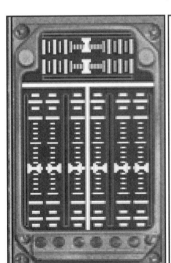

Figure 5.11:
The Concorde's Control Position indictors are located on the lower-right portion of the instrument panel.

Flying the Concorde

The first time many people look in the Concorde's cockpit, they tend to think that, as advanced as this aircraft obviously is, it seems strange to still see so many analog instruments. The Concorde's operators determined that advancing her systems to the latest and greatest "glass cockpit" displays couldn't be justified financially. Regardless, while flying this amazing aircraft you'll be even more appreciative of the designers' choices and engineering feats when you consider that its design is over 30 years old!

Crewing the Concorde

Like most large turbine-powered, commercial carrier aircraft, the Concorde's flight duties are assigned to a crew. Due to the complexity of the Concorde's flight operations, her flight crew consists of a pilot, copilot, and flight engineer. The way that the Concorde's flight crew operates tends to surprise people not familiar with the Concorde's systems. The Concorde flight crew operates like a crew on a ship. The pilot (captain) commands the crew. The autopilot would be the helmsman (who steers the ship), the copilot (first officer) handles the details related to the journey, and the flight engineer (chief engineer) handles all engine operations. But it's the extent of the duties of the flight engineer that's the most surprising.

In addition to the fuel juggling we covered earlier, the Concorde flight engineer's duties include starting, controlling, and optimizing the plane's massive engines. For example, the flight engineer, not the pilot or copilot, reduces power during climb and turns the afterburners on and off.

Aircraft Performance

The Concorde can be likened to an ultra-plush dragster—it goes like heck in a straight line, but its maneuverability suffers as a result. Nevertheless, as you'll see, the Concorde is quite nimble when she needs to be.

V Speeds

The Concorde has a total of three pitot tubes to measure airspeed/Mach: two for the computer and one standby located in the center of the nose. You can switch between the computer and standby pitot tubes by clicking the N S switches located in the lower-right corners of the ASI and ALT. ("N" is for Normal, and "S" is for Standby.)

As you're well aware of by now, V speeds are a function of total aircraft weight and OAT. The following numbers are based on a standard day, maximum gross weight at sea level.

V Speed	KIAS/MACH
V_1	165 KIAS
V_R	193 KIAS
V_2	214 KIAS
*V_N	250 KIAS
V_{2+40}	244 KIAS
Maximum nose down speed	270 KIAS
Maximum visor down speed	325 KIAS / 0.8 Mach
V_{MO} (5,000' - 32,000' MSL)	400 KIAS
(32,000' - 44,000' MSL)	400–530 KIAS
(44,000' - 50,000' MSL)	530 KIAS
M_{MO}(5,000' - 32,000' MSL)	.65–1.07 Mach
(44,000' - 50,000' MSL)	1.75–2.0 Mach
(51,000' - 60,000' MSL)	2.04 Mach
V_{LE}/V_{LO}	270 KIAS / 0.7 Mach
V_{MC}	185 KIAS
**VLA (15,000' - 41,000' MSL)	250 KIAS
(41,000' - 60,000' MSL)	300 KIAS
V_{REF}	162 KIAS

*Target speed

**Lowest authorized speed

Advanced Systems

Flying the Concorde is very different from flying just about every other civil aviation aircraft out there. Here are some of the more notable differences that you should be aware of:

Supercruise One of the Concorde's most outstanding capabilities is its ability to supercruise. *Supercruising* is an aircraft's ability to maintain supersonic speeds without the use of afterburners. (We'll talk about afterburners next.) What's more astonishing is that the Concorde will accelerate and maintain Mach 2.0 without using afterburners!

Afterburners Afterburners (or reheat, as the British call them) are a device used to gain huge increases in thrust from turbine engines. Basically raw fuel is sprayed (dumped is more like it) into the engine's exhaust and ignited. Unfortunately, while the increase in thrust is handy for transoceanic crossing, the use of reheat is extremely inefficient on fuel, which is why the ability to supercruise is so valuable. To toggle afterburners/reheat, press Shift+F4.

▶ **Note**

There are only thirteen Concorde supersonic transports in service around the world. Seven are operated by British Airways, and Air France operates the remaining six.

▶ **Note**

A 100-percent throttle setting without afterburners is known as full drive power.

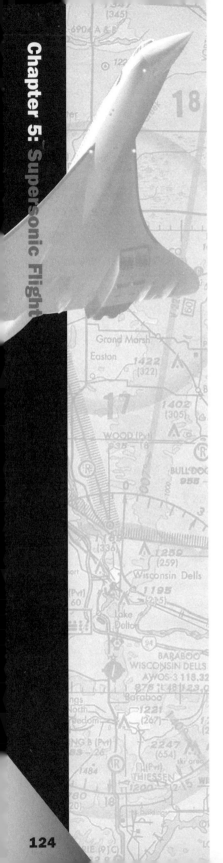

The Concorde's four engines are controlled by the center console throttle quadrant (see Figure 5.12). These are electronic throttles (fly-by-wire), and each engine has its own reheat toggle. To toggle reheat by individual engine, press E+[the engine number(s) you want to activate] followed by Shift+F4.

Figure 5.12:
Press Shift+4 to access the Concorde's throttle quadrant.

You can determine which engines have reheat activated by watching the fuel flow and primary nozzle (gas discharge area) gauges in the engine gauge cluster shown in Figure 5.13. When reheat is engaged, you'll notice that fuel flow will increase dramatically, and the lights in the upper-left corner of the primary nozzle gauges will light up.

Thrust Reversers Although most turbine engines have some sort of thrust reversal devices to help slow the aircraft, the Concorde's are used in supersonic flight as well. Reverser buckets close like a clam shell at the rear of the engine where thrust is expelled, redirecting it forward. Due to their shape, these reverser buckets produce additional thrust when fully open in supersonic flight. (Hey, every little bit helps!)

Reverser Bucket Positions	Flight Mode
0° (full open)	Supersonic flight
21°	Normal flight
Closed	Thrust reverse

Control of the reverser bucket positions is handled automatically, except for the closed/thrust reverse position. To operate the thrust reversers, press and hold F2.

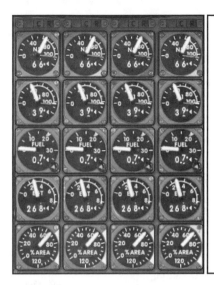

Figure 5.13:
The engine gauge
cluster houses (from
top to bottom) N_1, N_2,
fuel flow, EGT, and
primary nozzle gauges.

Nose and Visor System The Concorde's pointy nose is great for low-drag supersonic flight, but it's less than ideal for forward vision. To get the best of both worlds, the Concorde's designers devised a movable nose and visor system (the slanted glass greenhouse section of the cockpit), shown in Figure 5.14. During operation, the visor lowers first, and the nose tilts second.

The nose can be placed in three positions: full up, 5 degrees down (for taxi and flight below 250 KIAS), and 12.5 degrees down (used only for landing). To lower or raise the visor and nose, click on the VIS/NS control (Figure 5.15), on the upper-right side of the instrument panel.

Inlet Ramps and Spills There are three main sections of a supersonic-capable engine: intake, engine, and exhaust. A turbine engine will ignite only if the incoming air is at Mach 0.7 or lower. The Concorde handles this problem with computer-controlled inlet ramps. They slow the incoming air by creating a shock wave at each engine's inlet. Just like in the real Concorde, *Flight Simulator 2000*'s ramps are controlled automatically.

Cooling While the Concorde's passengers are no doubt traveling at a comfortable temperature (everyone is considered First Class passengers) within her cabin, supersonic flight is quite stressful to her hull. The Concorde's Mach 2.0 speed limit is due more to the limits in materials used than anything else. Speeds much over Mach 2.0 produce temperatures that cause aluminum alloys to lose their strength. (Aluminum loses its strength at temperatures exceeding 250°F.)

The heat and forces that are produced during a typical flight will cause the aircraft to stretch 8 to 10 inches longer. Although fuel is recirculated inside the aircraft to help cool the skin and engines, temperatures on the wings can still easily fry an egg.

▶ **Tip**

Across the very top of the engine gauge cluster are the engine management lights. Green means go, red means caution, and blue means reverse thrust.

▶ **Note**

To give you an indication of how much drag is cause by the visor system, consider this: when the real Concorde's visor is in the up position, it reduces cockpit noise by about half.

Figure 5.14:
Concorde's nose and
visor can tilt to provide
the best of both sub-
sonic and supersonic
operation efficiency.

While you won't need to worry about recirculating fuel to help cool the aircraft (it's another duty handled by the flight engineer), you will have to keep track of how hot you let the airplane get by monitoring the Outside/Skin temperature gauge. If the TOT temperature exceeds +127°C (243°F), you've got no choice but to slow down—or risk becoming a man-made meteor!

Radar The Concorde is equipped with three radar-based systems: the radar altimeter (Figure 5.16), TCAS (Traffic Collision Avoidance System), and weather radar (radar designed for tracking storms). The Concorde's radar altimeter is located just above the fuel gauge in the center of the instrument panel (the TCAS and Storm Scope aren't modeled in *Flight Simulator 2000*).

The radar altimeter uses radar to track and display the Concorde's height over the surface below (as opposed to the altitude based on the sea level reference plane of the ALT). In the real world, the Concorde's radar is used for terrain-proximity warnings as well as its automatic landing system. Use your mouse on the knob in the lower-left corner to adjust the radar altimeter's warning bug. When the set altitude is crossed, it will illuminate the DH (Decision Height) light located in the upper-right corner of the AI.

Figure 5.15:
Use this control
to lower and raise
Concorde's visor
and nose.

Figure 5.16:
The Concorde's radar
altimeter is located just
above the fuel gauge in
the center of the
instrument panel.

The Concorde's Brakes and Tires

Special equipment had to be developed to handle the Concorde's high ground speeds during take off and landing. To slow the airplane down, the Concorde is equipped with carbon fiber disc brakes. To keep the brakes from glazing and/or burning, each is equipped with electric cooling fans and temperature-monitoring sensors.

Special tires had to be designed and manufactured to take the abuse as well. The Concorde's tires are built to withstand speeds to 250 mph. To give you an idea of the sturdiness of their construction, the main landing gear tires are pressurized to about 232 PSI (Pound per Square Inch).

Flight Plan

In addition to the normal flight information we've used in the other chapters, we also need to talk about some of the special equipment and operational procedures and restrictions placed on supersonic flight.

Airports

As we mentioned at the beginning of this chapter, we'll be flying from London's Heathrow Airport (EGLL) from runway 27L to John F. Kennedy International Airport (JFK) in New York, runway 31R.

The runway lengths at Heathrow and JFK are 12,000 feet (3,658 meters) and 10,000 feet, respectively. The Concorde requires 9,000 feet to take off and land. Possible alternates for our flight include Boston's Logan International and New Jersey's Newark International.

Route

The real Concorde uses an Inertial Navigation System (INS) to navigate across the ocean (where ground-based radio navigation aids are sparse). This system uses accelerometers to keep track of where the aircraft is and where it's going. Even with a long, transoceanic flight, INS accuracy is in the 200–300 yard range at the end of the flight. Of course, as you might suspect, INS accuracy is only as good as the latitude and longitude information entered at the start point.

▶ **Note**

Normally with a long-distance trip we wouldn't know which runway we'd be landing on because it's determined by weather and traffic conditions. Nevertheless, Kennedy's runway 31R is used most often for incoming traffic. (Besides, we're flying Flight Simulator 2000 so we can pick and choose our weather!)

Flight Simulator 2000 doesn't have an INS system, but its GPS (Global Positioning System) navigation feature can be used to simulate one. We'll save the details of GPS until Chapter 7; for now we'll limit our discussion to how we can use it for this flight.

The INS waypoints for a typical transatlantic Concorde flight are listed in Table 5.3. The first three waypoints comply with the Compton Three DP out of EGLL. (See page 279 in *Flight Simulator 2000*'s *Pilot's Handbook*.) The next two waypoints are used to guide the Concorde to its acceleration point (more on this in a minute). Waypoint #5 marks the end of the Concorde's transatlantic track routing (we'll get to this, too), and waypoint #6 is the deceleration/descent reference. The final waypoint, #7, is an intersection that's used as an entry point for a vectored ATC arrival to JFK.

Table 5.3: INS Waypoints for a Typical Transatlantic Concorde Flight

Waypoint	Coordinates (Longitude/Latitude)	Description
#0	N051°27.69 / W000°26.69	Heathrow Concorde gate
#1	N051°27.20 / W000°52.70	Woodley (WOD 352 NDB)
#2	N051°29.50 / W001°13.20	Compton (CPT 114.35 VOR/DME)
#3	N051°35.50 / W002°03.60	North Eagle (GPS fix)
#4	N051°24.00 / W003°00.50	Acceleration point (Bristol Channel GPS fix)
#5	N042°46.00 / W065°00.00	(GPS fix) North Atlantic Track exit
#6	N042°00.00 / W067°00.00	(GPS fix) decelerate/descent
#7	N039°49.40 / W072°49.83	OWENZ intersection

Using the Flight Planner

We can use *Flight Simulator 2000*'s flight planner to input waypoints that will simulate our GPS waypoints. But due to some limitations of this GPS—we're unable to input/create our own waypoints—we'll have to use some nearby published jetway intersections as substitutes. These few variations won't appreciably affect our flight or experience.

Let's talk about how to input our modified flight route. First select Flight Planner from the Flight menu. Enter EGLL as the departure airport, runway 27R; KJFK as the destination airport, runway 31R; KLGA as the alternate airport, runway 22L; and click the IFR and Direct-GPS buttons as shown in Figure 5.17. Next click the Find Route button.

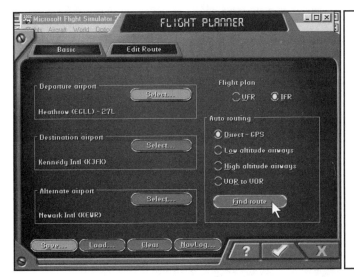

The Edit Route part of the Flight Planner will automatically appear. This is the place where we can tweak flight plans. If you've played with the flight planner at all, to recreate some of our tutorial flights for example, you're probably aware of some of its limitations. Like most flight planners, it's only able to create a basic framework that almost always needs to be modified. (Flight planners don't always select the optimal route, and they are usually oblivious to VFR airspace restrictions, MEAs, and so on.)

The toolbar buttons (Figure 5.18) at the top of the Map window are from left to right: Zoom In, Zoom Out, Reset Zoom, De-clutter, Print, Show Airports, Show VORs, Show NDBs, Show Intersections, Show Victor Airways, and Show Jet Routes. We'll be using these buttons to modify our flight plan, but first toggle off Show Intersections (they'll appear in green), Show Victor Airways (dark blue), and Show Jet Routes (dark green).

Figure 5.18:
The flight planner's Edit
Routes toolbar

For our flight we'll need to enter the waypoints used in the Compton Three Golf (CPT 3G) DP from London Heathrow runway 27L. Click on EGLL in the list on the right; Map view will zoom in on it. (You may need to click on KJFK first to get the zoom to work.)

Next, drag the red course line over the LON VOR (blue) as shown in Figure 5.19. This will bring up the Facilities window. When there's more than a single waypoint located in the same general area, this window will appear to let you make a selection. In this case, we want the LON VOR, so select it from the list, as shown in Figure 5.20, and click the green checkmark to close the window.

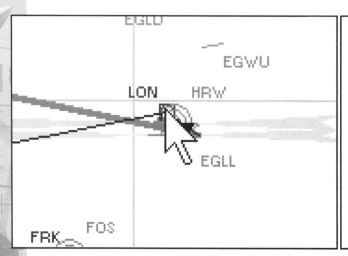

Figure 5.19:
Select LON VOR by
dragging the course
line over it.

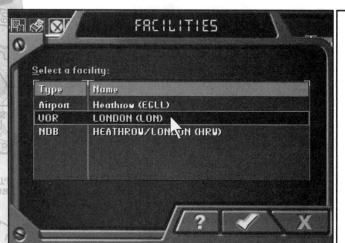

Figure 5.20:
When there's more
than a single waypoint
located in the same
general area, you can
select your choice here.

As you'll see when we return to the Edit Route window, LON VOR has
been added to our waypoint list. Next, click on the Zoom Out button once
and drag the course line to WOD NDB to add it to our waypoint list. Our
next waypoint is CPT VOR, but it isn't in our view right now. When you move
your cursor to the left edge of the map, it'll turn into an arrow as shown in
Figure 5.21. If you click your left mouse button when the cursor is changed
to an arrow, the map will scroll in the direction of the arrow. Go ahead and
scroll the map to the left. Now drag our course line over CPT.

The rest of our waypoints will be added essentially the same way.
The biggest difference is that we'll be doing a lot of scrolling to locate the
others. Fortunately, at certain zoom factors longitude and latitude numbers
will be displayed around the borders of each sector. The following table
lists the remaining waypoints and their coordinates. Note that in order to
find intersections, you need to enable View Intersections from the toolbar.

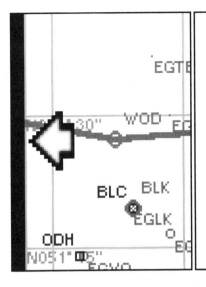

Figure 5.21:
Scroll the map by
moving your cursor
to the borders and
clicking when it turns
to an arrow.

Coordinates (Longitude/Latitude)	Description
N051°10.72 / W003°21.58	EXMOR intersection
N042°37.40 / W064°14.10	CUDAS intersection
N041°47.00 / W067°00.00	VITOL intersection
N039°49.40 / W072°49.83	OWENZ intersection
N040°32.62 / W073°32.38	LORAC intersection

Once you've entered all of the required waypoints, enter 60,000 feet in the Cruising Altitude box, then click the Save button to save the flight plan. Click the green checkmark button to close the flight planner and load the flight plan. When you load the flight plan, it'll place you on the runway at your departure airport.

Below is the modified flight plan for our trip:

Waypoint	Frequency	Course	Altitude	Distance	ETE
EGLL	ATIS 123.9	270°	580'	—	—
LON	113.6	260°	6,000'	7 nm	0:02
(7 DME) WOD	352	273°	6,000' (4,000' minimum)	13 nm	0:13
CPT	114.35	Direct	FL80 (6,000' minimum)	82.4 nm	0:085
EXMOR	GPS	Direct	FL500	2,473 nm	2:09
CUDAS	GPS	Direct	FL500	133 nm	0:07
VITOL	GPS	Direct	8,000'	290 nm	0:29
OWENZ	GPS	Direct	3,000'	54 nm	0:11
LORAC	111.5	313°	3,000'	11.5 nm	0:035
JFK	ATIS 128.725		TOTAL	3,064 nm	3:22

▶ **Warning**

One of the limitations of Flight Simulator 2000's Flight Planner is that it can accept only a single altitude, so always use the highest MEA along your route.

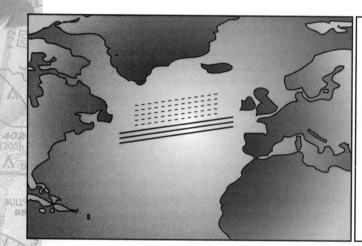

Following the CPT 3G DP, we fly runway heading and intercept LON R-260 degrees. At 7 DME out from LON we then make a right turn at magnetic bearing 273 degrees and track that inbound to WOD NDB. From there we fly CPT direct, EXMOR direct, CUDAS DIRECT, VITOL direct, OWENZ direct, and LORAC direct. At LORAC, we intercept JFK ILS RWY 31R for landing.

Concorde Routes

Commercial flights from Europe to North America are flown via the North Atlantic Tracks, as illustrated in Figure 5.22. These airways are the airborne equivalent of "one-way highways" for aircraft. There are five tracks dedicated for subsonic flights; their locations and altitudes are changed daily, but they're always evenly spaced about 60 miles apart from each other to prevent potential traffic problems.

Figure 5.22:
North Atlantic Tracks are the airborne equivalent of "one-way highways" for aircraft. (Spacing not to scale.)

> ▶ *Note*
>
> *ATC over the ocean is under the jurisdiction of Oceanic Control and is handled by Gander in Newfoundland and by Shanwick in the United Kingdom.*

The Concorde is unique in that there are three North Atlantic Tracks located to the south of the subsonic routes dedicated solely to high-altitude supersonic flight. These "autobahns" of the skies are named SQ, SN, and SM, and their midpoints are located at 30 degrees West longitude.

Concorde Climb

Because of the Concorde's extraordinary high speed and superb climb rate (it can accelerate to Mach 2.0 while in a climb), its normal climb has been dubbed "Concorde Climb." Concorde Climbs require special clearance from ATC. But typically, they're allowed only away from populated areas and other aircraft traffic.

From Heathrow, Concorde Climb is authorized over the Bristol Channel (we're using CUDAS intersection to identify it). If we were flying from JFK to EGLL, we'd have to fly past Nantucket Island before Concorde Climb would be authorized.

Altitude

CPT 3G DP requires us to climb to at least 580 feet before any turns. The MEA over WOD is 4,000 feet. The Concorde's best subsonic flight performance is found at FL280 and 0.95 Mach. So after leaving Heathrow and being cleared to climb above 10,000 feet, we'll fly at FL280 and 0.95 Mach until we're over the Bristol Channel—where we'll be cleared for Concorde Climb.

Maximum altitude for a typical supersonic cruise ranges from 50,000 to 60,000 feet. (The latter is the Concorde's maximum altitude.) We'll maintain supersonic cruise until we reach VITOL, where we'll decelerate and descend to FL280. At VITOL, we'll descend to 8,000 feet. Between OWENZ and LORAC we'll descend to 3,000 feet for the approach and slow down to 250 KIAS and lower from here on in.

Fuel/Performance

The Concorde is capable of carrying 100 passengers at Mach 2.0 for about 4,000 miles total. Our trip is approximately 3,064 nm total. We've got enough fuel for the trip.

Special Considerations

To save weight, the Concorde is not equipped with an onboard APU (Auxiliary Power Unit—it powers air-conditioning and electronics while on the ground until engines are started). Since *Flight Simulator 2000*'s passengers are only virtual passengers, we don't need to worry about keeping them cool while they enjoy their virtual caviar and champagne.

Noise Abatement

There are two noise abatement issues we need to consider. The first is the volume of sound produced by the Concorde's engines when reheat is engaged. The second is sonic booms.

In order to achieve minimum ground roll and maximum rate of climb, the Concorde uses full reheat on takeoff. To be good neighbors, reheat is turned off about 1.4 minutes after takeoff, and throttle is reduced to maintain V_N 250 KIAS until cleared for higher speed.

Sonic Booms

The areas of supersonic flow that occur on an airplane flying at speeds above an aircraft's critical Mach number are accompanied by the formation of shock waves. A supersonic aircraft typically generates two main shock waves while in supersonic flight—one at the nose (known as *bow shock*) and one off the tail (known as *tail shock*).

A sonic boom is produced by the pressure waves/pulse generated by the shock waves formed on the aircraft in supersonic flight. To someone on the ground, these pulses are experienced as an abrupt compression above atmospheric pressure followed by a rapid decompression below atmospheric pressure and a final recompression back to atmospheric

> ▶ *Note*
>
> *While in supersonic flight, the Concorde produces a shock wave that is 15 miles long and 20 miles wide.*

pressure. Because these changes happen so quickly (they take place in less than a tenth of a second), the experience is typically described as a double jolt or boom, as shown in Figure 5.23.

Although sonic booms are not particularly dangerous to people or property, the apprehension and disturbance created by them has caused restrictions to be placed on supersonic aircraft operations. The restrictions placed on the Concorde roughly read: "Boom must not be heard by anyone on land." In general, you should meet the regulations if you enter or exit supersonic flight when you're at least 55 miles offshore.

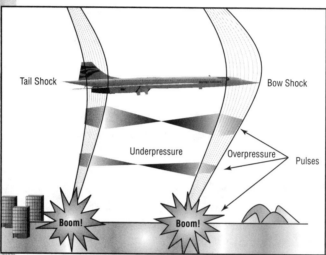

Figure 5.23:
A sonic boom is produced by the pressure waves/ pulse generated by the shock waves formed on an aircraft in supersonic flight.

Flight Tutorial

Because the Concorde is a commercial carrier, we're going to cover how this aircraft would fly a typical commercial flight. This means we'll talk about engine start and pushback from the airport passenger gate.

To set up this flight, choose Select Aircraft from the Aircraft menu, and then choose Concorde from the resulting submenu. Next load the Heathrow to Kennedy flight plan we created earlier from the Flight Planner screen (select Flight Planner from the Flight menu). We're now on runway 27L at EGLL.

Now move us to the British Airways Concorde Terminal using the Map View command (Figure 5.24) found under the World menu. Enter N51°27.69' Latitude, W0°26.69' Longitude, +93 Altitude, and Heading 320.

Weather isn't much of an issue here since we're flying IFR. As long as winds aren't so high that they're detrimental for takeoff or landing on our chosen runways, and visibilities are within minimums, we'll technically be okay. Regardless, consider using good weather for your first flights until you get used to flying the Concorde.

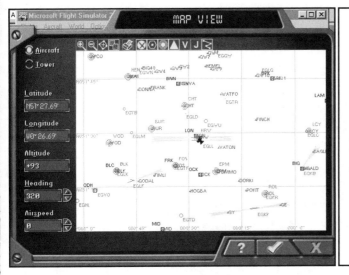

Figure 5.24:
Move us to the British
Airways Concorde
Terminal using these
settings in map view.

Before Engine Start

Start by shutting down the engines—press Ctrl+Shift+F1.

Action	Response
Master CBs	SET/CHECKED

CBs (Circuit Breakers) are not modeled in *Flight Simulator 2000*'s
Concorde.

Cockpit Preparation/Security	COMPLETE

Get your charts, plates, and flight logs in order.

Oxygen	CHECKED 100%
OV Windows	CLOSED
Flight Control Inverters	ON

The electrical power inverters operate Concorde's irreversible (meaning
external flight forces can't move them) control system.

Anti-Stall Systems	ON

These are the stall warning horns. They're always on in *Flight Simulator
2000* if you have sound and the cockpit sounds are enabled.

RAD/INS sw	RAD

This switch determines which source (radio or inertial navigation system)
is used to guide the HSI's CDI. *Flight Simulator 2000* modified this
switch, located on the lower-right corner of the HSI pictured in Figure

> ▶ *Note*
>
> *Several of these items are
> for information purposes
> only. For example, cabin
> oxygen for passengers and
> crew are obviously not
> simulated in* Flight
> Simulator 2000.

5.25, to read NAV/GPS. The NAV setting corresponds to RAD and GPS corresponds with INS, so set this to NAV. The light in the lower-right corner indicates when the autopilot is in HDG mode.

Figure 5.25:
The Concorde's HSI can be driven by standard radio NAVAIDs or GPS.

Instrument Transfer sw	SET

Each of the flight crew has some duplicate instruments at their stations. In an effort to reduce potential input errors that might occur if each of the crew were to enter duplicate information, instrument settings can be sent to all stations remotely with this switch.

Altimeters	CHECKED/SET

Press the B key to set the altimeter.

NAV/Radios	SET

We'll need to navigate with NAVAIDs in order to perform this DP. Set LON VOR frequency (113.6) in NAV1 radio (located to the left of the autopilot panel), 260 degrees on the HSI OBS, 352 on the ADF radio (press Shift+2 to bring up the radio stack), and EGLL ATIS (123.9) in COM1.

Note that COM1 allows you to enter two frequency selectors. Either one can be selected by the toggle switch in the center. Since we won't be actually talking to anyone during our flight, we can go ahead and enter JFK ATIS (128.725) in COM1's right side. We can then just toggle the switch to hear JFK ATIS when we arrive.

Brakes	PARK/CHECKED
NAV Lights	AS REQUIRED

Lights are located along the right side of the instrument panel. Go ahead and turn on the NAV lights.

Throttle Masters	MAIN/ALT
Ground Hyd Check Out	YELL. YELL/OFF
Fuel Heaters	AUTO
Engine Reset Valves	SELECT
Secondary Air Doors	SELECT/ALT

The Concorde's engines have secondary air doors that open outward in the event that too much air is entering the inlet, or they open inward if not enough air is getting to the engine.

Batteries	ON/NORMAL
INS 1,2, and 3	LOADING CHECKED/NAV MODE/MON

This is where the crew double-checks the INS waypoint data. We've already loaded our flight plan, so we're okay here.

Air Bugs and Pitch Index	SET

The real Concord has multiple bugs (indexes) that can be adjusted for critical airspeeds, such as V_1, V_2, and so on.

Set the pitch index (the little white indicator that enters from the left) on the D/AI (Direction/Attitude Indicator—this AI version has LOC and glideslope needles incorporated in it) to 13 degrees using the knob on the lower-left side of the instrument (Figure 5.26). Be aware that the pitch index should be set to 13 degrees above the airplane reference index and not above the AI's horizon line.

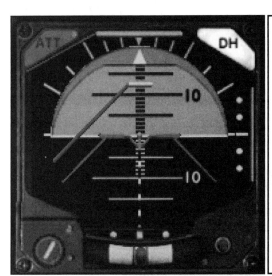

Figure 5.26:
The D/AI's pitch index bug is adjusted from the knob on the lower-right side of the instrument.

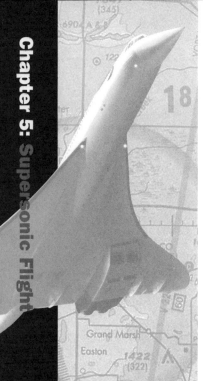

Fuel Flow and PT Bugs	SET
Clock and TLA Bugs	SET
Briefing	STATED

Whether it's sports or flying aircraft, a good captain informs their team/crew of the game plan.

Loadsheet	CHECKED

This point on the checklist is known as *below the line*. Cockpit operations stop here until a loadsheet is given to the flight crew from the cabin crew and ground crew. The loadsheet provides the weight of passengers and baggage and specifies where everything is loaded. This information is loaded into the CG computer (handled automatically for you in *Flight Simulator 2000*).

ZFW and ZFCG	SET/CHECKED

This is where the aircraft's zero fuel weight and zero fuel CG are entered into the CG computer. *Flight Simulator 2000* does this for you.

Fuel Rem and A/C Weight	SET/CHECKED

Next, the fuel load and weight are entered into the CG computer. This is also handled for you automatically. As mentioned earlier, the Concorde usually leaves the gate with the rear tank empty. To adjust our fuel load, open the Fuel dialogue box found under the Aircraft menu selection.

The rear tank is labeled Center 2. Adjust the % Quantity to read 0, as shown in Figure 5.27. Note that if you're planning on transferring fuel manually, you need to set the fuel pump control on the fuel panel (Shift+6) to the Off position.

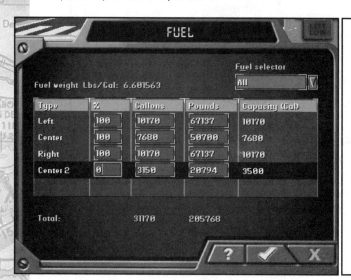

Figure 5.27:
Empty the rear
fuel tank.

Load Limits	SET
T.O. Data	CHECKED

This includes the computed runway takeoff distance, aircraft weight, CG, and airspeeds.

Start Clearance	OBTAIN
Door Lights	CHECKED
Master Warning	RECALL

Pressing recall on the master warning panel will alert you to anything that might require your attention. Do this by clicking on the Master Warning light (Figure 5.28) located in the upper-left side of the instrument panel next to the NAV1 radio or by pressing Shift+5.

Figure 5.28:
Click on this Master Warning button to see if anything needs your attention.

Anti-Collision Lights	ON
Throttles	IDLE

Press the F1 key.

Engine Feed Pumps	ON
Clearance to Start	OBTAIN

Pushback

While the Concorde is pushed back from the passenger gate, her engines are started. Most carriers typically start engines this way as a courtesy to passengers still in the terminal and ground crew working on aircraft still parked at the gate.

To simulate a ground tug pushback, press the Y key to enter Slew mode, then press the numpad 2 key (with Num Lock off) twice. When you've moved back enough, press numpad 5 to stop. Press the Y key again to exit Slew mode.

Action	Response
NOs 3 and 2 Engines	STARTED

Engines 3 and 2 are the inboard engines. These are started first as a courtesy to ground crew. The engine starters are found on the lower half of the Fuel Control Panel window (Shift+6).

Action	Response
Hydraulics	CHECKED
Ground Equipment	CLEAR
NOs 4 and 1 Engines	STARTED

Engines 4 and 1 are the outboard engines. They're started the same way as engines 3 and 2.

After Engine Start

After the engines are started, perform the After Start Checklist next.

Action	Response
Nosewheel Steering	CHECKED

Check that the nosewheel is steering by using the rudder pedals. It's typically disconnected from the hydraulic system to prevent damage that might occur during pushback when it's being towed.

Action	Response
Flt. Control AFCS and Trims	CHECKED

Check the settings in the AFCS (Automatic Flight Control System—a fancy name for the autopilot) and trim settings. Specifically on the autopilot, set 250 KIAS in the lower SPD window, 273 degrees in the HDG window, click the ALT mode button, then enter 6,000 feet in the ALT window. All trims should be centered (their indexes are located on the right half of the autopilot). Figure 5.29 shows the proper autopilot configuration.

Figure 5.29:
The autopilot is ready to go.

The next few items are just for your information.

Action	Response
Stab and Feel	ENGAGED
Eng Anti-Ice/Eng Schedule	AS REQUIRED
Brake Fans	ON
Idle Switches	LOW
Door Warnings	TESTED/OFF
Engine Feed Pumps	ALL/ON
Hydraulics	CHECKED
Electrics	CHECKED/GRD BYPASS
Ground Equipment	CLEAR

Taxi

Action	Response
Visor/Nose	**DOWN/5°**

Lower the visor, and lower the nose down to 5 degrees by clicking on the VIS/NS control twice or by pressing the F7 key twice.

Brakes	**CHECKED/NORMAL**
Flight Instruments	**CHECK**

Here's another chance to check your instrument settings (ALT, radio frequencies, course headings, and so on). Press the D key to set the DG portion of your HSI.

Flight Controls EFC	**BLUE LIGHTS/LIGHTS OUT**

Control Position indicators are used because the flight crew can't see the control surfaces move by looking out the cockpit window as you can in other aircraft. Check to see that the lights along the bottom are out.

Trims	**SET TAKEOFF 2.5**

The default settings are fine.

Reverse Air Throttle	**CHECK MAIN THROTTLE FORWARD, IDLE, IDLE REVERSE/IDLE**

This is a throttle control check. Press F4, quickly followed by F1, then press and hold F2, followed by a quick press of F1 to complete the check.

Seat	**ADJUSTED AND SET**
Takeoff CG	**CHECK**

The Concorde's takeoff CG is 53.5 percent +/−.3 percent. If you're manually transferring fuel, move the fuel pump switch to AFT position and monitor the fuel transfer progress during taxi. When the CG meter indicates 53.5 percent +/−.3 percent, place the fuel pump switch in the Off position. (Now you're beginning to see why a flight engineer is a vital crew member!)

After completing this checklist, make a right turn and taxi to the end of runway 27L.

> ▶ **Note**
>
> *The pilot can use a tiller, located to the left of the seat, to steer the Concorde's nosewheel. The copilot has a similar setup on the right.*

Before Takeoff

Action	Response
Briefing Takeoff Data	CHECK

The pilot will brief the crew on how they want the takeoff to proceed (information about noise abatement and airspeeds) and reiterate what they need from the crew.

Action	Response
Landing Lights	AS REQUIRED
XPNDR	ON/ALT
Wheel Lights	OFF
Master Warning	RECALL/INH

Check the Master Warning panel again to see if any last minute problems have cropped up.

Action	Response
Takeoff Monitor	ARMED
Reheat	SELECTED

Engage reheat on all four engines by pressing Shift+F4.

Action	Response
Pitch Index	13°

This is to double-check the setting we made earlier.

Action	Response
Radar	AS DESIRED

Radar is always enabled in *Flight Simulator 2000*.

Takeoff

When you're set, check for landing traffic first and then taxi out onto the runway.

Action	Response
Brakes	RELEASE

Press the "." (period) key.

Action	Response
Throttle	FULL

After full drive power is applied, reheat will automatically kick in because we've enabled it. Watch the ASI and call out V_1. At V_R, pitch up to 13 degrees (use the index we set earlier as your reference).

Noise Power/AB	OFF

Once a positive rate of climb is established, we need to reduce power for noise abatement purposes. If we're above 500 feet AGL, engage the autothrottle (Shift+R) in IAS MODE (Ctrl+R), select ALT mode on the autopilot (Ctrl+Z), and engage the autopilot by pressing the Z key. Finally, turn off reheat by pressing Shift+F4.

Landing Gear	RETRACT

Press the G key.

Landing Light	OFF
Master Warning	CHECK
Nose and Visor	0°, UP

Press F5.

Taxi Lights	OFF

Fly the runway heading until 580 feet AGL. Once clear of 580 feet AGL, set the autopilot to NAV mode. It will intercept LON R-260 degrees. We'll track that outbound until 7 DME out, when we'll make a right turn towards WOD and track WOD NDB bearing 273 degrees inbound (TO). The ADF is located to the lower right of the HSI. You'll know to turn when the green ADF needle points to 273 degrees, as shown in Figure 5.30. At this point you can either hand fly to WOD or place the autopilot into HDG mode (take it out of NAV mode first). (We set it earlier to turn to 273 degrees.)

Figure 5.30:
Turning to track WOD
NDB 270 degrees
bearing To

After crossing WOD NDB (you'll see the ADF needle swing around), we'll fly direct to CPT. We can now switch to the GPS (simulating INS) to fly the next few legs of our flight. Click the NAV/GPS switch to GPS, the set the autopilot back to NAV mode.

Typically by this time we'd be cleared for a higher altitude, so let's begin our climb to FL280. Dial in 28,000 feet in the autopilot ALT window. As we climb, begin transferring fuel to the rear tank again. (Just continue pumping rearward in preparation for Mach-speed flight.)

As we cross over 10,000 feet, switch the autopilot to Mach mode and change the top SPD window to read 0.95 Mach. Upon clearing FL180, reset the altimeter to 29.92. From here the autopilot will take us to EXMOR—where we'll begin our Concorde Climb.

Concorde Climb

At EXMORE the fun begins. First disengage autothrottle (Shift+R), then apply full drive power (press the F4 key) and engage reheat in pairs. Engage the center pair first, then the two outer pair. To do this first press E+2+3 to select the center engines. Then press Shift+F4. To toggle reheat on the outer engines press E+1+4, followed by Shift+F4 again.

Next switch the fuel selector to draw from the center tank (select Fuel from the Aircraft menu to open the dialogue). Now set the autopilot ALT window to 50,000 feet, Mach 2.0 in the top SPD window, and 650 FPM in the VS (Vertical Speed) window. (We want the aircraft to accelerate while climbing.)

At Mach 1.0, CG should be at least 55.8 percent and moving aft. At Mach 1.7, turn the reheats off (Shift+F4). We can supercruise up to our cruise altitude.

Concorde Cruise

Mach 2.0 should be achieved about FL500, and CG should now be at 58.8 percent, as shown in Figure 5.31. Fuel management duties typically transfer fuel from the front tank to rear (as we've been doing); when the front tank is empty, start drawing from the wing tanks. If you're trans-ferring fuel manually, this part of the flight is where you play the balancing act. When one wing tank gets light, balance it out by cross-feeding from the other thank. Try to keep the wing tanks balanced to offset any drag-inducing elevon differential.

> ### ▶ Warning
>
> *As you begin the Concorde Climb, be sure to double-check that your fuel is still being pumped to the rear tank after adjusting the fuel selector.*

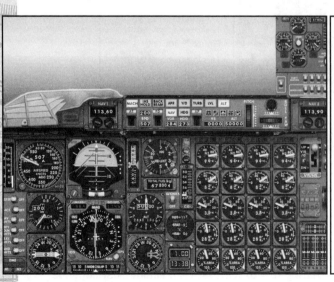

Figure 5.31:
Yehaw! Now *this* is flyin'!

We'll exit the North Atlantic Tracks at the CUDAS intersection waypoint. Then we'll proceed to VITOL.

Deceleration

About 40 miles before we cross VITOL, we'll begin our deceleration and descent. For noise abatement purposes, the Concorde must achieve subsonic flight at least 55 miles offshore. Because we're going so fast (and to minimize energy waste), slowing down and descent are taken in steps. Let's talk about decelerating first since it'll be your first task.

To decelerate, set the autopilot to ALT Hold (should still be set), turn the autothrottle off (Shift+R), and pull throttle back to about 2/3 full drive power (66 percent N_1) and maintain altitude.

Descent

At Mach 1.55 begin descending to 3,700 feet. (Use the autopilot.) If this were a real flight, we'd most likely receive vectors to JFK airport. We'll use our GPS/INS waypoints instead. As we decelerate, keep an eye on the CG indicator. We'll have to begin pumping fuel from the rear tank back to the forward tank again.

We want to cross Owens intersection at 8,000 feet, so set the autopilot ALT window to 8,000 feet. At 60 nm out from OWENZ we should slow down to Mach 1.0 with the power setting we have. We should decelerate to Mach 1.0 below 33,000 feet in any case. Also remember to slow to 250 KIAS when crossing below 10,000 feet. Set the throttle to idle if necessary.

After crossing OWENZ we'll set up for the approach. Set JFK ILS 31R frequency (111.5) in NAV1 and flip COM1 toggle switch to the JFK (right) side. If you had radar headings vectors, you should be slowed to 230 KIAS at 3,000 feet before the approach (being vectored to LORAC).

Approach

The Concorde's approach speed is 200 KIAS (set the autopilot again). About 5 miles out from LORAC, put the autopilot in LVL (wing leveler) mode, flip the NAV/GPS switch to NAV, and put the autopilot on APR mode. This will keep us on an intercept course with the ILS and allow the autopilot to use it.

Set the radio altimeter to decision height of 213 feet. Then set the pitch index to an 11-degree pitch attitude. Lower the visor (press F7 once) and extend the landing gear (the G key) about 5 miles out from JFK.

Landing

Once you're stabilized, turn off the autopilot. All that's left now is to go through the landing check and put 'er on the ground.

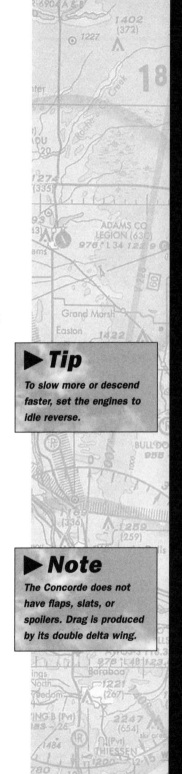

> ▶ **Tip**
>
> *To slow more or descend faster, set the engines to idle reverse.*

> ▶ **Note**
>
> *The Concorde does not have flaps, slats, or spoilers. Drag is produced by its double delta wing.*

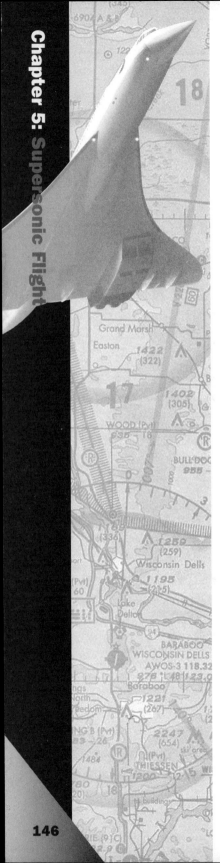

Action	Response
Gear	CHECK DOWN
Nose	DOWN FULL

Press the F8 key to lower the nose fully. V_{REF} is 162 KIAS for a standard 3-degree glideslope. Landings are made at an 11-degree pitch attitude. Good luck!

After touchdown, reverse thrust will be automatically applied. Reverse thrust is most effective at high speed, so it'll shut off (return reverse buckets to normal) below 40 KIAS. All you need to do is stand on the brakes (the "." [period] key) before running off the end of the runway.

Taxi

Action	Response
Raise Nose	5°

Press the F6 key once. This helps prevent damage during taxi. If you haven't moved all of the fuel from the rear tanks forward already, move the CG forward during taxi (as much as 4,000 kilos) forward to allow baggage to be removed safely.

Parking

Action	Response
Nose Full	UP
Visor	UP

Press the F5 key to return the nose and visor to the fully raised position. This not only helps prevent damage, but it also increases the Concorde's aesthetics while she readies for her next flight.

Parking Brakes	SET

Press Ctrl+"." (period).

There you have it. Welcome to the U.S.! You certainly know how to travel in style!

In through
the Out Door:
Flying a LOC BC

Chapter 6

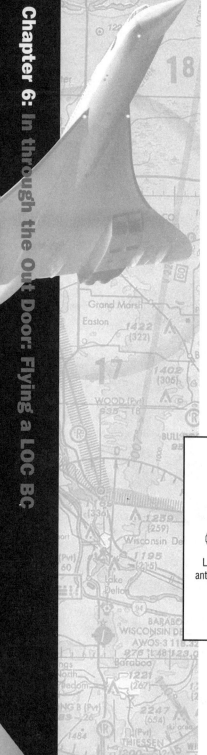

*T*he Mooney Bravo makes its debut in Flight Simulator 2000 Professional Edition. *Although it's a shame that owners of* Flight Simulator 2000 Standard Edition *won't be able to get a feeling for what it's like to fly one of the finest piston-driven aircraft ever built (even if only in simulation), the concepts in our navigation and tutorial sections are still applicable to other aircraft.*

In this chapter, in addition to flying the Mooney Bravo, we'll talk about how to fly a LOC (LOCalizer) BC (Back Course). Even though back course procedures, which include departures and approaches, are becoming rarer, they're still out there.

Nonprecision Approach Review

A LOC BC is a nonprecision approach, just like a VOR approach. People tend to think of the LOC BC as a precision approach because it utilizes an ILS LOC. While a LOC is a component of a precision approach (see Figure 6.1), what separates a precision approach from a nonprecision approach is the glideslope component. In other words, it takes both a LOC and a glideslope to make a precision approach.

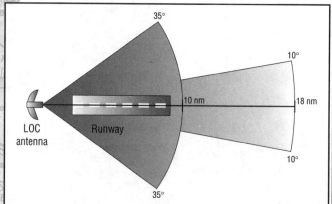

Figure 6.1:
The LOC provides horizontal guidance for an ILS.

Since LOC BCs are nonprecision approaches, we should review a few things that tend to be taken for granted, especially by pilots who mostly fly precision approaches.

Minimum Descent Altitude

Recall that an approach's MDA (Minimum Descent Altitude) is the lowest you can legally (most pilots would say *safely*) descend to without seeing the runway. MDAs are called out at the lower-left side of each respective approach plate in the Landing Minimums table section.

Landing minimums are based on the aircraft's approach category, which break down as follows:

Approach Category	A	B	C	D	E
Speed (knots)	0–90	91–120	121–140	141–165	Above 165

Approach categories are based on the aircraft's approach speed. For example, the C-182R RG is an approach category A aircraft because approaches are usually made below 90 knots.

The left column in the Landing Minimums table of an approach plate indicates which type of approach the minimums are for. (The prefix "S" stands for *straight-in approach*.) Minimums are specified as MDA followed by the visibility requirements. A "/" indicates an RVR value, and a "–" indicates visibility in statute miles.

Circle to Land

Many VOR and NDB (Non-Directional Beacon) approaches are not lined up with the runway, requiring you to circle the airport and land. (Circle-to-land procedures are required when the alignment of the runway and the approach course are 30° apart or greater.) Of course what makes this kind of approach difficult, or even dangerous, is that you have to keep sight of the airport while you circle. (You'll be off immediate instrument guidance, so you can't rely on it to get you on the runway.) When weather is at minimums, this task is even more difficult.

On the other hand, LOCs are aligned with the runway within a 3-degree maximum, but most are aligned exactly with the runway.

Localizer Back Courses

LOC BCs are used for both departures and approaches. The normal limits of LOC BC coverage are the same as the front side of the LOC. But what makes a LOC BC desirable for nonprecision approaches has to do with the LOC itself. If you recall, a LOC provides very accurate course guidance because the CDI is approximately four times as sensitive as when tracking a VOR radial.

So with all of these benefits, what makes the back course such a big deal? The biggest difference between a front course and back course is that you have to fly opposite the CDI reading while you're on a back course because the CDI reacts to the LOC the same way, regardless of whether your aircraft is on the front course or back course (see Figure 6.2).

> ▶ **Note**
> MDA should not be confused with ILS DH (Decision Height). The difference is that DH is where an ILS missed approach begins.

> ▶ **Note**
> LOCs not exactly aligned with the runway are annotated as an offset localizer on approach plates.

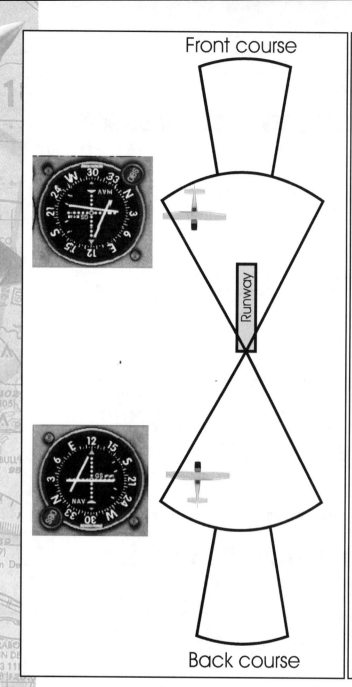

Front course

Runway

Back course

Figure 6.2:
A LOC BC is transmitted away from the airport directly opposite the ILS and shouldn't be used for navigation unless there's a published procedure for doing so. The CDI reacts to the LOC the same way regardless of the aircraft's orientation.

In other words, you need to fly away from the needle as opposed to flying towards it as we usually do. This issue is more of a mental adjustment than a motor-skill problem, but many pilots have trouble adjusting to it until they fly a couple for themselves.

> ▶ **Warning**
> *Ignore the glideslope indications when flying back courses!*

Flying the Mooney Bravo

Just as with cars, airplanes built by a single manufacturer tend to share many recognizable look-and-feel characteristics. This observation isn't too surprising because their design elements typically reflect the company's philosophical ideals. What sets Mooney airplanes apart from other single-engine piston aircraft is its melding of performance, quality, style, and comfort.

Flying a Mooney feels like flying a well-balanced sports car, or riding a fine touring motorcycle. The controls are very solid (very little slop) and extremely responsive. But don't let that well-refined demeanor fool you—the Bravo is all thoroughbred, and you need to think well ahead of the aircraft to keep up with its speed.

Aircraft Performance

The Mooney Aircraft Corporation has held many aviation speed records for the fastest single-engine, piston-driven production airplanes over the years. The Mooney Bravo continues the tradition. With a maximum level cruise speed of 220 KTAS at FL250 (its 1,130 FPM climb and 1,070 nm range are nothing to sneeze at, either), the Mooney Bravo continues its reign as the fastest single-engine production aircraft in the world.

V Speeds

V Speed	KIAS
V_R	—
(3,368#)	66
(3,100#)	64
(2,700#)	59
V_Y	105
V_X	85
V_A	—
(2,400#)	106
(2,600#)	111
(2,900#)	117
(3,200#)	127
V_S	66
V_{SO}	59
V_{NE}	195
V_{NO}	174
V_{LE}	165
V_{LO} (Extension)	140
(Retraction)	106
V_{FE}	110

continued on next page

V Speed	KIAS
Approach	—
Flaps 10°	80
Flaps 30°	75
Short Field 30°	70
Max Demonstrated Crosswind Component	13 knots
Max Range Glide	—
(3,368#)	91.5
(3,200#)	89
(2,900#)	84.5
(2,600#)	80
Emergency Descent (Gear Up)	—
(Smooth Air)	195
(Turbulent Air) (3,368#)	127
(3,200#)	123
(2,900#)	117
(2,600#)	111
Emergency Descent (Gear Down)	—
(Smooth Air)	165
(Turbulent Air) (3,368#)	127
(3,200#)	123
(2,900#)	117
(2,600#)	111

> ▶ **Note**
>
> *V_A in all aircraft increases with weight because the heavier the aircraft is, the less susceptible to outside forces (such as turbulence) it becomes.*

Advanced Systems

The Mooney Bravo has several advanced systems not typically found on most single-engine, piston aircraft. Four are modeled in *Flight Simulator 2000 Professional Edition*. They are prop de-ice, speed brakes, standby vacuum pump, and turbocharger.

Prop De-Ice As we mentioned in Chapter 4, the term *anti-ice* tends to get confused with the term *de-ice* quite often. Here's the difference: anti-ice describes a system that prevents ice from forming, and de-ice refers to systems that remove ice. If you think about it a little, you'll see that these systems are not the same. The main difference is although an anti-ice system might remove ice after it's formed, that's not what it was designed for and it may not help you after you've accumulated ice. (It should go without saying that finding out the differences between the two during a flight would be really bad.) *Flight Simulator 2000*'s Mooney Bravo prop anti-ice system is activated by clicking on the Prop De-Ice button on the lower center of the instrument panel, shown in Figure 6.3.

Figure 6.3:
Activate prop anti-ice
with this switch.

▶ *Tip*

Any time you enter icing
conditions or suspect ice,
always engage pitot heat.

Flying into Known Icing

The real Mooney Bravo has optional equipment that, when installed, will make
the aircraft legal to fly into known icing condition (places where other pilots
have reported icing). What makes this ability so notable is that most light
aircraft are prohibited from flying into known icing conditions. The Mooney
Bravo that comes in Flight Simulator 2000 *is only equipped with the propeller*
anti-ice system, so it's not certified to fly into known icing.

While preventing ice from building on the prop and causing a loss in thrust
may seem like a questionable design decision when the wings can still accumulate ice, there is some logic
behind it. When ice forms on airfoils, it causes disruptions in the airflow patterns around them—and subse-
quently reduces the maximum lift they're able to generate. But perhaps most importantly, it raises your stall
speed. So if you've got lowered lift and limited thrust (where you can't maintain airspeed without diving
towards the ground), you're in a really bad situation.

Speed Brake Another rather unusual feature for light, piston-driven
airplanes is speed brakes. As we saw when we flew the triple 7, a speed
brake creates aerodynamic drag. On the Mooney, speed brakes are small
x-shaped devices that extend from the top of the wing. Although there is
only one per wing, they're surprisingly effective for their small size. To
activate the Bravo's speed brakes, either click the Speed Brake control
button (Figure 6.4), located just above the NAV/GPS switch on the left
side of the instrument panel, or press the / key.

Figure 6.4:
Activate the Mooney
Bravo's speed brake by
clicking this button.

▶ *Note*

The Mooney Bravo's speed
brake can't be armed for
automatic deployment
upon landing.

Standby Vacuum Pump A standby vacuum pump is a really handy feature
for IFR flights. You may recall that your AI and DG are vacuum driven.
Typically, if your engine-driven vacuum pump that powers these instruments
fails, you're stuck flying partial-panel IFR until you can get the aircraft back
on the ground and have it repaired. A standby vacuum pump can save the
day by providing these instruments with the required vacuum power.

The standby vacuum pump is also engine driven, but it's activated with a switch that engages an electric clutch on the pump. To activate the standby vacuum pump, simply click on the Stby Vac switch, located to the left of the Prop De-Ice switch. (See Figure 6.5.)

Figure 6.5:
The standby vacuum pump will become your best friend if you're flying IFR and your main vacuum pump fails.

Turbocharger A *turbocharger* (besides being a really cool sounding word) is a mechanical device that uses engine exhaust pressure to turn a turbine that compresses the air going into the engine. It provides a better charge for the engine so the engine can develop more power. (Remember that air is the medium that's being consumed to produce power in internal-combustion engines.) In the simplest terms, the more air you can pack into the engine, the more power it can produce.

There are other benefits to turbochargers, in addition to raw horsepower. First off, they're rather simple devices mechanically. A turbocharger is fairly small as well, so it doesn't add much weight (although the piping/ducting can be quite complex), and it doesn't require any power-robbing, direct-drive connections to the engine itself.

What makes a turbocharger even more valuable to an aircraft is that it can delay the effects of altitude (thinning air) on the engine. In a normally aspirated engine, as the air thins with altitude, the maximum power the engine can generate decreases. A turbocharger (or its mechanical cousin, the supercharger) compresses the incoming air to a higher pressure, which helps the engine breathe as if it were flying at a lower (higher pressure) altitude.

Unfortunately, as with many good things, there are some tradeoffs to the turbocharger. Here are two situations that you should watch for, although only one has direct implications in *Flight Simulator 2000*:

✛ **Overboost**—Although the Bravo's turbocharger has a wastegate (a valve that automatically opens to reduce turbocharger compression pressure into the engine), it's still possible to overboost the engine under certain conditions (we'll talk about those later). The way to monitor overboost is to watch the MP gauge. If MP goes over redline, you're in overboost and have no choice but to reduce your throttle setting or risk damaging the turbocharger and/or engine.

✛ **Lack of cooling**—Heat is the enemy of all mechanical and electrical devices. Because a turbocharger is directly connected to an engine's exhaust system, it picks up a lot of heat. Before shutting down a turbocharged engine, most manufacturers specify a cool-down period, which usually means letting the engine run at a low power setting for five minutes or so.

> ▶ **Note**
>
> *When operating at less than full throttle or above FL200 with full throttle, changes in engine speed will cause a change in manifold pressure. For example, a decrease in engine speed (similar to what's produced with a prop pitch increase) produces an increase in manifold pressure.*

The reason for a cool-down period is that a turbocharger uses the same oil system as the engine. So while the engine is running, the turbocharger is being lubricated and subsequently cooled. If the engine were to be shut down with a hot turbocharger, it would literally cook the no-longer-circulating oil.

Flight Plan

We'll begin our flight by flying out of Los Angeles International Airport, one of the busiest airports in the United States. Naturally, we'll be ending our flight with a LOC BC approach into Santa Maria Public Airport, home of the Cessna Pilots Association (not that we care, 'cause we're flying a Mooney now) and the Museum of Flight.

Airports

LAX's longest runway is 12,091 feet, and SMX's longest runway is 6,300 feet. Both are more than long enough to accommodate the Mooney Bravo's 2,000-foot takeoff and 2,500-foot landing distances for a standard day.

The alternate airport for this flight is Santa Barbara (SBA). Its longest runway is 6,052 feet, and its weather minimums as an alternate are 800 feet and 2 miles visibility.

Route

Waypoint	Course	Altitude	Distance	ETE
CHATY2.RZS	040°	6,000'	(7 DME)	—
VECTORS	270°	6,000'	—	—
LAX 113.6	323°	6,000' (4,000' minimum)	20.0 nm	0:07
CHATTY INT FIM 112.5 R-100 (279° To)	323°	6,000' (5,400' minimum)	1.0 nm	0:004
FIM R-277 INT FIM 112.5	277° To	6,000'	16.0 nm	0:05
—	250° From	6,000'	—	—
RZS 114.9 DEANO	289° To	6,000'	27.0 nm	0:09
—	286° From	6,000'	21.0 nm	0:07
MADOO (14.9 DME)	286° From	4,600'	14.9 nm	0:05
KOAKS (SMX 108.9 11.6 DME)	286° From RZS	3,000'	14.1 nm	0:05
CAMCO SMX 108.9	300° LOC/BC	1,680'	5.8 nm	0:02
PATER	300° LOC/BC	800'	3.8 nm	0:01
MAP .5 DME	—	800'	1.5 nm	0:00.5
SMX	300° LOC/BC	—	0.7 nm	0:00.23
SMX ATIS 121.15		TOTAL	126.4 nm	42 minutes

We selected to leave LAX on runway 6L using the Chaty Two Departure, San Marcus Transition (CHATY2.RZS, see Appendix B), because it takes us in the right direction, and it's non-turbojet aircraft DP. Once we're at RZS, we can fly the SMX's LOC/DME BC-A (Figure 6.6) because RZS is the approach's IAF. How convenient!

Altitude

The CHATY2.RZS departure specifies a 6,000-foot MEA. Since this MEA is the highest for the whole flight, we'll use it as our cruise altitude. The reason why we'll only fly at the MEA is that because our flight is so short, we don't want to spend our flight time climbing and descending. We want to take advantage of the Mooney Bravo's speed, so we want to get to cruise as soon as possible and stay there as long as practical to achieve the lowest flight times.

After crossing the MADOO intersection, we'll descend to 4,600 feet, and step down to 3,000 feet at CAMCO, 1,680 feet at PAXTER, and end up at 800 feet (our category A MDA) per the procedure. We'll identify these intersections using DME.

> ▶ **Warning**
>
> *Remember that our DME counts for the approach are taken from both RZS and I-SMX.*

Fuel/Performance

Fuel burns at 2,400 RPM, 34 inches MP/best power at 6,000 is 20.1 gallons per hour. This rate will produce a TAS of 180 knots. The Bravo has a total usable fuel capacity of 89 gallons in its two tanks. So on a full tank we have enough fuel to fly for 4.23 hours and 761 nm—which is more than enough to make our 127 nm trip, as well as make it to our alternate destination with the required 45-minute fuel reserve.

Mooney Bravo Cruise Performance – Pressure Altitude Sea Level

RPM	MP	Peak TIT indicates Peak or 1,750°F TIT	20°C Below Standard Temp -5°C KTAS	GPH	Standard Temp 15°C KTAS	GPH	20°C Above Standard Temp 35°C KTAS	GHP
2400	34"	1,650°F	170	20.1	169	19.6	169	19.1
	34"	Peak	165	16.8	165	16.3	165	15.8
	32"	Peak	158	15.8	158	15.3	158	14.8
2200	27"	Peak	135	11.9	135	11.4	135	10.9
	24"	Peak	121	10.3	120	9.8	120	9.3

Mooney Bravo Cruise Performance – Pressure Altitude 5,000'

RPM	MP	Peak TIT indicates Peak or 1,750°F TIT	20°C Below Standard Temp -15°C KTAS	GPH	Standard Temp 5°C KTAS	GPH	20°C Above Standard Temp 25°C KTAS	GHP
2400	34"	1650	180	20.6	178	20.1	178	19.6
	34"	Peak	178	17.5	175	17.0	173	16.5
	32"	Peak	171	16.5	168	16.0	167	15.5
2200	27"	Peak	149	12.8	147	12.3	145	11.8
	24"	Peak	135	11.2	132	10.7	131	10.2

Mooney Bravo Cruise Performance – Pressure Altitude 10,000'

RPM	MP	Peak TIT indicates Peak or 1,750°F TIT	20°C Below Standard Temp -25°C KTAS	GPH	Standard Temp -5°C KTAS	GPH	20°C Above Standard Temp 15°C KTAS	GHP
2400	34"	1,650°F	191	20.9	188	20.4	186	19.9
	34"	Peak	187	17.9	185	17.4	183	16.9
	32"	Peak	182	16.9	180	16.4	177	15.9
2200	27"	Peak	159	13.3	158	12.8	154	12.3
	24"	Peak	148	11.8	145	11.3	142	10.8

Mooney Bravo Cruise Performance – Pressure Altitude 15,000'

RPM	MP	Peak TIT indicates Peak or 1,750°F TIT	20°C Below Standard Temp -35°C KTAS	GPH	Standard Temp -15°C KTAS	GPH	20°C Above Standard Temp 5°C KTAS	GHP
2400	34"	1,650°F	200	21.1	197	20.6	194	20.1
	34"	Peak	196	18.0	193	17.5	190	17.0
	32"	Peak	190	17.0	188	16.5	186	16.0
2200	27"	Peak	167	13.6	165	13.1	163	12.6
	24"	Peak	155	12.2	152	11.7	150	11.2

Mooney Bravo Cruise Performance – Pressure Altitude 20,000'

RPM	MP	Peak TIT indicates Peak or 1,750°F TIT	20°C Below Standard Temp -45°C KTAS	GPH	Standard Temp -25°C KTAS	GPH	20°C Above Standard Temp -5°C KTAS	GHP
2400	34"	1,650°F	210	21.1	205	20.6	202	20.1
	34"	Peak	—	—	202	17.6	198	17.1
	32"	Peak	201	17.1	196	16.6	193	16.1
2200	27"	Peak	173	13.8	170	13.3	168	12.8
	24"	Peak	160	12.5	158	12.0	157	12.5

Mooney Bravo Cruise Performance – Pressure Altitude 25,000'

RPM	MP	Peak TIT indicates Peak or 1,750°F TIT	20°C Below Standard Temp -55°C KTAS	GPH	Standard Temp -35°C KTAS	GPH	20°C Above Standard Temp -15°C KTAS	GHP
2400	34"	1,650°F	—	—	213	20.5	209	20.0
	34"	1,650°F	—	—	—	—	206	17.0
	32"	Peak	—	—	204	16.6	199	16.1
2200	27"	Peak	—	—	174	13.3	173	12.8
	24"	Peak	—	—	160	12.1	159	11.6

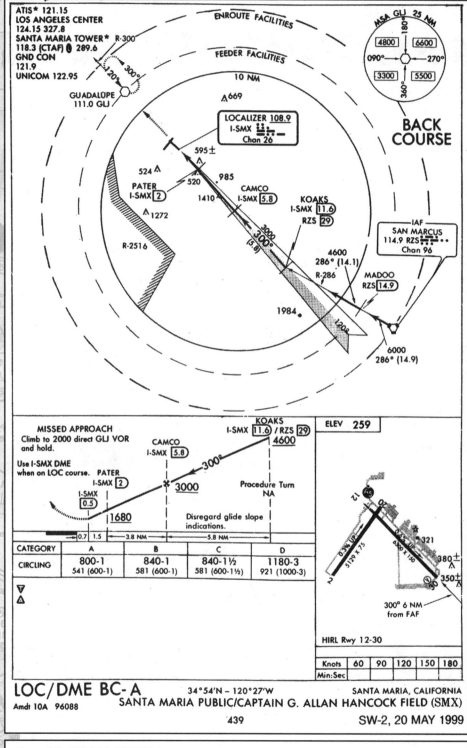

ATIS* 121.15
LOS ANGELES CENTER
124.15 327.8
SANTA MARIA TOWER* R-300
118.3 (CTAF) 289.6
GND CON
121.9
UNICOM 122.95

ENROUTE FACILITIES

FEEDER FACILITIES

10 NM

GUADALUPE
111.0 GLJ

LOCALIZER 108.9
I-SMX
Chan 26

MSA GLJ 25 NM

4800	6600
090°	270°
3300	5500

BACK
COURSE

595±

524

PATER
I-SMX 2

520

985

CAMCO
I-SMX 5.8

KOAKS
I-SMX 11.6
RZS 29

1272

1410

R-2516

3000
300°
(5.8)

4600
286° (14.1)
R-286

IAF
SAN MARCUS
114.9 RZS
Chan 96

MADOO
RZS 14.9

1984

120°

6000
286° (14.9)

MISSED APPROACH
Climb to 2000 direct GLJ VOR
and hold.

Use I-SMX DME
when on LOC course.

KOAKS
I-SMX 11.6 / RZS 29
4600

ELEV 259

CAMCO
I-SMX 5.8

300°

PATER
I-SMX 2

3000

I-SMX
0.5

1680

0.7 1.5

3.8 NM

Procedure Turn
NA

Disregard glide slope
indications.

5.8 NM

321

380±

350±

300° 6 NM
from FAF

HIRL Rwy 12-30

CATEGORY	A	B	C	D
CIRCLING	800-1 541 (600-1)	840-1 581 (600-1)	840-1½ 581 (600-1½)	1180-3 921 (1000-3)

Knots	60	90	120	150	180
Min:Sec					

LOC/DME BC-A
Amdt 10A 96088

34°54'N – 120°27'W

SANTA MARIA, CALIFORNIA
SANTA MARIA PUBLIC/CAPTAIN G. ALLAN HANCOCK FIELD (SMX)

439

SW-2, 20 MAY 1999

Figure 6.6: SMX LOC/DME BC-A

Special Considerations

What makes this flight different from other flights is in the approach. We're flying a BC, so you have to remember that the CDI will look backwards compared to what we're used to seeing.

▶ **Note**

Remember: The OBS disconnects when a LOC frequency is tuned in.

Flight Tutorial

To set up for this flight, first select the Mooney Bravo as your aircraft. You can fly this tutorial with the IFR Mooney panel, but since this panel is a little different from the standard panel, some of the operations we'll discuss won't apply. For example, you won't need to open the annunciator panel when using the IFR panel because it's displayed at all times.

Because this is an IFR flight, we're not really concerned with the weather, other than avoiding extremely high winds, winds coming from the wrong direction (which would prohibit the safe use of our chosen runways), and visibility below LAX's takeoff and SMX's landing minimums (both of which are 1 mile).

Next we'll move to LAX's west side by the gas pump by using map view. The settings are Latitude N33°56.53', Longitude W118°25.82', Altitude +130, Heading 341, and Airspeed 0.

Before Engine Start

Action	Response
Preflight Inspection	COMPLETED

Although a preflight inspection technically means that everything is checked before the airplane leaves the ground, what it means here is the exterior check—which we don't do in flight simulations.

Seats, Belts, Shoulder Harness	ADJUST AND SECURED
Magneto/Starter Switch	OFF

Turning the mags off prevents any unwanted engine starts. With the mags on, all it'd take is a little hand propping (turning the propeller by hand) and the engine could start. Press the M key followed by the – (hyphen) key three times, or click on the left side of the magneto/starter switch (Figure 6.7), located at the lower left of the instrument panel, three times.

Master Switch	OFF

The Bravo's master switch (Figure 6.8) is a split rocker switch. The left side connects the aircraft's electrical circuits to the alternator, and the right side connects them to the battery. The down position is off for either side.

Figure 6.7:
The magneto/starter switch can be operated by mouse or key commands.

Figure 6.8:
The Bravo's master switch is a split rocker switch.

Alternator Field Switches   OFF

An alternator generates power by spinning a magnet inside an electrical field. This electrical field needs to be connected (via the *field* wire) to a low voltage power source (like a battery) before the alternator can generate power. The *alternator field* is the term used to describe the alternator's electrical field circuit. The Bravo has two alternators, but *Flight Simulator 2000* doesn't model these switches.

Radio Master Switch   OFF

This is Mooney's designation for the avionics power switch, shown in Figure 6.9. It's found to the right of the master switch.

Figure 6.9:
The avionics switch

Fuel Boost Pump   OFF

The fuel boost pump is a secondary electric-powered fuel pump. In the real Bravo, it activates automatically when full power is given. You can activate it manually by using the switch shown in Figure 6.10.

Figure 6.10:
The Bravo's fuel boost pump is electrically driven.

Directional Gyro	SLAVED

The real Mooney Bravo has a feature that connects (*slaves* is the proper term) the DG portion of the HSI directly to the magnetic compass eliminating the problems caused by gyro drift (having to reset the DG at regular intervals). You can simulate this feature by disabling Gyro Drift under Realism Settings.

Circuit Breakers	CHECK
ELT Switch	ARMED

ELT is the Emergency Locator Transmitter. There are three positions for the ELT switch: Off, On, and Armed. On causes the ELT to transmit, and Armed activates the G-trigger so that in the event of a crash or really hard landing, it'll begin transmitting automatically. ELTs are not modeled in *Flight Simulator 2000*.

Rocker Switches	OFF

This item refers to turning off every switch in the aircraft, including those on the overhead panel located in the upper-right corner of *Flight Simulator 2000*'s screen.

Alternate Static Source	OFF

Not modeled.

Throttle	CLOSED

Pressing F1 on the keyboard will close the throttle completely.

Propeller	FULL FORWARD

Ctrl+F4 will advance the propeller control full forward.

Mixture	IDLE CUT-OFF

Press Ctrl+Shift+F1 to place the mixture control at Idle Cut-off.

Cowl Flaps	**FULL OPEN**

The Bravo's cowl flaps are electrically operated; the control and position indicator shown in Figure 6.11 is located below NAV2's indicator head. The cowl flap control works like a momentary toggle. In other words, you need to push and hold it (in our case, click and hold with your mouse) until the desired cowl flap position (as shown on the indicator) is reached. Of course, since it is an electrical system, in order to move the cowl flaps at this point, you need to turn the master switch on again.

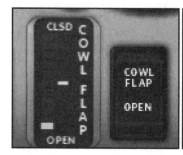

Figure 6.11:
Click and hold the position switch with your mouse to open or close the cowl flaps.

Parking Brakes	**SET**

Press Ctrl+"." (period) to set the parking brakes.

Wing Flaps Switch	**FLAPS UP**

The F5 key will retract the wing flaps to the full-up position. During the exterior preflight inspection, the flaps are usually deployed for easier inspection. Although wing flaps will not operate on the Bravo without the master switch turned on, the idea here is to have the flaps switch in the up position.

Defrost	**OFF**
Cabin Heat	**OFF**
Cabin Vent	**AS DESIRED**
Fuel Selector	**FULLEST TANK**

Generally, if both tanks are equally filled, the left tank is selected. In our case, since we're fully fueled, there's nothing to do here.

All Rocker Switches	**OFF**
Landing Gear Switch	**DOWN**
Emergency Gear Extension Handle	**DOWN AND LATCHED**

The emergency gear extension system in the Bravo is a little different from what we've seen before. The Bravo's landing gear is electrically driven (no hydraulics involved). The emergency gear extension handle in the real

Bravo must be locked and latched in order for the landing gear to work normally, because once the handle is unlatched, the drive gear from the electric extension/retraction motor is disengaged from the rest of the system. You don't need to worry about any of this in *Flight Simulator 2000*.

Internal Lights	OFF
Passenger Briefing	COMPLETED

The Passenger Briefing includes stuff like how to operate the seat belts, open the doors, what to do in an emergency, and where the "goodie" bags are in case they get airsick!

> ▶ *Tip*
>
> *The Bravo's real emergency gear extension system works like a lawnmower's pull start: you pull it, and it turns the extension system gears. Regardless, the manual gear extension pump command (Ctrl+G) will still work in the same capacity.*

Engine Start

Action	Response
Before Starting Checklist	COMPLETED
Throttle	OPEN ¼"

Pressing F3 about six times in rapid succession will open the throttle the proper amount.

Cowl Flaps	OPEN

Cowl flaps should still be open from the last checklist, but if they're not, remember to turn on the master switch or you won't be able to operate the cowl flaps.

Propeller	FULL FWD
Mixture	FULL RICH
Master Switch	ON
Alternator Field Switches	ON
Annunciator Lights	PRESS TO TEST

When you press the Test button in the real Bravo, all of the lights in the annunciator panel light up. The idea here is to discover any light bulbs that might be burned out. After all, if any are burned out, you won't see the associated warning light if there's a problem with that particular system. Although there's no way to check for this problem in *Flight Simulator 2000*, there isn't any need to because none of the lights can burn out.

Fuel Boost Pump	ON, THEN OFF

The idea here is to pressurize the fuel injection system so that you know the pump is actually working and so that less time is spent cranking the engine without it starting.

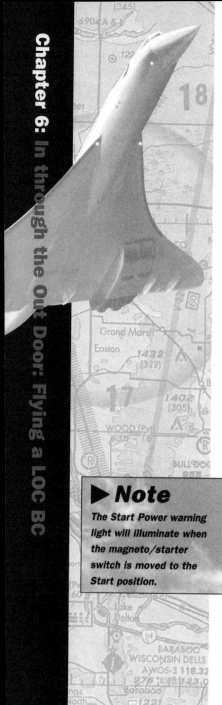

Propeller Area	CLEAR
Magneto/Starter Switch	TURN AND PUSH TO START

You can click on the right side of the magneto/starter switch a few times until it reaches the Start position and hold. Likewise, you can press the M key followed by the = (equal) key a couple of times. In either case, you need to hold the last position (with a mouse click or the = key) until the engine turns over.

Throttle	IDLE 700 RPM

Adjust the throttle using F2 and F3 keys to achieve 700 RPM on the RPM gauge (Figure 6.12), just above the rudder trim control on the lower-right side of the instrument panel.

Figure 6.12:
The Bravo's RPM gauge is located just above the rudder trim control.

Ammeter	CHECK

> ### ▶ Note
> The Start Power warning light will illuminate when the magneto/starter switch is moved to the Start position.

The ammeter is the upper-right instrument in the engine gauge cluster shown in Figure 6.13. You're looking to see that you're getting a positive rate of charge. If you're unsure, you can turn off the alternator side of the master rocker switch to see whether the alternator is providing power. (The ammeter needle will move to the left when the alternator is turned off.)

Interior/Exterior Lights	AS DESIRED

It's considered good practice to run the beacon and navigation lights any time the engine is running. These lights are labeled as Rot Bcn and Nav Lite and are located on the lighting panel above the instrument panel, as shown in Figure 6.14. They are operated by mouse clicks or by pressing the L key to toggle all of the lights on at once from your keyboard.

Engine Instruments	CHECKED

Check that all of the engine gauges are in the green or yellow arcs.

Figure 6.13:
The ammeter is the gauge at the top-right corner in the engine gauge cluster.

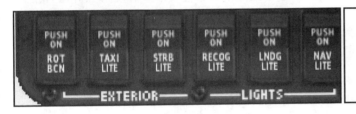

Figure 6.14:
Lights are operated from this panel above the instrument panel.

Before Taxi

Action	Response
Engine Start Checklist	COMPLETED
Radio Master Switch	ON
Elevator Trim Switch	ON

These items are handled for you automatically.

Internal/External Lights	AS DESIRED

No changes are required here.

Directional Gyro	SET

The HSI contains the DG. To set the DG to correspond with the magnetic compass, press the D key.

Standby Vacuum Pump	CHECK

Turn on the standby vacuum pump and verify its operation by clicking on the Warn light (Figure 6.15) on the left side of the instrument panel. This will bring up the annunciator panel. When the standby vacuum pump is operating, the Stby Vac light will illuminate. Turn the standby vacuum pump off again after verifying its operation.

Figure 6.15:
Click this Warn light to open the annunciator panel.

Instruments	NORMAL OPERATION
Radios	CHECKED AND SET

LAX ATIS is 135.65. Dial in LAX VOR in NAV1 (113.6), and 323 degrees on the HSI OBS. Enter FIM VOR (112.5) into NAV2, and 277 degrees on the OBS of NAV2's indicator head. These settings (Figure 6.16) set us up for our outbound departure radial and our transition intersection to FIM.

Figure 6.16:
Radios and autopilot set up for takeoff.

Altimeter	SET

Press the B key to set the ALT to the current altimeter setting.

Fuel Selector	SWITCH TANKS

Switch tanks by clicking on the fuel selector (Figure 6.17). The idea here is to verify whether the engine runs on the other tank. Because the fuel selector cycles in sequence, be sure to quickly cycle past Off on your way back to the fullest tank or the engine may quit from fuel starvation.

Figure 6.17:
The fuel selector cycles through every setting in sequence.

Cowl Flaps	FULL OPEN OR AS DESIRED

We'll leave them full open for taxi and takeoff.

Cabin Heat	AS DESIRED
Defroster	AS DESIRED
Cabin Vent	AS DESIRED

These last three items are not modeled.

Taxi

Action	Response
Before Taxi Checklist	COMPLETED
Rudder Trim	AS DESIRED

Rudder trim on the real aircraft is balanced by a bungee device. Having it set too far on one side or the other can restrict nose wheel authority to the opposite side. To adjust the rudder trim, simply click on the side of the rudder trim control (Figure 6.18) that you want to move the trim toward.

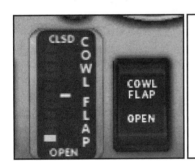

Figure 6.18:
Rudder trim is operated from this controller.

Parking Brake	RELEASE

Press the "." (period) key to release the parking brakes.

Brakes	CHECK

Press the "." (period) key again to check that the brakes are operating properly once you start rolling.

Directional Gyro	PROPER INDICATION DURING TURNS

As you're taxiing, do a couple of S-turns to check that the DG, TC, and AI (the next two items on the checklist) are operating properly.

Turn Coordinator	PROPER INDICATION DURING TURNS
Artificial Horizon	PROPER INDICATION DURING TURNS
Throttle	MINIMUM POWER
Cowl Flaps	OPEN OR AS DESIRED
Propeller	FULL FORWARD

Go ahead and make a left turn and taxi over to runway 6L. Note that you'll have to cross runway 6R to get there. Because we don't have the luxury of ground control, be especially careful to watch for traffic if you've got Dynamic Scenery enabled.

Before Takeoff (Run-up)

Hold short of runway 6L and perform your run-up check.

Action	Response
Taxi Checklist	COMPLETE
Parking Brake	SET

Use Ctrl+"." (period) to set the parking brake.

Fuel Selector	FULLEST TANK
Throttle	1,000 RPM

Press F3 or F2 to bring the throttle to 1,000 RPM.

Cowl Flaps	OPEN or AS DESIRED
Propeller	FULL FORWARD
Alternate Air	CLOSED

Alternate air is found on fuel-injected aircraft. It's essentially an alternate (typically unfiltered) engine air intake. When the primary air intake, which is filtered, becomes clogged with debris or ice, the spring-loaded alternate air intake door will automatically open, but the pilot can operate it manually, too. Alternate air in *Flight Simulator 2000* is modeled in the all-purpose prop anti-ice system, so just make sure the Prop De-Ice button is off.

Alternator Field Switch	VERIFY ON
Throttle	2,000 RPM

Bring the throttle up to 2,000 RPM using the F3 key.

> ▶ **Tip**
>
> *LAX is a big airport (you can literally taxi around for miles), so press Shift+] to use the top-down view window if you need it.*

> ▶ **Note**
>
> *Alternate air differs from cowl flaps, which cool the engine.*

Magneto/Starter Switch	CHECK—BOTH TO L, BOTH TO R, BOTH

Move the magneto/starter switch to the positions specified by using your mouse or by pressing the M key followed by the – (hyphen) and/or = (equal) keys. You're looking for a 150 RPM maximum drop in each magneto and 50 RPM maximum difference between magnetos.

Propeller	CYCLE

The quickest way to cycle the props without a dedicated prop controller is to use the Ctrl+F1 and Ctrl+F4 keys. Cycle the props three times.

Ammeter	CHECK

Check the ammeter for a positive rate of charge indication.

Throttle	1,000 RPM

Bring the throttle back to 1,000 RPM using the F2 key.

Fuel Boost Pump Switch	ON

Click on the fuel boost pump switch to verify that the annunciator light on the annunciator panel will illuminate.

Fuel Boost Pump Switch	OFF

The annunciator light should extinguish.

Elevator Trim	TAKEOFF SETTING

Use the rudder and elevator trim controls (next item on the checklist) to move the trims to the takeoff (T/O) positions.

Rudder Trim	TAKEOFF SETTING
Wing Flaps	10°

Drop the flaps one increment by using your mouse or by pressing F7 once. The flap position indicator should be within the T/O (takeoff) range.

Flight Controls	FREE AND CORRECT
Cabin Door	CHECK SECURED
Seats, Belts, Harnesses	SECURED
Avionics and Autopilot	CHECK

169

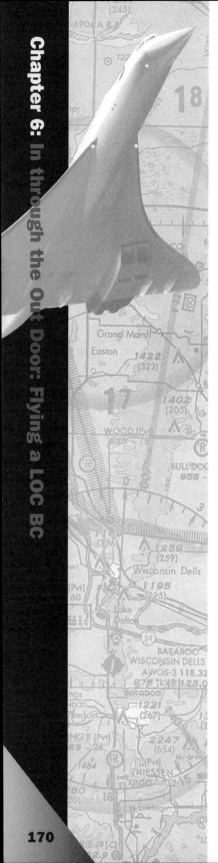

Whether you use the autopilot on this flight is up to you. We've already set up the avionics for takeoff, but if you're interested in using the autopilot, press Shift+2 to bring up the radio stack. Then hit the autopilot ALT button and set 6,000 feet for the altitude. Next set the DG heading bug by clicking on the right knob on the HSI to 040 degrees (our initial course after takeoff).

Annunciator Lights	**CHECK**
Internal/External Lights	**AS DESIRED**

For takeoff, all lights should be turned on even if it's daylight. This helps make your aircraft as visible as possible to other aircraft and ATC. Turn on all of your aircraft lights by pressing the I key.

Strobe Lights/Rotating Beacon	**ON**

See above.

Pilots Window	**CLOSED**
Emergency Gear Extension Handle	**DOWN AND LATCHED**
Oil Temperature	**100°F MINIMUM**

Temperatures below 100°F will produce an overboost in manifold pressure.

CHT	**250°F MINIMUM**
Parking Brake	**RELEASE**

Press the "." (period) key to release the parking brake.

When you're ready, note the time and then taxi out onto the runway. But again, if you've got Dynamic Scenery enabled, be sure to watch for landing traffic before moving onto the runway.

Takeoff

Action	Response
Power	**FULL THROTTLE**

Advance the throttle smoothly using the F3 key. Do not exceed 2,575 RPM and 38 inches MP.

Annunciator	**CHECK**

In the real Bravo, you'd check the annunciator panel for proper indications and for the boost pump light to light up (which goes on at full throttle automatically—but this is not modeled).

| Engine Instruments | CHECK |

You're just checking to see that everything is in the green. If not, you'd abort takeoff.

| Lift Off/Climb Speed | AS SPECIFIED |

Rotate at V_R (66 KIAS) and climb out at V_Y (106 KIAS).

| Landing Gear | RETRACT IN CLIMB |

As soon as a positive rate of climb is established, press the G key to retract the landing gear.

| Wing Flaps | UP |

Once V_Y is achieved, raise the flaps using the F5 key.

| Fuel Pressure | 24 PSI (MINIMUM) |

If your fuel pressure was below 24 PSI, you'd turn on the boost pump switch.

Once you're past the end of the runway, make a turn to heading 040 degrees. (If you're using the autopilot, click the HDG button and engage the autopilot by pressing the Z key.)

Climb

Action	Response
Power	34 in. Hg./2,400 RPM

At 500 feet AGL, adjust power and props to 34 inches MP and 2,400 RPM, using F2 and F3 keys and the Ctrl+F2 and Ctrl+F3 keys.

| Mixture | RICH |
| Cowl Flaps | FULL OPEN OR AS REQUIRED |

Unless it's extremely cold outside, cowl flaps are usually left open during climbs.

| Airspeed | 120 KIAS |

Adjust pitch to maintain 120 KIAS. If you're using the autopilot, increase the autopilot VSI rate to maintain 120 KIAS. This will be about 800 FPM.

At 7 DME out of LAX, make a climbing left turn to heading 270 degrees. (If you're flying the autopilot, move the DG heading to 270 degrees. Once your wings are level, leave HDG mode enabled and switch on NAV mode.)

We're now waiting to intercept LAX R-323 outbound. Figure 6.19 illustrates where you should be.

Figure 6.19:
Heading 270 degrees
and climbing to 6,000
feet while waiting for
LAX R-323 on the HSI
to come in.

Cruise

Depending on how organized you are in the cockpit (don't worry if you feel like you're swimming right now, that's pretty typical when you're in a new airplane), just about the time you should be leveling off we should intercept LAX R-323 degrees. Follow it outbound and place the airplane in cruise configuration by using the following checklist.

Be aware that while you're doing this, we're looking for the FIM R-277 degrees intersection to come in on NAV2. If NAV2's CDI needle comes in while you're changing flight configuration, remember the number one rule of piloting—*fly the airplane first!*

Action	Response
Airspeed	ACCELERATE TO CRUISE SPEED

Upon reaching 6,000 feet, level off. After leveling off, allow the aircraft to accelerate before adjusting power.

Throttle	SELECTED SETTING

Set power to cruise setting 2,400 RPM using the F2 and F3 keys. Also verify that fuel pressure remains within the green arc.

Propeller	SELECTED SETTING

We should already be set at 2,400 RPM. Use the Ctrl+F2 and Ctrl+F3 keys if necessary.

Mixture	LEAN TO PEAK TIT

Okay, putting aside the awkward acronym, TIT stands for Turbine Inlet Temperature. This is the exhaust gas temperature measured at the turbocharger turbine inlet. As the fuel mixture is leaned, the engine runs hotter (excess fuel tends to cool the engine). Maximum fuel economy is found at peak TIT. We're cruising at Best Power, so lean the fuel mixture to 1,650°F TIT.

Engine Instruments	CHECK
Cowl Flaps	AS REQUIRED

Cowl flaps are typically closed during cruise unless the OAT is pretty warm.

Rudder Trim	AS DESIRED

Once you see the NAV2's CDI start to center (see Figure 6.20), make a left turn and track FIM R-277 degrees inbound using NAV2. If you're not sure where you are in relation to the FIM R-277 degrees intersection, use the DME. This intersection is 21 DME from LAX VOR. So if your DME reading is greater than 21 DME, you've passed your turn/intersection—not good, so stay on top of it!

Figure 6.20: We're nearing FIM R-277's intersection—NAV2's CDI has "come alive."

For those using the autopilot, once you're about 19 DME from LAX VOR, disengage NAV mode on the autopilot. Enter FIM's frequency in NAV1 (you can read it from NAV2 if you forgot it and are in a rush), set NAV1/HSI's OBS to 277 degrees and reenter NAV mode on the autopilot.

For manual flyers, you should be tracking FIM R-277 degrees inbound using NAV2's indicator head at this point. Once you're established (stabilized), bring up the radio stack and set FIM VOR frequency in NAV1 and set 277 degrees on NAV1/HSI's OBS. Once this is done you can continue tracking inbound using the HSI.

After crossing FIM, rotate NAV1/HSI's OBS to 250 degrees and track that outbound. Regardless of which method you're using to control your aircraft, the next item on the agenda is to set up to find the DEANO intersection. To do this, enter RZS VOR frequency (114.9) into NAV2. Then set NAV2's OBS to 289 degrees.

Watching for DEANO is the same drill as when we were watching for the FIM R-277 degrees intersection. When NAV2's needle begins to center (DEANO is 27 DME from FIM), track R-289 degrees inbound. Once you're established, transfer NAV2 to NAV1, then track NAV1 inbound the rest of the way.

► **Tip**

The only item missing from the Cruise checklist is external lights. We chose to fly the tutorial without using this method, to illustrate BC concepts. Taxi and landing lights are usually turned off once you've entered cruise (and are outside traffic areas).

While we're waiting to cross RZS, let's set up for our LOC BC approach: set SMX's LOC frequency (108.9) in NAV2. (See Figure 6.21.) Although LOCs disengage the OBS setting, it's useful to set our approach course in the OBS anyway. This is helpful as a reminder of what our final approach course is, but more importantly, it reduces confusion when things start to get hectic in the cockpit.

Figure 6.21:
Inbound to RSZ and set
up for the approach

Descent

After crossing RZS, set 286 degrees on the NAV1/HSI OBS. Track it outbound while watching the DME. At MADOO (14.9 DME from RSZ), we'll descend to 4,600 feet by pulling the throttle back 19 inches MP. For those of you using the autopilot, pull the throttle back to about 19 inches MP before entering 4,600 feet in the autopilot.

Action	Response
Seats, Belts, Harnesses	ADJUST AND SECURE
Wing Flaps	UP
Landing Gear	UP
Throttle	ABOVE 15 IN. HG.

MP is kept above 15 inches Hg. to keep the engine's temperature up. The idea is to keep the CHT in the green arc. If you need to descend faster, instead of pulling the power off, drop the landing gear and/or deploy the spoilers.

Propeller	2,400 RPM
Mixture	PEAK TIT

Depending on your throttle setting, fuel mixtures may need to be enriched as you descend into the thicker air.

Cowl Flaps	CLOSED
CHT	MONITOR (250°F MINIMUM)
Airspeed	AS DESIRED

You can descend as fast as you like (assuming you stay below V_{NE} or V_A if conditions warrant), as long as you can slow down in enough time to make your approach. Here is where your skill and experience with the aircraft comes into play. But generally, if you descend at 700 FPM at 150 KIAS, it'll take about 13 minutes (36 nm) to descend 10,000 feet.

Rudder Trim	**AS DESIRED**

When you reach 4,600 feet, level off and add a little power (about 22 inches MP) to maintain altitude. Your airspeed will drop off to about a comfortable 110 KIAS. Now would be a good time to listen to SMX ATIS (121.15).

Once you reach KOAKS (29 DME from RZS), turn to heading 300 degrees, reduce power to 18 inches, and descend to 3,000 feet. For autopilot fliers, reduce power, turn off NAV mode, turn to heading 300 degrees, enter 3,000 feet in the autopilot, and then press the HDG mode button.

Approach for Landing

Enter the I-SMX (SMX's LOC) frequency (108.9) in NAV1. Be sure to enter the GLJ VOR frequency in NAV2 in preparation for a missed approach in case we need it.

The most important thing you need to remember is that the HSI needle will move in the opposite direction from what you're used to. Remember this is a BC—and now the fun begins. Good luck!

If you're flying the autopilot, once you're receiving I-SMX, pull the autopilot out of HDG mode and place it into BC mode by pressing the REV mode button. Now you can track the LOC BC properly.

Action	Response
Seats, Belts, Harnesses	**ADJUST AND SECURE**
Internal/External Lights	**AS DESIRED**

Time to turn on the landing lights and taxi lights again.

Landing Gear	**EXTEND**

Extend the landing gear by pressing the G key.

Mixture	**FULL RICH**

Advance the mixture control to full rich by pressing Ctrl+Shift+F4.

Propeller	**HIGH RPM**

Ctrl+F4 will move the prop control to high RPM.

▶ *Tip*

When using an HSI on a LOC BC you can set the OBS needle to the FRONT course. When flying a back course with OBS set like this you'll get normal (i.e., "fly-to") indications on the HSI. This capability is one of the reasons it's easier to fly with an HSI—you don't have to remember to fly away from the needle. But don't let that stop you from trying to fly the LOC BC like the rest of us that fly aircraft with less capable NAV instruments!

Fuel Boost Pump	ON

The fuel boost pump is turned on in preparation for a go-around in case one is needed.

Fuel Selector	FULLEST TANK
Wing Flaps	10°, FULL DOWN BELOW 110 KIAS

Press F7 to deploy wing flaps in increments. As your airspeed drops below 110 KIAS, press F7 once again to fully extend wing flaps.

Elevator Trim	AS DESIRED
Rudder Trim	AS DESIRED
Parking Brake	VERIFY OFF

This step prevents landing with the parking brake engaged—which can really ruin a good (not to mention expensive!) set of tires.

Watch the DME for CAMCO intersection. Note that DME readings are now coming from I-SMX, so they'll count down. At CAMCO (5.8 DME from I-SMX) descend to 1,680 feet. To enter odd numbers (in this case numbers that aren't even 100s) use the Autopilot window that opens when you select the Autopilot option from the Aircraft menu, as shown in Figure 6.22.

Figure 6.22:
The Autopilot window

At PATER (2 DME from I-SMX), you can descend to 800 feet. If you see the runway before any of these step-down intersections, you can just ignore them and land visually.

Landing

Once you've got the airport in sight, go ahead and grease 'er in. (Don't forget to disengage the autopilot first if you were using it!)

Action	Response
Approach for Landing Checklist	COMPLETE
Approach Airspeed	AS SPECIFIED

Approach speeds are listed in Table 6.1 for your convenience.

Table 6.1 Mooney Bravo Approach Speeds

Flap Setting	KIAS
Flaps 10°	80
Flaps 30°	75
Short field 30°	70

Action	Response
Touchdown	MAIN WHEELS FIRST
Landing Roll	LOWER NOSE WHEEL GENTLY
Brakes	MINIMUM REQUIRED

Unless you touched down really long or landed with the wind at your back, you won't need any brakes.

After Landing

Before taxiing to parking, complete the after-landing checklist.

Action	Response
Throttle	AS REQUIRED
Fuel Boost Pump	OFF
Cowl Flaps	OPEN
Wing Flaps	RETRACT

The F4 key will fully retract the flaps.

Action	Response
Elevator Trim	TAKEOFF SETTING
Avionics/Radios	AS REQUIRED
Interior/Exterior Lights	AS DESIRED

Strobe lights should be turned off while you're on the ground. (Press the O key to toggle them off.)

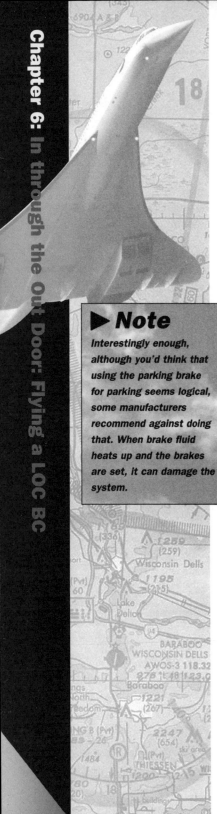

Engine Shut Down

Action	Response
Parking Brake	SET

Ctrl+"." (period) will set the parking brake.

Throttle	IDLE RPM
Radio Master Switch	OFF
Interior/Exterior Lights	OFF
Pitot Heat	OFF
Magneto/Starter Switch	GROUNDING CHECK

A grounding check tests whether the magneto grounding wire is still connected. If the grounding wire has been disconnected, the engine will continue running even if the mag switch is turned off. The way to check it is to quickly turn the mag switch off for a split second to see whether the engine will skip (stop running for a second).

Mixture	IDLE CUT-OFF

Press Ctrl+Shift+F1 to place the mixture control to Idle Cut-off quickly.

Alternator Field Switches (L/R)	OFF
Master Switch	OFF
Magneto/Starter Switch	OFF

You did great! Now let's try something a little more difficult—the often dreaded DME arc approach!

▶ **Note**

Interestingly enough, although you'd think that using the parking brake for parking seems logical, some manufacturers recommend against doing that. When brake fluid heats up and the brakes are set, it can damage the system.

Taking the Long Way Around

Chapter 7

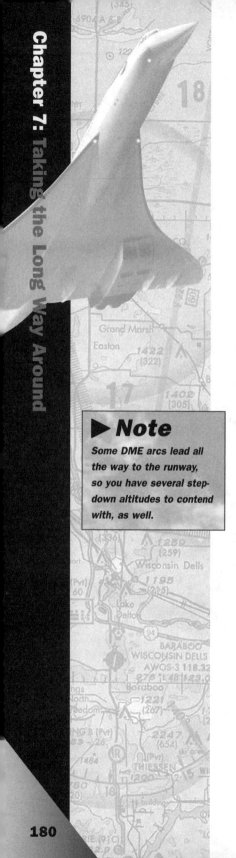

*T*he King Air 350 makes its debut in Flight Simulator 2000, and it's the first turboprop ever to be included in any version of Flight Simulator. Considering that turboprop aircraft make up the backbone of most commuter airlines in the U.S., it's a welcome addition for many Flight Simulator enthusiasts.

In this chapter we'll discuss the often dreaded DME arc. What makes the DME arc so feared is the high cockpit workload associated with it. Physically you're constantly tracking, turning, or twisting something throughout the arc. Once you factor in the mental processes required to fly the approach (not to mention planning for a potential missed approach), well, you've got one busy pilot. So let's talk about how to minimize the trauma.

DME Arc

The DME arc is a fairly common initial approach segment. It usually leads into an ILS, LOC, or VOR-DME approach. Although it may seem like DME arcs were simply invented to tax instrument piloting skills, there's a more practical reason for them. DME arcs are generally used in places where a more direct approach is prohibitive. For instance, you'll likely find a DME arc initial approach segment where there's a large obstruction near the instrument approach path, like a mountain range.

Flying Tangents

Flying a large, curved arc at a specific range from a VOR-DME or VORTAC (a combination VOR TACAN, essentially a military version of a VOR-DME) is practically an impossible maneuver. Even without the wind complicating matters, you'd be constantly changing your bank and wandering about the sky quite a bit.

Flying a DME arc means flying a series of tangents to the depicted circle, as shown in Figure 7.1. Each tangent is perpendicular to the radials that align the circle with the VOR-DME/VORTAC.

Although ideally we'd like to fly tangents for every degree/radial to make as perfect a circle as possible, that isn't practical. The accepted rate of tangent change is every 10 degrees. Of course, the smaller the DME arc, the shorter the tangents and the quicker you'll need to change headings. The following table lists tangent lengths of 10-degree segments for arcs within the FAA arc sizes range (7–30 nm):

> ▶ **Note**
>
> **Some DME arcs lead all the way to the runway, so you have several step-down altitudes to contend with, as well.**

Arc Radius	Tangent Length
7	1.2 nm
10	1.8 nm
15	2.6 nm
20	3.5 nm
25	4.7 nm
30	5.3 nm

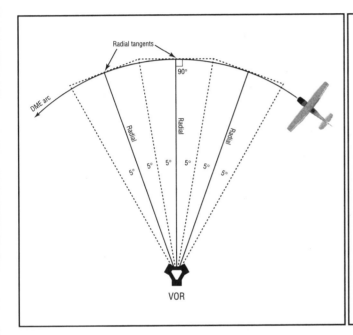

Figure 7.1: DME arcs are accomplished by flying a series of 10-degree tangents.

To illustrate how to fly tangents, let's look at the approach we'll be using in our tutorial (see Figure 7.2). As you'll see later, our routing will take us from PMD VOR to VCV VOR. From there we'll fly outbound on R-055 degrees to our IAF, TRNDL—which conveniently happens to be on our DME arc.

About a half mile from TRNDL (13.0 DME from VCV VOR), we'll make our first turn (at standard rate) to fly tangent to R-055 degrees. Since a tangent is 90 degrees to the radial and the arc runs counterclockwise, from our direction of travel we'll make a left turn to heading 325 degrees.

The way we keep track of each 10-degree segment is by watching the HSI CDI. If you recall, a full CDI deflection when tracking a VOR is 10 degrees. Because we're flying tangents on each radial (in this case VCV R-055 degrees), we count our 10-degree segment as extending from 5 degrees before the radial to 5 degrees after the radial. This means once we see a 5-degree CDI deflection from R-055 degrees, we'll have completed our 10-degree segment and should begin our next tangent turn.

▶ *Tip*

The biggest hurdle to mastering the DME arc is being able to visualize where you are and what you need to do. Granted, it's a tough proposition, but it can mean the difference between learning good situational awareness and "flying in a tube."

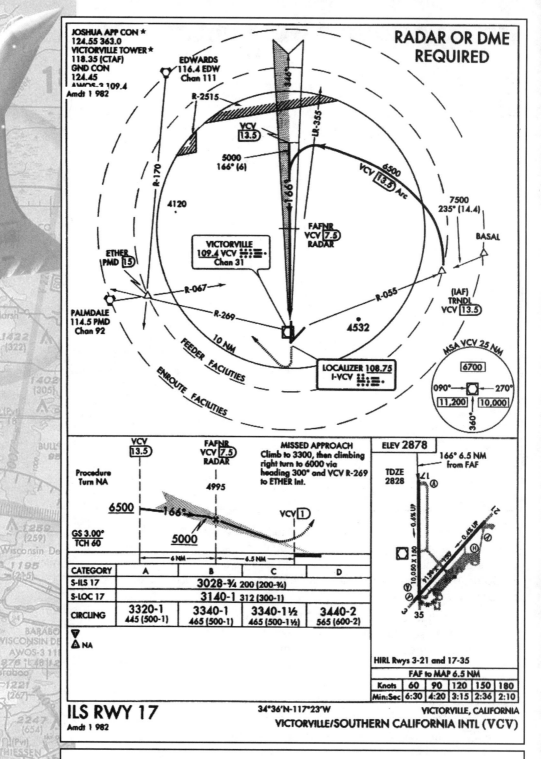

Figure 7.2: VCV ILS RWY 17

Because our arc circles to the left, we turn the airplane and the HSI OBS to the left. Specifically, we'll now turn 10 degrees to the left (heading 315 degrees) and twist the OBS 10 degrees to the left (045 degrees). We'll fly this heading until the CDI shows a half deflection to the right (remember we're flying with a From flag). At that point, we turn and twist another 10 degrees and fly the next tangent. We continue the process until we reach the *lead radial*. Before we cover that, we should say a few words about wind and how it'll make your arc flying tasks more difficult.

Dealing with Wind

During each segment, we need to keep an eye on the DME to watch our arc radius. With wind present, we'll need to make course corrections with each segment turn. This is fairly easy to visualize in your mind. If your arc is getting smaller (that is, the DME reading is getting lower), turn the airplane less than 10 degrees. If the arc is getting larger (DME is reading higher), turn the airplane a little more than 10 degrees.

Lead Radial

A lead radial is identified on approach plates with the letters "LR." They're placed there as an aid to alert pilots when it's time to turn inbound and switch over to the approach course NAVAID. Using our example approach, the lead radial is LR-355 degrees. Therefore, at LR-355 degrees, we'll make a left turn and intercept the ILS.

GPS

The Global Positioning System (GPS) is a satellite-based radio navigational, positioning, and time transfer system operated by the United States Department of Defense (DOD). Since December 8, 1993, the GPS has aimed to provide highly accurate position and velocity information and precise time on a continuous global basis.

The way that GPS works is based on the concept of ranging and triangulation from a group of satellites parked in orbit that provide precise reference points. There are currently 24 GPS satellites stationed in orbit so that a minimum of 5 are always observable by a user/receiver anywhere on the surface of the earth. Regulated radio signals are sent from the satellites and are timed and calculated by the receiver to determine how far the receiver is from the satellite transmitter. Although triangulation technically requires only three points to calculate a position, a fourth is used to increase accuracy and determine your altitude, and the fifth is used as a backup to allow the GPS unit to reject the worst signal.

As neat as GPS is, it's currently authorized only for terminal and en route navigation and nonprecision approaches. It is not authorized as the sole navigation instrument. Nevertheless, there are two features that make GPS really attractive for use in aviation. First, GPS overlays a moving map representation over the representation of your position. This provides a very literal representation of where you are that anyone can quickly grasp.

▶ **Tip**

Although you won't need to know this technical stuff to use the GPS navigation system in Flight Simulator 2000, it's just helpful to understand how it's modeled. This way you'll be able to understand its limitations and advantages.

Various Flavors of GPS

There are two levels of GPS service available: Standard Positioning Service (SPS), and Precise Positioning Service (PPS). SPS, which is used by civil aviation, provides horizontal positioning accuracy of 100 meters or less with a probability of 95 percent and 300 meters with a probability of 100 percent. PPS, on the other hand, is more accurate than SPS, but it's limited to authorized U.S. and allied military, government, and qualified civil users that meet specific requirements. This policy is called Selective Availability *or* SA *and the idea behind it is to make sure that no hostile force or terrorist group can use GPS to make accurate weapons. Aviation GPS navigation systems use SPS for en route flight and another form of GPS known as Differential GPS for GPS instrument approaches. Basically the way that the DOD "detunes" SPS GPS is by introducing some "noise" (or inaccuracy) into the satellite's clock data, which, in turn, adds noise into position calculations. (SA is the biggest single source of inaccuracy in the system.) Military receivers use a decryption key to remove the SA errors, restoring them to their highest accuracy. Fortunately SA inaccuracies still don't add up to a very large error and Differential GPS significantly reduces these problems.*

Differential GPS uses an additional ground-based signal to correct for any inaccuracies, including SA errors. This "local" solution lends itself very well to instrument approaches.

The second advantage to GPS is that you can select any waypoint in its database at any time. You don't have to deal with the reception problems/range limitations that plague ground-based NAVAIDs, so hopping from VOR to VOR, usually as a result of range limitations, is virtually eliminated (but not entirely, as you'll see later on).

▶ *Tip*

The GPS window, like all of the other windows in Flight Simulator 2000, *can be resized by dragging its corner.*

Flight Simulator 2000's GPS Features

Flight Simulator 2000 automatically loads any flight plans that you create in its flight planner into the GPS. So let's concentrate on the GPS's features.

Flight Simulator 2000's GPS has three main feature categories: Mode, Direct, and Menu. You can access these categories by clicking on the buttons across the top-left side of the GPS.

The Mode button has three submodes:

✛ **Moving Map**—This mode offers a very useful representation of where your aircraft is in relation to airports, NAVAIDs, fixes, and airways. You can adjust the scale (zoom) by using the up and down cursor buttons in the upper center of the GPS. Available zoom factors are from .025 nm to 1,000 nm. The current zoom factor is displayed in the lower-right corner.

The waypoint identifier, distance, and magnetic bearing to the waypoint, are displayed on the top-left side of this screen. On the right side are ground speed, magnetic course, and distance and direction off course. (The small arrow will point towards the direction of the set course.)

✛ **Waypoint Detail**—This screen displays the same waypoint identifier, distance, magnetic bearing to the waypoint, ground speed, and magnetic course information, but it adds ETE and ETA calculations

based on ground speed, as well as your exact current position in latitude and longitude.

✢ **Route Detail**—This mode displays the current loaded flight plan (if any). Identifier, magnetic bearing, and distance in nautical miles are listed for each waypoint. The current active waypoint is highlighted in green. You can switch to any waypoint at any time by using the up and down GPS cursor buttons.

   Along the bottom of this screen are the current leg ETE and ETA, the exact position of the active waypoint in longitude and latitude, and the total trip ETE and ETA estimates (see Figure 7.3).

Figure 7.3:
The GPS Route Detail submode displays your flight plan and flight progress information.

The second button causes the GPS to enter Direct mode, which has two submodes:

✢ **Direct To**—This mode lets you select any airport or NAVAID waypoint and bypass the current flight plan (if any). The GPS cursor buttons are used to choose a waypoint, and the Enter button to the right selects it. To do this, first select the type of waypoint you want using the left and right GPS cursor buttons. Then use the up and down arrows to cycle thought the available choices and use the Enter button to activate your new waypoint. Waypoint info (magnetic bearing, distance, and exact location in latitude and longitude) are displayed on the lower half of the screen.

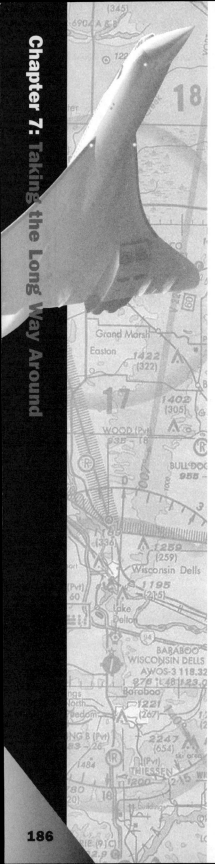

✛ **Emergency**—This mode constantly updates a list of the nearest airports and presents them in order of range. Information for each airport ID, magnetic bearing, range, name, and position in latitude and longitude is provided. Use the up and down GPS cursor keys to select an airport, then click the Enter button to make your selection the active waypoint.

The third button accesses the Configuration menu. This mode allows you to select the options for how information is displayed on the Map screen. Except for Orientation, which we'll talk about in a minute, everything else here is self-explanatory. As with the other GPS functions, use the up and down GPS cursor buttons to select an item, and use the left and right buttons to change the option. The Enter button will make the selection active.

Orientation refers to the Moving Map orientation. The default is Track Up, which means the top of the GPS will always align with the nose of the aircraft. The two other options are Desired Up and North Up. Desired Up freezes the Moving Maps orientation to whatever direction the aircraft is pointing when you make it active. North Up causes the Moving Map to remain oriented with (what else?) North at the top of the GPS.

Flying the King Air 350

Known as the Super King Air B300, the King Air 350 comes in two flavors: the B300 and B300C. The most noticeable differences between the two are a couple of aft seating arrangement changes and the C version's big cargo door in the rear of the fuselage. Otherwise, they're pretty much the same.

These aircraft have the performance to get you where you need to go on short hauls in more than reasonable time, as well as take off and land at smaller airports with passengers and luggage or cargo. King Air pilots have been known to refer to the King Airs as turbine-powered air taxis that feel like limousines, with the capabilities and ruggedness of all-terrain vehicles. But it's the King Air's simplicity of operation, combination of speed, load-hauling capability, relatively low cost of operation (compared to most jets), and short-field performance that make it so versatile and popular.

Aircraft Performance

For anyone not familiar with it, a turboprop is a turbine-powered, propeller-driven aircraft. In other words, the propeller is powered by a jet engine. Although this may seem like a strange combination, the reality is that it brings together the best parts of low-speed aviation propulsion systems—the reliability of turbine engines and the efficiency of propellers. But as you'll see, the King Air 350 offers many other sensible choices that contribute to making it one of the most popular turboprops in the world.

The King Air 350 turboprop represents the high end of low-speed range aircraft because high-speed aerodynamics is considered to begin at 350 mph and the King Air 350 cruises in this range.

V Speeds

Takeoff speeds are for sea level, maximum gross weight, on a standard day.

V Speed	KIAS
V_1	106
V_R	110
V_2	117
V_{35}	$V_2 + 6$
V_X	125
V_Y	140
V_{MCA} (Propeller Feathered)	—
(Flaps UP)	94
(Flaps Approach)	93
V_{SSE}	110
V_{XSE}	125
V_{YSE}	125
V_A	184
V_{MO} (Sea Level to FL210)	263
(FL210-FL350)	263–194 (0.58 Mach)
V_{LE}	184
V_{LO} (Extension)	184
(Retraction)	166
V_{FE} (Approach)	202
(Full Down)	158
Emergency Descent	184
Max Range Glide	135
Turbulent Air Penetration	170
Max Demonstrated Crosswind Component	20 knots
VREF Flaps DOWN (15,000#)	109
(14,000#)	105
(13,000#)	102
(12,000#)	100
(11,000#)	100
(10,000#)	100
Flaps UP	(V_{REF} + 20)

Advanced Systems

The King Air 350 features two advanced systems that you should be familiar with. They are autosynch and autofeather.

Autosynch Autosynch (known as the propeller synchrophaser) is a mechanism that synchronizes the propeller RPMs for both engines on the

King Air by raising the RPM on the slower prop and lowering the RPM on the faster prop. While having one prop spinning at a much higher RPM than the other (an out-of-phase condition) causes a thrust imbalance (and subsequently unwanted yaw), be aware that autosynch is designed only to fine tune small variations in RPM. Although small RPM differences between props isn't very hazardous, the "wah, wah, wah" sound and vibration that accompanies unsynchronized props is an unnecessary annoyance and discomfort for passengers, as well as a needless stress (however minor) on the airframe.

There are two parts of the autosynch system visible in the cockpit—the Prop Sync button and the propeller synchroscope (see Figure 7.4). Operating autosynch is very simple: set your prop controls and click on the Prop Synch button with your mouse.

Figure 7.4: Prop autosynch is controlled by this switch next to the synchroscope display.

The synchroscope (the thing that looks like a black and white nuclear radiation warning sign) provides a visual indication of prop synchronization. When both props are synchronized, the black and white cross pattern will remain stationary. When the props are out of synch, the synchroscope will appear to spin, and the faster it spins the more out of synch the props are.

The direction of the synchroscope rotation will be in the same direction as the engine that's rotating faster. In other words, a clockwise rotation indicates the right prop's RPM is faster than the left prop's, and a counterclockwise rotation indicates a higher RPM on the left prop. As you'd expect, the synchroscope is very handy for manual prop synchronization.

Autofeather *Feathering* is a propeller term that's used to indicate an extreme prop pitch position that places the blade at as close to zero angle of attack as the prop governor (the device that controls how fast the propeller is allowed to spin) will allow. A prop is typically feathered when an engine stops running while in flight to stop it from windmilling. The feathered blade's orientation is virtually parallel to the oncoming airflow, so it produces the least amount of drag on a stationary prop, as illustrated in Figures 7.5 and 7.6.

The King Air 350 is equipped with an autofeather system. If you recall, prop governors use oil pressure to maintain settings other than minimum positive or negative prop pitch. A full-feathering system uses springs and counterweights to achieve a prop blade pitch of zero AOA and lock it in that position, which, of course, requires very low governor oil pressure to achieve.

► Tip

The synchrophaser will never reduce propeller RPM below the lowest propeller control lever setting selected.

► Note

Angle of Attack (AOA) is the angle between the chord line (the distance between the leading and trailing edges of an airfoil) of a wing and the oncoming airflow.

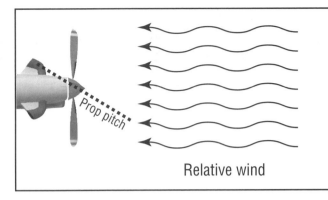

Figure 7.5:
A stationary feathered prop blade produces the least amount of drag.

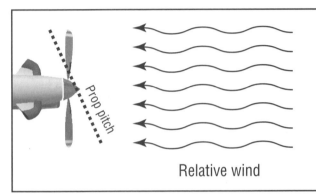

Figure 7.6:
An unfeathered propeller presents its largest surface area to the oncoming air flow. This causes it to windmill.

One of the most deadly situations faced by all aircraft is engine loss upon takeoff. Because you're so close to the ground, any spin will usually end tragically—you won't have sufficient altitude to recover. Due to the yawing forces produced by a windmilling prop on a multiengine aircraft, an engine loss at takeoff is perhaps the most potentially hazardous situation that a turboprop pilot will ever face. The autofeather system provides a faster means of dumping oil from the governor, allowing the feathering springs and counterweights to operate quickly. One less thing to worry about in the cockpit during an emergency helps the pilot remain focused on flying the airplane.

In order for the autofeather mechanism to work, it must be armed. To arm autofeather, all you need to do is click on the Autofeather switch (Figure 7.7), located on the lower-left side of the instrument panel. Illumination of the autofeather annunciator lights (Figure 7.8) requires that the system be armed and the power lever advanced above 90 percent N_1.

Figure 7.7:
The Autofeather switch has two positions, Arm and Off.

▶ *Note*

Although the term feather *is used to indicate maximum prop pitch, not all prop governors are full-feathering (able to achieve zero AOA).*

L AUTOFEATHER   R AUTOFEATHER

Flight Plan

We'll be taking an IFR flight in the King Air 350, and we'll end with (what else?) a DME arc approach. For navigation, we'll be using *Flight Simulator 2000*'s GPS and its Navigation log to illustrate how they work and how they can lighten your flight planning duties.

Airports

Starting at Seattle-Tacoma International Airport (commonly referred to as Sea-Tac) in Washington state, we'll fly all the way down to Victorville/Southern California International Airport. The longest runway at Sea-Tac is 11,900 feet. The longest runway at Victorville is 10,500 feet long. The sea level, minimum required hard-surface runway lengths at maximum gross weight on a standard day (15°C) are 3,000 feet for takeoff and 2,700 feet for landing in zero wind—no problems.

For an alternate, we've selected Ontario Airport (ONT), which is just south of Victorville, but it's on the other side of the San Gabriel and San Bernardino mountains. Although the high desert (where VCV is) doesn't usually get fogged in, the weather is usually radically different on opposite sides of the mountains, so ONT is a good choice.

Route

Here's the navigation log for your flight to Victorville/Southern California International Airport:

Waypoint	Frequency	Course	Altitude	Distance	ETE
SEA	ATIS 118.0	158°	FL250	793 nm	2:45
PMD	114.5	079°	6,700'	33.3 nm	0:08
VCV	109.4	055°	6,500'	13.5 nm	0:07
TRNDL	109.4	325°	6,500'	13.5 nm	0:07
LR-355	109.4	166°	5,000'	13.5 nm	0:07
VCV	ATIS/ AWOS 109.4*		TOTAL	866.8 nm	3:14

* *Flight Simulator 2000* can't receive AWOS (Automated Weather Observation Service) or other voice communication signals from NAVAIDS.

We'll be departing on runway 16R using the Seattle Two DP (Figure 7.9), which is essentially a straight-out departure that ATC vectors you to your assigned route. Our route is direct via GPS to Palmdale (PMD) VORTAC. From there we'll fly to VCV VOR and finish with the VCV ILS RWY 17 approach.

We're flying directly to PMD rather than directly to VCV to avoid restricted airspace R-2515 to the north and northwest of VCV. (Ah, now it makes sense that VCV has a DME arc approach, doesn't it?)

Altitude

We'll be cruising at FL250 for the whole flight. FL250 was selected because it offers the shortest flight time balanced by a compromise between cruise speed and fuel economy for the distance and direction of the flight. FL250 is also above the MEAs (FL240 is the highest) throughout our route.

Flying at a higher altitude may increase your fuel economy, but it also extends your flight time. (You're essentially in slower climb configuration longer, so your total flight time increases.) Conversely, flying at something below 10,000 feet would limit our speed to 250 KIAS—and that would be a waste of the King Air's speed.

We'll descend to 6,700 feet (the MEA between PMD and VCV) after crossing PMD. We can descend at 1,500 FPM and fly at 250 KIAS. It should only take 48 nm. (24,000 − 6,700 = 17,300 feet to descend. At 1,500 FPM, it'll take 11.5 minutes. Traveling at 250 KIAS, we'll cover 48 nm.)

The first part of the approach specifies 6,500 feet. Descending 200 feet in the 13.5 miles beyond VCV should be easy. After turning to intercept the ILS, we'll descend to 5,000 feet as the approach profile outlines.

Fuel/Performance

The King Air 350 carries 539 gallons (3,611 pounds) of fuel in four tanks (two main and two auxiliary tanks). Total distance from SEA to VCV along our route is 826.3 nm. We'll add another 41 nm for the approach (about 13.5 x 3), so our grand total is 867.3 nm. Maximum range with a full load of fuel is 1,894 nm.

Having made it this far in the book, you're no doubt prepared to see more of the details of flight planning. Up until now we've been basically using cruise fuel consumption figures to estimate fuel requirements, which works out fine if your trip is well within total range of the aircraft.

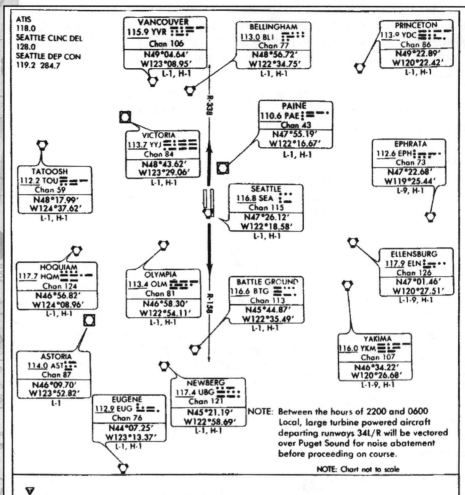

ATIS
118.0
SEATTLE CLNC DEL
128.0
SEATTLE DEP CON
119.2 284.7

NOTE: Between the hours of 2200 and 0600 Local, large turbine powered aircraft departing runways 34L/R will be vectored over Puget Sound for noise abatement before proceeding on course.

NOTE: Chart not to scale

DEPARTURE ROUTE DESCRIPTION

TAKE-OFF RUNWAYS 16L/R: Intercept and proceed via the SEA R-158, expect radar vectors to assigned route.

TAKE-OFF RUNWAYS 34L/R: Intercept and proceed via the SEA R-338, expect radar vectors to assigned route.

SEATTLE TWO DEPARTURE
(VECTOR) 94342

SEATTLE-TACOMA INTL (SEA)
SEATTLE, WASHINGTON

NW-1, 9 SEP 1999

Figure 7.9: Seattle Two Departure

Fuel usage for this flight is calculated using the following:

Configuration	Fuel Rate	Rate	Speed
Climb	975#/hr.	1,500 FPM	130 KIAS*
Cruise	685#/hr.	—	300 KTAS
Descent	500#/hr.	1,500 FPM	250 KIAS
Approach	515#/hr.	—	120 KIAS

*V_y above 25,000 feet is 130 KIAS, and we always take the slowest speed for an added margin of safety.

Calculations to our alternate destination adds 13 minutes of flight, and 290 pounds of fuel. Therefore the total fuel required for this flight (including the required IFR 45-minute reserve) is 2,992 pounds.

Maximum Cruise Power: 14,000lbs/6350kg				
1500 RPM/ISA -30°C				
OAT	Torque per ENG	Fuel Flow per ENG	Total Fuel Flow	TAS
°C	(%)	(lbs/hour)	(lbs/hour)	(Kn)
-15	99	522	1044	246
-19	100	512	1024	252
-23	100	500	1000	257
-27	100	490	980	262
-31	100	481	962	267
-35	100	472	944	272
-39	100	464	928	278
-43	100	457	914	283
-47	100	451	902	290
-51	100	448	896	296
-55	100	447	894	302
-59	100	447	894	309
-63	100	448	896	316
-87	94	427	854	315
-70	83	381	762	308
-72	80	365	730	306
-76	74	341	682	303
-80	70	320	640	302
-84	64	294	588	296

Maximum Cruise Power: 14,000lbs/6350kg

1500 RPM/ISA -10°C

OAT	Torque per ENG	Fuel Flow per ENG	Total Fuel Flow	TAS
°C	(%)	(lbs/hour)	(lbs/hour)	(Kn)
5	100	530	1060	254
1	100	517	1034	259
-3	100	505	1010	264
-7	100	495	990	269
-11	100	486	972	274
-15	100	477	954	280
-19	100	469	938	285
-23	100	462	924	291
-27	100	456	914	297
-31	100	450	900	303
-35	100	448	896	310
-39	99	441	882	314
-43	93	417	834	315
-47	87	391	782	314
-50	81	364	728	311
-52	78	351	702	310
-56	72	324	648	306
-60	65	298	596	300
-64	59	272	544	293

Maximum Cruise Power: 14,000lbs/6350kg

1500 RPM/ISA -20°C

OAT	Torque per ENG	Fuel Flow per ENG	Total Fuel Flow	TAS
°C	(%)	(lbs/hour)	(lbs/hour)	(Kn)
-5	100	526	1052	250
-9	100	514	1028	255
-13	100	520	1004	260
-17	100	492	981	265
-21	100	483	966	271
-25	100	475	950	277
-29	100	467	934	282
-33	100	460	920	288
-37	100	454	908	294
-41	100	450	900	300
-45	100	447	894	306
-49	100	447	894	313
-53	100	448	896	319
-57	94	423	846	319
-60	88	395	790	317
-62	84	381	762	316
-66	78	353	708	313
-70	71	324	648	307
-74	64	293	586	300

Maximum Cruise Power: 14,000lbs/6350kg
1500 RPM/ISA

OAT °C	Torque per ENG (%)	Fuel Flow per ENG (lbs/hour)	Total Fuel Flow (lbs/hour)	TAS (Kn)
15	100	532	1064	256
11	100	520	1040	261
7	100	508	1016	266
3	100	497	994	272
-1	100	488	976	277
-5	100	479	958	282
-9	100	470	940	288
-13	100	463	926	294
-17	100	456	912	300
-21	100	451	902	306
-25	97	435	870	309
-29	92	410	820	309
-33	86	385	770	309
-37	80	360	720	307
-40	75	335	670	304
-42	72	322	644	303
-46	66	297	594	298
-50	60	274	548	292
-54	54	249	498	283

Maximum Cruise Power: 14,000lbs/6350kg
1500 RPM/ISA +10°C

OAT °C	Torque per ENG (%)	Fuel Flow per ENG (lbs/hour)	Total Fuel Flow (lbs/hour)	TAS (Kn)
25	100	534	1068	259
21	100	521	1042	264
17	100	510	1020	269
13	100	499	998	274
9	100	489	978	279
5	100	480	960	285
1	100	471	942	291
-3	100	464	928	297
-7	98	448	896	300
-11	94	427	854	302
-15	90	405	810	303
-19	84	380	760	303
-23	79	355	710	302
-27	74	331	662	300
-30	68	308	616	297
-32	66	297	594	295
-36	61	294	548	290
-40	55	252	504	282
-44	50	228	456	270

Maximum Cruise Power: 14,000lbs/6350kg
1500 RPM/ISA +30°C

OAT	Torque per ENG	Fuel Flow per ENG	Total Fuel Flow	TAS
°C	(%)	(lbs/hour)	(lbs/hour)	(Kn)
45	97	532	1064	261
41	95	510	1020	263
37	94	493	986	267
33	93	475	950	271
29	90	457	914	274
25	88	439	878	277
21	85	419	838	280
17	82	398	796	282
13	79	378	756	283
9	76	357	714	284
5	71	334	668	283
1	67	314	628	282
-3	63	293	586	280
-7	59	274	548	278
-10	56	256	512	275
-12	54	247	494	273
-16	50	229	458	265
-20	45	209	418	252
-24	—	—	—	—

Maximum Cruise Power: 14,000lbs/6350kg
1500 RPM/ISA +20°C

OAT	Torque per ENG	Fuel Flow per ENG	Total Fuel Flow	TAS
°C	(%)	(lbs/hour)	(lbs/hour)	(Kn)
35	100	539	1078	261
31	100	525	1050	266
27	100	513	1026	271
23	100	501	1002	277
19	100	490	980	282
15	97	471	942	285
11	94	451	902	288
7	92	433	886	291
3	89	414	828	293
-1	85	394	788	295
-5	81	370	740	294
-9	76	348	696	294
-13	72	325	650	293
-17	67	304	608	291
-20	63	283	566	288
-22	60	273	546	286
-26	55	252	504	280
-30	50	231	462	270
-34	45	208	416	253

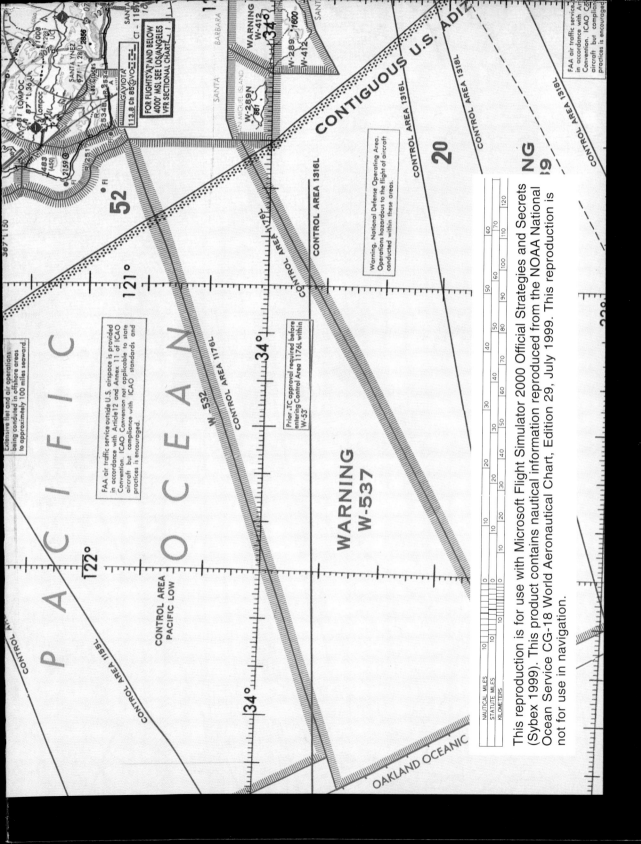

Maximum Cruise Power: 14,000lbs/6350kg
1500 RPM/ISA -30°C

OAT	Torque per ENG	Fuel Flow per ENG	Total Fuel Flow	TAS
°C	(%)	(lbs/hour)	(lbs/hour)	(Kn)
-15	99	522	1044	246
-19	100	512	1024	252
-23	100	500	1000	258
-27	100	490	980	262
-31	100	481	962	267
-35	100	472	644	272
-39	100	464	628	278
-43	100	457	614	283
-47	100	451	602	290
-51	100	448	896	298
-56	100	447	894	302
-59	100	447	894	309
-63	97	433	866	311
-67	90	404	808	310
-70	84	377	754	308
-72	81	363	726	307
-78	74	335	670	303
-80	67	306	612	297
-84	60	276	552	289

Maximum Cruise Power: 14,000lbs/6350kg
1500 RPM/ISA -20°C

OAT	Torque per ENG	Fuel Flow per ENG	Total Fuel Flow	TAS
°C	(%)	(lbs/hour)	(lbs/hour)	(Kn)
-5	100	526	1052	250
-9	100	514	1028	255
-13	100	502	1004	260
-17	100	492	984	265
-21	100	483	966	271
-25	100	475	950	277
-29	100	467	934	282
-33	100	460	920	288
-37	100	454	908	294
-41	100	450	900	300
-45	100	447	894	306
-49	97	435	870	309
-53	91	406	812	308
-58	85	378	756	306
-60	79	352	704	304
-62	76	339	678	302
-66	70	314	628	299
-70	65	293	586	295
-74	59	271	542	289

Maximum Cruise Power: 14,000lbs/6350kg
1500 RPM/ISA

OAT	Torque per ENG	Fuel Flow per ENG	Total Fuel Flow	TAS
°C	(%)	(lbs/hour)	(lbs/hour)	(Kn)
15	100	532	1064	256
11	100	520	1040	261
7	100	508	1016	266
3	100	497	994	272
-1	100	488	976	277
-5	100	479	958	282
-9	100	470	940	288
-13	100	463	926	294
-17	100	456	912	300
-21	96	437	874	302
-25	91	408	816	301
-29	85	382	764	300
-33	79	355	710	299
-37	74	330	660	296
-40	68	307	614	294
-42	66	295	590	292
-46	61	274	548	287
-50	56	254	508	282
-54	51	234	468	273

Maximum Cruise Power: 14,000lbs/6350kg
1500 RPM/ISA -10°C

OAT	Torque per ENG	Fuel Flow per ENG	Total Fuel Flow	TAS
°C	(%)	(lbs/hour)	(lbs/hour)	(Kn)
5	100	530	1060	254
1	100	517	1034	259
-3	100	505	1010	264
-7	100	495	990	269
-11	100	486	972	274
-15	100	477	954	280
-19	100	469	938	285
-23	100	462	924	291
-27	100	456	914	297
-31	100	450	900	303
-35	97	435	870	306
-39	91	407	814	305
-43	85	379	758	304
-47	79	353	706	301
-50	73	328	656	299
-52	71	316	632	297
-56	65	294	588	294
-60	60	273	546	289
-64	55	252	504	282

Maximum Cruise Power: 14,000lbs/6350kg 1500 RPM/ISA +10°C				
OAT	Torque per ENG	Fuel Flow per ENG	Total Fuel Flow	TAS
°C	(%)	(lbs/hour)	(lbs/hour)	(Kn)
25	100	534	1068	259
21	100	521	1042	264
17	100	510	1020	269
13	100	499	998	274
9	100	489	978	279
5	100	480	960	285
1	98	464	928	289
-3	96	446	892	292
-7	92	426	852	284
-11	88	405	810	286
-15	83	379	758	285
-19	78	356	712	284
-23	74	333	666	283
-27	69	310	620	281
-30	64	287	574	287
-32	61	276	552	285
-36	56	255	510	280
-40	52	236	472	272
-44	47	217	434	261

Maximum Cruise Power: 14,000lbs/6350kg 1500 RPM/ISA +20°C				
OAT	Torque per ENG	Fuel Flow per ENG	Total Fuel Flow	TAS
°C	(%)	(lbs/hour)	(lbs/hour)	(Kn)
35	99	535	1070	260
31	97	515	1030	263
27	96	499	998	267
23	95	483	966	271
19	94	467	934	275
15	92	452	904	279
11	90	433	866	282
8	87	414	828	285
3	84	394	788	287
-1	80	374	748	288
-5	76	351	702	288
-9	72	329	658	287
-13	67	307	614	285
-17	63	286	572	282
-20	58	266	532	279
-22	56	257	514	276
-26	52	237	474	270
-30	47	219	438	261
-34	43	199	398	243

Maximum Cruise Power: 14,000lbs/6350kg

1500 RPM/ISA +30°C

OAT	Torque per ENG	Fuel Flow per ENG	Total Fuel Flow	TAS
°C	(%)	(lbs/hour)	(lbs/hour)	(Kn)
45	89	503	1006	253
41	87	481	962	255
37	86	464	928	259
33	85	449	898	263
29	84	436	872	267
25	84	423	846	272
21	81	404	808	275
17	78	384	768	277
13	75	363	726	278
9	72	343	686	278
5	68	321	642	277
1	64	301	602	276
-3	60	281	562	274
-7	56	262	524	271
-10	52	244	488	267
-12	50	235	470	264
-16	47	217	434	255
-20	42	199	398	240
-24	—	—	—	—

Maximum Cruise Power: 14,000lbs/6350kg

1500 RPM/ISA -30°C

OAT	Torque per ENG	Fuel Flow per ENG	Total Fuel Flow	TAS
°C	(%)	(lbs/hour)	(lbs/hour)	(Kn)
-15	48	338	676	186
-19	47	322	644	187
-23	46	308	616	189
-27	45	293	586	190
-31	43	278	556	191
-35	42	265	530	192
-39	42	253	506	194
-43	42	243	486	197
-37	41	233	466	200
-51	40	223	446	202
-55	40	215	430	205
-59	40	208	416	208
-63	40	201	402	211
-67	40	196	392	214
-70	40	192	384	219
-72	40	191	282	221
-76	41	190	380	226
-80	42	191	382	233
-84	41	188	376	233

Maximum Cruise Power: 14,000lbs/6350kg
1500 RPM/ISA -20°C

OAT	Torque per ENG	Fuel Flow per ENG	Total Fuel Flow	TAS
°C	(%)	(lbs/hour)	(lbs/hour)	(Kn)
-5	47	335	670	186
-9	47	323	646	189
-13	46	311	622	192
-17	46	299	598	195
-21	45	285	570	196
-25	44	272	544	198
-29	43	258	516	199
-33	42	248	496	202
-37	42	240	480	205
-41	42	231	462	209
-45	42	223	446	213
-49	42	217	434	216
-53	42	210	420	220
-57	42	204	408	223
-60	42	199	398	226
-62	41	196	392	227
-66	41	191	392	228
-70	42	194	388	236
-74	42	194	388	240

Maximum Cruise Power: 14,000lbs/6350kg
1500 RPM/ISA -10°C

OAT	Torque per ENG	Fuel Flow per ENG	Total Fuel Flow	TAS
°C	(%)	(lbs/hour)	(lbs/hour)	(Kn)
5	46	335	670	187
1	46	322	644	190
-3	45	310	620	193
-7	45	298	596	196
-11	45	287	574	199
-15	44	275	550	201
-19	44	264	528	204
-23	43	253	506	206
-27	43	243	486	209
-31	42	233	466	211
-35	42	224	448	214
-39	42	216	432	217
-43	41	209	418	220
-47	42	205	410	224
-50	42	203	406	230
-52	43	202	404	233
-56	43	199	398	237
-60	43	197	394	240
-64	43	199	388	245

Maximum Cruise Power: 14,000lbs/6350kg
1500 RPM/ISA

OAT °C	Torque per ENG (%)	Fuel Flow per ENG (lbs/hour)	Total Fuel Flow (lbs/hour)	TAS (Kn)
15	47	339	678	190
11	45	322	644	191
9	45	310	620	194
3	45	298	596	198
-1	44	286	572	199
-5	44	274	548	202
-9	43	263	526	205
-13	43	254	508	208
-17	43	245	490	211
-20	43	236	472	214
-25	43	229	458	219
-29	43	222	444	223
-33	43	216	432	226
-37	43	209	418	228
-40	43	204	408	232
-42	43	204	408	236
-46	44	205	410	243
-50	43	199	398	241
-54	40	190	380	229

Maximum Cruise Power: 14,000lbs/6350kg
1500 RPM/ISA +10°C

OAT °C	Torque per ENG (%)	Fuel Flow per ENG (lbs/hour)	Total Fuel Flow (lbs/hour)	TAS (Kn)
25	46	338	676	192
21	46	325	650	195
18	46	315	630	198
13	46	304	608	202
9	45	292	584	204
5	45	280	560	206
1	44	268	536	209
-3	44	258	516	212
-7	43	248	496	214
-11	43	238	476	217
-15	43	230	460	221
-19	43	225	450	225
-23	44	220	440	231
-27	44	217	434	236
-30	44	210	420	238
-32	43	206	412	237
-36	43	204	408	241
-40	45	210	420	251
-44	47	217	434	261

Maximum Cruise Power: 14,000lbs/6350kg
1500 RPM/ISA +20°C

OAT	Torque per ENG	Fuel Flow per ENG	Total Fuel Flow	TAS
°C	(%)	(lbs/hour)	(lbs/hour)	(Kn)
35	44	330	660	189
31	44	321	642	194
27	45	313	626	199
23	46	304	608	203
19	46	294	588	207
15	45	281	562	209
11	44	267	534	210
7	43	256	512	212
3	43	248	496	216
-1	43	241	482	220
-5	44	235	470	225
-9	44	228	456	228
-13	43	218	436	229
-17	43	213	426	232
-20	45	216	432	241
-22	45	216	432	245
-26	47	219	438	254
-30	47	219	438	261
-34	43	199	398	243

Maximum Cruise Power: 14,000lbs/6350kg
1500 RPM/ISA +30°C

OAT	Torque per ENG	Fuel Flow per ENG	Total Fuel Flow	TAS
°C	(%)	(lbs/hour)	(lbs/hour)	(Kn)
45	45	336	672	192
41	43	319	638	192
37	44	311	622	198
33	45	304	608	204
29	45	293	586	208
25	44	280	560	209
21	43	267	534	211
17	43	258	516	214
13	43	249	498	218
9	43	240	480	221
5	43	232	464	223
1	44	231	462	231
-3	46	229	458	239
-7	46	227	454	245
-10	47	225	450	252
-12	48	225	450	255
-16	47	217	434	255
-20	42	199	398	240
-24	—	—	—	—

Special Considerations

As we briefly mentioned earlier, Edwards Air Force Base's R-2515 restricted airspace lies directly to the north and northwest of VCV. The name Edwards may sound familiar—it's where many of the most advanced military aircraft are tested. (It used to be named Muroc Air Force Base— where Chuck Yeager and other brave pilots made history.)

Anyway, to the civil aviation world restricted airspace means you can't fly in it without clearance. If you do, you risk flying in formation with a couple of F-16 fighters while they take your picture so they can send it to the FAA!

Flight Tutorial

As we've done in our earlier tutorials, we first need to switch to the aircraft in question—this time, the King Air 350. Because we'll be flying IFR and using the GPS, we need to create and load a flight plan into the GPS next. We'll come back to the other particulars of this flight in a minute.

Loading the GPS

To program the GPS for this trip, we use *Flight Simulator 2000*'s flight planner. Enter KSEA as your departure airport, KVCV as your destination airport, then KONT as your alternate. Next click the IFR Flight Plan button and the Direct-GPS Auto Routing button. When you're done, click the Find Route button (see Figure 7.10).

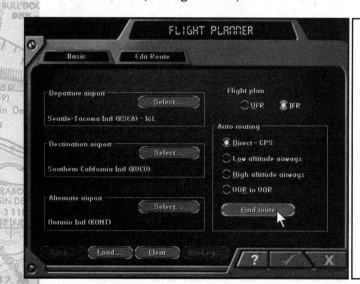

Figure 7.10:
Enter the basic flight plan info here.

Once the route is generated, the flight planner will automatically bring us to the Edit Route screen. Enter our cruise altitude (25,000 feet) in the Cruising Altitude box in the lower-left corner. Next click on KVCV on the

Waypoint list box on the right side of the screen, as shown in Figure 7.11. This will zoom KVCV up in the Map view.

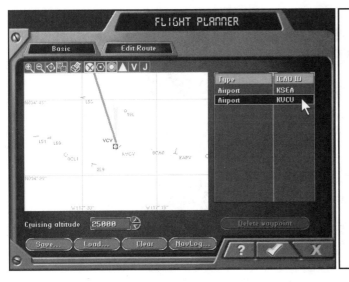

Figure 7.11:
Selecting a waypoint from the list will cause the Map window to zoom in on it.

We need to enter PMD VOR as a waypoint, so click on the Zoom Out icon (the magnifying glass with the minus sign in it) above the Map view twice. Now drag the red course line over to KPMD, as shown in Figure 7.12. This will bring up the Facilities window. Select VOR PALMDALE (PMD) from the list (Figure 7.13) and click the green checkmark button to close the window.

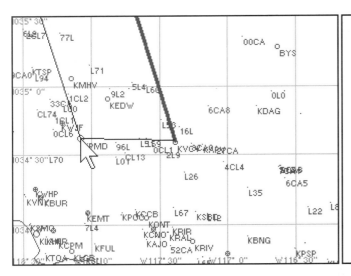

Figure 7.12:
Dragging the red course line over a NAVAID or airport will add it the waypoint list.

Now we need to add VCV VOR as a waypoint. (Remember, the flight planner has us going to the airport, but we need to fly to the VOR.) To do this, click on KVCV in the list box on the right side of the screen again; the Map view will zoom back on KVCV. Drag the red course line over VCV

VOR (see Figure 7.14). The Facilities window will appear again. Select VOR VICTORVILLE (VCV) from the list and click the green checkmark button.

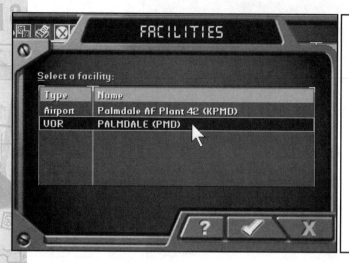

Figure 7.13:
If more than one NAVAID or airport exists in an area, this Facilities window will appear to let you select the one you want.

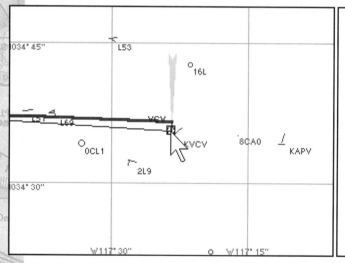

Figure 7.14:
The flight planner has us going to the KVCV airport, but we need to fly to the VOR for the approach.

When you're finished, click the green checkmark button at the bottom of the Flight Planner window and save your flight plan. Once you've saved the file, it'll automatically be loaded into the GPS.

Navigation Log

One of the neatest things about using the flight planner in *Flight Simulator 2000* is that it automatically creates a navigation log for you. You can access the navigation log by selecting Navigation Log from the Flights menu (Figure 7.15).

▶ **Warning**

The navigation log is a pretty neat feature, but be wary of its ETE times and fuel estimates. They're all based on a single ground speed.

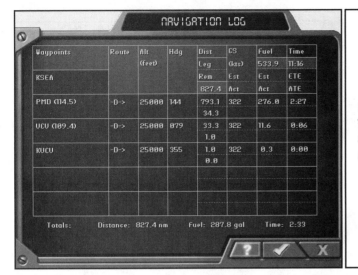

NAVIGATION LOG

Waypoints	Route	Alt (feet)	Hdg	Dist Leg	CS (kts)	Fuel	Time
				Leg	(kts)	533.9	11:16
KSEA				Rem	Est	Est	ETE
				827.4	Act	Act	ATE
PMD (114.5)	-D->	25000	144	793.1	322	276.0	2:27
				34.3			
UCU (109.4)	-D->	25000	079	33.3	322	11.6	0:06
				1.0			
KUCU	-D->	25000	355	1.0	322	0.3	0:00
				0.0			

Totals: Distance: 827.4 nm   Fuel: 287.8 gal   Time: 2:33

Figure 7.15:
The flight planner automatically creates a navigation log for you.

Setting Up the Tutorial Flight (Part 2)

Now that we've got the flight plan and GPS out of the way, we'll move the aircraft to North 47°29.09', West 122°18.20', Altitude +433, and Heading 1 using the Map View dialogue. We'll be at the North Satellite Ramp, which is about midfield on the east side of the airport (see Figure 7.16 for details).

On this IFR flight, we'll be performing the now much better understood DME arc approach. As such, the time and weather at VCV won't make as much of a difference to us as it might if we were to attempt this trip VFR. But we still need to watch for very low visibility (3/4 mile, 200-foot ceiling) and extremely high winds that might prevent us from landing on runway 17. We also need to meet the standard for twin-engine aircraft takeoff minimums at SEA (1 statute mile visibility).

Before Engine Start

If you're going to start the engines, you'll need to shut them down first by pressing Ctrl+Shift+F1.

Action	Response
Weight and CG	CHECKED
Airstair Door/Cargo Door	LOCKED

Airstair is a fancy name for the door that has a built-in staircase/ladder.

Load and Baggage	SECURE
Aft Exit Sign Switch	ON-TEST, OFF-RESET

An internal G switch will automatically activate this light in the event of a crash or very hard landing. Placing the switch in Reset mode arms it. (This option is not modeled in *Flight Simulator 2000*.)

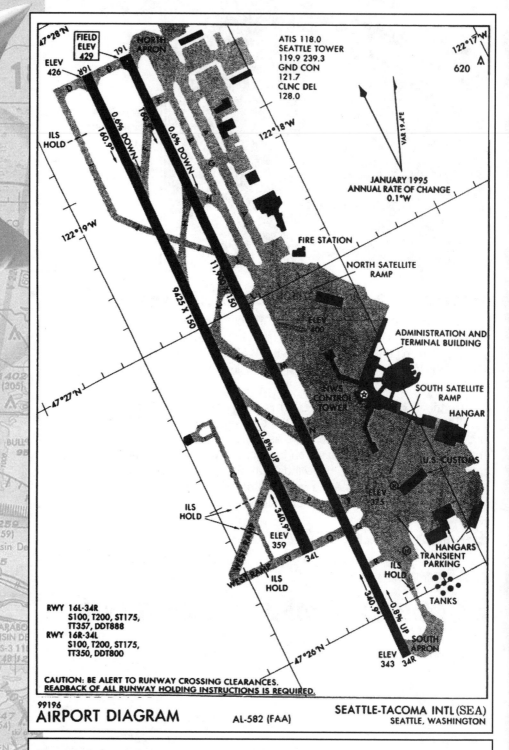

Figure 7.16: Seattle-Tacoma International Airport Diagram

Emergency Exits	**SECURE AND UNLOCKED**
Seats	**POSITIONED, UPRIGHT**
Seatbelts and Shoulder Harnesses	**FASTENED**
Parking Brake	**SET**

Press Ctrl+"." (period) to engage the parking brake.

Control Locks	**REMOVE**

Control locks are locking pins used to keep the flight controls from moving in the wind while the aircraft is parked.

Left Panel Circuit Breakers	**IN**
Fuel and Pilot's Subpanel Switches	**AS REQUIRED**
Engine Anti-Ice	**ON**

The engine anti-ice system is a centrifugal diverter that prevents ice and/or other debris from entering the engine intakes. All of the anti-ice systems (engines, tail, wings, and brakes) in *Flight Simulator 2000*'s King Air 350 are operated by a single control (Figure 7.17) located next to the pitot heat switch on the bottom-left side of the instrument panel.

Figure 7.17:
This anti-ice switch toggles all of the King Air 350's anti-ice systems.

Landing Gear Relay Circuit Breaker	**IN**
Landing Gear Control	**DN**

The default landing gear handle position is down, so you won't have to do anything here.

Landing Gear Alternate Extension Handle	**STOWED**

This is the emergency gear extension pump handle. If this handle isn't stowed, it can cause a loss of hydraulic pressure in the landing gear system. Although the handle itself isn't modeled in *Flight Simulator 2000*, you can still pump down the gear in an emergency, as if there were a handle, by repeatedly pressing Ctrl+G.

Power Levers	**IDLE**

Power levers are another name for the throttle controls. Press Shift+4 to bring up the Throttle Quadrant window (Figure 7.18). Bring the throttles down to idle by using your throttle controller (if you have one)—drag them with your mouse or press E+1+2 followed by F1.

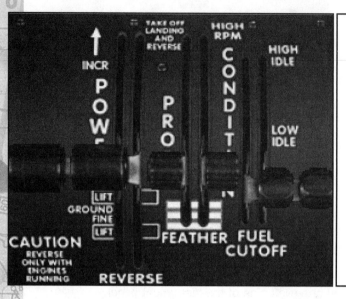

Figure 7.18:
The King Air 350's throttle quadrant

Propeller Controls   FULL FORWARD

With the throttle quadrant still visible, drag the prop controls to full forward (to the top of the screen) with your mouse or press E+1+2 followed by Ctrl+F4.

Condition Levers   FUEL CUTOFF

Condition levers act as fuel controls for the engines. They perform the same cut off function as mixture controls on internal combustion engines, but they won't lean the mixture/increase fuel economy on turbine engines. To move the condition levers, drag them with your mouse all the way down towards the bottom of the screen, or press E+1+2 followed by Ctrl+Shift+F1.

Vent Blower   AUTO

The vent blower is a cockpit ventilation fan. It and other environmental devices are turned off to reduce power consumption/drain in preparation for engine start.

Cabin Temp Mode	OFF
Aft Blower	OFF

The aft blower is another ventilation fan. It is in the rear cabin. (Not modeled.)

Electric Heat	OFF
Aft Heat	AS REQUIRED
Right Panel Circuit Breakers	IN
Pilot's Static Air Source	NORMAL

Both the pilot and copilot have their own individual pitot-static systems (pitot tubes and static sources) and related instruments. The pilot's static air source has two positions: Normal and Alt. Normal uses the external static source, and Alt uses the alternate interior static source.

Battery Bus	NORM

The battery bus can be thought of as a battery circuit panel. Every electrical item connected to the battery bus is hooked up to the battery when the battery bus is, in turn, connected to the battery. Separate electrical buses allow alternate means of providing power to electrical equipment. This operation is handled automatically for you.

Battery	ON

The battery switch is located on the far-left side of the instrument panel.

Oxygen Control	PULL ON SYSTEM STANDBY
Oxygen System Preflight Inspection	CONFIRM COMPLETE
Firewall Fuel Valves	CLOSE

This and the next three steps allow you to pressurize the fuel system without forcing excess fuel into the engines (by closing the fuel valves first). All of these steps are handled for you automatically.

Standby Fuel Pumps	ON
Firewall Fuel Valves	OPEN
Standby Fuel Pumps	OFF
Crossfeed	ALTERNATELY LEFT AND RIGHT

The crossfeed pump allows you to pump fuel from one side of the aircraft to the other. It comes in handy if you have an engine out and need to

balance the wings or to extend the range on the remaining engine. The crossfeed pump control (Figure 7.19) is located between the two fuel gauges along the bottom center of the control panel.

Crossfeed	OFF
Fuel Quantity	CHECK (MAIN AND AUXILIARY)

Check your fuel on board by selecting Fuel from the Aircraft menu.

Figure 7.19:
The crossfeed pump control is located between these two fuel gauges.

Cabin Altitude Warn	TEST

Aircraft pressurization systems only pressurize cabins to the level of a lower altitude than what the aircraft is flying at (not sea level or "ground altitude"). It's impractical to maintain very low cabin altitudes because the *differential pressure* (the difference in pressure between the outside air and inside the cabin) would require increased structural strength. Humans can tolerate altitudes up to 12,500 feet without detriment, so adding the ability to pressurize an aircraft below that level at the highest cruise altitude simply adds unnecessary weight to the aircraft.

The cabin altitude warning lets the flight crew know that the cabin pressure has become lower (that is, equivalent to a higher altitude) than the cabin pressure setting. Testing this warning ensures that the warning light and warning horn are working properly. These systems are not modeled in *Flight Simulator 2000*.

Cabin Differential Warn	TEST

This test is the same as above, but it's for the cabin differential pressure system.

Overspeed Warn	TEST

The overspeed warning is just what it sounds like: it warns you when you fly faster than the aircraft can tolerate (V_{MO}). This system is modeled as part of *Flight Simulator* but not as an individual aircraft system, which means you can't test it. But on the bright side, it means it'll never fail either!

Stall Warn/Landing Gear Warn   **TEST**

The stall warning system is like the overspeed warning because it's also built into *Flight Simulator 2000* and not into individual aircraft (so you can't test it). The landing gear warning can't be tested either, but it's aircraft dependent. The King Air 350's gear warning system horn will sound and indicate a gear unsafe condition (red lights on the gear handle will light up) when the flaps are in the Up or Approach setting and either or both power levers are set below 85 percent N_1. Figure 7.20 shows the landing gear warning lights and the landing gear extension handle.

Figure 7.20:
The gear warning lights are located to the right of the gear handle.

Engine Fire Test   **DET AND EXT**

Not modeled.

Annunciator Lights   **TEST**

The King Air has two sets of annunciator lights, shown in Figure 7.21. One set is for warning items and the other is for caution items. To view the annunciator panels, click on the Master Warning and Master Caution lights above the AI on the instrument panel. The Master Warning lights are for oil and fuel pressure.

Figure 7.21: Master Warning (left) and Master Caution (right) annunciator light panels.

The caution panel lights and indications, from top left to right, are shown in Table 7.1.

Table 7.1 Caution Panel Lights

Light	Indication
L DC GEN	Left engine DC generator not operating
L FUEL QTY	Left tank fuel quantity; illuminates at less than 265 pounds fuel
RVS NOT READY	Thrust reversers not ready
AUTOFEATHER OFF	Autofeather disarmed
R FUEL QTY	Right tank fuel quantity; illuminates at less than 265 pounds fuel
R DC GEN	Right engine DC generator not operating
TAIL DE-ICE	Tail surface de-ice activated
WING DE-ICE	Wing surface de-ice activated
L IGNITION ON	Left engine ignition engaged
L ENGINE ANTI-ICE	Left engine anti-ice engaged
*L BK DE-ICE ON	Left wheel brake de-ice engaged
FUEL CROSSFEED	Crossfeed pump activated
*R BK DE-ICE ON	Right wheel brake de-ice engaged
R ENGINE ANTI-ICE	Right engine anti-ice engaged
R IGNITION ON	Right engine ignition engaged
LDG/TAXI LIGHT	Landing light activated

These next two tests are just to make sure that the warning lights are not burned out.

Action	Response
Landing Gear HDL LT	TEST
Hyd Fluid Sensor	TEST
Beacon	ON

Click the beacon switch on the lighting panel (Figure 7.22) with your mouse.

Figure 7.22:
This lighting panel is located just to the right of the fuel gauges.

Engine Starting

Action	Response
Right Ignition and Engine Start	ON

Click and hold the right engine start switch (Figure 7.23).

Figure 7.23:
The left and right ignition and engine start switches are on the lower-left side of the instrument panel, above the anti-ice switch.

▶ **Tip**

This engine start procedure requires a lot of keyboard gymnastics. So keep in mind that, as with all of Flight Simulator 2000's aircraft, both engines can be started automatically by pressing Ctrl+E.

Right Condition Lever	LOW IDLE (AFTER N1 12% MINIMUM)

Press Shift+4 to bring up the throttle quadrant, and either use your mouse to advance the right condition lever to the Low Idle position or press E+2 and then repeatedly press Ctrl+Shift+F3.

ITT and N1	MONITOR (1,000°C MAXIMUM)

The ITT (Interstage Turbine Temperature) gauges monitor the temperature between the turbine and the compressor. The ITT and N_1 gauges are located in the center engine gauge cluster, shown in Figure 7.24.

Figure 7.24:
The N_1 gauges are the fourth gauges down (labeled RPM) from the top, and they indicate the turbine's RPM.

Right Oil Pressure	CHECK

Oil pressure is on the right side of the bottom gauges in the engine gauge cluster. Check that the oil pressure reading is within the green range. If it isn't, you'll need to shut the engine down by placing the right condition lever to the Fuel Cutoff position before the engine is damaged.

Right Condition Lever	HIGH IDLE

Move the right condition lever to High Idle (to prevent the engine from stalling while starting the other engine) by pressing Ctrl+Shift+F4.

Right Ignition and Engine Start	OFF (AT 50% N_1 OR ABOVE)
Right Generator	RESET, THEN ON

Each engine's starter doubles as a power generator (motors can generate power when they're turned externally). What you're doing here is resetting the generator's circuit breaker and then placing the generator online to generate power. The right generator (GEN 2) is located just to the left of the starter switches.

Left Ignition and Engine Start	ON

Starting the left engine is identical to the right engine start procedure. The only change command-wise is to use the 1 key (reflecting the left engine number) instead of 2.

Left Condition Lever	LOW IDLE (AFTER N_1 12% MINIMUM)
ITT and N_1	MONITOR (1,000°C MAXIMUM)
Left Oil Pressure	CHECK
Left Ignition and Engine Start	OFF (AT 50% N_1 OR ABOVE)
Right Condition Lever	REDUCE TO LOW IDLE
Voltmeter Bus Select	L GEN (CONFIRM 27.5 – 29.0 VOLTS)
Left Generator	RESET, THEN ON
Gen Ties	OPEN

Gen ties are essentially generator circuit couplings. They connect the two generator bus relays to the same circuit. The Open position isolates the generator buses from the center bus. These operations are handled for you automatically.

Voltmeter Bus Select	TPL FED (CONFIRM 26.5–28.0V)

Just for your information, this step connects the voltmeter to the three buses (TPL=Triple). It and the three next items are not modeled in *Flight Simulator 2000*'s King Air 350.

Bus Sense	TEST
Bus Sense	RESET
Generator Load	OBSERVE PARALLELED WITHIN 10%

Before Taxi

Action	Response
Panel Lights	AS REQUIRED
Mic Switches	NORMAL
Cabin Lights/Furnishings	AS REQUIRED
Cabin Signs	NO SMK/FSB

These are the No Smoking and Fasten Seat Belts signs.

Inverters	CHECK

Inverters change DC power to AC.

Avionics Master	ON

The King Air 350's avionics master switch (Figure 7.25) is located in the lower-left corner of the instrument panel.

**Figure 7.25:
The avionics master switch**

Lights	AS REQUIRED
Environmental Cabin Controls	AS REQUIRED
Instruments	CHECK

This is your basic instrument check. Bring up the radio stack (Shift+2) and dial up SEA ATIS (118.0) on COM1. Press the B key to set your ALT and the D key to set your DG.

Brakes	RELEASED AND CHECKED

Release the brake by pressing the "." (period) key, then increase power slightly to begin rolling. As soon as the aircraft starts to roll, reduce power and press the "." key to check whether the brakes are working. It's far better to find out now about brake problems then when you need to stop while taxiing or after a landing.

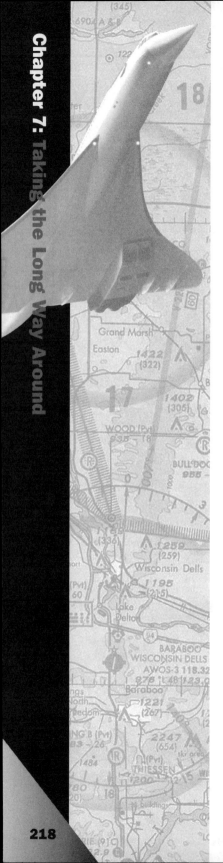

When you're set, go ahead and taxi out to runway 16R. Be sure to keep an eye out for landing traffic when you cross 16L.

Before Takeoff

Action	Response
Avionics and Radar	CHECK

Double-check that radios and navigation equipment are on and not on standby. To prepare for our flight, first slave the HSI (Figure 7.26) to the GPS by toggling the NAV/GPS switch located at the base of the HSI. You don't need to worry about radar because our airplane isn't equipped with it.

Figure 7.26:
The NAV/GPS switch is located at the base of the HSI.

Pressurization	CHECK AND SET
Autopilot	CHECK

There's a whole autopilot testing procedure that a pilot runs through to check the system. Needless to say, the reliability of the autopilot in *Flight Simulator 2000* is exemplary, so we don't need to test it.

Yaw Control	CHECK

The yaw damper switch is located on the autopilot panel. To check the real King Air's yaw damper, the pilot engages it and tests the rudder pedal movement for increased resistance. Of course, we don't get that kind of feedback; nevertheless to toggle the yaw damper, click the Y/D button (alternately you can press Ctrl+D).

Electric Pitch Trim Control	CHECK
Trim Tabs	SET

Set the trim tabs for takeoff positions by using the KP7 and KP1 (KeyPad) keys (with Num Lock off) for elevator trim, Ctrl+KP4 and Ctrl+KP6 (Num Lock off) for aileron, and rudder trim with Ctrl+KP0 and Ctrl+KPEnter. The default positions (centered) are fine.

Engine Control Friction Locks	SET

These mechanical friction clamps keep the engine control levers in the position that the pilot left them at. They are hardware related, so there's nothing to do in *Flight Simulator 2000*.

Flaps	CHECK AND SET

We won't be using any flaps for takeoff.

Flight Controls	FREE AND CORRECT
Engine Anti-Ice	CHECK
Primary Governors	EXERCISE AT 1500 RPM

Exercising the prop governors lets you stress them a bit (so if there's a problem, hopefully it'll expose itself while you're still on the ground) and circulate oil through them. Increase power using the F3 key to 1,500 RPM, then either use your mouse or press Ctrl+F1 and Ctrl+F4 to minimum RPM for a second and return the props back to minimum pitch/maximum RPM. Three cycles is standard. Return the engines back to idle at 1,150–1,250 RPM.

Ground Idle Low Pitch Stops	CHECK

In the real King Air, you need to lift the throttle levers over a gate to enter Ground Idle Low pitch. In *Flight Simulator 2000*, press F1 once and then F2 twice.

Autofeather	CHECK
Autofeather	ARM
Propeller Feather (manual)	CHECK

To manually feather the props, press and hold Ctrl+F2. Press Ctrl+F4 to return the props back to high RPM.

Instrument Vacuum/De-Ice Pressure System	CHECK (AT IDLE)

Recall that your gyro instruments (except for the turn and slip indicator) run on vacuum pressure. The de-icing systems that require air pressure are the de-icing boots on the wings and tail. De-icing boots are like balloons that inflate to break off any accumulated ice. There isn't any suction gauge modeled for the King Air 350 in *Flight Simulator 2000*.

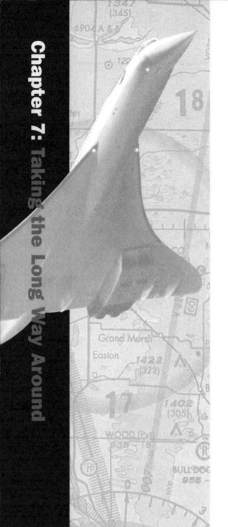

Fuel Quantity, Flight, and Engine Instruments	CHECK
Electric Heat	OFF
Aft Blower	OFF
Bleed Air Valves	AS REQUIRED
Envir Bleed Air	NORMAL OR LOW (AS REQUIRED)
Cabin Temp Mode	AS REQUIRED
Ice Protection	AS REQUIRED
Eng Auto Ignition	AS REQUIRED

Eng auto ignition automatically keeps the engines from losing combustion (flaming out) by providing an ignition source if required. It's used during take off and landing and when flying through rain, icing conditions, and turbulence, to back up the primary ignition system. This system is handled automatically by *Flight Simulator 2000*.

Generator Load	CHECK
Annunciator Lights	EXTINGUISHED
Lights	AS REQUIRED

As a safety precaution, you'd turn on all of your exterior lights (including taxi lights) even in the daylight to make your aircraft as visible as possible.

Transponder	ON
V_1, V_R, V_2, Static Take-off Power	CONFIRM

Now is the time to confirm your takeoff calculations. Static take-off power is the maximum power available (that will meet takeoff requirements of course) without exceeding any engine limitations.

Takeoff

Taxi out to the runway and do your thing.

Action	Response
Brakes	HOLD
Power Levers	SET STATIC TAKE-OFF POWER

Advance the throttle with your throttle controller or mouse or press E+1+2 and F4 on your keyboard. Keep ITT (Interstage Turbine Temperature) and TORQ indicators below redline.

> **▶ Tip**
>
> *You can achieve the same effect as holding the brakes by applying the parking brakes (Ctrl+"." [period] instead).*

Autofeather Annunciator	ILLUMINATED
Brakes	RELEASE

Press the "." (period) key to release the brakes.

V_R	ROTATE TO APPROXIMATELY 10° PITCH ATTITUDE
Landing Gear	UP

After establishing a positive rate of climb, press the G key to retract the landing gear.

Airspeed	MAINTAIN V35 (UNTIL CLEAR OF OBSTACLES)

Recall that V_{35} is V_2+6 knots. Use pitch to maintain airspeed until clear of any obstacles.

Flaps	UP (BLUE LINE, 125 KIAS MINIMUM)

If you had flaps deployed, you can raise them above 125 KIAS by pressing the F5 key.

Maintain runway heading on climb out. Upon climbing through 500 feet AGL (930 feet), we can engage the autopilot. Another way to access the autopilot settings is by selecting Autopilot from the Aircraft menu. Activate the autopilot, then click the HDG box and enter 166 degrees in it. Next click the ALT mode selection. Enter 25,000 feet in the Altitude Hold box and +1,500 feet in the Vertical Speed box.

Climb

Action	Response
Bleed Air Valves	OPEN
Yaw Damp	ON

Click the Y/D button or press Ctrl+D to engage the yaw damper.

Climb Power	SET

The maximum climb power is 100 percent torque or ITT 820°C, as read by engine gauges.

Propellers	1,600 RPM

Reduce prop RPM by pressing Ctrl+F2 several times until N_2 reads 1,600 RPM.

Propeller Synchrophaser	ON

Click on the Prop Sync button once.

Engine Instruments	MONITOR

You're just checking that everything is still in the green ranges. If there are any discrepancies, it's better to turn back to the airport now than wait until you get too far away and are unable to glide back.

Cabin Sign	AS REQUIRED
Pressurization	CHECK
Lights	AS REQUIRED

Once you're outside of traffic areas, it's okay to turn off your landing and taxi lights.

After climbing through 7,300 feet, go ahead and turn on the NAV mode on the autopilot. It is coupled to the GPS, so it'll take us directly to PMD.

> ▶ **Note**
>
> *Don't forget to set your ALT to 29.92 after crossing FL180.*

Cruise

Upon reaching cruise altitude, set your aircraft's cruise configuration.

Action	Response
Cruise Power	SET PER CRUISE POWER TABLES

We'll be using 1,500 RPM and 77 percent torque for cruise.

Autofeather	OFF
Aft Blower	AS REQUIRED
Engine Instruments	MONITOR
Auxiliary Fuel Gauge	MONITOR

While we've got some time to kill, let's set up our avionics for the approach. First enter VCV VOR frequency (109.4) in NAV1, then enter I-VCV frequency in NAV2 (108.75). (We can use NAV2 as a reference while we change frequencies from the arc to the ILS.) Finally, we dial VCV ATIS in COM1.

That's about all we can do now. Sit back and enjoy the flight—while you can!

Descent

About 15 DME before crossing PMD VOR, we need to begin our descent to 6,700 feet. We won't have to fiddle with the radios because we're running on the GPS, and it changes all of our waypoints for us.

Action	Response
Pressurization	SET
Altimeter	SET

You'll have the new ALT setting from ATIS. Pressing the B key will set the ALT after descending below FL180.

Action	Response
Cabin Sign	AS REQUIRED
Windshield Anti-Ice	AS REQUIRED
Window Defog	ON
Autofeather	ARM
Fuel Balance	CHECK
Power	AS REQUIRED

Reduce power as required, but keep ITT in the green arcs to keep the engines within their normal operating ranges. Bring the power back to about 75 percent N_1 and dial 6,700 feet in the autopilot.

Approach

About 5 DME from crossing VCV VOR, flip the NAV/GPS switch to NAV and dial in 055 degrees on the HSI OBS. Once we cross VCV VOR, the autopilot will track the 055 radial outbound. At this point we also need to descend a bit further to 6,500 feet, then dial the new altitude into the autopilot. You may need to increase power a bit to 80 percent N_1 to maintain airspeed after you level off at 6,500 feet.

Watch the DME click up towards 13.5 (that will mark TRNDL) while you complete the approach checklist.

Action	Response
Approach Speeds	CONFIRM
Pressurization	CHECK
Cabin Sign	NO SMK/FSB
Flaps	APPROACH

Set flaps to the Approach setting by pressing F7 once or by clicking on the flap control. (See Figure 7.27.)

Action	Response
Landing Gear	DN

Extend landing gear by pressing the G key, then watch for three green lights indicating gear is down and locked.

Lights   **AS REQUIRED**

Figure 7.27:
Flaps can be controlled
from here.

Same drill again—when you're near traffic areas (such as an airport), turn on all of your lights.

Radar	AS REQUIRED
Envir Bleed Air	LOW
Surface De-Ice	CYCLE (AS REQUIRED)

At 13.0 DME from TRNDL, take the autopilot out of NAV mode and make a left turn to heading 225 degrees. Hold that heading until the CDI deflects/moves to the first index (the dot), then turn to heading 215 degrees and twist the OBS to 045 degrees. (You may find it easier to press the V key followed by the – (hyphen) key to do this.) The sequence of OBS settings and the related course heading changes are listed in the table that follows, for your convenience:

OBS Setting	Course Heading
055°	255°
045°	245°
035°	235°
025°	225°
015°	215°
005°	205°
355°	195°

▶ *Tip*

You can quickly determine the first tangent heading by looking at the heading under the nine o'clock position on the HSI for left turn arcs. For right turn arcs, look under the three o'clock position.

One of the neatest things about flying DME arcs with GPS is that you can track your progress on the moving map. Figure 7.28 shows that we're right on course.

When you get to 355 radial (the CDI centers with the OBS on 355 degrees), remember to turn inbound to the ILS. First tune in the ILS frequency on NAV1 (it's the same as what's in NAV2 right now—108.75). Even though the OBS won't change the radial it reads on an ILS, it's best to rotate it on an HSI to avoid any possible confusion. So set the OBS to 166 degrees.

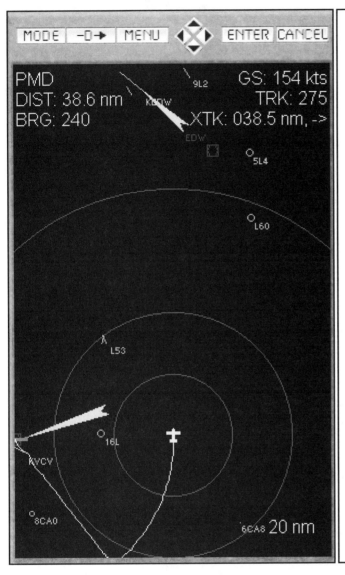

MODE −□→ MENU ◀◆▶ ENTER CANCEL

PMD
DIST: 38.6 nm
BRG: 240

9L2
KBQW

GS: 154 kts
TRK: 275
XTK: 038.5 nm, ->

EDW

5L4

L60

L53

16L

KVCV

SCA0

6CA8 20 nm

Figure 7.28:
The GPS Moving Map mode is wonderful for showing your DME arc progress.

You can descend to 5,000 feet after you begin your turn, so lower the autopilot altitude setting to 5,000. Once you intercept the glideslope, you can either hand fly the ILS or you can let the autopilot do it by pressing the APPR button. (Most commercial carriers require that pilots hand-fly approaches.) The MDA is 3,028 feet.

Landing

When landing is assured, perform the landing checklist. If you're allowing the autopilot to fly the ILS, be sure to disengage it above 500 AGL.

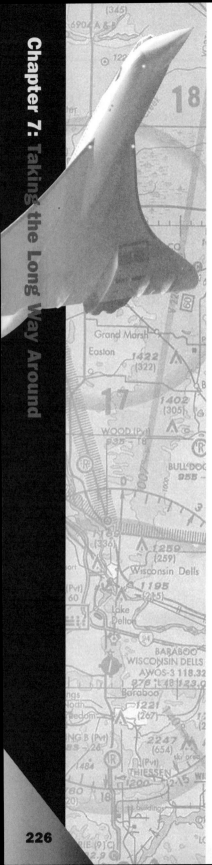

Action	Response
Flaps	DOWN

Deploy full flaps by pressing F7 again.

Action	Response
Airspeed	V_{REF}
Yaw Damp	OFF

You don't want the airplane fighting you if you're landing in a crosswind or if you need to fly in a slip. Turning the yaw damper off lets you move the nose of the airplane where you need it without any correctional resistance from the aircraft.

Action	Response
Condition Levers	HIGH IDLE

This setting is in preparation for reverse thrust application after touchdown. Reverse thrust is maximized when the engines are running at high idle.

Action	Response
Propellers	FULL FORWARD

Press Ctrl+F4 to move the props full forward. This is done in preparation in case a go-around is necessary. Having one less thing to worry about should a go-around become necessary will lighten your workload in that potentially dangerous procedure.

After touchdown, follow this checklist:

Action	Response
Power Levers	LIFT AND SELECT GROUND FINE AND LIFT TO REVERSE

Pressing and holding the F2 key will place the engines in reverse thrust mode.

Action	Response
Brakes	AS REQUIRED
Condition Levers	LOW IDLE

Once the aircraft is sufficiently slowed (to taxi speed), return the throttles to ground fine (press F1 once, followed by F2 twice) and move the condition levers to Low Idle by pressing Ctrl+Shift+F2 several times until N_1 is at the bottom of the green arc.

After Landing

Action	Response
Lights	AS REQUIRED
Engine Anti-Ice	ON
Ice Protection	OFF
Transponder	STBY
Radar	STANDBY OR OFF
Trim	SET

This checklist isn't just a courtesy for the next crew—it's to prevent possible damage to trim tabs that aren't in line with their control surfaces.

Action	Response
Flaps	UP

Press F5 to return the flaps to their fully retracted position. This action helps prevent damage and reduces aerodynamic forces during windy conditions.

Shutdown

Action	Response
Parking Brake	SET

Press Ctrl+"." (period).

Action	Response
Electric Heat	OFF
Avionics Master	OFF
Inverters	OFF
Autofeather	OFF
Exterior Lights	OFF
Vent Blower	AUTO
Cabin Temp Mode	OFF
Aft Blower	OFF
Aft Heat	AS DESIRED
Oxygen Controls	PUSH OFF
Battery	CHARGED

Some earlier models of the King Air 350 series had rechargeable ni-cad batteries.

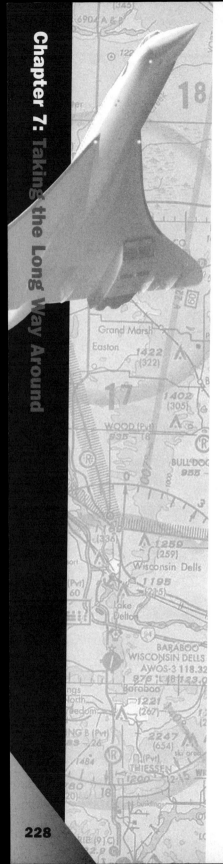

Brake De-Ice	ON, THEN OFF
ITT	STABILIZED AT MINIMUM TEMPERATURE FOR ONE MINUTE

Shutting an engine down while it's still very hot can cause all kinds of mechanical and lubrication problems.

CONDITION LEVERS	FUEL CUTOFF

Press Ctrl+Shift+F1.

You made it! You should feel proud. Tackling the DME arc requires good situational awareness. You can't even bluff your way through these approaches without having at least a clue where you are, so if you made it you must have done it right. Well done!

Expanding
Flight Simulator
2000's Horizons

Chapter 8

F light Simulator 2000 *functions as the nucleus of a total simulation environment. Its fundamental elements include the world, an aircraft, its instrumentation, and its movement through the environment (air and weather). Microsoft has always included a robust complement of these features with its product, including detailed aircraft realism, accurate procedures, and photo-realistic scenery. In addition, thousands of freeware, shareware, and commercial components are available for items ranging from history's most exotic aircraft to down-to-the-button realistic flight management computers (FMCs) and real-time air traffic control. Each* Flight Simulator *release incorporates many of the best such features as a natural part of its evolution.*

Both commercially oriented aviation software developers and labor of love-driven individuals have invested countless hours of their own resources to create what many people consider to be their personal "ultimate" simulation experience. The following paragraphs outline some of the possibilities, including types of, and sources for, add-ons and some caveats about using them. You'll also find ideas for creating features of your own with which to augment Flight Simulator 2000*'s already vast array.*

—Bill Hoscheit

The Simulation Platform

Unfortunately, in the past *Flight Simulator* has been considered an "entertainment" software product. However, *Microsoft Flight Simulator*'s features are more realistic and diverse than many high-end commercial products. It has evolved to include real-world, real-time weather, detailed and accurate operating procedures, and tools for managing and navigating flights as it's done in reality. Even the novice can enjoy the thrill of jumping into the left seat and parting the clouds without first investing thousands of flight hours.

What makes this possible? Microsoft's team of developers and designers has ensured that *Flight Simulator*'s features extend well beyond itself. Scores of specialized products help designers create realistic aircraft, instruments, scenery, and a variety of other specialties. A Software Development Kit (SDK) provides instruction in creating custom components with today's popular development tools, including Visual C++. Like the *Windows* operating system itself, *Flight Simulator* is as much an environment in which other components run as it is a simulator. The possibilities are endless.

Everything but the Kitchen Sink

On the hard disks of tens of thousands of flight simulation enthusiasts, you can find virtually any aircraft, instrument panel, or airline livery that's ever existed. Some developers are known for creating highly detailed regional and local scenery areas that bring most hometown geography and airports to life. Commercial software developers provide an endless variety of companion products for adding or improving features. Regardless of origin, some basic companion categories exist:

1. Aircraft, including instrument panels, sounds, checklists, and some truly breathtaking liveries

2. Scenery, with detailed global, regional, and local supplements covering virtually the entire world

3. Navigation, instrumentation, and other flight management tools

4. Capabilities for extended interactivity, multipilot interaction, and air traffic control

   The hundreds of other items are too diverse to mention. Each can add something special, like Adventures that can challenge even the most seasoned flyers.

Aircraft

Aircraft is the most prolific type of Flight Simulator add-on. Aircraft development tools are affordable and readily available, and creating an aircraft doesn't require weeks or months of sweat and tears. Because you can substitute texture files, paint scheme, and external appearance, a single model can become scores of different aircraft.

The aircraft developer community is vast and offers virtually every conceivable plane and paint combination. Commercial products vary, from specialized themes, featuring a single aircraft or aircraft family, to comprehensive collections of hundreds of types. Relatively small file sizes make them quick and easy downloads and *Flight Simulator*'s aircraft structure makes adding them a breeze.

Scenery

Each pilot has a favorite kind of scenery. Perhaps it covers the area where a pilot lives, or details a hometown airport. *Flight Simulator* comes with several highly detailed renderings, mostly of the areas around large cities, like Chicago and Los Angeles. Its comprehensive database also provides many secondary, tertiary, and grass strip fields. In fact, you'd be hard pressed to find an airport that *Flight Simulator* doesn't include in some manner. Unlike the photo-realistic areas, many of these airports are made up of rudimentary runways, taxiways, and control towers that are only identifiable by their layout. However, an endless variety of scenery products can bring virtually every type of scenery area to life. *Flight Simulator 2000* offers mesh terrain scenery, which provides realistic hills, canyons, and mountain ranges, as well as local airports and navigation aids (NAVAIDs).

▶ **Note**

Scenery areas vary in size and detail. Smaller areas may be download-friendly, but larger or highly detailed areas may exist only on CD-ROM.

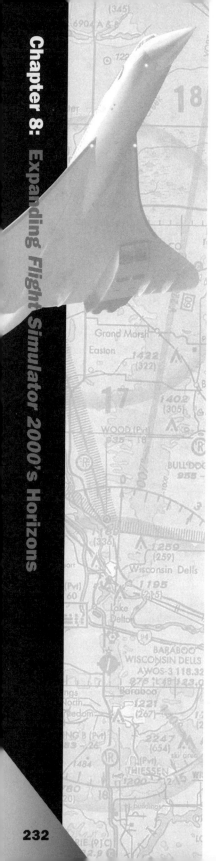

Navigation, Instrumentation, and Flight Tools

Although aircraft and scenery can enhance and augment depth and visual realism, a growing number of specialized instruments and tools make the process of flight more realistic each day. It's possible to find a historic DC-3's realistic instrument panel or a complete commercial flight management computer (FMC) for true immersion into technical flight processes. You'll find products that offer custom gauges, flight data recording—just about every imaginable aircraft feature. Many such products are available commercially, and even more are available as freeware or shareware for download from scores of Internet flight simulation sites.

Interactive Components

With the proliferation of the World Wide Web and its unlimited potential for connecting people, computers, and data, practical multiplayer functionality has become a reality for the masses. *Flight Simulator* offers a multiplayer component that supports pilots hosting or joining a group flight. External facilities, such as Microsoft's Internet Gaming Zone, (http://www.zone.com) offer a convenient, friendly place to meet other pilots and join in the fun.

An exciting development affords real-time air traffic control (ATC): the Internet provides access to a world of skilled air traffic controllers who can guide your aircraft around the virtual world. Most such sites offer free subscriptions or access. However, if you seek ATC precision, be prepared to bear down and learn real-world ATC fundamentals.

Best of all, the *Flight Simulation* community includes hundreds of thousands of participants who are eager and happy to help others learn.

Too Many to Mention

Given all the creative people in the world, you're sure to find some kind of enhancement that adds extra fun or a greater challenge. Adventures are among the most popular, because they offer interactive feedback and instruction. You'll find them useful for learning and testing one's mettle (the infamous "Checkerboard Approach" to Hong Kong's Kai Tak Airport, for example). Others offer graceful glider soaring on a lazy Sunday afternoon.

Flight Simulator 2000 lists hundreds of possible aircraft choices, numerous adventures, and an endless variety of options beyond the original. Building a personal fleet of aircraft and scenery is a great way to ensure that you fly the most exciting planes to the most exciting places under the best conditions. Whether geared toward enlightening the novice or challenging the seasoned veteran, something exists for everyone.

Getting the Goods

Almost as many add-on sources exist as there are add-ons. Retail commercial products are available from traditional computer software stores, mail order, and online distributors. Many are available for immediate download and installation. Prices vary depending on product, features, and a host of other factors, but most are affordable (although a few exceed the cost of *Flight Simulator* itself). Commercial products typically provide expert technical support, from both a computer and aviation perspective.

To locate freeware, shareware, or public domain components, just type a few keywords into your favorite Internet search engine—"flight sim," "aircraft," "FS2000," "add-on," and "scenery" are a few good ones. Many individuals provide *Flight Simulation* Web pages that offer links to their favorite Internet flight sim resources. The challenge won't be to locate them—it'll be deciding on a specific item!

The most convenient sources for many files may be the larger *Flight Simulation* Web sites. Most hold a treasure-trove of files, advice, conversation, news, tips, and tricks for just about any *Flight Simulation* subject. These sites' large servers allow them to offer an amazing selection. Most include search capabilities that make finding an aircraft, area, or instrument quick and easy.

Many of these products come from individuals who make them only to share them with the world. If you're going to use them, it's good form to acknowledge the authors or participate in a product's shareware program.

When it comes to something for nothing, *Flight Simulation* add-ons take the cake. Popular add-on sites included www.microwings.com, www.simflight.com, www.avsim.com, and www.flightsim.com. Specialty sites feature a particular aircraft or genre, especially those dedicated to military aviation. These include www.simcombat.com and www.combatsim.com. AVSIM Online's Combat 1 forums offer specialized content.

Using Add-Ons

It's important to remember that add-on products, although intended to function within *Flight Simulator*, aren't Microsoft products. Although many authors gladly provide product support free of charge, others provide little or no support at all. In most cases, a downloadable component will include instructions—a text file or other electronic document. Most are a snap for expert and novice alike. In all cases however, support lies outside Microsoft.

Be prepared for some "variety," owing to differences between individuals and cultures. The same instrument created by different authors is unlikely to employ the same key command or control device input combinations. Read the documentation that accompanies the component to learn its full features.

Managing scenery areas can also be a challenge. *Flight Simulator's* three-tiered world offers global, regional, and local areas that may have duplicate NAVAIDs, conflicting frequencies, or, in one case, a second control tower at Amsterdam's Schiphol Airport. In most cases, the cause and a solution are nearby. Internet-based discussion forums are excellent places to begin finding answers to all questions, big and small.

► **Warning**

As with all Internet downloads, be sure to scan for viruses before installing anything on your computer. You can never be too safe—in the air or with your computer.

► **Note**

Users can find many links on the Flight Simulator Web Site at www.microsoft.com/games/fs2000.

Creating Add-Ons

If you're ready to roll up your sleeves and get to work, you'll find a wide variety of options available to help you make realistic, dynamic, and artistic add-ons. An entire *Flight Simulator* subcategory offers development tools to create everything from aircraft and scenery to dynamic objects and adventures—virtually any other component. No prior experience is required. Whether for fun or profit, creating add-ons can be a wonderful way to enjoy a wonderful hobby.

> ▶ **Note**
>
> *Most design tools are available only as commercial software products, but in general prices remain well within reach.*

Designing Aircraft

The most popular aircraft development tool was *FlightShop* from BAO—the original *Microsoft Flight Simulator* authors. Its graphical interface and thousands of pre-existing source files have become a staple item, in its various forms. The best part is you don't have to be a programmer to create an aircraft. You need only patience and an eye for detail.

Over the years, other utilities have enhanced the aircraft creation process. Authors have pinpoint control over an aircraft's flight dynamics and can add, among other things, moving parts, retracting landing gear, and extending flaps to enhance realism and detail still further. The number of utilities is growing at a phenomenal rate. The aforementioned flight simulation enthusiast Web sites are great places to start.

Creating Scenery

A number of components make up the scenery, but the two most obvious are texture and terrain. Commercial products can place textures atop a terrain mesh to simulate virtually every square inch of the earth. More subtle scenery components include airports, buildings, structures, and other ground objects. *Flight Simulator* also offers moving dynamic scenery. Scenery products provide just about everything conceivable for recreating the world below.

> ▶ **Note**
>
> *As scenery files grow in size and detail, they may migrate to the capacious DVD format.*

Perhaps the most exciting aspect of scenery creation is the implementation of highly detailed topographical elevation points and digital aerial photography, provided by both government and private sources. Some of this data is available free of charge; others range in price from nominal to exorbitant. Using such real-world data, you can develop realistic scenery areas that rival the best.

Other standardized data sources are available for navigational and airport information, including runway placement and lengths, surfaces, frequencies, and almost every type of NAVAID. *Flight Simulator* includes the Jeppesen NavData database, a worldwide database that includes virtually all airports, navigation aids, high- and low-altitude airways, intersections, and other data. Whether you fly across the county or the North Atlantic on the Great Circle Route, *Flight Simulator 2000* can provide NAVAIDs the entire way.

Building Instrumentation and Tools

Most instrumentation and tools derive from conventional programming tools and languages. Visual C++ is a gauge designer's favorite, and Visual Basic's friendliness allows many to create robust and powerful add-ons for the first time. You'll find many technical details available in Microsoft's *Flight Simulator* SDK, available for earlier versions at the Microsoft Web site. This is an excellent way to delve into both the highly technical aspects of developing software and the simulator itself.

With all that it has to offer, and all that it allows, *Microsoft Flight Simulator 2000* promises to continue its predecessors' tradition of excellent value and never-ending levels of realism. The sheer number of high-quality add-ons ensures that no one ever flies the same sim twice. The availability of these products adds amazing realism and value to the core *Flight Simulator* software, making the world's most famous flight product the most fun. Over time, these add-ons will further erode the line between "serious" and "entertainment" use, helping *Flight Simulator* live up to its claim of being "As real as it gets!"

▶ *Tip*

Watch http:// www.microsoft.com/ games/fs2000/ for the release of Flight Simulator 2000 *SDK.*

Flight Simulator as a Training Aid

Chapter 9

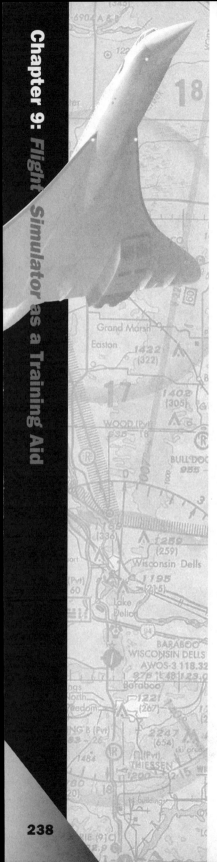

*I*f you've read this far, you've probably given Flight Simulator a thorough workout. You've got a handle on the Cessna 182RG, and you've seen the sights, flown under the Eiffel Tower, and looped the 737.

Perhaps you're a student, a private pilot working on an instrument rating, or an IFR pilot who wants to stay proficient. Maybe you're an instructor trying to find new ways to teach students. In short, you're ready to get serious about flying. And you wonder if flying Flight Simulator *can help when you take the controls of a real airplane.*

The short answer to that question is yes. Flight Simulator is helping train pilots today. For example, as part of the Career Pilot Program at the Flight Safety International Academy in Vero Beach, Florida, students must complete 27 hours of instruction in a Microsoft Flight Simulator *lab, where they practice running checklists, following ATC (Air Traffic Control) clearances, performing basic flight maneuvers, and learning IFR (Instrument Flight Rules) skills.*

In this chapter, I'll pass along tips on how you can take advantage of specific features in Flight Simulator *and make it an effective training aid. But first, a little background.*
—Bruce Williams

The Mental Game

Baseball is 90 percent mental; the other half is physical.
—Yogi Berra

I've never tried to hit a major-league fastball. But having taught people to fly and struggled to learn the finer points of aviating myself, I know Berra's aphorism applies equally well to flying. Most difficulties students (and rusty pilots) encounter stem from misunderstandings of principles and procedures, not from a lack of basic motor skills. Unless you're trying to win aerobatic competitions, the physical part of flying ain't that tough.

It's true, though, that all the theory in the world won't have you hovering a helicopter the first time you pull up on the collective. And understanding the aerodynamics of sideslips alone can't keep you out of the weeds when a gusty crosswind shoves you off the runway centerline. Some skills take practice to master. Muscles need training.

But you can't fly regulation traffic patterns, make smooth approaches, or impress the controllers with textbook holding-pattern entries unless you understand what you're supposed to do before you start wiggling the controls. And that's where *Flight Simulator* comes in. Whether you're a student, a licensed pilot working on an instrument rating, or an IFR veteran trying to stay current, *Flight Simulator* is a great training and proficiency tool, as the example in Figure 9.1 indicates.

Figure 9.1: Quick—ATC just cleared you to direct to a VOR to hold northwest on the 310 radial, right turns. What type of entry should you fly, and what's the initial heading after you cross the fix?

By the way, instructors will find *Flight Simulator* a great tool for testing students. With all the books, videos, and study guides available today, it's easy to parrot the correct answers to tricky questions. But put your students at the controls in *Flight Simulator*, give them a complex exercise, such as VOR orientation and navigation, and you'll soon determine who can apply theory to practical problems in real time. Most important, you'll find out *before* you get into the airplane.

Cutting Through the Noise

Used as part of a training or proficiency program, *Flight Simulator* also can help isolate tasks and divide complicated procedures into manageable pieces.

Consider a typical instructional flight: The lesson begins with preflight briefing on a specific task or tasks—for example, steep turns and slow flight. On the ground, the student seems to understand the theory and the steps required to accomplish the task.

But to apply that knowledge in the airplane, the student must first dispatch the aircraft, complete a preflight inspection, run checklists, follow ATC instructions to taxi, take off, and exit the traffic pattern, navigate to the practice area while looking for other aircraft, avoid controlled airspace, and endure an instructor's incessant patter about altitude, heading, trim, right rudder, and power settings.

By the time students are ready to practice what was discussed 20 or 30 minutes before, they may well have forgotten details such as specific

pitch attitudes, the horizontal component of lift, power, and flap settings, and elevator forces.

Flight Simulator can cut through that clutter to help both instructors and students focus on specific tasks and concepts. You can start a practice flight in the air, ready to work on a particular skill, and easily repeat it many times without the distractions that occur during actual flight.

Think of *Flight Simulator* as an inexpensive, PC-based procedure and task trainer. It brings to your desktop many of the benefits airline, corporate, and military pilots have enjoyed for years. Used properly and as part of a plan, *Flight Simulator* can tone the brain—the most important piece of equipment in any aircraft. It's not a substitute for formal ground and flight instruction, but it can help you sharpen that 90 percent of flying that's mental.

And along the way, you just might learn a few tips that can help with the other 50 percent.

Getting the Most from *Flight Simulator*

So what's the best setup for flying *Flight Simulator*? Pilots often wonder whether they need an expensive flight yoke, a joystick, rudder pedals, a throttle quadrant, or consoles to simulate the avionics stack.

All of these items make flying more fun, especially if you carry the "gizmo gene" that encodes a fascination with blinky lights, dials, and knobs. And you can reinforce some stick-and-rudder skills from flying a PC-based simulation. For example, if you have a force-feedback joystick or yoke, *Flight Simulator* can help you understand the control forces associated with acceleration, deceleration, and power changes. Extend the flaps on the Cessna 182, and, as in the real airplane, you'll feel a pitch-up force as the center of lift moves. Roll into a steep turn, and you'll need to pull back a bit on the stick to hold the nose up as some of the wing's lift is deflected horizontally. Stick time with *Flight Simulator* can help you learn to anticipate and compensate for such effects, even if the forces and control displacements don't match an airplane's precisely.

But I don't think you need a *Flight Simulator* "fort" in your basement to use it effectively as a training aid. Certainly, a joystick or basic flight yoke is important, but all the other goodies really aren't necessary. Regardless of how sophisticated your desktop setup is, when you climb into a real airplane, you'll need a few hours to learn to identify and use all the controls and switches properly and get used to each airplane's unique feel, especially under IFR. But having trained your *brain* with *Flight Simulator*, you'll be a few steps ahead on the procedures.

Do acquire recent (but not necessarily current) aviation charts. You'll learn more and develop good habit patterns if you have a training manual, as well—such as the book that comes with the "Cleared for Takeoff" multimedia private pilot course from Cessna, or *Rod Machado's Private Pilot Handbook*—and an IFR training manual.

The *Flight Simulator 2000* Web site has links to many aviation partners who create training scenarios, challenging flights, aviation charts, and other products for *Flight Simulator* pilots (see Figure 9.2). I especially recommend sites created by the Aircraft Owners and Pilots Association (AOPA), publisher of *AOPA Flight Training* magazine; Jeppesen, leading publisher of charts and aviation data for pilots; and King Schools, which creates multimedia training programs for all FAA pilot certificates and ratings.

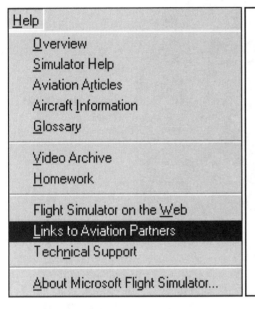

Figure 9.2:
You'll find links to the
Flight Simulator 2000
Web site and to avia-
tion partners in the
Help menu.

Check out the back of the *Pilots Handbook* for details about the Cessna training program, Machado's book, and offers from the aviation partners. You'll also find up-to-date information on the Web. From the *Flight Simulator 2000* Help menu, click Links to Aviation Partners. Or use the links on the *Flight Simulator 2000* Web site (http://www.microsoft.com/games/fs2000).

Training Features in *Flight Simulator 2000*

Flight Simulator 2000 incorporates many features that make the simulation more realistic, easy to use, and entertaining. You can also use most of these features to help you learn more efficiently and effectively— and have fun along the way.

The following sections describe my favorite *Flight Simulator 2000* training features and how they can help you acquire and hone your flying skills. You'll find details on how to use these features elsewhere in this

book, in the *Flight Simulator 2000 Pilot's Handbook,* and in the Simulator Help section of online Help.

Flights

Called "situations" in some earlier versions of *Flight Simulator*, Flights get you started quickly in a specific aircraft at a particular location with weather, realism settings, views, and other conditions already set up.

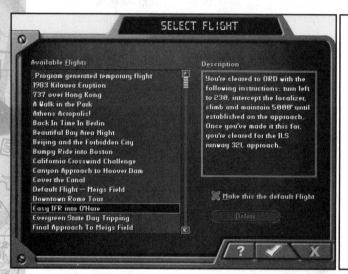

Figure 9.3:
To start a training session quickly, select a Flight.

You can create and save a Flight to practice flying an approach to your hometown airport in a stiff crosswind. Set up everything once, save that situation as a Flight, and, with just a couple of mouse clicks, you can start from that position under those conditions whenever you like. Creating a Flight eliminates the need to reposition the aircraft at the airport, adjust the weather, take off, and fly to where you want to start the approach every time you want to practice.

Flight Simulator 2000 includes many such Flights. Plus, you can create your own, download others from the Microsoft *Flight Simulator 2000* and other Web sites, and swap Flights with fellow pilots.

Instructors may want to create Flights for their students. To illustrate proper arrival procedures, for instance, you can create a set of Flights that position the airplane at various locations around your home base. Use those Flights during preflight briefings and have your students practice entering the traffic pattern from different locations.

Flights also come in handy for practicing specific skills, such as flying instrument approaches, entering holding patterns, or VOR navigation. Load a Flight and jump right into the action, focusing on specific tasks without spending time taking off, flying to the practice area, and configuring all the aircraft systems.

Devious instructors (and who among us isn't?) can set up Flights where certain instruments or aircraft systems fail. Students won't see you poking around menus and dialog boxes to mess with the airplane's

► Tip

Flight Simulator saves Flights in the Pilots folder. To share a Flight, copy it from the Pilots folder to a floppy disk or Web site. Flight files use an FLT extension. They're quite small—typically just a few kilobytes each.

equipment, so they'll be all the more surprised when the electrical system goes on the fritz or the attitude and heading indicators roll over and take a nap.

To view a list of Flights, go to the Flights menu and click Select Flight. To save a Flight, first choose an airplane, set its position and weather, adjust the avionics and system settings, and then click Save Flight in the Flights menu.

Weather

With *Flight Simulator 2000*, you can practice flying through the gray, moist skies of the Pacific Northwest even if you live in Arizona. Its advanced weather features make it easy to create cloud layers, pea-soup fog, cross-winds, and other challenges. This ability to create low clouds and reduced visibility comes in handy for teaching and learning how weather affects flying (see Figure 9.4). For example, you can set up VFR or IFR weather minimums and practice the transition from instrument to visual cues during the last stages of an approach.

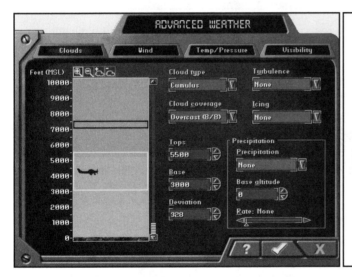

Figure 9.4: You can play weather god in the Advanced Weather dialog box.

And remember, time-of-day is "weather," too. Simulating night flights is a great way to learn about, and stay up to speed with, the challenges of flying after dark. To change the time-of-day, click the digits on the clock on the instrument panel, or, on the World menu, click Time & Season.

To create a dark and stormy night, a foggy morning, or the liquid sunshine of a summer day in Seattle, from the World menu, click Weather, and then click Advanced Weather.

System and Instrument Failures

Flight Simulator 2000 allows pilots to experience realistic, random instrument and systems failures (see Figure 9.5). Instead of watching an instructor's hand reach to cover the attitude indicator to simulate

▶ *Tip*

Use the Deviation option in the Advanced Weather dialog box to experience "landing anticipation." This "gotcha" has quickened the pulse of many an IFR pilot who arrived at the missed approach point, looked up, and didn't see the approach lights or runway. Deviation varies the cloud tops and bases from defined values. Set the base of the lowest cloud layer at the minimums for a particular approach and add a deviation: sometimes you'll break out of the clouds in time to see the runway, and sometimes you won't.

"failure," you must keep the suction gauge in your scan to watch for the far subtler signs of a realistic vacuum system failure.

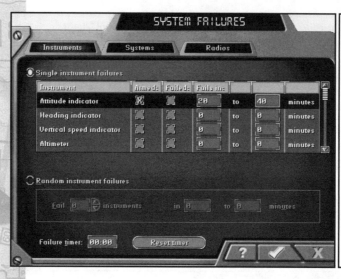

Figure 9.5:
You can break things in the System Failures dialog box.

Systems failures in *Flight Simulator 2000* are far more sophisticated and challenging than in previous versions. You can arm an instrument or system and schedule its failure for between, say, 20 and 40 minutes into a flight. You can set up random failures, so even if you're the one messing with the equipment, you'll never be sure what will bite you when.

These failures are extremely realistic. For example, if the vacuum system dies, the gyro in the attitude indicator slowly winds down and the indicator gradually tips and dips, just as in an airplane.

To set up system and instrument failures, click System Failures in the Aircraft menu.

Map View

The new Map View in *Flight Simulator 2000* isn't just for checking your position. It displays the locations of navigation aids, low- and high-altitude airways, intersections, and your track over the ground (see Figure 9.6).

Perhaps the coolest feature, however, is drag-and-drop. You can drag the airplane (or the tower, for Tower view) quickly to a new location, and then set a heading, altitude, and airspeed to use when you return to the cockpit. After moving the airplane, save the new position and conditions as a Flight.

You can also use the map to compare your position relative to a navigation aid to readings on the VOR/ILS and ADF indicators. If you're learning (or demonstrating) how to interpret those readings, drag the airplane around the map and then return to the cockpit to see how the needles have moved.

To bring up Map View, click on it in the World menu.

▶ Tip

Try saving a set of instrument and system failures as part of a Flight. Build a library of such Flights to jump quickly into a situation that will challenge a student or break the rust off an experienced pilot's technique.

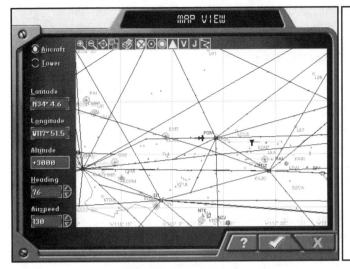

Figure 9.6:
Use Map View to reposition an aircraft or get information about airports and navigation aids.

Multiple Views and Windows

There's nothing quite like the view from the left seat of a real airplane. But if you're trying to connect what you see from the pilot's seat to the airplane's attitude during takeoffs, landings, and other maneuvers, *Flight Simulator 2000*'s multiple views come in handy (Figure 9.7).

For example, you can use one window to see the picture from the left seat, with all instruments in view. Open another window to display your aircraft from Spot Plane view. As you practice flaring during the final stages of landing with this bird's-eye view, you'll learn quickly when and how high to raise the nose as you settle onto the runway. Using Spot Plane view this way simulates the help chase plane pilots give their colleagues when a new aircraft begins test flights.

To set up multiple views, on the Views menu click New View. Or click View Options to set options for individual windows.

▶ *Tip*

Map View also serves as the Airport/Facility directory. To look up information about an airport, VOR, or NDB, switch to Map View, zoom in, and double-click on the item you're interested in. Flight Simulator 2000 includes the worldwide Jeppesen NavData database of airports and navigation aids.

Figure 9.7:
Make your own chase plane using *Flight Simulator 2000*'s multiple windows.

Flight Simulator 2000 includes multiple views for looking ahead, behind, and to each side as you fly. Use the hat switch on a joystick, or the arrow keys, to look around. Instructors can help students build good scanning habits by insisting they look before they turn, even in *Flight Simulator.*

Flight Videos

Because pilots like to admire their handiwork, *Flight Simulator* has long included a Flight Video recorder. You can put this feature to work as a training aid, just as the U.S. Navy uses videos to review every carrier landing a pilot makes.

Flight Simulator's Flight Videos aren't "videos," as such. Instead, the recorder acts like an airliner's flight data recorder (the so-called black box). It periodically samples airspeed, altitude, heading, and so on, and saves the information in a small file. When you play back a Flight Video, you run those data back through the simulation engine.

To record or play back a Flight Video, go to the Options menu and click Flight Video. Flight Videos save to the Pilots folder in the *Flight Simulator 2000* directory.

Autopilot

Yogi Berra also said, "You can observe a lot just by watchin'." Many flight schools incorporate that wisdom in their training programs by encouraging students to fly in pairs. One trainee sits in the left seat, next to the instructor, and gets hands-on practice at the controls. The other student rides in back to watch, listen, and learn. These backseat flyers needn't divide their attention between flying and other tasks, so they can concentrate on studying procedures, navigating, interpreting instrument readings and air traffic control instructions, and learning from the other student's mistakes.

You can use *Flight Simulator*'s autopilot to accomplish the same goal (Figure 9.8). (I'm not going to enter the debate about how much a pilot should use an autopilot in real flying. That's a matter of technique best left to the judgment of the pilot and the instructor considering the type of airplane and specific situations.)

When you're trying to learn how ADF or VOR needles move as you fly complex procedures, don't complicate things by struggling to hold altitude and heading. Turn on the autopilot, select ALT and HDG hold modes, and watch the show. Use the heading bug or autopilot control panel to steer the airplane until you thoroughly understand what's going on. Then add to your workload gradually by turning off ALT mode. When you can maintain altitude, keep track of your position, and anticipate heading changes, you're ready to turn autopilot off and juggle all the tasks simultaneously.

To activate autopilot, click controls on the instrument panel (or in the avionics stack, in some aircraft), or select options in the Autopilot dialog box.

▶ **Tip**

Create a series of Flight Videos to illustrate tasks such as entering holding patterns and using a VASI (Visual Approach Slope Indicator) or PAPI (Precision Approach Path Indicator) to fly the proper approach path. Because Flight Videos are saved as small files, it's easy to share them with students and fellow pilots who have Flight Simulator. *Just copy VID files from the Pilots folder in your* Flight Simulator 2000 *directory.*

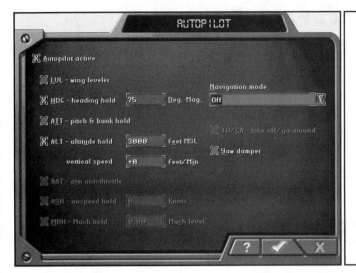

Slew Mode

The new Map View in Flight Simulator has made Slew Mode less important as a way of quickly moving the aircraft to a new location. Map View is much better, because you can use it to set a position, altitude, heading, and airspeed precisely.

But Slew Mode is still a handy tool for demonstrations and for learning to interpret navigation instrument readings. For example, in Cockpit view, you can slew around and observe how VOR, ILS, and NDB needles move as you scoot north, south, east, and west of a navigation aid. Slew Mode also provides a quick way to reposition the aircraft for another landing, or to enter the traffic pattern from another direction.

Press Y to switch Slew Mode on and off. To learn how to change direction and altitude in Slew Mode, see the Simulator Help section in the *Flight Simulator* online Help.

IFR Training Panels

Flight Simulator 2000 Professional Edition includes IFR training panels for the Cessna 182S and the Mooney Bravo to help pilots who want to learn or practice IFR skills.

These panels combine the flight instruments and avionics stack in one window, so all important controls and instruments remain in view. The "scenery" window is small, but because you're in the clouds when you practice IFR procedures, that doesn't matter.

To use these IFR training panels, go to the Aircraft menu in *Flight Simulator 2000 Professional Edition* and click C182S IFR or Mooney Bravo IFR.

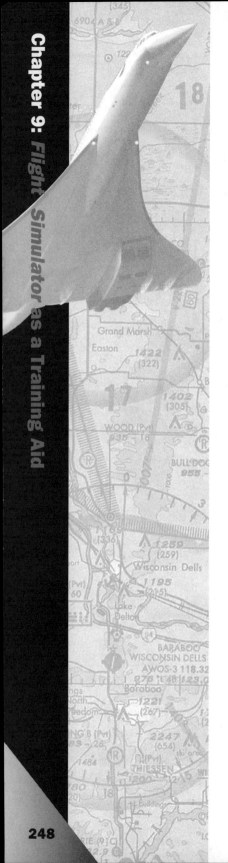

Instrument Panel Editor

If you have *Flight Simulator 2000 Professional Edition*, you also have FS2000 Aircraft Editor for customizing aircraft and instrument panels. With this editor, you can rearrange the instrument panels in *Flight Simulator* to better match the aircraft you fly. You can also create panels that include instruments you'd like to learn about or practice using—for example an HSI (Horizontal Situation Indicator) or RMI (Radio Magnetic Indicator).

The FS2000 Aircraft Editor is a separate utility (FSEDIT.EXE) installed in the *Flight Simulator 2000 Professional Edition* directory during setup. For details about using the editor, see online Help.

Creative Approaches

Don't hesitate to use *Flight Simulator 2000*'s other capabilities to make it a more effective training aid. Be creative.

It's also important to step back occasionally and look at *Flight Simulator* as more than a tool to use only when you want "fly." The following tips are geared particularly toward instructors.

A White Board for the Graphically Challenged

I find *Flight Simulator* makes an excellent white board. By creating Flights and Flight Videos, I can use *Flight Simulator* to illustrate important concepts during a ground school class or pre- or post-flight briefing.

For example, after I make my best attempt to draw an FAA-recommended parallel entry to a holding pattern at the intersection of two VOR radials, I usually turn around to face a class that looks like a museum tour group straining to find the nose in a Picasso portrait. But with *Flight Simulator* displayed on a large monitor, I can play a Flight Video that shows the entire class how the VOR needles move during that maneuver. Using the same technique, I can demonstrate a specific IFR procedure and have the students compare the instrument readings with details shown on a chart or approach plate in real time. And I can press P to stop and start the simulation at key points along the way.

Fly Before You Fly

Airline pilots take airport qualification courses before they fly to new airports. Why shouldn't the rest of us? If you're heading off on a long trip to an unfamiliar airport, you can use *Flight Simulator* to practice the flight ahead of time.

Because *Flight Simulator 2000* includes the Jeppesen NavData database, you can fly to more than 21,000 airports around the world. Practice flying along low- and high-altitude airways and get familiar with instrument departures, arrivals, and approaches before you set off on a long cross-country flight. Or use *Flight Simulator* to practice circle-to-land approaches or flights into airports guarded by mountains or other obstructions.

I like to have student pilots show me portions of their solo cross-country flights in *Flight Simulator* before I send them out alone. They gain confidence by identifying checkpoints visually and using VORs, becoming familiar with approaches to each airport, and considering alternatives should weather or other circumstances require a change in plans. I can confirm that they gain a real understanding of the tasks involved in the flights they're about to make.

Don't Do This in a Real Airplane

The airlines use sophisticated simulators to train pilots to deal with abnormal situations and emergencies. Use *Flight Simulator* in a similar way to demonstrate maneuvers and situations that are impractical or unsafe to practice in a real airplane.

For example, many pilots never really understand accelerated stalls and the concept that a stall can occur at any airspeed and with aircraft in any attitude. In flight training, they experience stalls only with the nose at or above the horizon and at relatively low speed. Using *Flight Simulator*, however, you can show a student what happens when, during a steep dive with the airspeed well into the yellow arc, you suddenly yank back on the yoke.

I use *Flight Simulator* to demonstrate how a steep spiral can develop if a pilot neglects to maintain a good instrument scan. And *Flight Simulator* can show a pilot—dramatically—why it's a bad idea to turn back to the airport if the engine quits shortly after takeoff.

Flying for Fun

Remember, learning should be fun. *Flight Simulator* is a great tool for setting up challenges that stimulate students and keep them motivated, especially when weather or maintenance problems cancel a flight.

You can also set up challenges for your fellow pilots. Dare them to record a Flight Video of their best ILS approaches or holding pattern entries starting from the same initial conditions (which you've saved as a Flight). Dig through your Jeppesen binders and find complex instrument departure or arrival procedures and then surprise students or fellow pilots by asking them to fly them on the spot—as if ATC had uttered the dreaded phrase, "We have an amendment to your clearance."

The real work in these situations isn't controlling the airplane. It's figuring out where you are, how to set up the avionics, and what to do two or three steps down the road. Such exercises can keep your mental flying skills sharp when hours of routine flying leave your brain flabby. And you may win a few beer bets.

▶ *Tip*

If you've ever wondered whether you have the right stuff, try a shuttle landing in the 737-400. Use Map View to set yourself up on final approach to a long runway. Shut down the engines, hang out the gear, flaps, and spoilers, and see if you can land without breaking anything (and don't forget to record a Flight Video to send to NASA's recruiting department along with your résumé).

Logging Time

Pilots often ask whether they can log the time they spend "flying" Flight Simulator. At present, in the U.S., the answer is no. With Advisory Circular AC61-126, "Qualification and Approval of Personal Computer-Based Aviation Training Devices" (May 12, 1997), the FAA took a small first step toward recognizing the value of PC-based simulations. The AC lays out the requirements for an approved training device. Only a few systems have been approved, in part because requirements include expensive consoles for switches and controls.

More to the point, even if you're using an approved PCATD, you can log only up to 10 hours of the training required for an initial instrument rating, provided the practice time is conducted under the direct supervision of an authorized flight instructor. You can't use a PCATD to log the approaches and other maneuvers required to maintain IFR currency. Nor can you use an approved PCATD for instrument proficiency checks, to log solo time, or to meet any of the flight time requirements for a private pilot certificate.

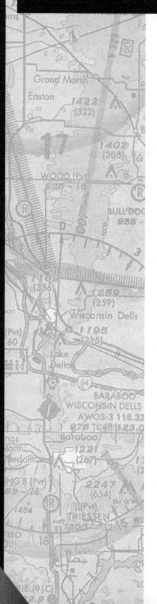

You're Never Alone... When You're Flying on the Zone

Chapter 10

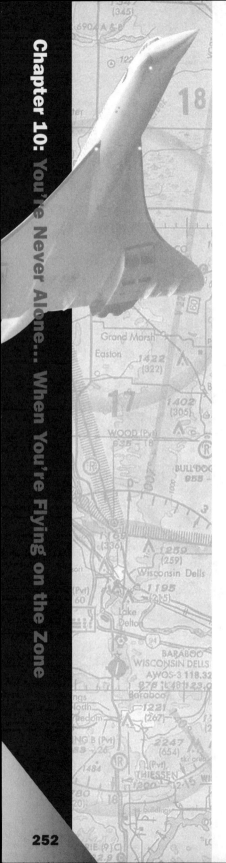

*A*s Bill mentioned in Chapter 8, Microsoft's Internet Gaming Zone (http://www.zone.com) is one of the best places to experience multiplayer flying in Flight Simulator 2000. *Although you may think you'll need to master all of your piloting skills before giving multiplayer flight a try, nothing could be further from the truth. The Zone, as frequent visitors call it, is a great place to learn and practice what you don't know.*

Everyone's a beginner at some time, even though there may be a few who'll deny it. If you're just starting out, you'll find that Flight Simulator *buffs are almost always willing to help newbies. As long as you make an effort to learn what you can on your own (no one likes to answer the really obvious questions that are covered in the manual, for instance), you'll find that Zoners are as helpful as they come. The only thing that anyone asks in return is that you extend the same courtesy to other newcomers when you can.*

This chapter gives you some advice for getting the most out the Zone. In the process, we'll also talk about latency issues, explore your communications options, and even take a look at ATC (Air Traffic Control) conventions as they apply to online Flight Simulator.

Zone Tips

Getting started on the Zone is fairly intuitive, but on the off chance that you have problems in the early going, you'll discover that most issues are well documented in the Zone's online help. If that fails, you can get assistance from Zone volunteers. So we'll skip the basic stuff here and go straight to specific things that'll affect your *Flight Simulator 2000* multiplayer experience.

Online Overhead

As we discussed way back in the beginning of the book, *Flight Simulator 2000*'s many configuration options let you tune *Flight Simulator*'s performance to meet your particular needs. But even though you may have the ultimate silky-smooth configuration for standalone offline play, flying online requires additional computing horsepower. This extra workload can render some marginal offline setups un-flyable.

Online overhead is caused by a number of factors that can impose as much as a 50%, or greater, performance hit. Adjusting some detail/resolution, traffic, and window settings for multiplayer flight can help, and obviously the closer your offline setup already is to "marginal" (roughly 15 frames per second if you're interested in flying rather than sight-seeing), the more problematic this online overhead will become.

Conversely, if you're getting 60+ frames per second offline with all detail settings maxed out, you probably won't even notice the overhead that online flying adds. Your only problem will be dealing with the rest of us pestering you to lend your system out!

Game Latency

As with all online activities, low peer-to-peer (in this case player-to-player) latency is very important for smooth gaming. When you're considering joining a particular game, you can quickly gauge the game table's latency by viewing each game table's latency indicator (see Figure 10.1).

Figure 10.1: Low peer-to-peer latency is very important for smooth gaming. You can gauge the latency of each game by viewing each game table's latency indicator.

Located at the upper-right corner of the title bar of each occupied game table, game table latency indicators graphically display the average latency for the system currently hosting the game. Sample peer-to-peer latency indicator bars are shown in Figure 10.2 and their descriptions are as follows:

- ✛ **Four bright green bars** indicates very low average latency. Players can expect excellent gameplay conditions.

- ✛ **Three dark green bars** indicates low average latency. Players can expect good gameplay conditions.

- ✛ **Two yellow bars** indicates medium average latency. Players may experience slight gameplay problems.

- ✛ **One red bar** indicates high average latency. High latency is not conducive to multiplayer flight.

If you see no bars, latency is still being calculated.

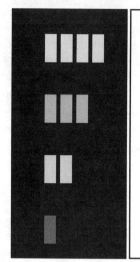

Figure 10.2:
The four types of
latency indicator bars,
minus color.

Multiplayer Settings

Flight Simulator 2000 also has several multiplayer options that can impact your online performance. While all of these affect overall flight performance, some may seem to only affect initial connect times, and others can cause some of the occasional pauses that you may experience while flying online.

The first option has to do with the number of players in your game. The more airplanes your system has to render, the more processing power you'll need. As you'd expect, this principle also applies to inter-player communications, and the situation can be easily aggravated by bandwidth limitations and latency problems.

The general rule of thumb is that the more players you have in a game, the more communications and processing power you need to maintain a smooth simulation. Again, the closer you are to marginal performance in these areas, the more likely it is that these factors will impact your multiplayer games.

To select the next set of options to configure *Flight Simulator* for multiplayer flying, from the Flight menu, choose Multiplayer, and then choose Settings (see Figure 10.3). In particular we're talking about the Send Detailed Aircraft Information and the Receive Detailed Aircraft Information options in the Visual Details box. Un-checking these options will improve your online performance. We'll talk more about these features later on.

Finally, the Update Date & Time feature (it only becomes accessible when you're connected to a multiplayer game) will cause *Flight Simulator 2000* to pause while it makes the data transfer, so you may want to wait until everyone is on the ground before using this feature!

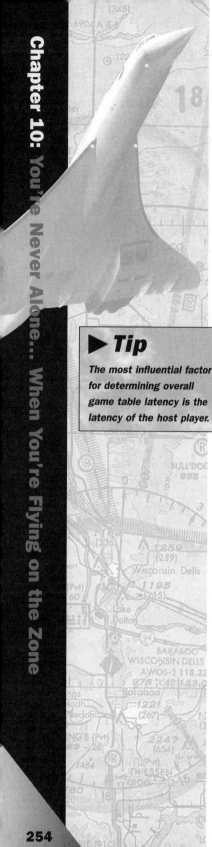

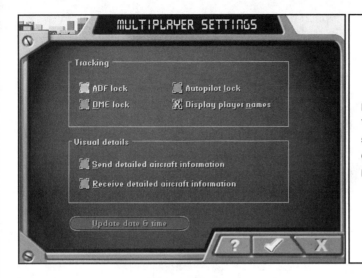

Figure 10.3:
Your multiplayer
settings affect the
quality of your multi-
player experience.

The Name Game and Setting the Pace

Hosts can add useful information about their games in a game table description. With add-ons such as Z-Planes and programs such as Roger Wilco™ (we'll get to what both of these are a little later on) in fairly wide use, this feature comes in very handy.

For example, people running Roger Wilco need to know which IP (Internet Protocol) address is being used before they can connect with each other. The game table description is where you'll often find that information, as well as game settings, particulars about the flight such as what airport you'll be flying around, and even the details of a flight plan (see Figure 10.4).

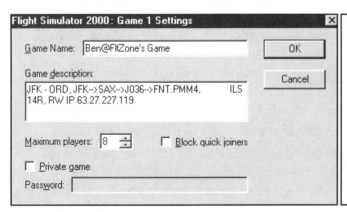

Figure 10.4:
You can find game table
descriptions by clicking
on the game table's
Info button.

To add a description to a game table, simply click on the Settings button shown in Figure 10.5. The information you type in the pop-up window will then appear in the game table's window.

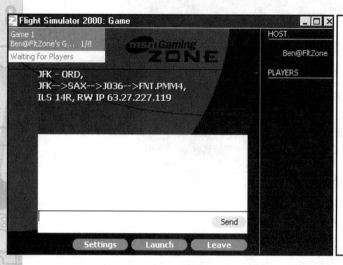

Figure 10.5:
Hosts can add long descriptions of their Zone game by clicking on the Settings button from the game table screen.

Conversely, if you're thinking about joining a game in progress, be sure to click the Info buttons on game tables to have a look at the game table description for more details about the flight. This ability to preview a flight can be really helpful for selecting a game that fits your mood, and it can also reduce game interruptions caused by basic questions such as "where's everyone flying?"

Joining the Fun

One of the neatest features of playing *Flight Simulator 2000* on the Zone is that you can join a session that's already underway. However, there will be occasions when you won't be able to join a game that's already started. Although it may seem like your ability to join a game already in progress depends on the phase of the moon, there really is a logic behind it.

You can join any game in progress as long as the following conditions are met:

1. The original host remains in the game as host.
2. The maximum number of players (set by the host) is not exceeded.
3. The new player joining a password-protected game has the password (also set by the host).

You'll occasionally find "hung" games where the host was lost but the Zone hasn't yet updated that fact. Obviously you won't be able to join those games because they don't meet the first criterion in the list above, but the Zone may still let you enter that particular game table. You can tell when a game's hung by looking at the name of the host on the game table's player list. Player names are dimmed when they're playing, as opposed to just hanging around the game table's chat window. So if the host's name is not dimmed, and the table is listed as In Progress, you'll know that game is hung.

Lost and Found

Although it's good Zone etiquette to name your game something that reflects the activity in progress, there are times when even long descriptions will be insufficient to help players who are joining a game that's already underway. This often happens when someone joins a game that's hosting a long cross-country flight. The new player enters the game in progress and starts typing "Where is everyone?" or something similar. Of course, Zoners are more than happy to supply geographical positioning and GPS coordinates, but there's a simpler way to play "catch up."

First, select the player you want to catch up with by repeatedly pressing Ctrl+Shift+T to cycle through the players in the session. Once the name of the chosen player appears in the upper-right corner of the Flight window, as shown in Figure 10.6, press Ctrl+Shift+F to transport your aircraft comfortably behind the selected player.

Tip

In some aircraft, such as the Mooney Bravo, the name of a selected player may be hidden behind overhead instrument panels. Press Shift+1 to temporarily remove the instrument panel from view.

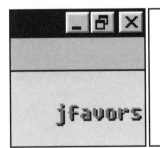

Figure 10.6: Press Ctrl+Shift+T to cycle through the players in the session, and the chosen player's handle will appear in the upper-right corner of the Flight window.

Be sure to get into level cruise flight before transporting your aircraft. If you transport yourself while sitting on the runway, you could drop out of the sky when you reappear—until you can gain airspeed and start flying. As you can imagine, this can be hazardous if the person you're following is low to the ground or getting ready to land. Talk about making an embarrassing entrance!

Add-on Aircraft in Multiplayer Flight

There are literally thousands of *Flight Simulator 2000*-compatible aircraft floating around on the Web and on retail shelves. If you have a favorite airplane (real, historical, or fictional!), there's a good chance that there's a *Flight Simulator*-compatible version out there.

We won't get into the steps of converting or importing after market add-on aircraft because the overwhelming majority come with installation directions. Instead, let's just concentrate on how imported aircraft affect multiplayer flights.

The problem with using imported aircraft in multiplayer flight is that, unless everyone in the game has the same aircraft installed on their system, no one will be able to ogle your new aircraft. *Flight Simulator 2000* has the ability to transfer the visual models of imported aircraft during an online multiplayer session, but as we mentioned earlier, this can cause some multiplayer gameplay problems.

Sending and Receiving Aircraft Information

In order to enable visual model transmission during multiplayer sessions, you need to activate the Visual Details Send and Receive features found in the Multiplayer Settings window. (To get to the Settings window, go the Flights menu, choose Multiplayer, and select Settings.)

This is one way to make sure your new aircraft can be enjoyed (and envied) by other pilots. Very cool, right? Unfortunately, the downside is that even on a 10Mbps network (note that modem speeds are substantially slower) it can take 20 minutes or more to transfer a single aircraft! Let's talk about one solution.

Z-plane, Z-plane!

If you've hung around the *Flight Simulator 2000* chat room for any time at all, you've probably already seen the word *Zplanes*. Zplane is short for Zone planes. These are a compilation of freeware aircraft assembled by a Zone pilot, Forkboy2.

Using Zplanes solves the problems that we just outlined by letting you download and install a standardized set of aircraft models (some with panels and sounds) at your convenience. This way it won't cut into your multiplayer flight time. Also, once they're installed, you'll be able to see everyone else's Zplanes in flight without hurting the quality of your gameplay.

Two of the Zplane sets are Zplanes 98C and Zplanes 98G. Zplanes 98C is comprised of 40 commercial regional and international class aircraft. Zplanes 98G has some 41 general aviation aircraft. That should keep you busy for a while!

Observer Fervor

Just as you'd expect, *Flight Simulator 2000*'s Multiplayer Observer feature lets a player act as an observer during multiplayer games. As an observer, you'll be able to see what's going on within a game from more perspectives than are normally available. For example, as an observer, you can watch the action from inside an aircraft that another player is flying!

Before we discuss how to engage Observer mode, there are some quirks and restrictions that you should be aware of:

+ Once you become an observer, you won't be able to fly again until you begin another multiplayer session.

+ The host determines how many (if any) observers can join the game.

+ The number of observers can't exceed the maximum number of players allowed in the game. In other words you can't have more than 8 players and/or observers in a game at one time.

+ Not all of the flight instruments will work from the observer's point of view when flying aboard someone else's aircraft.

+ Finally, if you don't have the same third-party aircraft (and accompanying instrument panel if applicable) already installed on your system

> **▶ Tip**
> You can download Zplanes from my Web site at http://www.benchiu.com.

> **▶ Note**
> The host determines the number of observers from the Host Settings screen (go to the Flights menu, choose Multiplayer, and select Host Settings).

as the player you're observing, *Flight Simulator* will use the closest default aircraft and instrument panel.

If the host allows observers, you can switch to Observer mode by taking the following steps:

1. After entering a multiplayer game, press Ctrl+Shift+O (see Figure 10.7).

Are you sure you wish to convert to an observer for the remainder of this session?

Yes   No

Figure 10.7:
Press Ctrl+Shift+O to enter Observer mode.

2. Press Ctrl+Shift+D the first time you enter Observer mode to lock your view.

3. Press the S key to cycle through the alternate views that are now available to you.

4. Press Ctrl+Shift+T to cycle your view through the various players in the session.

Amaze Your Friends!

Some of the features available in stand-alone flight also work in multi-player flight. You can use these features to stay ahead of your aircraft, save your bacon, or play tricks on your friends. A few of these features are listed below. What you do with them is your business!

✛ **Pause**—Press the P key to pause your multiplayer flight. Everyone else will continue to fly normally. This can come in handy if you need to play with your NAV radios or if you just get overwhelmed. But be especially careful using this while playing follow the leader—pity the pilot following you when you stop cold in mid-air!

✛ **Rate**—Can a Cessna fly faster than a Learjet 45? In multiplayer, you betcha! By increasing the simulation rate (press the R key, then press the = (equal) key), your aircraft will fly at a faster rate while everyone else in the game will fly at their normal rate, unless they change their rates as well. To decrease the simulation rate, press the – (hyphen) key. To reset it back to normal, press Backspace. If you changed to another instrument/feature from the simulation rate, you'll need to press the R key again first.

✛ **Slew**—You may recall that slewing is a way to move around without actually flying. Press the Y key to enter slew mode. Manipulate your joystick to move and press F1 through F4 to control your altitude. If you're careful, slewing around in the JetRanger can make you look like a hover expert!

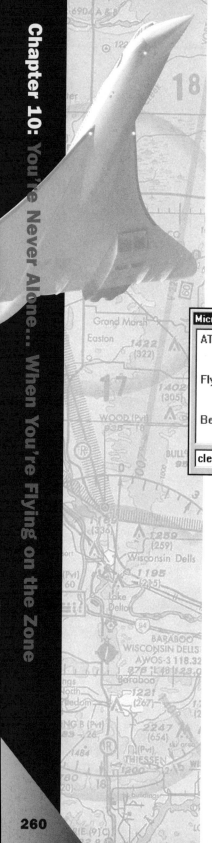

Online Communications

At the very heart of multiplayer flight is the ability to communicate with other pilots. You might as well be flying offline if you can't interact with others. Let's talk about a few useful tips that'll help make your online communications more enjoyable and realistic.

Let Your Fingers Do the Talking

The most common way to communicate with other pilots during multiplayer sessions is through the *Flight Simulator* chat window (see Figure 10.8). Press Ctrl+Enter to toggle the chat window on and off, and press the Enter key to switch window focus to the chat window. (This comes in very handy for those of you with 3-D accelerated video cards who need to run the game in full-screen mode. Although you can't see the chat window, it's there and you can still type messages. You'll still be able to see what others are typing because their messages will scroll across the screen.)

Figure 10.8:
Typing in the *Flight Simulator* chat window is the most common way to communicate during multiplayer flights.

Roger Wilco

One of the most exciting new utilities that'll work with *Flight Simulator 2000* incorporates live-voice communications during multiplayer flights. Resounding Technology, Inc. (www.rogerwilco.com) was one of the leaders in multiplayer real-time voice communication. Their product, *Roger Wilco*, shown in Figure 10.9, has been available for free downloading from their Web site, and Roger Wilco has become a de facto standard. However, as of this writing, this program has been sold to another company, Mpath Interactive, Inc., and its future as a freeware product remains unknown.

Nevertheless, Roger Wilco works very well with *Flight Simulator 2000* (and *Combat Flight Simulator* if you have that too) and performance degradation is generally imperceptible. Roger Wilco currently allows simultaneous real-time voice communications between 32 players without requiring a dedicated server or an additional sound card. If this freeware is still available when you're reading this, check it out. It'll change your multiplayer experience.

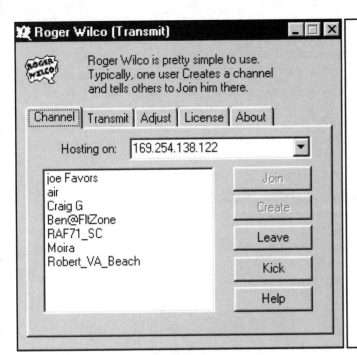

Figure 10.9:
Roger Wilco offers real-time voice communications while playing *Flight Simulator 2000* and other games on the Zone.

Virtual pilots use Roger Wilco to simulate ATC (Air Traffic Control) radio communications. With that in mind, let's switch fight configurations and discuss how ATC procedures work.

Basic ATC Airport Operations

Although you may be equipped with all of the right hardware and software to communicate with other virtual pilots, if you're not familiar with air traffic control procedures, it can be difficult to communicate your intentions (or instructions, if you're ATC for the session). So let's talk about the basic format of aviation communications. Once you're aware of the sequence of communications, you'll be better equipped to understand what's being said or asked.

The basic aviation communications format is:

+ **Whom you're calling**—The name of the airport tower or ground control if you're a pilot, or the aircraft ID if you're ATC. For example, "O'Hare tower" and "Kennedy ground control" would be used if you were a pilot. "Cessna 123" would be appropriate for a call from ATC.

+ **Your callsign (or ATC designation if you're ATC)**—Although ATC usually uses the last three digits or characters of your aircraft number to communicate with you, you should always announce your complete callsign upon initial contact with ATC. Your Zone handle will usually work well for this purpose and it'll help the person playing ATC keep track of everyone because your handle will be displayed on their screen.

▶ **Warning**

As with all downloads off the Internet, please be sure to scan everything for viruses before installing anything on your computer. You can never be too safe in the air or with your computer.

✛ **Your location (not used when you're ATC)**—Where you are. This includes vertical (height) as well as lateral position. Generalities are sufficient. For example, "over the Rosebowl" or "five miles south of the airport" are appropriate.

✛ **Your request (or reply/instructions if you're ATC)**—Here's where you say what you want to do. Do you want to "taxi to parking," or do you want to do a "touch and go?" If you're ATC, this is where you announce your instructions.

Taxiing

Requesting permission to taxi is fairly straightforward. Simply follow the format we just discussed. But if you're looking to taxi to the runway for takeoff, announce the current ATIS (Automated Terminal Information Services) information designation (e.g. "with Echo" or "with information Echo"). This will let ATC know that you want to takeoff. One example would be "Meigs ground, Cessna 700MS at transient parking with Gulf, taxi for takeoff."

Departure

When you're ready for takeoff, contact the tower and use our handy communications format. You also need to indicate which direction you intend to depart the airport from. For example, "downwind departure," "straight out departure," "left crosswind departure," and "right crosswind departure" are all valid. ATC will either clear you or tell you to "hold short" (move up to the runway, but don't move onto it).

Arrival

Arrivals usually make initial contact with the tower at least five miles outside of the airport. Again, if you announce the current ATIS information after following our radio procedure guidelines, ATC will assume you want to land.

At this point, ATC will tell you which way they want you to enter the traffic pattern (Figure 10.10), which runway they want you to land on, when/where they want you to contact them again, and any traffic and/or sequencing instructions. For example, ATC might respond "Cessna 123, ABC tower; enter left traffic runway 23, downwind on a 45, report downwind; there are two Mooney's in the pattern." See Figure 10.11 for an illustration of the traffic pattern when entering "on a 45."

> ▶ *Note*
>
> *ATC will usually include traffic and sequencing information in their replies, if appropriate.*

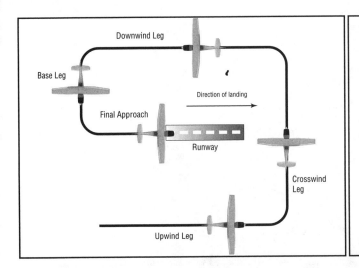

Direction of landing

Downwind Leg

Base Leg

Final Approach

Runway

Crosswind Leg

Upwind Leg

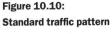

Figure 10.10:
Standard traffic pattern

Listening to the Pros

If you're interested in hearing what ATC communications sound like, here are a couple of links that will allow you to actually listen to what's going on in real time. That's right, you can listen to what's happening as it happens through the Internet. Enjoy!

☩ *Abilene Regional, KS: http://www.bitstreet.com/ra_test/abi.ram*

☩ *Bankstown, Australia: http://www.basair.com.au/bktower.htm*

☩ *Battle Creek, MI: http://www.aviation.wmich.edu/liveatc.html*

☩ *Calgary Terminal, Canada: http://yyc.calgaryweb.net/yyc.ram*

☩ *Chicago Approach: http://www.cyberair.com/audio/chiapp/index.html*

☩ *Dallas/Fort Worth, TX: http://www.audionet.com/simuflite/*

☩ *Denver, CO: http://www.airparts.com/livefeed/tower.ram*

☩ *Miami, FL: http://www.silverexpress.com/mialive.ram*

☩ *New York, NY: http://realserver.brooklyn.cuny.edu:8080/ramgen/encoder/jfk.rm*

☩ *Omaha, NB: http://r90.natca.net/liveatc.htm*

☩ *Providence, RI: http://www.ids.net/airport/airport.ram*

☩ *Santa Ana, CA: http://pv801.pv.reshsg.uci.edu/~jfeise/Flying/SNA.ram*

☩ *San Diego, CA: http://www.sdmedia.net/lindberghatc.ram*

☩ *Toronto Arrival, Canada: http://www.interlog.com/~danamar/yyz.ram*

Figure 10.11:
The traffic pattern when entering "on a 45."

Online ATC Tips

Here are a couple of *Flight Simulator 2000*'s features that will help assist you with your ATC duties.

God's Eye View

Opening a top-down View window (Figure 10.12) can give you a great view of the local area. When used at the right zoom levels (press Backspace, then either the – (hyphen) and/or = (equal) key to adjust), player names and their positions relative to your position will appear on the map.

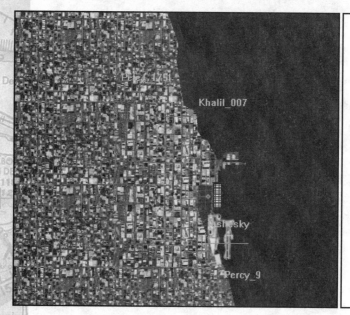

Figure 10.12:
Press Shift+] to open a top-down view window. You can then right-click on the map and select Maximize Window from the pop-up menu.

The only thing missing is altitude information, but that's not such a big deal. In the real world, controllers can still do their jobs even if an aircraft's not equipped with a Mode C transponder (which transmits altitude as reported by the aircraft's altimeter). They simply ask each aircraft to report its altitude over the radio. Sometimes the best solutions to minor problems are the simplest ones.

Tower of Power

One of the neatest things you can do as an observer is switch to Tower view. Press the S key and cycle through the views as you normally would. Although you can go to Tower view in Player mode as well, combining Tower view with Observer mode lets you "lock" your view on to other aircraft by pressing Ctrl+Shift+T (see Figure 10.13). This is very handy for simulating Air Traffic Control. One player/observer can offer clearances from the airport to the other players flying around in the pattern.

**Figure 10.13:
Observer mode and the Tower view are perfect for simulating ATC (Air Traffic Control) in multiplayer sessions.**

The Flight Zone

The Flight Zone (Figure 10.14), written by yours truly, is a Zone-based online column dedicated to multiplayer *Flight Simulator*. You'll find a link in the main *Flight Simulator* rooms and at the Zone's Simulator hub.

Each installment covers helpful tips and pointers designed to enhance your enjoyment of multiplayer flight plus news about the latest *Flight Simulator* add-ons, products, and events.

▶ **Note**

My handle on the Zone is Ben@FltZone. If you see me there, please say hello. I'm always honored to fly with anyone willing, when I've got the time.

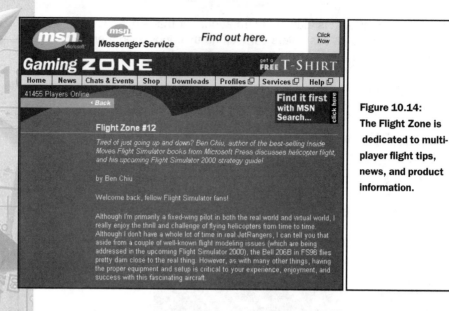

Figure 10.14:
The Flight Zone is dedicated to multi-player flight tips, news, and product information.

Other Web Resources

Here are some handy additional Web resources that you can use to meet other *Microsoft Flight Simulator* fans, share your experiences, and seek answers to technical questions. Don't be surprised if you run into people with very similar interests.

Flight Simulator Newsgroups

Below are three Usenet newsgroup servers that contain newsgroups you may find useful. The first two are specifically for *Microsoft Flight Simulator*, and the others have *Flight Simulator*-related content.

msnews.microsoft.com

Next to the information found directly at www.microsoft.com/games/fs2000 you'll find the most useful information about *Microsoft Flight Simulator* in these Usenet newsgroups, which are frequented by Microsoft volunteers who are always ready to offer advice and encouraging words.

+ microsoft.public.simulators

+ microsoft.public.games.zone.simulators

msnnews.msn.com

These newsgroups also contain *Flight Simulator 2000* content, but they're less active than the ones just mentioned.

+ msn.computingcentral.flightsimulator.fs98

+ msn.computingcentral.flightsimulator.general.help

+ msn.computingcentral.combatflightsimulator

▶ **Tip**

You can access msnews.msn.com *news-groups directly from* http://computingcentral. msn.com/topics/ flightsimulator/

Public Newsgroups

Purely public newsgroups tend to get a little more coarse (not all that uncommon for public newsgroups) than the others, so be prepared. Nevertheless, there's often good information to be found here.

- alt.games.microsoft.flight-sim
- rec.aviation.simulators

MSN *Microsoft Flight Simulator* Chat

If you've got questions about *Flight Simulator*, or just want to enjoy the company of fellow simulation enthusiasts in a less hectic environment, there's MSN Computing Central's *Microsoft Flight Simulator* chat. This is the official *Microsoft Flight Simulator* chat room on MSN Computing Central, also hosted by yours truly.

Regulars range from veteran sim and real-world pilots to virtual pilots just getting started, and from prominent add-on developers to *Flight Simulator* development team members. You won't find a nicer group of people anywhere.

We meet every Tuesday and Thursday from 7–8 pm PST/10–11 pm EST, and everyone is welcome!

There are two ways to access MSN Computing Central's *Flight Simulator* chat:

1. If you prefer a Web-based chat client, you can use this URL: http://computingcentral.msn.com/topics/flightsimulator/chat.asp

2. If you have a chat client such as Microsoft Chat (see Figure 10.15), simply start Microsoft Chat and type publicchat.msn.com in the Server box, enter #Chat_Hangar in the chat room box, and then click OK. Hope to see you there!

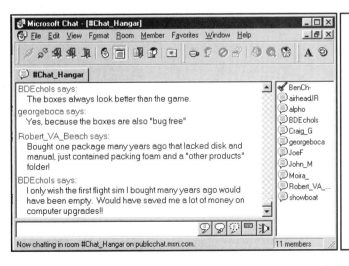

Figure 10.15: MSN Computing Central's *Microsoft Flight Simulator* Chat

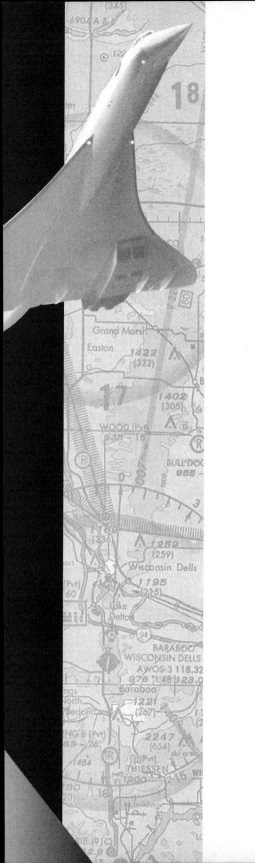

Los Angeles VFR Terminal Area Chart

Refer to this chart for the tutorials in Chapters 2 and 3. You can use it to plan your own VFR flights, as well. For a greater challenge, set the weather to VFR minimums and test your navigation and piloting skills.

Appendix A

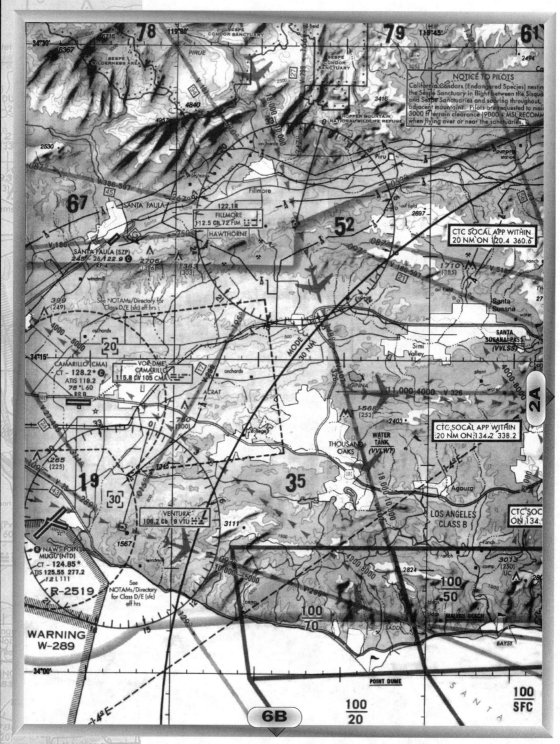

Maps not to be used for navigational purposes

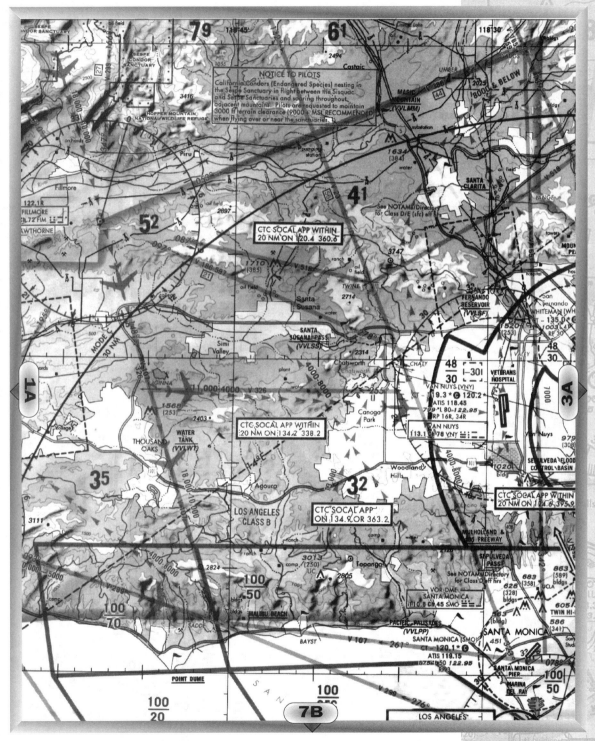

Maps not to be used for navigational purposes

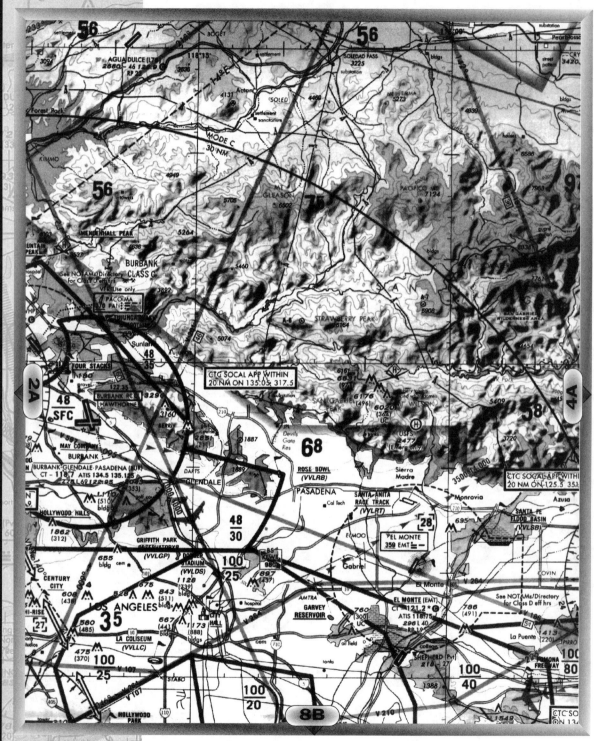

Maps not to be used for navigational purposes

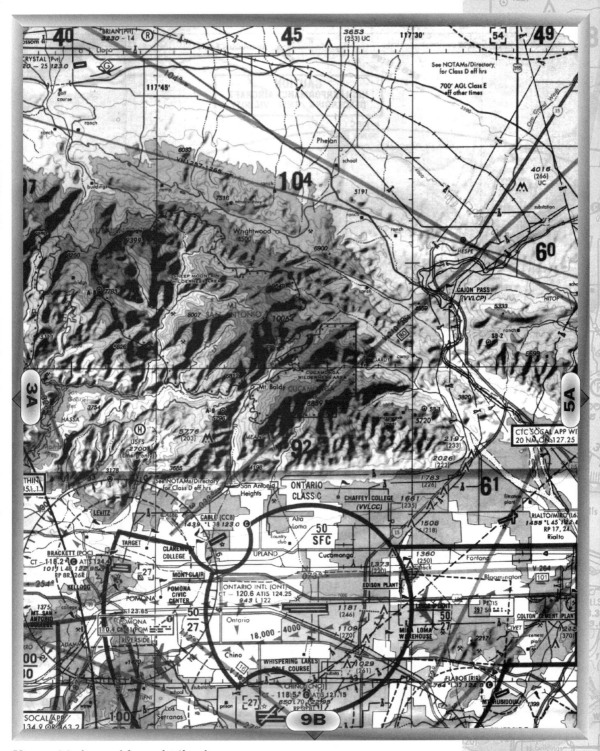

Maps not to be used for navigational purposes

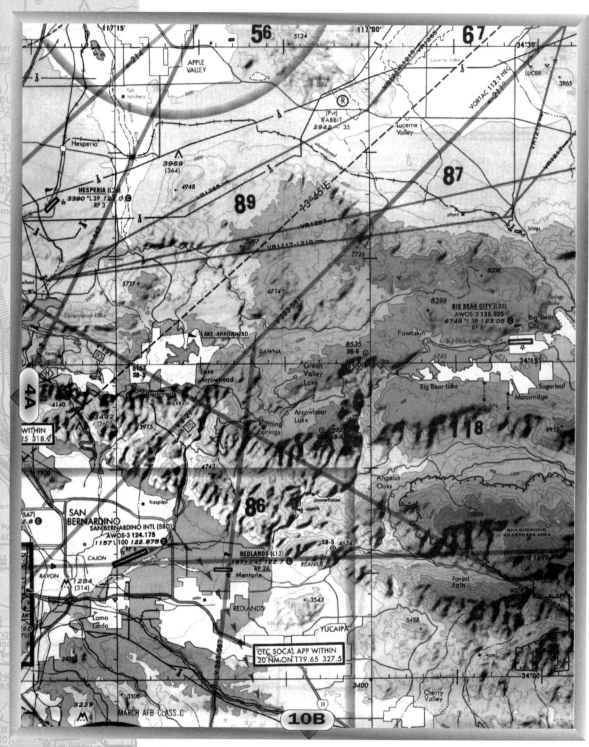

Maps not to be used for navigational purposes

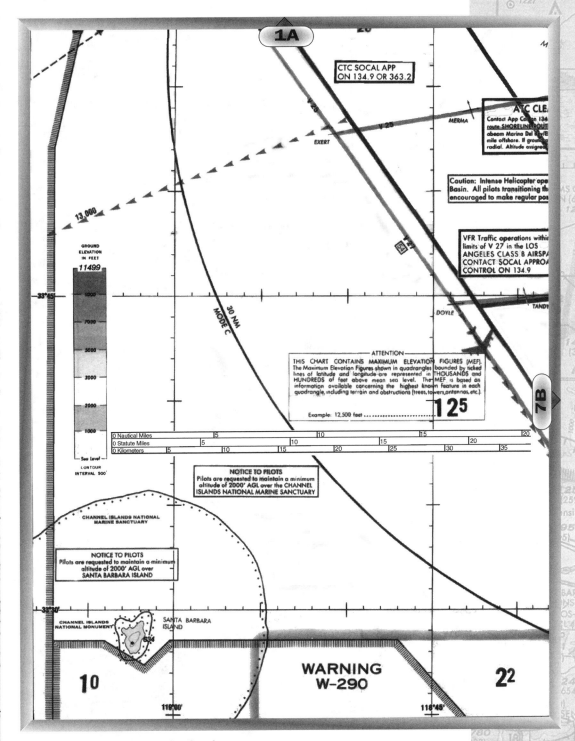

CTC SOCAL APP
ON 134.9 OR 363.2

ATC CLEA.

Contact App Co.ton 134.
route SHORELINE ROUTE
abeam Marina Del Rey/E.
mile offshore. If ground.
radial. Altitude assigned

Caution: Intense Helicopter ope.
Basin. All pilots transitioning th.
encouraged to make regular pos.

VFR Traffic operations within.
limits of V 27 in the LOS
ANGELES CLASS B AIRSPA
CONTACT SOCAL APPROA
CONTROL ON 134.9

GROUND
ELEVATION
IN FEET

11499

13,000

33°45'

30 NM
MODE C

ATTENTION

THIS CHART CONTAINS MAXIMUM ELEVATION FIGURES (MEF).
The Maximum Elevation Figures shown in quadrangles bounded by ticked
lines of latitude and longitude are represented in THOUSANDS and
HUNDREDS of feet above mean sea level. The MEF is based on
information available concerning the highest known feature in each
quadrangle, including terrain and obstructions (trees, towers, antennas, etc.).

Example: 12,500 feet 12⁵

DOYLE

TANDV.

7B

0 Nautical Miles	5	10	15	20
0 Statute Miles	5	10	15	20
0 Kilometers	5	10	15	20	25	30	35

CONTOUR
INTERVAL 500'

NOTICE TO PILOTS
Pilots are requested to maintain a minimum
altitude of 2000' AGL over the CHANNEL
ISLANDS NATIONAL MARINE SANCTUARY

CHANNEL ISLANDS NATIONAL
MARINE SANCTUARY

NOTICE TO PILOTS
Pilots are requested to maintain a minimum
altitude of 2000' AGL over
SANTA BARBARA ISLAND

33°30'

CHANNEL ISLANDS
NATIONAL MONUMENT

SANTA BARBARA
ISLAND

634

10

WARNING
W-290

2²

119°00'

118°45'

Maps not to be used for navigational purposes

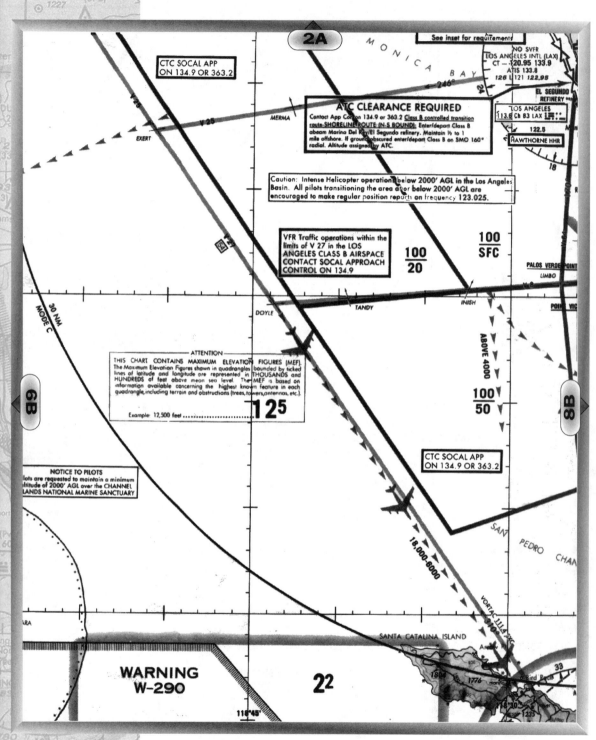

2A

MONICA BAY

See inset for requirements

NO SVFR
LOS ANGELES INTL (LAX)
CT – 120.95 133.9
ATIS 133.8
126 L 121 122.95

CTC SOCAL APP
ON 134.9 OR 363.2

246°

24

EL SEGUNDO
REFINERY

LOS ANGELES
113.6 Ch 83 LAX

122.5

HAWTHORNE HHR

ATC CLEARANCE REQUIRED
Contact App Control on 134.9 or 363.2 Class B controlled transition
route-SHORELINE ROUTE (N-S BOUND): Enter/depart Class B
abeam Marina Del Rey/El Segundo refinery. Maintain ½ to 1
mile offshore. If ground obscured enter/depart Class B on SMO 160°
radial. Altitude assigned by ATC.

18

MERMA

EXERT

V 25

Caution: Intense Helicopter operations below 2000' AGL in the Los Angeles
Basin. All pilots transitioning the area after below 2000' AGL are
encouraged to make regular position reports on frequency 123.025.

VFR Traffic operations within the
limits of V 27 in the LOS
ANGELES CLASS B AIRSPACE
CONTACT SOCAL APPROACH
CONTROL ON 134.9

100
20

100
SFC

PALOS VERDE POINT

DOYLE

TANDY

INISH

LIMBO

30 NM
MODE C

ABOVE 4000

POINT VIC

— ATTENTION —
THIS CHART CONTAINS MAXIMUM ELEVATION FIGURES (MEF).
The Maximum Elevation Figures shown in quadrangles bounded by ticked
lines of latitude and longitude are represented in THOUSANDS and
HUNDREDS of feet above mean sea level. The MEF is based on
information available concerning the highest known feature in each
quadrangle, including terrain and obstructions (trees, towers, antennas, etc.).

Example: 12,500 feet 12⁵

100
50

CTC SOCAL APP
ON 134.9 OR 363.2

— NOTICE TO PILOTS —
Pilots are requested to maintain a minimum
altitude of 2000' AGL over the CHANNEL
ISLANDS NATIONAL MARINE SANCTUARY

18,000-6000

SAN
PEDRO CHAN

6B

8B

VORTAC 111.4 PVC

SANTA CATALINA ISLAND

WARNING
W-290

2²

118°45'

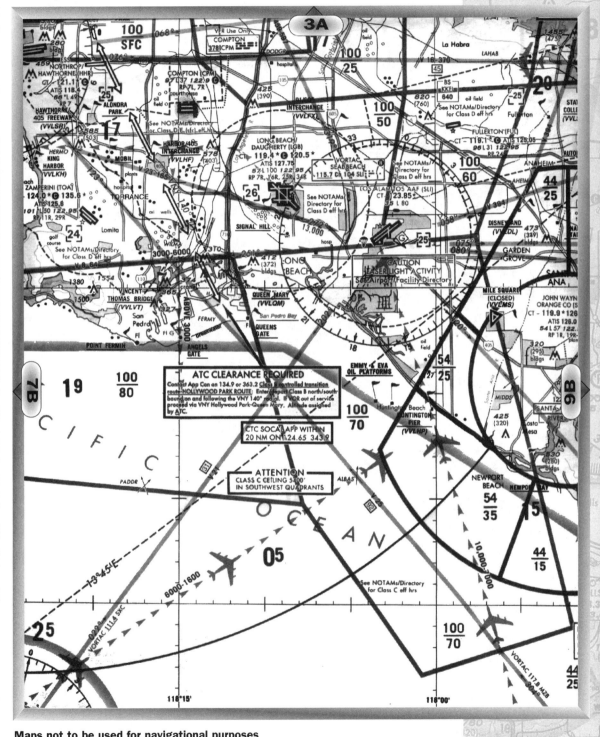

Maps not to be used for navigational purposes

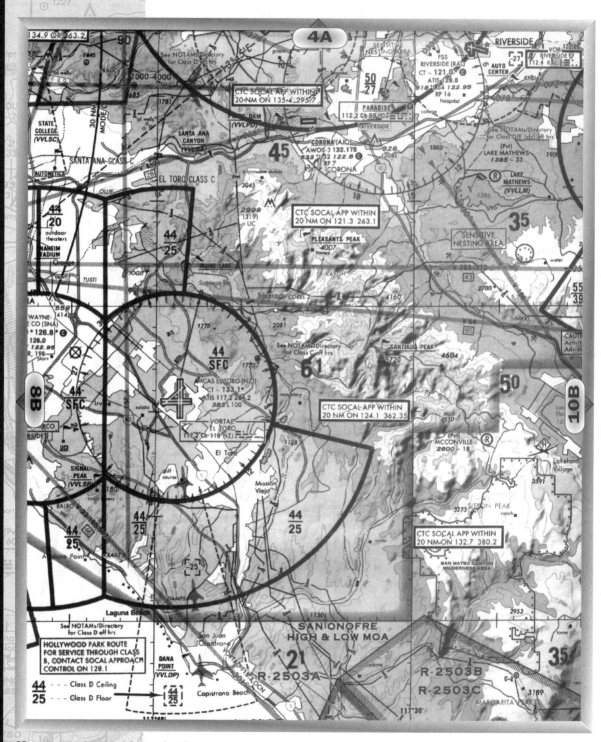

Maps not to be used for navigational purposes

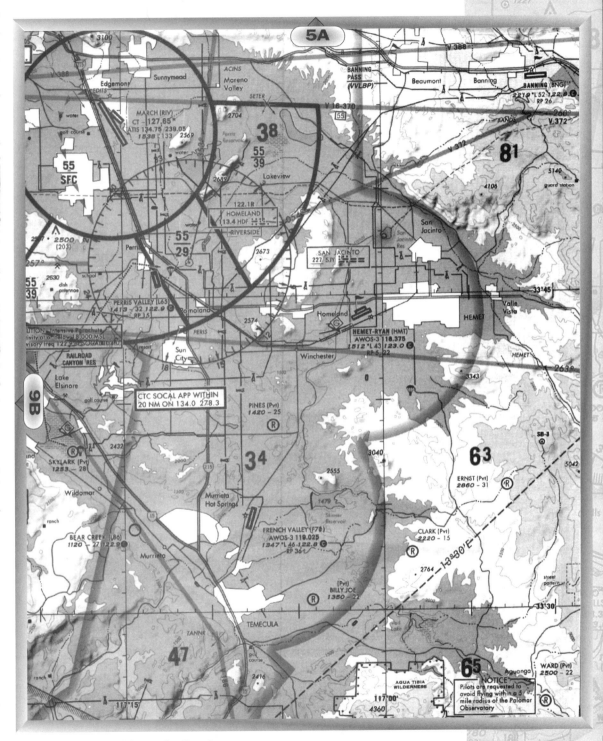

Maps not to be used for navigational purposes

IFR Terminal Procedures

Chapters 4, 5, and 6 refer you to these Terminal Procedures for Los Angeles International Airport, New York John F. Kennedy International Airport, and Chicago O'Hare International Airport. They're three of the most popular Flight Simulator 2000 airports that virtual pilots love to fly from (nice big runways!). You're sure to find them useful for creating other flights of fancy.

Appendix B

BASET ONE ARRIVAL Chart

LOS ANGELES INTL (LAX)
LOS ANGELES, CALIFORNIA

(BASET.BASET1) 99084
BASET ONE ARRIVAL

NOTE: DME Required

(NARRATIVE ON FOLLOWING PAGE)

NOTE: Chart not to scale.

ST-237 (FAA)

SOCAL APP CON
124.5 381.6
ATIS 133.8

LOS ANGELES, CALIFORNIA
LOS ANGELES INTL (LAX)
SW-2, 15 JUL 1999

BASET ONE ARRIVAL
(BASET.BASET1) 99084

TAKE-OFF MINIMUMS AND (OBSTACLE) DEPARTURE PROCEDURES ▽

SW-2
SW-2, 15 JUL 1999

LA VERNE, CA
BRACKETT FIELD
TAKE-OFF MINIMUMS: Rwys 8L, 8R, 26L, 26R, 300-1.
DEPARTURE PROCEDURE: Rwys 8L, 8R, climb runway heading 1400, then climbing right/turn heading 195°. Rwys 26L, 26R, climb runway heading to 1400, then climbing left/turn heading 130°. All aircraft intercept and climb via GYO R-278 to GYO VORTAC. Aircraft departing GYO R-120 CW R-020 climb on course. All others climb in GYO holding pattern (NW, right/turns, 127° inbound) to depart GYO VORTAC at or above 5000.

LAKEPORT, CA
LAMPSON FIELD
TAKE-OFF MINIMUMS: Rwy 10, 1700-3 or std. with min. climb of 910' per NM to 3300. Rwy 28, 1500-3 or std. with min. climb of 620' per NM to 2200.
DEPARTURE PROCEDURE: Rwy 10, climbing left/turn to heading 275°. Rwy 28, climbing right/turn to heading 035°. Intercept and climb northwestbound via the LOP NDB 336° bearing to 4000, then climbing left/turn direct ENI VORTAC. Cross ENI VORTAC at or above 6000.

LANCASTER, CA
GENERAL WILLIAM J. FOX AIRFIELD
DEPARTURE PROCEDURE: Climb southeastbound on R-299 to PMD VORTAC. Depart PMD at published MCA for direction of flight.

LINCOLN, CA
LINCOLN REGIONAL AIRPORT/
KARL HARDER FIELD
DEPARTURE PROCEDURE: Rwy 15, climbing right turn. Rwy 33, climbing left/turn. All aircraft climb direct MYV VOR/DME, then climb on course.

LIVERMORE, CA
LIVERMORE MUNI
TAKE-OFF MINIMUMS: Rwys 7L, 7R, 1500-2 or std. with a min. climb of 260' per NM to 2200. Rwys 25L, 25R, 2300-2 or std. with a min. climb of 375' per NM to 3100.
DEPARTURE PROCEDURE: Rwys 7L, 7R, climb direct REIGA LOM, then climbing left/turn via the I030° bearing from REIGA LOM to intercept V109, then proceed on course. Rwys 25L, 25R, climb runway heading to 1200, then climbing right/turn via heading I20° and OAK R-050 to ALTAM Int, then proceed on course.

LODI, CA
LODI
DEPARTURE PROCEDURE: Climb direct to LIN VORTAC.

LOMPOC, CA
LOMPOC
TAKE-OFF MINIMUMS: Rwy 7, 2900-2 or std. with a min. climb of 240' per NM to 1800. Rwy 25, turn right heading 130°. All aircraft intercept and climb via GVO R-278 to GVO VORTAC. Aircraft departing GVO R-120 CW R-020 climb on course. All others climb in GVO holding pattern (NW, right/turns, 127° inbound) to depart GVO VORTAC at or above 5000.

LONG BEACH, CA
LONG BEACH (DAUGHERTY FIELD)
TAKE-OFF MINIMUMS: Rwy 16L, 500-1 or std. with min. climb of 270' per NM to 400. Rwy 16R, 500-1 or std. with min. climb of 464' per NM to 400. Rwy 26L, 300-1 or std. with min. climb of 284' per NM to 300. Rwys 34L, 34R, 300-1.
DEPARTURE PROCEDURE: Rwys 7L, 7R, climb to 800, turn right direct SLI VORTAC and proceed to PADDR Int via R-210. Rwy 12, climb runway heading to intercept and proceed via SLI VORTAC R-210 to PADDR Int. Rwys 16L, 16R, climb to 600, turn right heading 190° to intercept and proceed via SLR R-210 to PADDR Int. Rwys 25L, 25R, 30, climb to 800, turn left heading 200° to intercept and proceed via LAX R-145 to PADDR Int.

LOS ANGELES, CA
LOS ANGELES INTL
TAKE-OFF MINIMUMS: Rwys 25L, 25R, turbojet std. non-turbojet std. with a min. climb of 360' per NM to 600.
DEPARTURE PROCEDURE: Rwys 6L, 6R, 7L, 7R, climb to 2000 heading 070°, then climbing right/turn. Rwys 24L, 24R, climb to 3000 heading 250°, then climbing left/turn. Rwys 25L, 25R, turbojet climb to 3000 heading 250°, then climbing left/turn, non-turbojet climb via heading 250°, at the SMO 154° radial turn left heading 200°. Then all aircraft climb direct SLI VORTAC, then climb on course.

WHITEMAN
TAKE-OFF MINIMUMS: Rwys 12, 30, 2900-2 or std. with a min. climb of 350' per NM to 4300.
DEPARTURE PROCEDURE: Rwy 12, climbing right turn direct VNY VOR/DME. Rwy 30, climbing left/turn heading 260°. All aircraft climb to 4500 via VNY R-325, then climbing left/turn direct VNY VOR/DME.

LOS BANOS, CA
LOS BANOS MUNI
DEPARTURE PROCEDURE: Aircraft departing 320° CW 120° climb on course. All others climb via heading 240° to intercept V109. Southeastbound via V109 requires a climb rate of 300' per NM to 4000.

C5
98337

CIVET FOUR ARRIVAL (CIVET.CIVET4) 98225

LOS ANGELES INTL
LOS ANGELES, CALIFORNIA

ST-237 (FAA)

SW-2, 15 JUL 1999

NOTE: DME or RADAR required.

NOTE: Chart not to scale.

From over CIVET INT via I-LAX to FUELR DME fix.
Expect ILS approach.

CIVET
N34°02.07'
W117°23.45'
Cross at or below 17,000'
Cross at or above 14,000'

ARNES
N33°59.93'
W117°45.92'
Cross at or below 11,000'

FUELR
N33°59.16'
W117°53.81'
Cross at or above 10,000'

BREMR
N34°00.67'-W117°38.16'
Cross at or above 12,000'

SUZZI
N33°59.46'
W117°50.70'
Cross at or above 9,000'

Cross at or above 8,000'

PARADISE
112.2 PDZ Chan 59

SEAL BEACH
115.7 SLI Chan 104

LOS ANGELES
113.6 LAX Chan 83

LOCALIZER 109.9
I-LAX Chan 36

SANTA MONICA
110.8 SMO Chan 45

RWY 25L

LAX R-068
R-073
R-030

I-LAX

SOCAL APP CON
124.9 269.0
ATIS 133.8
LOS ANGELES TOWER
N133.9 239.3
S120.95 379.1

P11

CIVET FOUR ARRIVAL (CIVET.CIVET4) 98225

LOS ANGELES, CALIFORNIA
LOS ANGELES INTL

SW-2, 15 JUL 1999

BASET ONE ARRIVAL (BASET.BASET1) 97254

P6   ST-237 (FAA)

SW-2, 15 JUL 1999

LOS ANGELES INTL (LAX)
LOS ANGELES, CALIFORNIA

ARRIVAL DESCRIPTION

HECTOR TRANSITION (HEC.BASET1): From over HEC VORTAC via HEC R-211 and PDZ R-030 to CIVET INT, then via LAX R-068 to BASET INT. Thence. . . .

PEACH SPRINGS TRANSITION (PGS.BASET1): From over PGS VORTAC via PGS R-229 and PDZ R-046 to RUSTT INT, then via LAX R-068 to BASET INT. Thence. . . .

TWENTYNINE PALMS TRANSITION (TNP.BASET1): From over TNP VORTAC via TNP R-245 and PDZ R-069 to PDZ VORTAC, then via PDZ R-265 to BASET INT. Thence. . . .

. . . From over BASET INT/DME via LAX R-068 to REEDR DME. REEDR DME via heading 210° for radar vector to final approach course for Runways 6 or 7.

LOST COMMUNICATIONS: DEPART REEDR heading 210° to intercept the SLI R-251 to TANDY INT/SLI 30 DME.

LOS ANGELES INTL (LAX)
LOS ANGELES, CALIFORNIA

BASET ONE ARRIVAL (BASET.BASET1) 97254

283

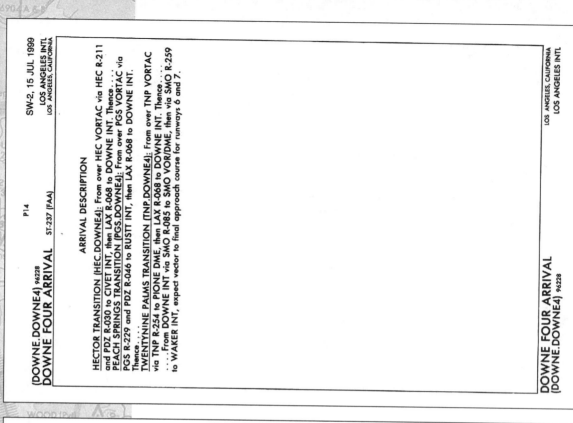

ARRIVAL DESCRIPTION

HECTOR TRANSITION (HEC.DOWNE4): From over HEC VORTAC via HEC R-211 and PDZ R-030 to CIVET INT, then LAX R-068 to DOWNE INT. Thence.....

PEACH SPRINGS TRANSITION (PGS.DOWNE4): From over PGS VORTAC via PGS R-229 and PDZ R-046 to RUSTT INT, then LAX R-068 to DOWNE INT. Thence.....

TWENTYNINE PALMS TRANSITION (TNP.DOWNE4): From over TNP VORTAC via TNP R-254 to PIONE DME, then LAX R-068 to DOWNE INT. Thence.....

.... From DOWNE INT via SMO R-085 to SMO VOR/DME, then via SMO R-259 to WAKER INT, expect vector to final approach course for runways 6 and 7.

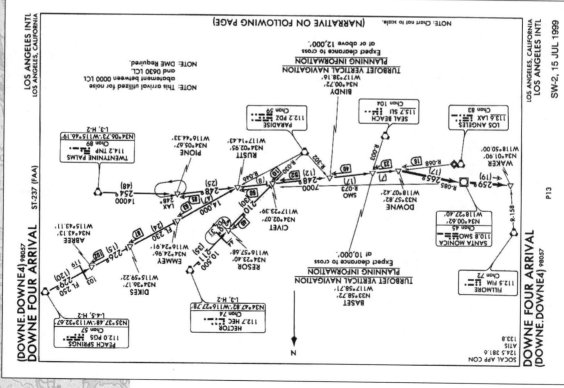

NOTE: Chart not to scale.   (NARRATIVE ON FOLLOWING PAGE)

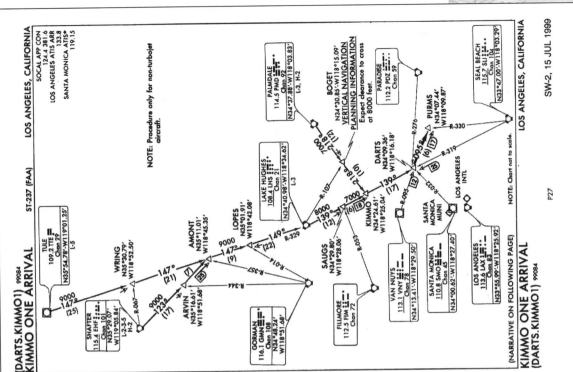

KIMMO ONE ARRIVAL

SOCAL APP CON
124.4 381.6
LOS ANGELES ATIS ARR
133.8
SANTA MONICA ATIS*
119.15

NOTE: Procedure only for non-turbojet aircraft.

TULE
109.2 TTE ≡
N35°54.78'-W119°01.25'
L-5

SHAFTER
115.4 EHF ≡
N35°29.07'-W119°05.84'
L-2-3-5 H-2

9000
147°
(25)

147°
(21)

WRING
N35°30.79'
W119°52.50'

9000
123° R-067
(17)

ARVIN
N35°16.61'
W118°51.68'

R-344

GORMAN
116.1 GMN ≡
N34°48.24'
W118°51.68'
Chan 108

AMONT
N35°11.01'
W118°45.35'

147°
(9)

R-357
R-014

LOPES
N35°01.61'
W118°42.08'

149° R-329

FILLMORE
112.5 FIM ≡
Chan 72

SAUGS
W118°28.06'
W118°28.06'

R-053

LAKE HUGHES
108.4 LHS ≡
Chan 21
L-3

8000
139°
(12)

7000
139°
(17)

KIMMO
N34°24.61'
W118°25.04'

R-095

VAN NUYS
113.1 VNY ≡
N34°13.41'-W118°29.50'
Chan 78

SANTA MONICA
110.8 SMO ≡
N34°00.62'-W118°27.40'
Chan 45

LOS ANGELES
113.6 LAX ≡
N33°55.99'-W118°25.92'
Chan 83

SANTA MONICA MUNI

LOS ANGELES INTL

R-033

7000
218°
(6)

8000
218°
(10)

7000
218°
(13)

R-107

PALMDALE
114.5 PMD ≡
N34°37.88'-W118°03.83'
Chan 92
L-3, H-2

BOGET
N34°30.85'-W118°15.09'
VERTICAL NAVIGATION PLANNING INFORMATION
Exped clearance to cross at 8000 feet.

DARTS
N34°09.36'
W118°16.18'

139°
(17)

R-276

R-319

PURMS
N34°07.44'
W118°09.87'

R-330

PARADISE
112.2 PDZ ≡
Chan 59

SEAL BEACH
115.7 SLI ≡
N33°27.00'-W118°03.29'
Chan 104

NOTE: Chart not to scale.

(NARRATIVE ON FOLLOWING PAGE)

KIMMO ONE ARRIVAL
(DARTS.KIMMO1) 99084

LOS ANGELES, CALIFORNIA

P27   SW-2, 15 JUL 1999

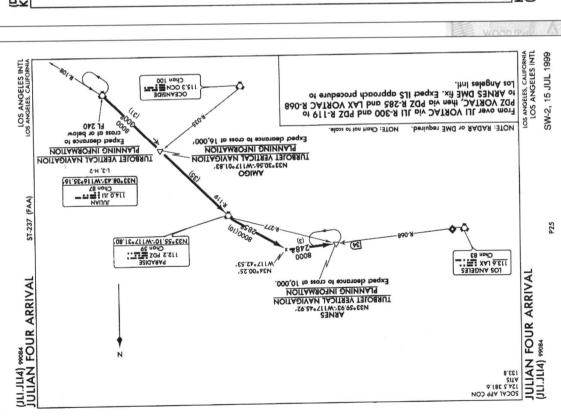

JULIAN FOUR ARRIVAL

SOCAL APP CON
124.5 381.6
ATIS
133.8

N

LOS ANGELES INTL
LOS ANGELES, CALIFORNIA

R-108

OCEANSIDE
115.3 OCN ≡
Chan 100

8000
(31)

FL 240
Exped clearance to cross at or below

TURBOJET VERTICAL NAVIGATION PLANNING INFORMATION
Exped clearance to cross at 16,000'

AMIGO
N33°30.56'-W117°01.83'
L-3, H-2

JULIAN
114.0 JLI ≡
N33°08.43'-W116°35.16'
Chan 87

R-300
R-035

R-119

8000 (10)
R-271
24 S5 28 S8

PARADISE
112.2 PDZ ≡
N33°55.10'-W117°31.80'
Chan 59

TURBOJET VERTICAL NAVIGATION PLANNING INFORMATION
Exped clearance to cross at 10,000.

ARNES
N33°59.93'-W117°45.92'

8000
248°
(3)

8000
R-068

34

LOS ANGELES
113.6 LAX ≡
Chan 83

NOTE: RADAR or DME required.

From over JLI VORTAC via JLI R-300 and PDZ R-119 to PDZ VORTAC, then via PDZ R-285 and LAX VORTAC R-068 to ARNES DME fix. Exped ILS approach procedure to Los Angeles Intl.

NOTE: Chart not to scale.

LOS ANGELES, CALIFORNIA
LOS ANGELES INTL

SW-2, 15 JUL 1999

JULIAN FOUR ARRIVAL
(JLI.JLI4) 99084

P25

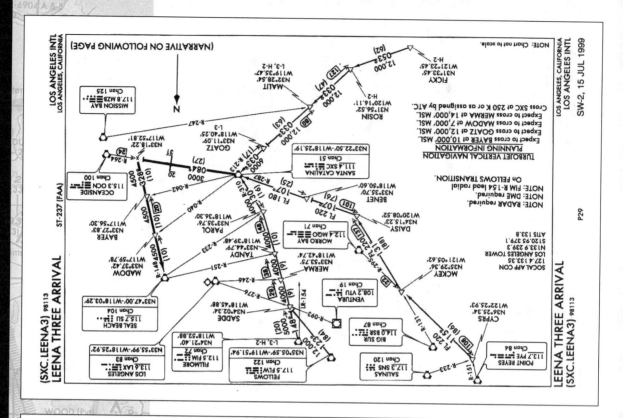

ARRIVAL ROUTE DESCRIPTION

LAKE HUGHES TRANSITION (LHS.KIMMO1): From over LHS VORTAC via LHS R-139 to DARTS INT. Thence. . . .

PALMDALE TRANSITION (PMD.KIMMO1): From over PMD VORTAC via PMD R-218 to KIMMO INT, then via LHS R-139 to DARTS INT. Thence. . . .

TULE TRANSITION (TTE.KIMMO1): From over TTE VOR/DME via TTE R-147 and LHS R-329 to LHS VORTAC, then via LHS R-139 to DARTS INT. Thence. . . .

SHAFTER TRANSITION (EHF.KIMMO1): From over EHF VORTAC via EHF R-123 and LHS R-329 to LHS VORTAC, then via LHS R-139 to DARTS INT. Thence. . . .

. . . . LANDING LOS ANGELES INTL: From over DARTS INT via VNY R-095 to PUMS INT. Expect radar vectors to final approach course.

. . . . LANDING SANTA MONICA MUNI: From over DARTS INT via VNY R-095 to DARTS INT. Expect radar vectors to final approach course.

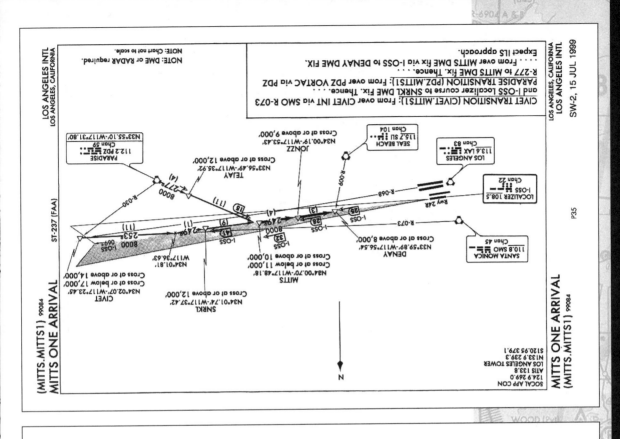

(MITTS.MITTS1) 99084 — MITTS ONE ARRIVAL

SOCAL APP CON
124.9 269.0
ATIS 133.8
LOS ANGELES TOWER
N133.9 239.3
S120.95 379.1

MITTS ONE ARRIVAL
(MITTS.MITTS1) 99084

NOTE: DME or RADAR required.
NOTE: Chart not to scale.

CIVET TRANSITION (CIVET.MITTS1): From over CIVET INT via SMO R-073 and I-OSS Localizer course to SNRKL DME Fix. Thence . . . .
PARADISE TRANSITION (PDZ.MITTS1): From over PDZ VORTAC via PDZ R-277 to MITTS DME Fix. Thence . . . .
. . . . From over MITTS DME Fix via I-OSS to DENAY DME FIX.
Expect ILS approach.

P35

(SXC.LEENA3) 97086 — LEENA THREE ARRIVAL

ARRIVAL DESCRIPTION

CYPRS TRANSITION (CYPRS.LEENA3): From over CYPRS INT via MQO R-295 to MCKEY INT, then via BSR R-131 to DAISY INT, and SXC R-287 to SXC VORTAC. Thence . . . .

FELLOWS TRANSITION (FLW.LEENA3): From over FLW VORTAC via FLW R-123 to SADDE INT, then via FIM R-148 to PAROL INT, and SXC R-310 to SXC VORTAC. Thence . . . .

FICKY TRANSITION (FICKY.LEENA3): From over FICKY direct ROSIN DME, then via SXC R-213 to SXC VORTAC. Thence . . . .

FILLMORE TRANSITION (FIM.LEENA3): From over FIM VORTAC via FIM R-148 to PAROL INT, then via SXC R-310 to SXC VORTAC. Thence . . . .

GOATZ TRANSITION (GOATZ.LEENA3): From over GOATZ DME via SXC R-213 to SXC VORTAC. Thence . . . .

MALIT TRANSITION (MALIT.LEENA3): From over MALIT DME via SXC R-213 to SXC VORTAC. Thence . . . .

ROSIN TRANSITION (ROSIN.LEENA3): From over ROSIN DME via SXC R-213 to SXC VORTAC. Thence . . . .

. . . . From over SXC VORTAC via SXC R-084 and OCN R-264 to intercept the SLI R-148 to SLI VORTAC. Expect radar vectors to ILS approach for Rwy 25L.

LEENA THREE ARRIVAL
(SXC.LEENA3) 97086

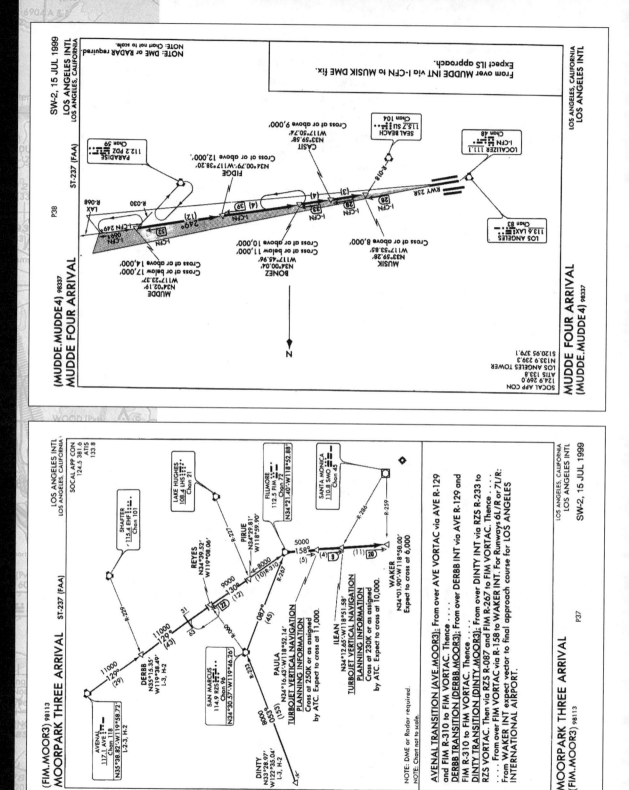

(MUDDE.MUDDE4) 98113
MUDDE FOUR ARRIVAL   ST-237 (FAA)   SW-2, 15 JUL 1999
LOS ANGELES INTL
LOS ANGELES, CALIFORNIA

NOTE: DME or RADAR required.
NOTE: Chart not to scale.

From over MUDDE INT via I-CFN to MUSIK DME fix.
Expect ILS approach.

SEAL BEACH 115.7 SLI Chan 104
N33°59.58' W117°50.74'
Cross at or above 9,000'

CASIT
Cross at or above 12,000'
FIDGE N34°00.79' W117°38.20'

PARADISE 112.2 PDZ Chan 59

LAX R-068
R-030
I-CFN 249°

CROSS at or below 14,000'
MUDDE N34°02.19' W117°23.37'
Cross at or below 17,000'

BONEZ N34°00.04' W117°45.96'
Cross at or above 11,000'

Cross at or above 10,000'

MUSIK N33°59.28' W117°53.85'
Cross at or above 8,000'

RWY 25R
LOCALIZER 111.1 I-CFN Chan 48
LOS ANGELES 113.6 LAX Chan 83

N
SOCAL APP CON 124.9 269.0
LOS ANGELES TOWER ATIS 133.8
N133.9 239.3
S120.95 379.1

MUDDE FOUR ARRIVAL
(MUDDE.MUDDE4) 98337

LOS ANGELES, CALIFORNIA
LOS ANGELES INTL

(FIM.MOOR3) 98113
MOORPARK THREE ARRIVAL   ST-237 (FAA)
LOS ANGELES INTL
LOS ANGELES, CALIFORNIA

SOCAL APP CON 124.5 381.6
ATIS 133.8

SHAFTER 115.4 EHF Chan 101

LAKE HUGHES 108.4 LHS Chan 21

REYES N34°39.52' W119°08.06'
R-227

PIRUE N34°29.81' W118°59.90'

FILLMORE 112.5 FIM Chan 77
N34°21.40' W118°52.88'

SANTA MONICA 110.8 SMO Chan 45

AVENAL 117.1 AVE Chan 118
N35°38.82' W119°58.72'
L-2,3, H-2

11000 129° (29)

DERBB N35°15.35' W119°38.49'
L-3, H-2

SAN MARCUS 114.9 RZS Chan 96
N34°30.57' W119°46.26'

11000 129° (43)

31
53

R-267
R-310

8000
130° (12)

9000

5000
158° (5)
(4) 9
(11) 20

WAKER N34°01.90' W118°50.00'
Expect to cross at 6,000'

R-259
R-286

ILEAN N34°12.65' W118°51.58'
TURBOJET VERTICAL NAVIGATION PLANNING INFORMATION
Cross at 230K or as assigned by ATC. Expect to cross at 10,000.

PAULA N34°16.43' W118°52.14'
TURBOJET VERTICAL NAVIGATION PLANNING INFORMATION
Cross at 250K or as assigned by ATC. Expect to cross at 11,000.

DINTY N33°28.97' W122°35.04'
L-3, H-2

9000 053° (153)

R-233
087° (45)

AVENAL TRANSITION (AVE.MOOR3): From over AVE VORTAC via AVE R-129
and FIM R-310 to FIM VORTAC. Thence . . . . .
DERBB TRANSITION (DERBB.MOOR3): From over DERBB INT via AVE R-129 and
FIM R-310 to FIM VORTAC. Thence . . . . .
DINTY TRANSITION (DINTY.MOOR3): From over DINTY INT via RZS R-233 to
RZS VORTAC. Then via RZS R-087 and FIM R-267 to FIM VORTAC. Thence . . . . .
. . . From over FIM VORTAC via FIM R-158 to WAKER INT. For Runways 6L/R or 7L/R:
From WAKER INT expect vector to final approach course for LOS ANGELES
INTERNATIONAL AIRPORT.

NOTE: DME or Radar required.
NOTE: Chart not to scale.

MOORPARK THREE ARRIVAL
(FIM.MOOR3) 98113

LOS ANGELES, CALIFORNIA
LOS ANGELES INTL
SW-2, 15 JUL 1999   P37

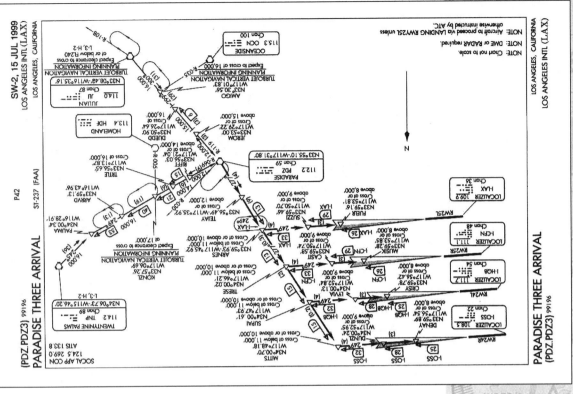

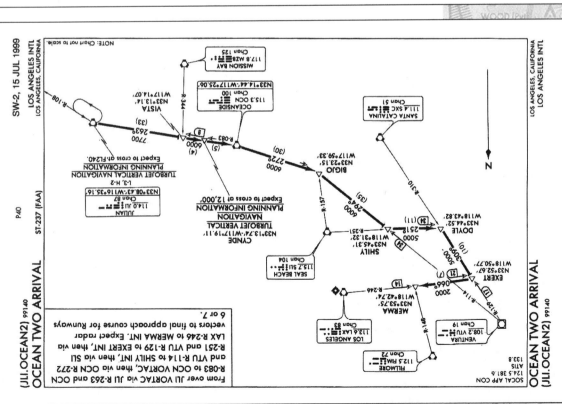

REDEYE ONE ARRIVAL chart

(DOWNE.RDEYE1) 98057
REDEYE ONE ARRIVAL

P46
ST-237 (FAA)

SW-2, 15 JUL 1999
LOS ANGELES INTL (LAX)
LOS ANGELES, CALIFORNIA

NOTE: DME Required.

NOTE: This arrival utilized to noise
abatement between 0000 LCL
and 0630 LCL.

(NARRATIVE ON FOLLOWING PAGE)

NOTE: Chart not to scale.

HOMELAND
113.4 HDF

PARADISE
112.2 PDZ
Chan 59
N33°55.10'-W117°31.80'
Cross at or above 14,000'

SEAL BEACH
115.7 SLI
Chan 104

LOS ANGELES
113.6 LAX
Chan 83

ARRVD
N33°59.13'
W117°06.69'

KONZL
N33°57.26'
W116°43.96'

TRTLE
N33°56.65'
W117°13.87'
Cross
at 16,000'

CACTS
N33°56.14'
W117°38.90'

WAKER
N34°01.90'
W118°50.00'
Chan 59

TWENTYNINE PALMS
114.2 TNP
Chan 89
N34°06.73'-W115°46.19'

R-069(15)
9000

R-046

R-230

R-003

R-068

2498 (14)
(19)
40
21
(6)

248.6
205
(9)
(17)
23
18 (7)

RUSH
N34°02.95'
W119°14.92'

GRAMA
N34°06.41'
W117°06.41'

DIKES
N34°36.17'
W115°59.22'

SMO
N34°06.73'
7000
7000

2248.8
(12)
40
(17)
(7)

7000 or above 10,000'

DOWNE
N33°57.82'
W118°07.42'

SANTA MONICA
110.8 SMO
Chan 43

ABREE
N34°43.13'
W115°43.10'

2210.6
39)
EL 230
(17)

EMMEY
N34°24.96'
W116°24.91'

10500
2211.6
(35)

DAWNA
N34°15.90'
W117°06.78'
Cross at
or below 13,000'

BINDY
N34°00.77'
W117°38.16'
Cross at
or above 12,000'

CIVET
N34°02.07'
W117°23.45'
Cross at
14,000'

259.6
2265.8
259
(19)
Cross at
or above 10,000'
R-085
R-158

FILLMORE
112.5 FIM
Chan 72

103
FL 250
229.8
119 (120)

2228

14,000

RESOR
N34°23.40'
W116°57.68'

BASET
N33°58.72'
W117°58.71'

HECTOR
112.7 HEC
Chan 74
N34°47.82'-W116°27.28'

PEACH SPRINGS
112.0 PGS
Chan 57
N35°37.48'-W113°32.67'

L-3, H-2

L-4-5, H-2

SOCAL APP CON
124.5 381.6
ATIS 133.8

N

REDEYE ONE ARRIVAL
(DOWNE.RDEYE1) 98057

LOS ANGELES, CALIFORNIA
LOS ANGELES INTL (LAX)

PARADISE THREE ARRIVAL chart

(PDZ.PDZ3) 99084
PARADISE THREE ARRIVAL

ST-237 (FAA)

LOS ANGELES INTL (LAX)
LOS ANGELES, CALIFORNIA

ARRIVAL DESCRIPTION

JULIAN TRANSITION (JLI.PDZ3): From over JLI VORTAC via JLI R-300 and PDZ
R-119 to PDZ VORTAC. Thence....

TWENTYNINE PALMS TRANSITION (TNP.PDZ3): From over TNP VORTAC via
TNP R-245 to PAUMA INT, then via PDZ R-069 to PDZ VORTAC. Thence....
....From over PDZ VORTAC via PDZ R-277 to TEJAY DME fix thence via one of the four
Landing Rwy routes beginning at TEJAY.

Landing Rwy 25L: From over TEJAY INT via PDZ R-277 to ARNES DME, then via
I-LAX (Rwy 25L) to FUELR INT. Expect ILS approach.

Landing Rwy 25R: From over TEJAY INT via PDZ R-277 to TRESE DME, then via
I-CFN (Rwy 25R) to MUSIK INT. Expect ILS approach.

Landing Rwy 24L: From over TEJAY INT via PDZ R-277 to SUPAI DME, then via
I-HQB (Rwy 24L) to CRISY INT. Expect ILS approach.

Landing Rwy 24R: From over TEJAY INT via PDZ R-277 to MITTS DME, then via
I-OSS (Rwy 24R) to DENAY INT. Expect ILS approach.

LOS ANGELES, CALIFORNIA
LOS ANGELES INTL (LAX)

SW-2, 15 JUL 1999

P43

PARADISE THREE ARRIVAL
(PDZ.PDZ3) 99084

ARRIVAL DESCRIPTION

HECTOR TRANSITION (HEC.RDEYE1): From over HEC VORTAC via HEC R-211 and PDZ R-030 to CIVET INT, then LAX R-068 to DOWNE INT. Thence. . . .

PEACH SPRINGS TRANSITION (PGS.RDEYE1): From over PGS VORTAC via PGS R-229 and PDZ R-046 to RUSTT INT, then LAX R-068 to DOWNE INT. Thence. . . .

TWENTYNINE PALMS TRANSITION (TNP.RDEYE1): From over TNP VORTAC via TNP R-245 and PDZ R-069 to PDZ VORTAC, then PDZ R-265 to BASET INT, then LAX R-068 to DOWNE INT. Thence. . . .

. . . . From DOWNE INT via SMO R-085 to SMO VOR/DME, then via SMO R-259 to WAKER INT. Expect vector to final approach course for runways 6 and 7.

LOS ANGELES, CALIFORNIA
LOS ANGELES INTL (LAX)
SW-2, 15 JUL 1999

P47

REDEYE ONE ARRIVAL
(DOWNE.RDEYE1) 97254

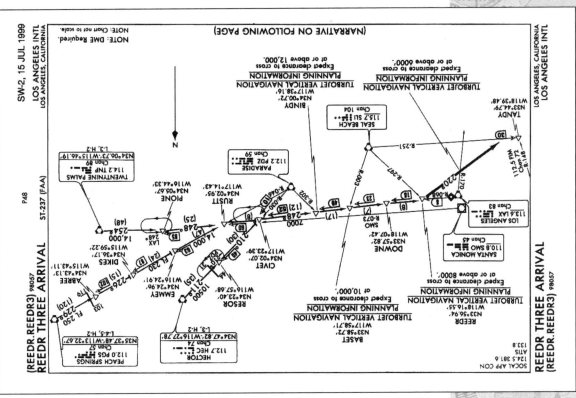

SW-2, 15 JUL 1999
LOS ANGELES INTL
LOS ANGELES, CALIFORNIA

(REEDR.REEDR3) 98057   P48   ST-237 (FAA)
REEDR THREE ARRIVAL

REEDR THREE ARRIVAL
(REEDR.REEDR3) 98057
LOS ANGELES, CALIFORNIA
LOS ANGELES INTL

(NARRATIVE ON FOLLOWING PAGE)

NOTE: DME Required.
NOTE: Chart not to scale.

LAX

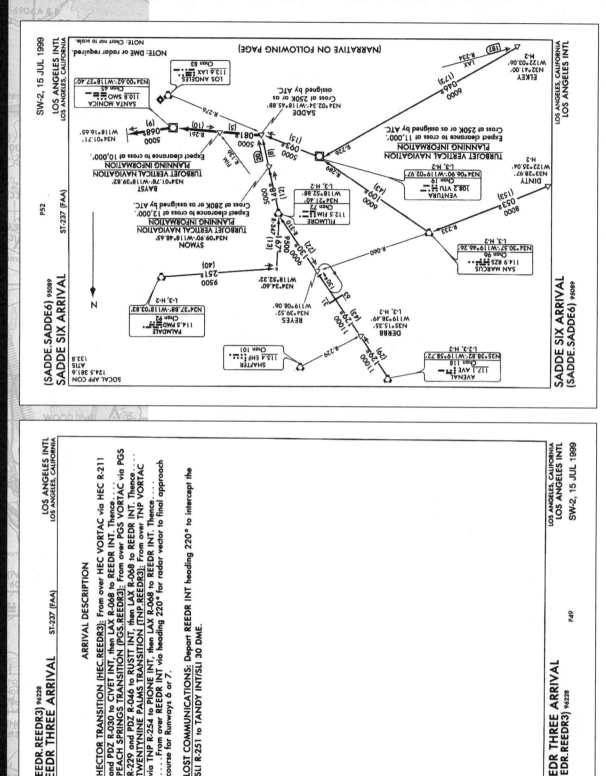

(SADDE.SADDE6) 95089
SADDE SIX ARRIVAL

SW-2, 15 JUL 1999
LOS ANGELES INTL
LOS ANGELES, CALIFORNIA

SOCAL APP CON
124.5 381.6
ATIS
133.8

P52   ST-237 (FAA)

NOTE: DME or radar required.
NOTE: Chart not to scale.
(NARRATIVE ON FOLLOWING PAGE)

SADDE SIX ARRIVAL
(SADDE.SADDE6) 95089
LOS ANGELES, CALIFORNIA
LOS ANGELES INTL

(REEDR.REEDR3) 96228
REEDR THREE ARRIVAL   ST-237 (FAA)

LOS ANGELES INTL
LOS ANGELES, CALIFORNIA

ARRIVAL DESCRIPTION

HECTOR TRANSITION (HEC.REEDR3): From over HEC VORTAC via HEC R-211 and PDZ R-030 to CIVET INT, then LAX R-068 to REEDR INT. Thence....
PEACH SPRINGS TRANSITION (PGS.REEDR3): From over PGS VORTAC via PGS R-229 and PDZ R-046 to RUSTT INT, then LAX R-068 to REEDR INT. Thence....
TWENTYNINE PALMS TRANSITION (TNP.REEDR3): From over TNP VORTAC via TNP R-254 to PIONE INT, then LAX R-068 to REEDR INT. Thence....
....From over REEDR INT via heading 220° for radar vector to final approach course for Runways 6 or 7.

LOST COMMUNICATIONS: Depart REEDR INT heading 220° to intercept the SLI R-251 to TANDY INT/SLI 30 DME.

REEDR THREE ARRIVAL
(REEDR.REEDR3) 96228
P49

LOS ANGELES, CALIFORNIA
LOS ANGELES INTL
SW-2, 15 JUL 1999

LAX

SADDE SIX ARRIVAL

(SADDE.SADDE6) 95089

(SADDE.SADDE6) 95089
SADDE SIX ARRIVAL

ST-237 (FAA)

LOS ANGELES INTL
LOS ANGELES, CALIFORNIA

ARRIVAL DESCRIPTION

AVENAL TRANSITION (AVE.SADDE6): From over AVE VORTAC via AVE R-129 and FIM R-310 to FIM VORTAC, then via FIM R-148 to SADDE INT. Thence. . . .
DERBB TRANSITION (DERBB.SADDE6): From over DERBB INT via AVE R-129 and FIM R-310 to FIM VORTAC, then via FIM R-148 to SADDE INT. Thence. . . .
DINTY TRANSITION (DINTY.SADDE6): From over DINTY INT via RZS R-233 to RZS VORTAC; then via RZS R-109 and VTU R-289 to VTU VOR/DME, and then via VTU R-093 to SADDE INT. Thence. . . .
ELKEY TRANSITION (ELKEY.SADDE6): From over ELKEY INT via VTU R-226 to VTU VOR/DME then via VTU R-093 to SADDE INT. Thence. . . .
FILLMORE TRANSITION (FIM.SADDE6): From over FIM VORTAC via FIM R-148 to SADDE INT. Thence. . . .
PALMDALE TRANSITION (PMD.SADDE6): From over PMD VORTAC via PMD R-251 and FIM R-347 to FIM VORTAC, then via FIM R-148 to SADDE INT. Thence. . . .
SAN MARCUS TRANSITION (RZS.SADDE6): From over RZS VORTAC via RZS R-109 and VTU R-289 to VTU VOR/DME then via VTU R-093 to SADDE INT. Thence. . . .
VENTURA TRANSITION (VTU.SADDE6): From over VTU VOR/DME via VTU R-093 to SADDE INT. Thence. . . .
. . . . From over SADDE INT via SMO R-261 to SMO VOR/DME, then via SMO R-068 to SMO 9 DME for Runways 24 and 25. From SMO 9 DME expect vector to final approach course for Los Angeles Intl Airport.

SADDE SIX ARRIVAL
(SADDE.SADDE6) 95089

LOS ANGELES, CALIFORNIA
LOS ANGELES INTL
SW-2, 15 JUL 1999

P53

VISTA ONE ARRIVAL

(JLI.VISTA1) 96228

(JLI.VISTA1) 96228
VISTA ONE ARRIVAL

ST-237 (FAA)

LOS ANGELES INTL
LOS ANGELES, CALIFORNIA

SOCAL APP CON
124.5 381.6
ATIS
133.8

From over JLI VORTAC via JLI R-263 and OCN R-083 to OCN VORTAC, then via the OCN R-259 and SLI R-148 to SLI VORTAC. Expect radar vectors to final approach course for runways 24 or 25.

N

NOTE: DME Required.
NOTE: Chart not to scale.

SEAL BEACH
115.7 SLI
Chan 104
N33°47.00'-W118°03.29'

R-148

4000
328°
(32)

CYNDE
N33°13.75'-W117°19.16'
TURBOJET VERTICAL
NAVIGATION
PLANNING INFORMATION
Expect to cross at 12,000'.

JULIAN
114.0 JLI
Chan 87
N33°08.43'-W116°35.16'
L-3, H-2
TURBOJET VERTICAL NAVIGATION
PLANNING INFORMATION
Expect to cross at or below FL240.

SHIVE
N33°15.97'
W117°52.00'

259°
(23)

R-083
(5)

4000
(4) 9

7700
263°
(33)

R-108

OCEANSIDE
115.3 OCN
Chan 100
N33°14.44'-W117°25.06'

VISTA
N33°13.14'
W117°14.07'

R-344

MISSION BAY
117.8 MZB
Chan 125

VISTA ONE ARRIVAL
(JLI.VISTA1) 96228

LOS ANGELES, CALIFORNIA
LOS ANGELES INTL
SW-2, 15 JUL 1999

P63

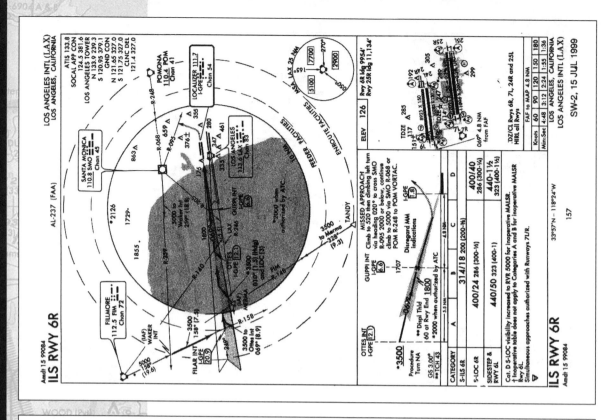

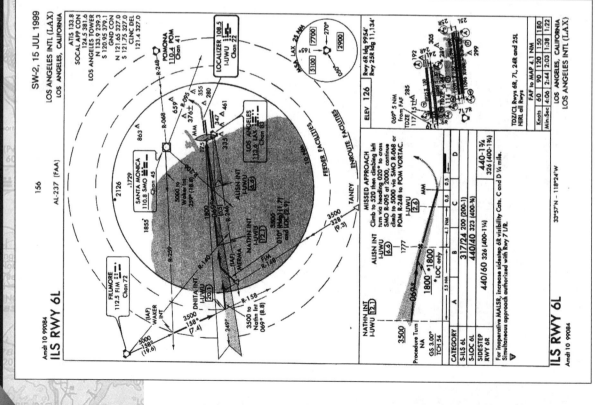

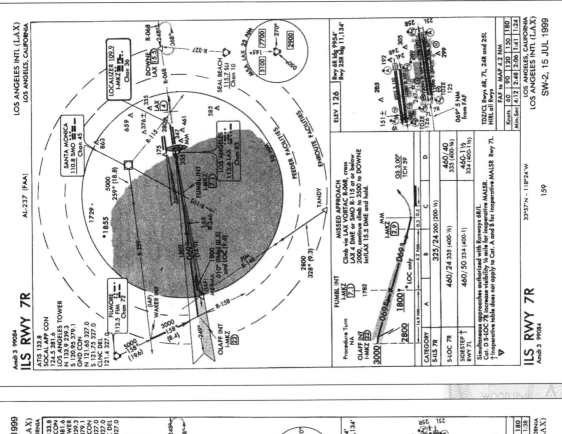

ILS RWY 7R

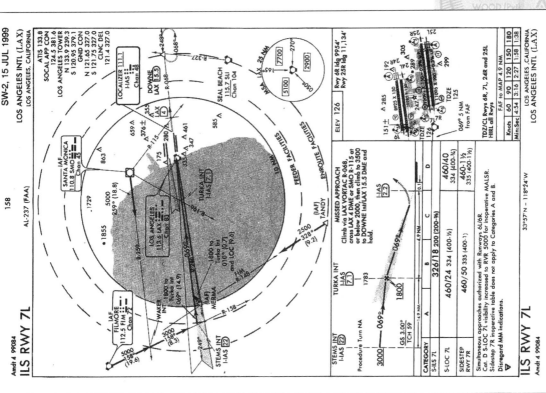

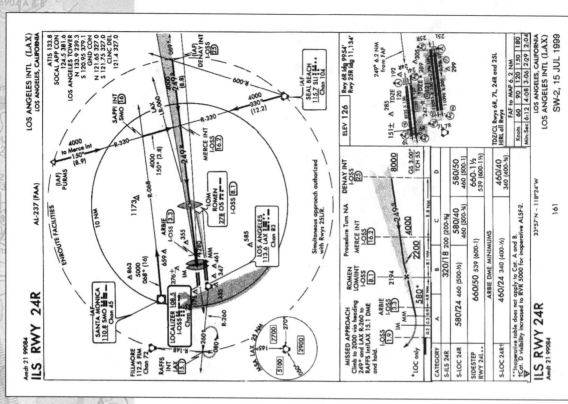

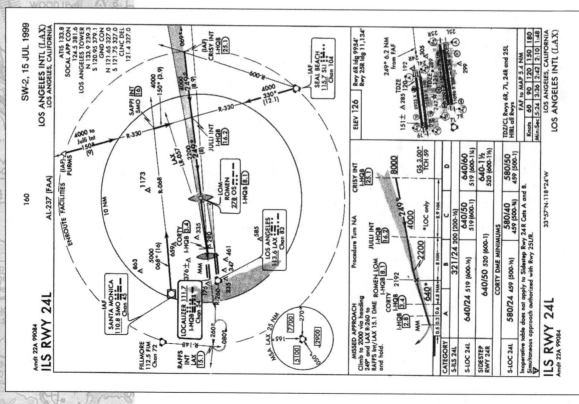

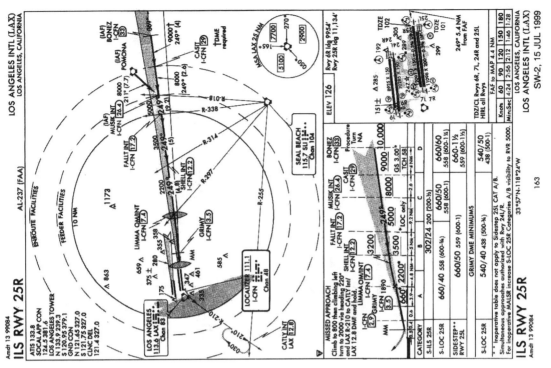

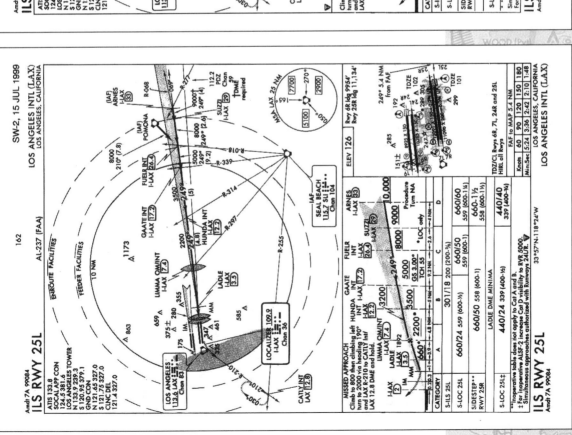

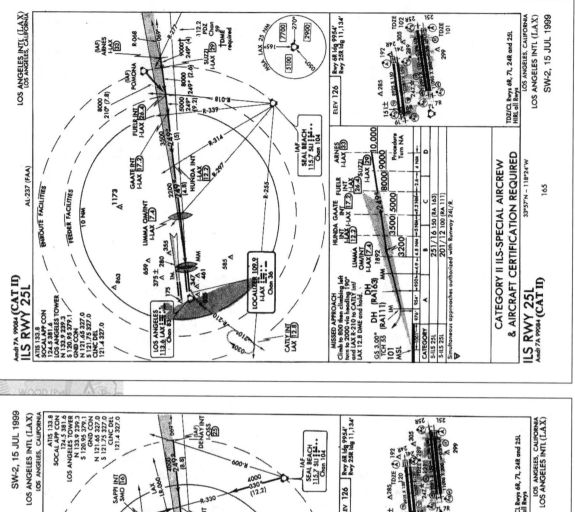

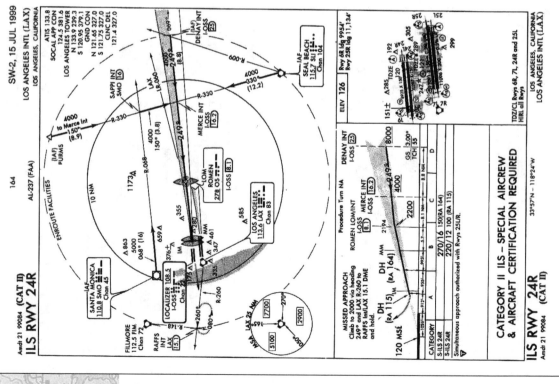

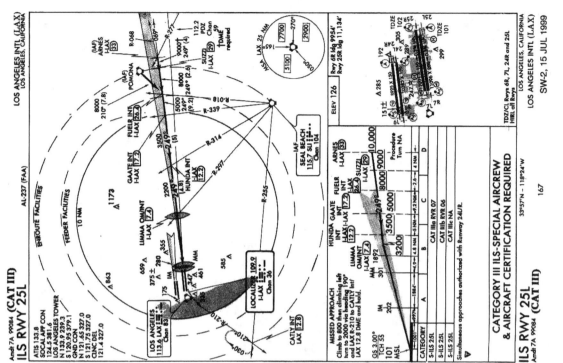

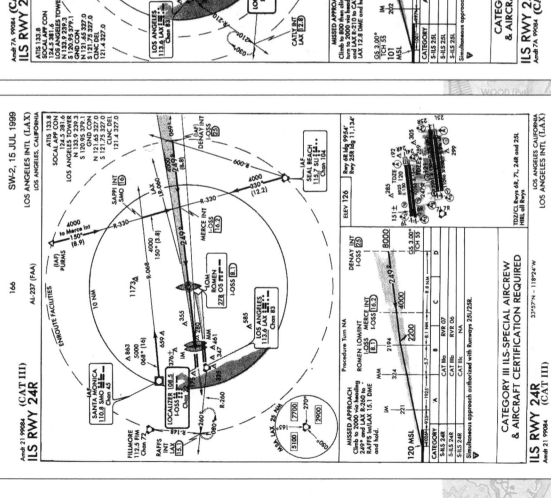

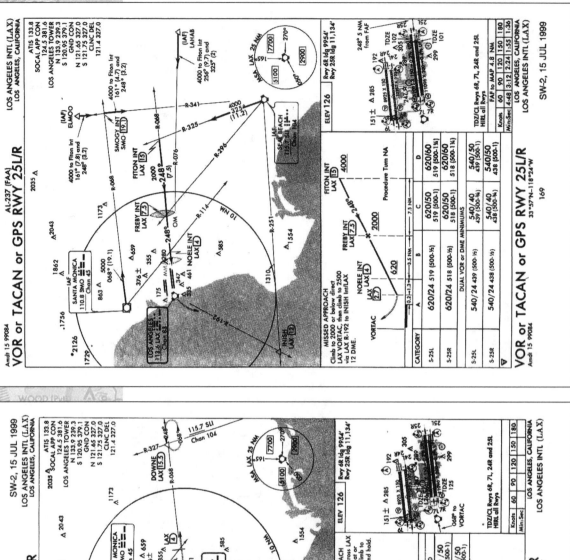

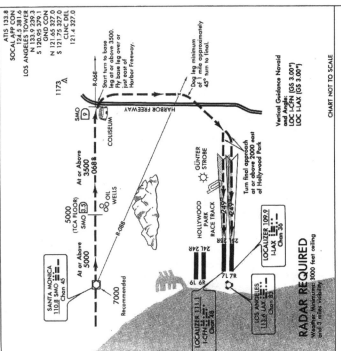

Harbor Visual RWY 25L/R

Amdt 4 96228
HARBOR VISUAL RWY 25L/R AL-237 (FAA)

LOS ANGELES INTL (LAX)
LOS ANGELES, CALIFORNIA

ATIS 133.8
SOCAL APP CON
124.5 381.6
LOS ANGELES TOWER
N 133.9 239.3
S 120.95 379.1
GND CON
N 121.65 327.0
S 121.75 327.0
CLNC DEL
121.4 327.0

SANTA MONICA
110.8 SMO
Chan 45

1173

At or Above 5000
7000 Recommended

5000 (TCA FLOOR)
SMO 8.5

OIL WELLS

At or Above 3500
068 8

Start turn to base leg at or above 3500. Fly base leg over or just east of Harbor Freeway.

Dog leg minimum of 1 mile approximately 45° turn to final.

R-068

SMO 9
COLISEUM
HARBOR FREEWAY

GÜNTER STROBE

Turn final approach at or above 2000 east of Hollywood Park

HOLLYWOOD PARK RACE TRACK

25L 25R
251 25R
249°
249°

24L 24R
19 6R

7L 7R

LOCALIZER 109.9
I-LAX
Chan 36

LOCALIZER 111.1
I-CFN
Chan 48

LOS ANGELES
113.6 LAX
Chan 83

Vertical Guidance Navaid and Angle:
LOC I-CFN (GS 3.00°)
LOC I-LAX (GS 3.00°)

CHART NOT TO SCALE

RADAR REQUIRED
Weather Minimums: 3000 feet ceiling and 3 miles visibility.

HARBOR VISUAL APPROACH

When visual approaches to Runways 25L/R are in progress, clearances to aircraft from the north and northwest will be given utilizing the following phraseology:

"(IDENT) CLEARED FOR HARBOR VISUAL RUNWAY 25 LEFT/RIGHT APPROACH."

A descent profile of approximately 3° starting at 7000 over SMO VOR/DME may be made with reference to the minimum altitudes above.

Amdt 4 96228
HARBOR VISUAL RWY 25L/R 33°57'N-118°24'w

LOS ANGELES INTL (LAX)
LOS ANGELES, CALIFORNIA
SW-2, 15 JUL 1999

171

NDB or GPS RWY 24R

SW-2, 15 JUL 1999

170

Amdt 12 99084
NDB or GPS RWY 24R AL-237 (FAA)

LOS ANGELES INTL (LAX)
LOS ANGELES, CALIFORNIA

ATIS 133.8
SOCAL APP CON
124.5 381.6
LOS ANGELES TOWER
N 133.9 239.3
S 120.95 379.1
GND CON
N 121.65 327.0
S 121.75 327.0
CLNC DEL
121.4 327.0

FILLMORE
112.5 FIM
Chan 72

A 1173

LOM ROMEN
278 OS

2200
256° (7.6)
256°
R-068
R-076

249°
355
280
247
325
175
378 ±
659 A

LOS ANGELES
113.6 LAX
Chan 83

A 863
A 585
A 461

RAFFS INT
LAX 15.1

R-260

(IAF)
LAHAB

3000 to Downe Int
256° (9.3)
and 327° (2.2)

IAF
SEAL BEACH
115.7 SLI
Chan 104

3000
327° (11.4)

DOWNE
R-327

ENROUTE FACILITIES

10 NM

NSA OS 25 NM

4800
9100
5100
2600

ELEV 126

Rwy 6R ldg 9954'
Rwy 25R ldg 11,134'

TDZE 120

249° 6.2 NM from FAF

TDZ/CL Rwys 6R, 7L, 24R and 25L
HIRL all Rwys

151 ±

285

299

192

305

7L 7R

Knots	60	90	120	150	180
Min:Sec	6:12	4:08	3:06	2:29	2:04

FAF to MAP 6.2 NM

MISSED APPROACH
Climb to 2000 via heading 249° and LAX R-260 to RAFFS Int/LAX 15.1 DME and hold.

DOWNE INT
3000
256°
7.5 NM
Procedure Turn NA

ROMEN LOM
*2200
249°
6.3 NM

CATEGORY	A	B	C	D
S-24R	680/40 560 (600-¾)		680/50 560 (600-1)	680-1½ 560 (600-1½)
SIDESTEP RWY 24L	680/50 560 (600-1)			680-1¾ 560 (600-1¾)

Inoperative table does not apply to sidestep categories A and B.

Amdt 12 99084
NDB or GPS RWY 24R 33°57'N - 118°24'w

LOS ANGELES INTL (LAX)
LOS ANGELES, CALIFORNIA

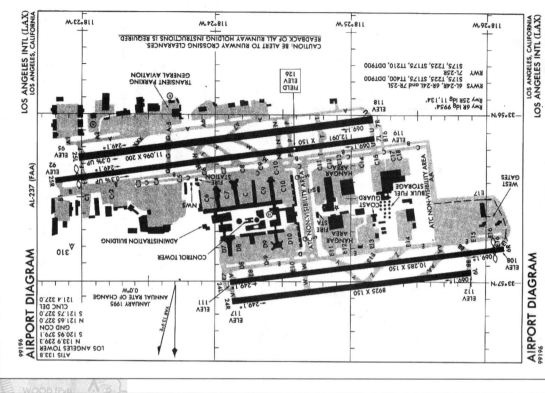

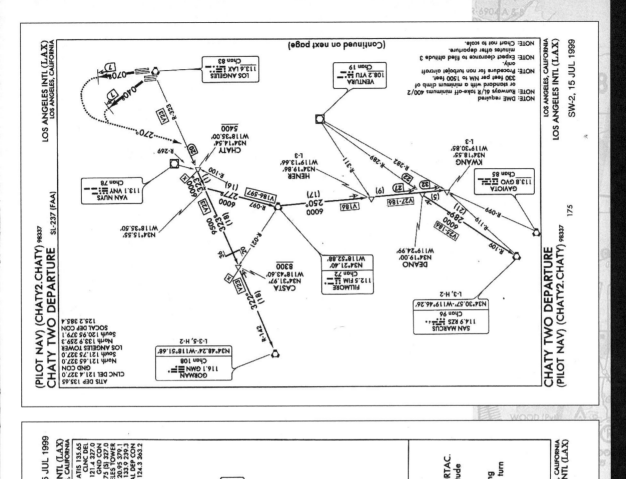

Chaty Two Departure

(PILOT NAV) (CHATY2.CHATY) 98337

SL-237 (FAA)

CHATY TWO DEPARTURE

ATIS DEP 135.65
CLNC DEL 121.4 327.0
GND CON
North 121.65 327.0
South 121.75 327.0
LOS ANGELES TOWER
North 133.9 259.3
South 120.95 379.1
SOCAL DEP CON
125.2 385.4

Van Nuys 113.1 VNY Chan 78

Los Angeles 113.6 LAX Chan 83

Ventura 108.2 VTU Chan 19

Gaviota 113.8 GVO Chan 85

San Marcus 114.9 RZS Chan 96

Gorman 116.1 GMN Chan 108

Casta 112.5 FIM W118°43.60' N34°31.97'

Fillmore 112.5 FIM Chan 72 N34°21.40' W118°52.88'

Hener N34°19.86' W119°13.66' L-3

Kwang N34°18.55' W119°30.85' L-3

Deano N34°19.00' W119°24.99'

Chaty N34°14.54' W118°35.00'

(Continued on next page)

NOTE: Expect clearance to filed altitude 3 minutes after departure.

NOTE: Chart not to scale.

NOTE: Procedure for non turbojet aircraft only.

NOTE: Standard with a minimum climb of 330 feet per NM to 1500 feet.

NOTE: Runways 6L/R take-off minimums 400/2 or

NOTE: DME required

LOS ANGELES, CALIFORNIA
LOS ANGELES INTL (LAX)

CHATY TWO DEPARTURE
(PILOT NAV) (CHATY2.CHATY) 98337

SW-2, 15 JUL 1999

175

(VECTOR) (SXC5.SXC) 96284

SL-237 (FAA)

CATALINA FIVE DEPARTURE

ATIS 135.65
CLNC DEL
121.4 327.0
GND CON
121.65 (N) 121.75 (SI) 327.0
LOS ANGELES TOWER
S 120.95 379.1
N 133.9 259.3
SOCAL DEP CON
124.3 363.2

Seal Beach 115.7 SLI Chan 104

Los Angeles 113.6 LAX Chan 83

Santa Catalina 111.4 SXC Chan 51 N33°22.50' W118°25.19'

NOTE: This is a radar vector departure to SXC VORTAC. Route depicted is a lost communication procedure only.

NOTE: Chart not to scale.

DEPARTURE ROUTE DESCRIPTION

TAKE-OFF RUNWAYS 6/7: Climb via heading 070° for vector to SXC VORTAC. Then via (assigned route). All aircraft expect further clearance to filed altitude three minutes after departure.

LOST COMMUNICATIONS

Take-off Runways 6/7: If not in contact with Departure Control after reaching 2000', turn right heading 245°. Cross LAX R-170 at or above 5000', then turn left proceed direct SXC VORTAC. Cross SLI R-235 at or below 9000'.

LOS ANGELES, CALIFORNIA
LOS ANGELES INTL (LAX)

CATALINA FIVE DEPARTURE
(VECTOR) (SXC5.SXC) 96284

(PILOT NAV)(GABRE5.GABRE) 6284
SW-2, 15 JUL 1999
GABRE FIVE DEPARTURE   SL-237 (FAA)
LOS ANGELES INTL (LAX)
LOS ANGELES, CALIFORNIA

ATIS 135.65
CLNC DEL
121.4 327.0
GND CON
121.65 (N) 121.75 (S) 327.0
LOS ANGELES TOWER
S 120.95 379.1
SOCAL DEP CON
125.2 385.4

DAGGETT
113.2 DAG •–•
Chan 79
N34°57.75'-W116°34.69'
L-3.5, H-2

GABRE
N34°18.12'
W118°03.29'
MCA
11000

R-227

SEAL BEACH
115.7 SLI •••
Chan 104

R-345

345°

LOS ANGELES
113.6 LAX •–••
Chan 83

070°
055°
070°

NOTE: This SID requires a minimum climb of 330' per NM to 12000'.

NOTE: Expect radar vector to SLI R-345.

NOTE: RADAR Required.

NOTE: DME required.

NOTE: Chart not to scale.

DEPARTURE ROUTE DESCRIPTION

TAKE-OFF RUNWAY 6: Climb via heading 070° until the LAX VORTAC 3 DME, then turn left heading 055° for vector to SLI R-345. Thence . . . . .
TAKE-OFF RUNWAY 7: Climb via heading 070° for vector to SLI R-345.
Thence . . .
. . . via SLI R-345 to GABRE INT. Then via (transition) or (assigned route). All aircraft expect further clearance to filed altitude three minutes after departure.
DAGGETT TRANSITION (GABRE5.DAG): From over GABRE INT via DAG R-227 to DAG VORTAC.

GABRE FIVE DEPARTURE
(PILOT NAV)(GABRE5.GABRE) 6284
177
LOS ANGELES, CALIFORNIA
LOS ANGELES INTL (LAX)
SW-2, 15 JUL 1999

(PILOT NAV) (CHATY2.CHATY) 98337
176
SW-2, 15 JUL 1999
CHATY TWO DEPARTURE   SL-237 (FAA)
LOS ANGELES INTL (LAX)
LOS ANGELES, CALIFORNIA

DEPARTURE ROUTE DESCRIPTION

TAKE-OFF RUNWAYS 6L/R: Climb via heading 040° for vector to V23; thence via (transition) or (assigned route).
TAKE-OFF RUNWAYS 7L/R: Climb via heading 070° for vector to V23; thence via (transition) or (assigned route).
LOST COMMUNICATIONS
RUNWAYS 6L/R and 7L/R: If no transmissions are received upon reaching the LAX 7 DME, turn left heading 270°, intercept V23 to CHATY INT and resume the CHATY TWO DEPARTURE. Continue climb on course.
GORMAN TRANSITION (CHATY2.GMN): From over CHATY INT via V23 to GMN VORTAC. Cross CHATY INT at or above 5400', and CASTA INT at or above 8300'.
HENER TRANSITION (CHATY2.HENER): From over CHATY INT via V23 and FIM R-097 to FIM VORTAC. Cross CHATY INT at or above 5400'. Then proceed via FIM R-250 to HENER INT.
KWANG TRANSITION (CHATY2.KWANG): From over CHATY INT via V23 and FIM R-097 to FIM VORTAC. Cross CHATY INT at or above 5400'. Then proceed via FIM R-250 to KWANG INT.
SAN MARCUS TRANSITION (CHATY2.RZS): From over CHATY INT via V23 and FIM R-097 to FIM VORTAC. Cross CHATY INT at or above 5400'. Then proceed via FIM R-250 and RZS R-109 to RZS VORTAC.

CHATY TWO DEPARTURE
(PILOT NAV) (CHATY2.CHATY) 98337
LOS ANGELES, CALIFORNIA
LOS ANGELES INTL (LAX)

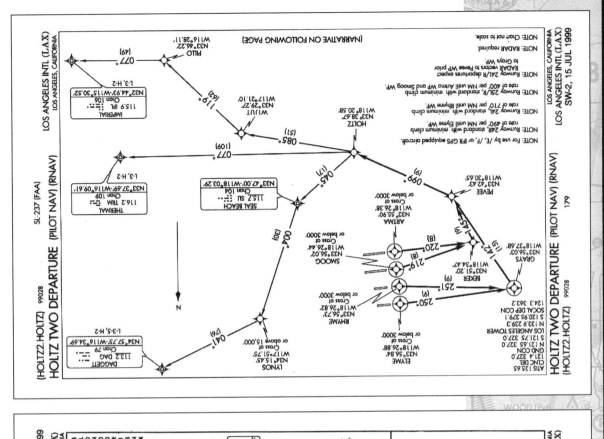

(PILOT NAV) (IPL3.IPL) %284
IMPERIAL THREE DEPARTURE SL-237 (FAA)

```
ATIS 135.65
CLNC DEL
121.4 227.0
GND CON
121.65 (N) 121.75 (S) 327.0
LOS ANGELES TOWER
N 133.9 239.3
SOCAL DEP CON
124.3 363.2
```

SEAL BEACH
115.7 SLI ⁝⁝⁝⁝⁝⁝⁝
Chan 104
N33°27.00'-W118°03.29'

JULIAN
114.0 JLI ⁝⁝⁝⁝⁝⁝⁝
Chan 87
N33°08.43'-W116°35.16'

IMPERIAL
115.9 IPL ⁝⁝⁝⁝⁝⁝⁝
Chan 106
N32°44.93'-W115°30.51'

LOS ANGELES
113.6 LAX ⁝⁝⁝⁝⁝⁝⁝
Chan 83

OCEANSIDE
115.3 OCN ⁝⁝⁝⁝⁝⁝⁝
Chan 100
N33°14.44'-W117°25.06'

NOTE: Chart not to scale.

DEPARTURE ROUTE DESCRIPTION

<u>TAKE-OFF RUNWAYS 6/7:</u> Maintain heading 070° for vector to SLI VORTAC.
Then via SLI R-120 and OCN R-301 to OCN VORTAC; via OCN R-083 and JLI
R-263 to JLI VORTAC; via JLI R-115 and IPL R-258 to IPL VORTAC. Then via
(assigned route). Thence . . . .
<u>TAKE-OFF RUNWAYS 24/25:</u> Maintain heading 250° for offshore vector to LAX
R-160. Then via LAX R-160 and OCN R-270 to OCN VORTAC; via OCN R-083
and JLI R-263 to JLI VORTAC; via JLI R-115 and IPL R-258 to IPL VORTAC. Then
via (assigned route). Thence . . . .
. . . . All aircraft expect further clearance to filed altitude three minutes after
departure.

IMPERIAL THREE DEPARTURE
(PILOT NAV) (IPL3.IPL) %284

180
SL-237 (FAA)

HOLTZ TWO DEPARTURE (PILOT NAV) (RNAV)

DEPARTURE ROUTE DESCRIPTION

TAKE-OFF RUNWAY 24R: Climb via 249° course to ELYME WP, 250° course to GRAYS
WP, 142° course. Thence . . . .
TAKE-OFF RUNWAY 24L: Climb via 249° course to RHYME WP, 251° course to GRAYS
WP, 142° course. Thence . . . .
TAKE-OFF RUNWAY 25R: Climb via 249° course to SMOOG WP, 219° course to BEKER
WP, 145° course. Thence . . . .
TAKE-OFF RUNWAY 25L : Climb via 249° course to ARTMA WP, 220° course to BEKER
WP, 145° course. Thence . . . .
. . . . To PEVEE WP, 099° course to HOLTZ WP, then assigned (Transition/Altitude).

DAGGETT TRANSITION (HOLTZ2.DAG): From over HOLTZ WP via 045° course to
SLI VORTAC. Then via 004° course to LYNOS WP and 041° course to DAG VORTAC.
IMPERIAL TRANSITION (HOLTZ2.IPL): From over HOLTZ WP via 085° course to
WIJUT WP. Then via 119° course to PILLO WP. Then via 077° course to IPL VORTAC.
THERMAL TRANSITION (HOLTZ2.TRM): From over HOLTZ WP via 077° course to
TRM VORTAC.

HOLTZ TWO DEPARTURE (PILOT NAV) (RNAV)

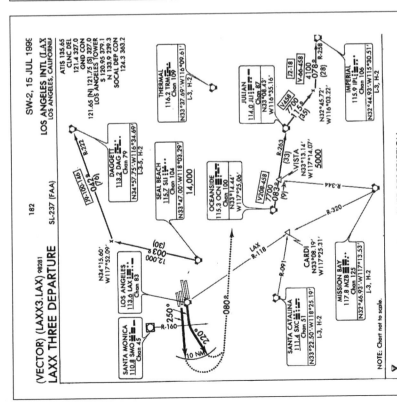

LOOP TWO DEPARTURE (Top Chart)

(PILOT NAV) (LOOP2.LAX) 98281
LOOP TWO DEPARTURE

SW-2, 15 JUL 1999

SL-237 (FAA)

LOS ANGELES INTL (LAX)
LOS ANGELES, CALIFORNIA

ATIS 135.65
CLNC DEL
121.4 327.0
GND CON
121.65 (N) 121.75 (S) 327.0
LOS ANGELES TOWER
S 120.95 379.1
N 133.9 239.3
SOCAL DEP CON
124.3 363.2

DAGGETT
113.2 DAG ≡••
Chan 79
N34°57.75'-W116°34.69'
[-3.5; H-2]

R-222

19-100-146
[
15,000
041°
(9)

COOPP
N34°07.27',
W118°06.03'
15,000

(12)

12,000
041°
(8)

KEGGS
N34°00.51',
W118°17.98'
13,000

SANTA MONICA
110.8 SMO ≡••
Chan 45

R-160

250°
235°

LOS ANGELES
113.0 LAX ≡••
Chan 83
N33°55.99'-W118°25.92'
10,000

NOTE: Remain within 10 NM of LAX VORTAC until established on (transition) or (assigned route).

NOTE: Minimum climb rate 500 feet per NM to 10,000 feet. If unable, use the LAXX SID.

NOTE: Use the LAXX DEPARTURE during the period 2100-0700 local time in lieu of the LOOP SID.

NOTE: Radar Required.

NOTE: DME Required.

DEPARTURE ROUTE DESCRIPTION

TAKE-OFF RUNWAY 24: Climb via heading 250° for vector to LAX VORTAC. Expect left turn direct LAX VORTAC. Thence . . .
TAKE-OFF RUNWAY 25: Climb via heading 250° at the SMO R-160 turn left heading 235° for vector to LAX VORTAC. Expect left turn direct LAX VORTAC. Thence . . .
. . . via (transition) or (assigned route). Aircraft filing FL240 or above expect further clearance to filed flight level ten minutes after departure.
DAGGETT TRANSITION (LOOP2.DAG): From over LAX VORTAC via LAX R-041 and DAG R-222 to DAG VORTAC.

NOTE: Chart not to scale.

LOOP TWO DEPARTURE
(PILOT NAV) (LOOP2.LAX) 98281

LOS ANGELES, CALIFORNIA
LOS ANGELES INTL (LAX)

183

SW-2, 15 JUL 1999

LAXX THREE DEPARTURE (Bottom Chart)

(VECTOR) (LAXX3.LAX) 98281
LAXX THREE DEPARTURE

SW-2, 15 JUL 1999

SL-237 (FAA)

182

LOS ANGELES INTL (LAX)
LOS ANGELES, CALIFORNIA

ATIS 135.65
CLNC DEL
121.4 327.0
GND CON
121.65 (N) 121.75 (S) 327.0
LOS ANGELES TOWER
S 120.95 379.1
N 133.9 239.3
SOCAL DEP CON
124.3 363.2

THERMAL
116.2 TRM ≡••
Chan 109
N33°37.69'-W116°09.61'
[-3; H-2]

R-222

DAGGETT
113.2 DAG ≡••
Chan 79
N34°57.75'-W116°34.69'
[-3.5; H-2]

19-100-146
042°
(76)

N34°15.60'
W117°52.09'
12,000
003°
(30)

SEAL BEACH
115.7 SLI ≡••
Chan 104
N33°47.00'-W118°03.29'
14,000

JULIAN
114.0 JLI ≡••
Chan 87
N33°08.43'
W116°35.16'
[J2-18]

V66-458
4100
078°
(28)

IMPERIAL
115.9 IPL ≡••
Chan 106
N32°44.93'-W115°30.51'
[-3; H-2]

V458
7700
115.3°
(35)

N32°45.72'
W116°03.22'

R-263
(33)

VISTA
N33°13.14',
W117°14.07'
5000

083°
(9)

OCEANSIDE
115.3 OCN ≡••
Chan 100
N33°12.44'
W117°25.06'

V208-458
7700

R-344

LOS ANGELES
113.0 LAX ≡••
Chan 83

SANTA MONICA
110.8 SMO ≡••
Chan 45

R-160
250°
220°

10 NM

080°

R-320

R-091

LAX
R-118

CARDI
N33°08.19'
W117°25.31'

MISSION BAY
117.8 MZB ≡••
Chan 125
N32°46.93'-W117°13.53'
[-3; H-2]

SANTA CATALINA
111.4 SXC ≡••
Chan 51
N33°22.50'-W118°25.19'
[-3; H-2]

DEPARTURE ROUTE DESCRIPTION

TAKE-OFF RUNWAY 24: Climb via heading 250°, thence . . . . .
TAKE-OFF RUNWAY 25: Climb via heading 250°, at the SMO R-160 turn left heading 220°, thence . . .
. . . expect vectors to assigned route/fix/transition. Expect further clearance to filed flight level ten minutes after departure.
LOST COMMUNICATIONS: If not in contact with departure control by 10 NM west of LAX, turn left heading 080°, climb to FL230 or filed altitude, whichever is lower, and when able, proceed direct route/fix/transition. Climb to filed flight level ten minutes after departure.
DAGGETT TRANSITION (LAXX3.DAG)
IMPERIAL TRANSITION (LAXX3.IPL)

NOTE: Chart not to scale.

LAXX THREE DEPARTURE
(VECTOR) (LAXX3.LAX) 98281

LOS ANGELES, CALIFORNIA
LOS ANGELES INTL (LAX)

Left chart — PERCH SEVEN DEPARTURE

SW-2, 15 JUL 1999

(VECTOR) (PRCH7.LAX) 96284
184
LOS ANGELES INTL (LAX)
LOS ANGELES, CALIFORNIA
PERCH SEVEN DEPARTURE SL-237 (FAA)

ATIS 135.65
CLNC DEL
121.4 327.0
GND CON
121.65 (N) 121.75 (S) 327.0
LOS ANGELES TOWER
S 120.95 379.1
N 133.9 239.3
SOCAL DEP CON
125.2 385.4

NOTE: Departure off runways 25: Turns for radar vectors shall commence within one mile after passing LAX VORTAC. Departures off runways 24: Turns for radar vectors shall commence crossing the LAX R-310.

NOTE: MRA DINTY DME FL 220 to receive LAX and R25 DME.

NOTE: This is a radar vector departure to DINTY DME or FICKY DME. Route depicted is a lost communication procedure only.

NOTE: Chart not to scale

SAN MARCUS
114.9 RZS ≡·≡·
Chan 96

DINTY
N33°28.97'
W122°35.04'
H-2

CONTROL 1316

FICKY
N31°33.46'
W121°23.51'
H-2

VENTURA
108.2 VTU ≡·≡·
Chan 19

PERCH
N33°52.04'
W119°09.45'

SANTA MONICA
110.8 SMO ≡·≡·
Chan 45

LOS ANGELES
113.6 LAX ≡·≡·
Chan 83

DEPARTURE ROUTE DESCRIPTION

TAKE-OFF RUNWAYS 6/7: Climb via heading 070° for vector to DINTY DME or FICKY DME. Cross SMO R-160 at or above 5000'. Cross SMO R-210 at or below 10,000'. Thence . . . .
TAKE-OFF RUNWAYS 24/25: Climb via heading 250° for vector to DINTY DME or FICKY DME. Thence . . . .
. . . . Via (assigned route). All aircraft expect further clearance to filed altitude three minutes after departure.
LOST COMMUNICATIONS:
TAKE-OFF RUNWAYS 6/7: If not in contact with Departure Control after reaching 2000', turn right heading 250'. Cross SMO R-160 at or above 5000'. Cross SMO R-210 at or below 10,000'. After leaving 10,000', turn right heading 270° to intercept and proceed via LAX R-249 to PERCH INT. Then via DINTY DME or FICKY DME as assigned.
TAKE-OFF RUNWAYS 24/25: If not in contact with Departure Control one minute after crossing the shoreline or the LAX R-190 or R-305, proceed outbound via LAX R-249 to PERCH INT. Thence via direct DINTY DME or FICKY DME, as assigned.

PERCH SEVEN DEPARTURE
(VECTOR) (PRCH7.LAX) 96284
LOS ANGELES, CALIFORNIA
LOS ANGELES INTL (LAX)

Right chart — SAN DIEGO THREE DEPARTURE

(PILOT NAV) (SNGO3.CARDI) 96284
LOS ANGELES INTL (LAX)
LOS ANGELES, CALIFORNIA
SAN DIEGO THREE DEPARTURE SL-237 (FAA)

ATIS 135.65
CLNC DEL
121.4 327.0
GND CON
121.65 (N) 121.75 (S) 327.0
LOS ANGELES TOWER
S 120.95 379.1
N 133.9 239.3
SOCAL DEP CON
124.3 363.2

SEAL BEACH
115.7 SLI ≡·≡·
Chan 104
N33°47.00'·W118°03.29'

CARDI
N33°08.19'
W117°25.31'

TORIE
N32°51.47'
W117°16.03'

MISSION BAY
117.8 MZB ≡·≡·
Chan 125
N32°46.93'·W117°13.53'
L-3, H-2

LOS ANGELES
113.6 LAX ≡·≡·
Chan 83

SANTA CATALINA
111.4 SXC ≡·≡·
Chan 51

NOTE: Radar required.

NOTE: Off runways 24/25 this SID is for non-turbojet aircraft. Turbojet aircraft use LAXX Departure.

NOTE: Chart not to scale.

DEPARTURE ROUTE DESCRIPTION

TAKE-OFF RUNWAYS 6/7: Climb via heading 070° for vector to SLI VORTAC, then via SLI R-148 and LAX R-118 to CARDI INT. Thence . . . .
TAKE-OFF RUNWAYS 24/25: Climb via heading 250° for vector to intercept and proceed via SXC R-091 to CARDI INT. Thence . . . .
. . . . via (transition) or (assigned route). All aircraft expect further clearance to filed altitude three minutes after departure.
MISSION BAY TRANSITION (SNGO3.MZB)

SAN DIEGO THREE DEPARTURE
(PILOT NAV) (SNGO3.CARDI) 96284
LOS ANGELES, CALIFORNIA
LOS ANGELES INTL (LAX)

SW-2, 15 JUL 1999
185

SEBBY ONE DEPARTURE (top chart)

(PILOT NAV) (SEBBY1.SEBBY) 96284   SL-237 (FAA)

SEBBY ONE DEPARTURE

LOS ANGELES INTL (LAX)
LOS ANGELES, CALIFORNIA

ATIS 135.65
CLNC DEL
121.4 327.0
GND CON
121.65 (N) 121.75 (S) 327.0
LOS ANGELES TOWER
S 120.95 379.1
N 133.9 239.3
SOCAL DEP CON
124.3 363.2

SANTA MONICA
110.8 SMO :⋯:⋯
Chan 45

LOS ANGELES
113.6 LAX :⋯:⋯
Chan 83

250°

R-160

160°

R-225

SEAL BEACH
115.7 SLI :⋯:⋯
Chan 104
N33°47.00'-W118°03.29'
14000
L-3, H-2

*3500
R-022
(23)
*14000

SEBBY
N34°05.38'
W117°46.62'

*1400
*1500
034°
(16)
(23)

DAGGETT
113.2 DAG :⋯:⋯
Chan 79
N34°57.75'-W116°34.69'
R-214
L-3-5, H-2

LOS ANGELES INTL (LAX)
LOS ANGELES, CALIFORNIA

NOTE: SID to be used when assigned by ATC only.
NOTE: DME Required.
NOTE: Chart not to scale.

DEPARTURE ROUTE DESCRIPTION

TAKE-OFF RUNWAY 25L/R: Climb via heading 250°, at the SMO R-160 turn left heading 220° until 10 DME west of LAX VORTAC. Turn left heading 160° for vector to SLI VORTAC. Expect left turn to intercept the SLI R-225 to SLI VORTAC, thence via assigned route. All aircraft expect further clearance to filed altitude three minutes after departure.

LOST COMMUNICATIONS: If not in contact with departure control after established on 160° heading, turn left direct SLI VORTAC, climb to FL230 or filed altitude whichever is lower, and when able, proceed via assigned route. Climb to filed flight level ten minutes after departure.
DAGGETT TRANSITION (SEBBY1.DAG): From over SLI VORTAC via SLI R-022 and DAG R-214 to DAG VORTAC.

SEBBY ONE DEPARTURE
(PILOT NAV) (SEBBY1.SEBBY) 96284

LOS ANGELES, CALIFORNIA
LOS ANGELES INTL (LAX)

SW-2, 15 JUL 1999   187

SEAL BEACH THREE DEPARTURE (bottom chart)

SW-2, 15 JUL 1999   186

LOS ANGELES INTL (LAX)
LOS ANGELES, CALIFORNIA

(VECTOR) (SLI3.SLI) 96284   SL-237 (FAA)

SEAL BEACH THREE DEPARTURE

ATIS 135.65
CLNC DEL
121.4 327.0
GND CON
121.65 (N) 121.75 (S) 327.0
LOS ANGELES TOWER
S 120.95 379.1
N 133.9 239.3
SOCAL DEP CON
124.3 363.2

SANTA MONICA
110.8 SMO :⋯:⋯
Chan 45

R-154

LOS ANGELES
113.6 LAX :⋯:⋯
Chan 83

070°

250°

250°

200°

SEAL BEACH
115.7 SLI :⋯:⋯
Chan 104
N33°47.00'-W118°03.29'
L-3, H-2

NOTE: Off Runways 24/25 this SID is for non-turbojet aircraft. Turbojet aircraft use LAX Departure.
NOTE: Take-off minimums Runways 25L/R are STANDARD with a minimum climb of 360' per NM to 600'.
NOTE: Chart not to scale.

DEPARTURE ROUTE DESCRIPTION

TAKE-OFF RUNWAYS 6/7: Climb via heading 070° for vectors to SLI VORTAC. Then via (assigned route).
TAKE-OFF RUNWAY 24: Climb via heading 250° for vectors to SLI VORTAC. Then via (assigned route).
TAKE-OFF RUNWAY 25: Climb via heading 250°. At the SMO R-154, turn left heading 200° for vectors to SLI VORTAC. Then via (assigned route).

LOST COMMUNICATIONS:
All aircraft expect further clearance to filed altitude three minutes after departure.

SEAL BEACH THREE DEPARTURE
(VECTOR) (SLI3.SLI) 96284

LOS ANGELES, CALIFORNIA
LOS ANGELES INTL (LAX)

NE-2, 15 JUL 1999

C6

TAKE-OFF MINIMUMS AND (OBSTACLE) DEPARTURE PROCEDURES

MONTICELLO, NY
MONTICELLO
TAKE-OFF MINIMUMS: Rwy 1, 400-2 or std. with a min. climb of 220' per NM to 2100, Rwy 33, 300-1 or std. with a min. climb of 280' per NM to 1900.
NOTE: Rwy 1, 1849' power line/tower 3200' from departure end of runway, 200' right of centerline. Rwy 33, 1785' power line/tower 5000' from departure end of runway, 1200' right of centerline.

SULLIVAN COUNTY INTL
DEPARTURE PROCEDURE: Rwy 33, climb straight ahead to 2500 before departing on course.

MOUNT JOY/MARIETTA, PA
DONEGAL SPRINGS AIRPARK
DEPARTURE PROCEDURE: Rwy 9, climb to 3000 direct LRP VORTAC before proceeding on course. Rwy 27, climbing right turn 3000 direct LRP VORTAC before proceeding on course.

MOUNT POCONO, PA
POCONO MOUNTAINS MUNI
DEPARTURE PROCEDURE: All runways, climb straight ahead to 2500 feet before turning on course.

NEW CASTLE, PA
NEW CASTLE MUNI
TAKE-OFF MINIMUMS: Rwy 13, 300-1 or std., with a min. climb of 320' per NM to 1300.

NEW YORK, NY
JOHN F. KENNEDY INTL
TAKE-OFF MINIMUMS: Rwy 13R, 300-1 or std. with min. climb of 230' per NM to 300

LA GUARDIA
TAKE-OFF MINIMUMS: Rwys 4, 13, 31, 400-1 or std. with min. climb of 220' per NM to 500.   Rwy 22, 400-1.
DEPARTURE PROCEDURE: Comply with La Guardia departure procedure or . Rwys 4, 13, climb to 1100 before proceeding westbound. Rwy 22, climb to 2000 before proceeding westbound. Rwy 31, climb to 1400 before proceeding southbound

NEWBURGH, NY
STEWART INTL
TAKE-OFF MINIMUMS: Rwy 16, 1100-1 or std. with min. climb of 205' per NM to 1500. Rwy 27, 300-1 or std. with min. climb of 270' per NM to 700.   Rwy 34, 300-1.
DEPARTURE PROCEDURE: Rwy 9, climb runway heading to 1800 before turning southbound.   Rwy 16, climb runway heading to 1500 before turning. Rwy 27, climb runway heading to 1000 before turning southbound.

NIAGARA FALLS, NY
NIAGARA FALLS INTL
TAKE-OFF MINIMUMS: Rwys 10L, 10R, 24, 300-1 or std. with a min. climb of 300' per NM to 1700.
DEPARTURE PROCEDURE: Rwys 10L, 10R, 24 climb runway heading to 1700 before proceeding on course.

NORWICH, NY
LT. WARREN EATON
TAKE-OFF MINIMUMS: Rwys 1, 19, 700-2 or std. with a min. climb of 400' per NM to 1900.
DEPARTURE PROCEDURE: Rwy 1, 19, climb runway heading to 2500 before proceeding on course.

OGDENSBURG, NY
OGDENSBURG INTL
DEPARTURE PROCEDURE: Rwys 9, 27, climb runway heading to 700 before proceeding on course.

OLEAN, NY
CATTARAUGUS COUNTY-OLEAN
TAKE-OFF MINIMUMS: Rwy 16, 300-1 or std. with a min. climb of 340' per NM until passing 2500.   Rwy 34, 300-1 or std. with a min. climb of 300' per NM until passing 2500.

ONEONTA, NY
ONEONTA MUNI
TAKE-OFF MINIMUMS: Rwys 6, 24, 300-1.

PENN YAN, NY
PENN YAN
TAKE-OFF MINIMUMS: Rwy 1, 500-2 or std. with a min climb of 230' per NM to 1700. Rwy 19, 600-2 or std. with a min. climb of 230' per NM to 1700. Rwy 28, 600-2, or std. with a min climb of 320' per NM to 1700.
NOTE: Rwy 10, 40' AGL trees at departure end of runway, 96' right of centerline.

PERKASIE, PA
PENNRIDGE
TAKE-OFF MINIMUMS: Rwy 8, 300-1.
Rwy 26, 500-1.

PHILADELPHIA, PA
PHILADELPHIA INTL
TAKE-OFF MINIMUMS: Rwy 9L, 300-1 or std. with min. climb of 300' per NM to 500. Rwy 9R, 300-1 or std. with min. climb of 250' per NM to 500. Rwy 17, 300-1 or std. with min. climb of 400' per NM to 500. Rwy 35, 300-1 or std. with min. climb of 315' per NM to 500.

WINGS FIELD
DEPARTURE PROCEDURE: Rwys 6, 24, climb runway heading to 700 before turning.

TAKE-OFF MINIMUMS AND (OBSTACLE) DEPARTURE PROCEDURES

NE-2

[PILOT NAV] (VTU2.VTU) 96284
VENTURA TWO DEPARTURE SL-237 (FAA)
188   SW-2, 15 JUL 1999
LOS ANGELES INTL (LAX)
LOS ANGELES, CALIFORNIA

ATIS 135.65
CLNC DEL 121.4 327.0
GND CON 121.65 (N) 121.75 (S) 327.0
LOS ANGELES TOWER S 120.95 379.1 N 133.9 239.3
SOCAL DEP CON 125.2 385.4

NOTE: RADAR required.
NOTE: Chart not to scale.

DEPARTURE ROUTE DESCRIPTION

TAKE-OFF RUNWAYS 6/7: Climb via heading 070° for vector to VTU VOR/DME.
Thence . . . . . .
TAKE-OFF RUNWAYS 24/25: Climb via heading 250° for vector to VTU VOR/DME.
Thence . . . . . .
. . . via (transition) or (assigned route). All aircraft expect further clearance to filed altitude three minutes after departure.

DINTY TRANSITION (VTU2.DINTY)
SAN MARCUS TRANSITION (VTU2.RZS)

VENTURA TWO DEPARTURE
(PILOT NAV) (VTU2.VTU) 96284
LOS ANGELES, CALIFORNIA
LOS ANGELES INTL (LAX)

CAMRN THREE ARRIVAL (SIE.CAMRN3)

CAMRN THREE ARRIVAL (SIE.CAMRN3)

NEW YORK APP CON
127.4 269.0
JOHN F. KENNEDY INTL ATIS ARR 128.725
(NE) 117.7 (SW) 115.4
REPUBLIC ATIS*
126.65

DEEP PARK
117.7 DPK
Chan 124

REPUBLIC

JOHN F. KENNEDY INTL

R-221

CAMRN
N40°01.04'-W73°51.66'
TURBOJET VERTICAL NAVIGATION
PLANNING INFORMATION
Expect clearance to cross at 11,000'
and 250 KT.

KARRS
N39°50.45'
W73°59.16'

PANZE
N39°40.56'
W74°10.09'

HOGGS
N39°34.97'-W74°16.24'
TURBOJET VERTICAL NAVIGATION
PLANNING INFORMATION
Expect to cross at FL190.

BOTON
N39°24.87'
W74°27.29'

ROBBINSVILLE
113.9 RBV
Chan 85

COYLE
113.4 CYN
Chan 81

ATLANTIC CITY
108.6 ACY
Chan 23

SEA ISLE
114.8 SIE
Chan 95
N39°05.73'
W74°48.02'
L-24-28, H-3-4-6

R-121
R-143
R-135
R-162
R-124

049°
049°
210K (12)
049° (12)
(13)
(8)
(13)
(25)

NOTE: STAR applicable to Turbojet and
Turboprop aircraft operating at
250KT IAS or greater.

NOTE: Chart not to scale.

From over SIE VORTAC via SIE R-049 and DPK R-221 to CAMRN INT. Expect radar
vectors to final approach fix in use.

CAMRN THREE ARRIVAL (SIE.CAMRN3)

⚠ ALTERNATE MINS

ALTERNATE MINIMUMS

NAME

HARRISBURG, PA
CAPITAL CITY .... ILS Rwy 8
Categories A,B, 900-2; Categories C,D,
900-2¼.
NA when control tower closed.

HARRISBURG INTL .... ILS Rwy 13[1]
ILS Rwy 31[1]
VOR or GPS Rwy 31[2]
[1]ILS, Categories C,D, 700-2. LOC, NA.
[2]Categories A,B, 900-2, Category C, 900-2¼,
Category D, 900-3.

ISLIP, NY
LONG ISLAND MAC ARTHUR ...... ILS Rwy 24
LOC, NA.

ITHACA, NY
TOMPKINS COUNTY .... ILS Rwy 32[1]
VOR or GPS Rwy 14[2]
VOR or GPS Rwy 32#
[1]Categories A,B, 1100-3; Categories C,D.
1100-3.
[2]NA when control tower closed, except for
operators with approved weather reporting
service.
#Categories A,B, 1500-2; Categories C,D,
1500-3.

JAMESTOWN, NY
CHAUTAUQUA COUNTY
/JAMESTOWN .... VOR/DME RNAV or GPS
Rwy 13[1]
VOR/DME RNAV or GPS Rwy 31[1]
VOR/DME or GPS Rwy 7[2]
VOR or GPS Rwy 25[2]
[1]NA when Class E airspace not effective.
[2]NA when control zone not in effect.

JOHNSTOWN, PA
JOHNSTOWN-CAMBRIA
COUNTY .... ILS Rwy 33[1]
VOR Rwy 15,1000-3
[1]ILS, Categories A,B,C, 700-2;Category D,
700-2¼. LOC, Category D, 800-2¼.

ALTERNATE MINIMUMS

NAME

LANCASTER, PA
LANCASTER .... ILS Rwy 8[1]
VOR/DME or TACAN or GPS Rwy 8[2]
VOR/DME or GPS Rwy 26[1]
VOR/DME or GPS Rwy 31[1]
VOR Rwy 8[2]
VOR Rwy 31[1]
[1]NA when control tower closed.
[2]NA when control zone not in effect.
[3]Categories A,B, 1000-2; Categories C,D.
1000-3.

LATROBE, PA
ARNOLD PALMER REGIONAL ...... ILS Rwy 23
NDB Rwy 23
NA when control tower closed.
Categories A,B, 1100-2;Category C, D,1200-3.

MASSENA, NY
MASSENA INTL-RICHARDS
FIELD .... VOR/DME RNAV or GPS Rwy 5
VOR/DME RNAV or GPS Rwy 23
VOR or GPS Rwy 27
Category D, 800-2¼.

NEWBURGH, NY
STEWART INTL .... ILS Rwy 9[1]
VOR/DME RNAV or GPS Rwy 27[2]
VOR Rwy 27[2]
[1]ILS, Categories C,D. 700-2.
[2]Category D, 800-2¼.

NEW YORK, NY
JOHN F. KENNEDY INTL .... ILS Rwy 22R[1]
ILS Rwy 22L[1]
ILS Rwy 4L[1]
ILS Rwy 4R[1]
ILS Rwy 13L[1]
ILS Rwy 31L[1]
ILS Rwy 31R[1]
VOR or GPS-D,1000-3
VOR/DME or GPS Rwy 31L[2]
VOR or FMS or GPS Rwy 13L/R,1000-3
[1]ILS, 700-2.
[2]Category D, 800-2¼.

⚠ ALTERNATE MINS

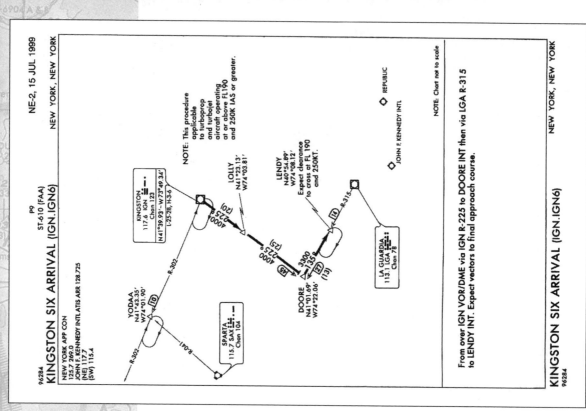

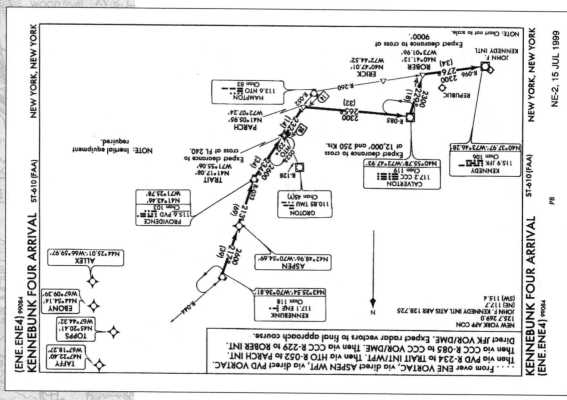

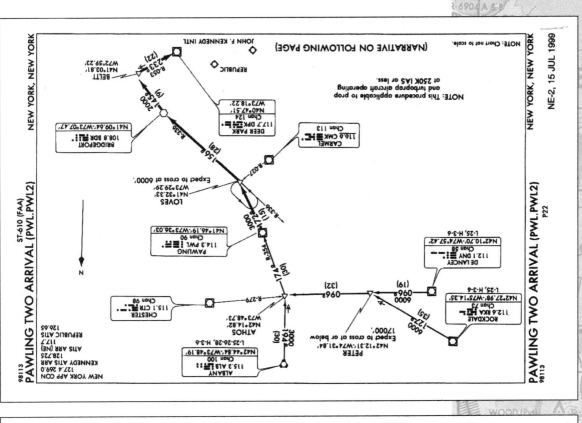

PAWLING TWO ARRIVAL (PWL.PWL2)
NEW YORK, NEW YORK
NE-2, 15 JUL 1999
P22

ST-610 (FAA)
PAWLING TWO ARRIVAL (PWL.PWL2)
NEW YORK, NEW YORK

NOTE: Chart not to scale.

NOTE: This procedure applicable to prop and turboprop aircraft operating at 250K IAS or less.

(NARRATIVE ON FOLLOWING PAGE)

NEW YORK APP CON
127.4 269.0
KENNEDY ATIS ARR
128.725
117.7
ATIS ARR (NE)
REPUBLIC ATIS 126.65

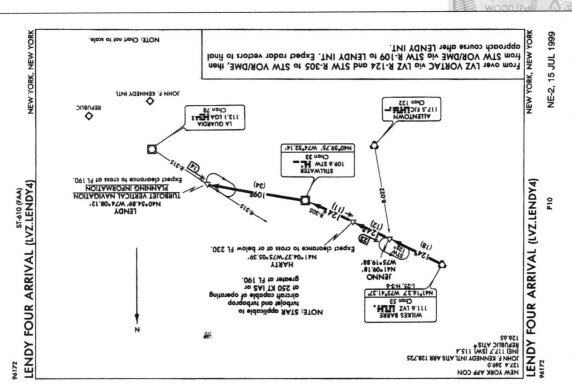

LENDY FOUR ARRIVAL (LVZ.LENDY4)
NEW YORK, NEW YORK
NE-2, 15 JUL 1999
P10

ST-610 (FAA)
LENDY FOUR ARRIVAL (LVZ.LENDY4)
NEW YORK, NEW YORK

NOTE: Chart not to scale.

From over LVZ VORTAC via LVZ R-124 and STW R-305 to STW VOR/DME, then from STW VOR/DME via STW R-109 to LENDY INT. Expect radar vectors to final approach course after LENDY INT.

NOTE: STAR applicable to turbojet and turboprop aircraft capable of operating at 250 KT IAS or greater at FL 190.

NEW YORK APP CON
127.4 269.0
JOHN F. KENNEDY INTL ATIS ARR 128.725
(NE) 117.7 (SW) 115.4
REPUBLIC ATIS
126.65

313

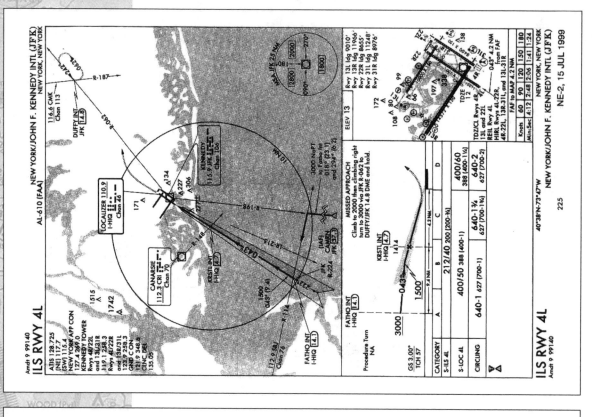

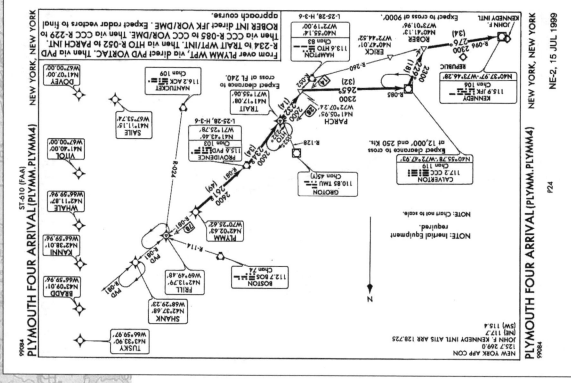

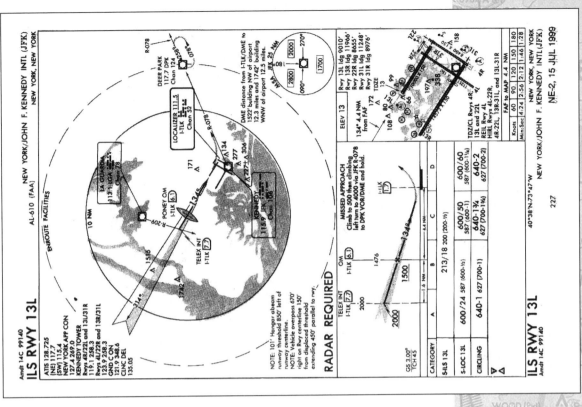

JFK

Left chart:

Amdt 28C 99140 — 226 — NE-2, 15 JUL 1999 — AL-610 (FAA) — NEW YORK/JOHN F. KENNEDY INTL (JFK) — NEW YORK, NEW YORK

ILS RWY 4R

ATIS 128.725
(NE) 117.7
(SW) 115.4
NEW YORK APP CON
127.4 269.0
KENNEDY TOWER
Rwys 4R/22L and 13L/31R
119.1 258.3
Rwys 4L/22R and 13R/31L
123.9 258.3
GND CON
121.9 348.6
CLNC DEL
135.05

DEER PARK 117.7 DPK Chan 124
ENROUTE FACILITIES
FEEDER FACILITIES
R-078

LOCALIZER 109.5 I-JFK Chan 32
KENNEDY 115.9 JFK Chan 106
CANARSIE 112.3 CRI Chan 70
SOLBERG 112.9 SBJ Chan 76

134
277
304
171
R-172
R-221

3000 to Narro Int
JFK R-192 (15.3) and SBJ R-114 (7.3)

1500 to Ebbee Int 044° (9.5)
EBBEE INT I-JFK 6 DME
NARRO INT I-JFK 15.5 DME

(IAF) SATES

MISSED APPROACH
Climb to 500 then climbing right turn to 4000 via heading 100° and V44 to DPK VOR/DME and hold.

10 NM
25 NM
2800 | 2000
270°
180°
090°
1700

ELEV 13
Rwy 13L ldg 9010'
Rwy 13R ldg 11966'
Rwy 22R ldg 8655'
Rwy 31L ldg 11248'
Rwy 31R ldg 8976'
TDZE 12
TDZ/CL Rwys 4R, 13L and 22L
REIL Rwy 4L
HIRL Rwys 4L-22R, 4R-22L, 13L-31L, and 13R-31R
044° 4.5 NM from FAF
FAF to MAP 4.5 NM

Knots	60	90	120	150	180
Min:Sec	4:30	3:00	2:15	1:48	1:30

NARRO INT I-JFK 15.5 DME   Procedure Turn NA
3000

GS 3.00° TCH 53

CATEGORY	A	B	C	D
S-ILS 4R		212/18 200 (200-⅜)		
S-LOC 4R	480/24 468 (500-½)		480/40 468 (500-¾)	480/50 468 (500-1)
CIRCLING	640-1 627 (700-1)	640-1¾ 627 (700-1¾)	640-2 627 (700-2)	

NOTE: 23' Blast fence 540 feet left of Rwy centerline 540 feet North of Rwy 4R threshold and 158' tower 1517 feet East of Rwy 4R centerline.

ILS RWY 4R
Amdt 28C 99140

40°38'N-73°47'W — NEW YORK, NEW YORK — NEW YORK/JOHN F. KENNEDY INTL (JFK)

Right chart:

Amdt 14C 99140 — AL-610 (FAA) — NEW YORK/JOHN F. KENNEDY INTL (JFK) — NEW YORK, NEW YORK

ILS RWY 13L

ATIS 128.725
(NE) 117.7
(SW) 115.4
NEW YORK APP CON
127.4 269.0
KENNEDY TOWER
Rwys 4R/22L and 13L/31R
119.1 258.3
Rwys 4L/22R and 13R/31L
123.9 258.3
GND CON
121.9 348.6
CLNC DEL
135.05

DEER PARK 117.7 DPK Chan 124
R-078
ENROUTE FACILITIES

LOCALIZER 111.5 I-TLK Chan 52
LA GUARDIA
KENNEDY 115.9 JFK Chan 106
PONEY OM I-TLK
TELEX INT I-TLK
R-209
R-078

134
277
306
171

NOTE: 101' Hangar abeam runway threshold 850' left of runway centerline.
NOTE: Vehicle overpass 670' right on Rwy centreline 150' from displaced threshold extending 450' parallel to rwy.

DME distance from I-TLK/DME to 1522 building NW of airport 12.3 miles and 1746' building WNW of airport 12.5 miles.

10 NM
25 NM
2800 | 2000
270°
180°
090°
1700

RADAR REQUIRED

MISSED APPROACH
Climb to 500 then climbing left turn to 4000 via JFK R-078 to DPK VOR/DME and hold.

TELEX INT I-TLK
PONEY OM I-TLK
2000
1500
1476

ELEV 13
Rwy 13L ldg 9010'
Rwy 13R ldg 11966'
Rwy 22R ldg 8655'
Rwy 31L ldg 11248'
Rwy 31R ldg 8976'
TDZE 13
TDZ/CL Rwys 4R, 13L and 22L
REIL Rwy 4L
HIRL Rwys 4L-22R, 4R-22L, 13L-31L, and 13R-31R
13.4° 4.4 NM from FAF
FAF to MAP 4.4 NM

Knots	60	90	120	150	180
Min:Sec	4:24	2:56	2:12	1:46	1:28

GS 3.00° TCH 45

CATEGORY	A	B	C	D
S-ILS 13L		213/18 200 (200-½)		
S-LOC 13L	600/24 587 (600-½)		600/50 587 (600-1¼)	600/60 587 (600-1¼)
CIRCLING	640-1 627 (700-1)	640-1¾ 627 (700-1¾)	640-2 627 (700-2)	

ILS RWY 13L
Amdt 14C 99140

40°38'N-73°47'W — 227 — NE-2, 15 JUL 1999 — NEW YORK, NEW YORK — NEW YORK/JOHN F. KENNEDY INTL (JFK)

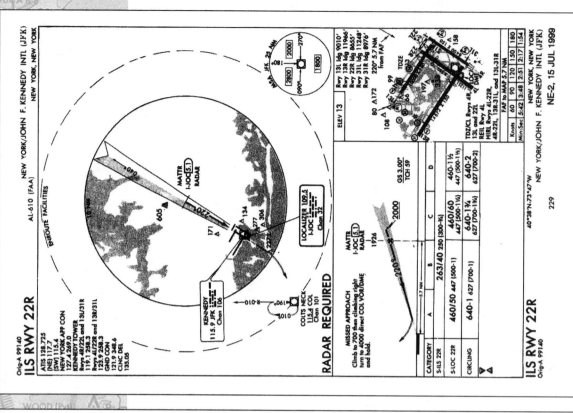

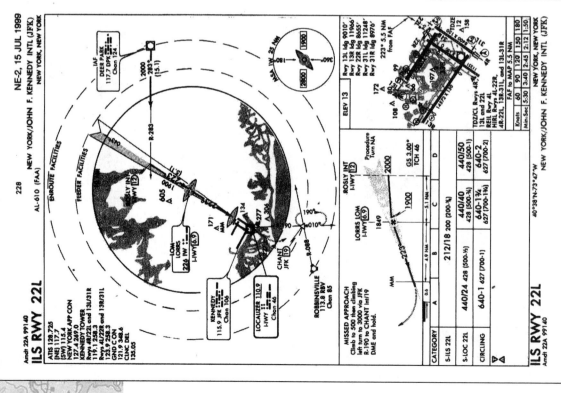

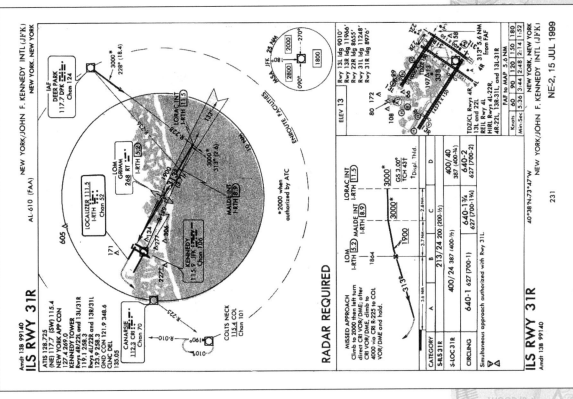

Amdt 13B 99140
ILS RWY 31R
AL-610 (FAA)   NEW YORK/JOHN F. KENNEDY INTL (JFK)
NEW YORK, NEW YORK

NEW YORK, NEW YORK
ILS RWY 31R   NE-2, 15 JUL 1999
Amdt 13B 99140   231

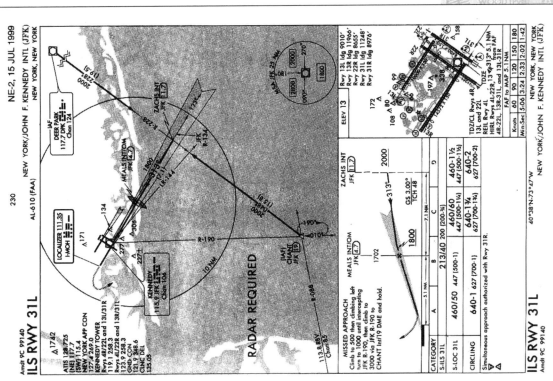

230   NE-2, 15 JUL 1999
Amdt 9C 99140
ILS RWY 31L
AL-610 (FAA)   NEW YORK/JOHN F. KENNEDY INTL (JFK)
NEW YORK, NEW YORK

NEW YORK/JOHN F. KENNEDY INTL (JFK)
ILS RWY 31L
Amdt 9C 99140

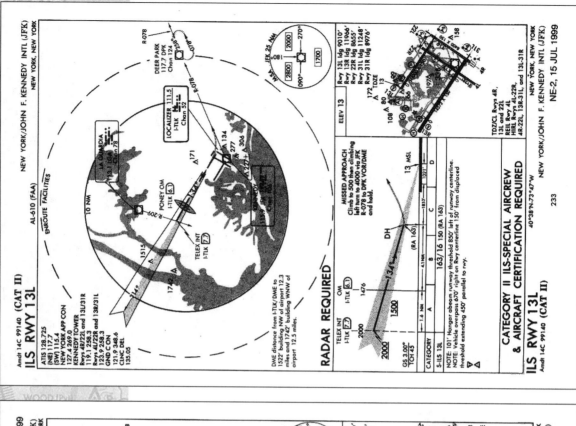

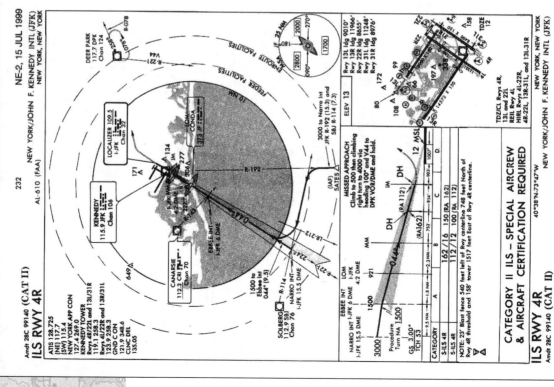

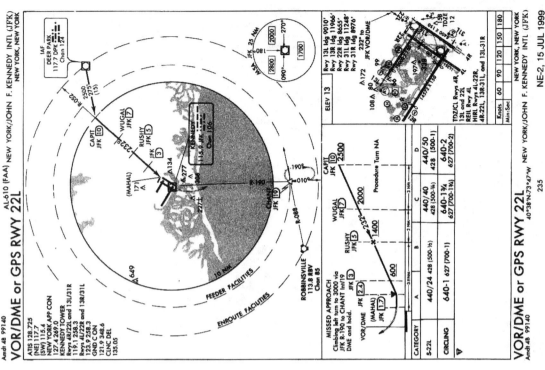

Amdt 4B 99140

VOR/DME or GPS RWY 22L
AL-610 (FAA)   NEW YORK/JOHN F. KENNEDY INTL (JFK)
NEW YORK, NEW YORK

ATIS 128.725
(NE) 117.7
(SW) 115.4
NEW YORK APP CON
127.4 269.0
KENNEDY TOWER
119.1 258.3
Rwys 4R/22L and 13L/31R
123.9 258.3
Rwys 4L/22R and 13R/31L
GND CON
121.9 348.6
CLNC DEL
135.05

MISSED APPROACH
Climbing left turn to 3000 via JFK R-190 to CHANT Int/19 DME and hold.

CATEGORY	A	B	C	D
S-22L	440/24 428 (500-½)		440/40 428 (500-¾)	440/50 428 (500-1)
CIRCLING	640-1 627 (700-1)	640-1¼ 627 (700-1¼)	640-1¾ 627 (700-1¾)	640-2 627 (700-2)

VOR/DME or GPS RWY 22L
Amdt 4B 99140

NEW YORK, NEW YORK
NEW YORK/JOHN F. KENNEDY INTL (JFK)
40°38'N-73°47'W
NE-2, 15 JUL 1999

ELEV 13
235

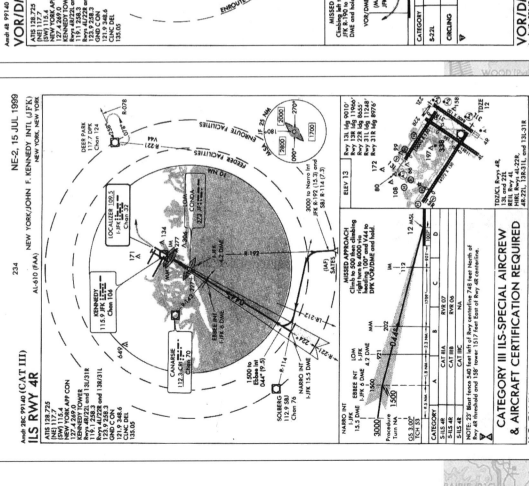

Amdt 28C 99140 (CAT III)

ILS RWY 4R
AL-610 (FAA)   NEW YORK/JOHN F. KENNEDY INTL (JFK)
NEW YORK, NEW YORK
NE-2, 15 JUL 1999
234

ATIS 128.725
(NE) 117.7
(SW) 115.4
NEW YORK APP CON
127.4 269.0
KENNEDY TOWER
119.1 258.3
Rwys 4R/22L and 13L/31R
123.9 258.3
Rwys 4L/22R and 13R/31L
GND CON
121.9 348.6
CLNC DEL
135.05

MISSED APPROACH
Climb to 500 then climbing right turn to 4000 via heading 100° and V44 to DPK VOR/DME and hold.

CATEGORY	A	B	C	D
S-ILS 4R				
S-ILS 4R				
S-ILS 4R				

NOTE: 23' Blast fence 540 feet left of Rwy centerline 748 feet North of Rwy 4R threshold and 158' tower 1517 feet East of Rwy 4R centerline.

CATEGORY III ILS-SPECIAL AIRCREW
& AIRCRAFT CERTIFICATION REQUIRED

ILS RWY 4R (CAT III)
Amdt 28C 99140
NEW YORK, NEW YORK
NEW YORK/JOHN F. KENNEDY INTL (JFK)
40°38'N-73°47'W

ELEV 13

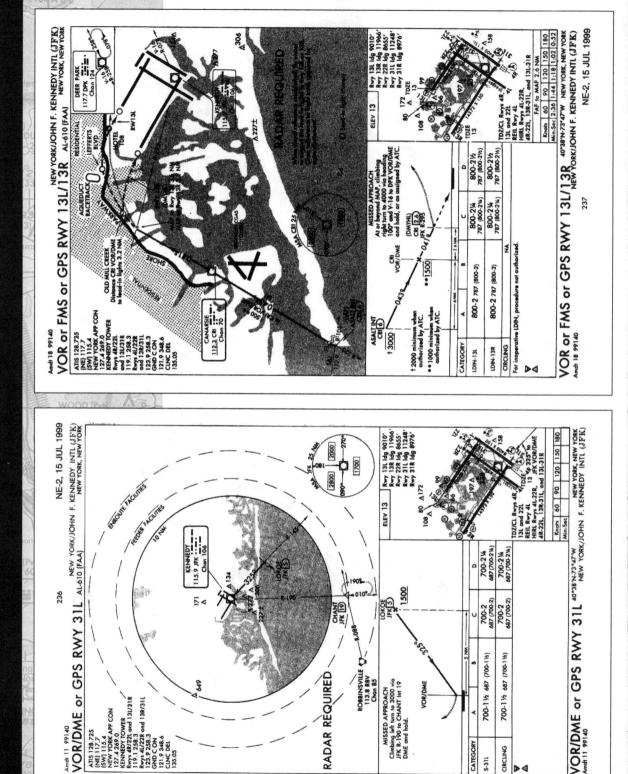

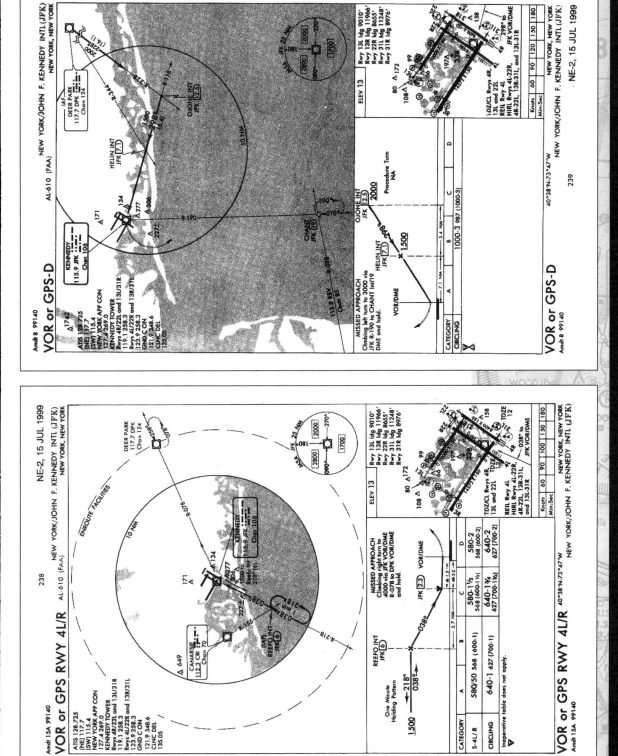

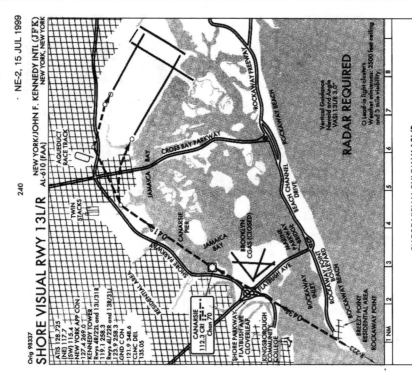

AIRPORT DIAGRAM

99028

NEW YORK/JOHN F. KENNEDY INTL (JFK)
NEW YORK, NEW YORK

AL-610 (FAA)

ATIS 128.725
(NE) 117.7
(SW) 115.4
KENNEDY TOWER
119.1 258.3
Rwys 13R/22L,
13L/31R
Rwys 4L/22R,
13R/31L
123.9 258.3
GND CON
121.9 348.6
CLNC DEL
135.05

JANUARY 1995
ANNUAL RATE OF CHANGE
0.1°W

CAUTION: BE ALERT TO
RUNWAY CROSSING CLEARANCES.
READBACK OF ALL RUNWAY
HOLDING INSTRUCTIONS IS REQUIRED.

NORTH
PASSENGER
TERMINAL

AUX ARFF

Rwy 13L ldg 9010'
Rwy 13R ldg 11966'
Rwy 22R ldg 8655'
Rwy 31L ldg 11248'
Rwy 31R ldg 8976'

INTERNATIONAL
ARRIVAL TERMINAL
U.S. CUSTOMS

CONTROL
TOWER
338

ELEV 161
ELEV 12
ELEV 12
ELEV 197
ELEV 11

ARFF

GENERAL
AVIATION
BUILDING

RWYS 4R-22L, 4L-22R, 13R-31L, 13L-31R
S100, T185, ST175, TT550, TDT823

FIELD
ELEV 13

CAT 2
HOLD

10000 X 150
8400 X 150
11351 X 150
14572 X 150

AIRPORT DIAGRAM

NEW YORK, NEW YORK
NEW YORK/JOHN F. KENNEDY INTL (JFK)
NE-2, 15 JUL 1999

99028

241

Orig 98337

SHORE VISUAL RWY 13L/R

NEW YORK/JOHN F. KENNEDY INTL (JFK)
NEW YORK, NEW YORK

AL-610 (FAA)

ATIS 128.725
(NE) 117.7
(SW) 115.4
NEW YORK APP CON
127.4 269.0
KENNEDY TOWER
119.1 258.3
Rwys 4L/22L and 13L/31R
Rwys 4L/22R and 13R/31L
123.9 258.3
GND CON
121.9 348.6
CLNC DEL
135.05

AQUEDUCT
RACE TRACK

TWIN
STACKS

JAMAICA
BAY

CROSS BAY PARKWAY

ROCKAWAY FREEWAY

ROCKAWAY BEACH

BEACH CHANNEL DRIVE

CANARSIE
PIER

JAMAICA
BAY

BROOKLYN
CGAS (CLOSED)

CANARSIE
112.3 CRI •—•••
Chan 70

SHORE PARKWAY
FLATBUSH AVE
CLOVERLEAF

KINGSBOROUGH
COMMUNITY
COLLEGE

FLATBUSH AVE

RESIDENTIAL AREA
ROCKAWAY BEACH

BREEZY POINT
RESIDENTIAL AREA
ROCKAWAY POINT

MARINE
PARKWAY
BRIDGE

ROCKAWAY
INLET
ROCKAWAY POINT
BOULEVARD

Vertical Guidance
Nonstd and Angle
VASI 13L/R 3.0°

RADAR REQUIRED

Ⓛ Lead-in Light System.
Weather minimums: 2500 foot ceiling
and 3 mile visibility.

1 NM 1 2 3 4 5 6 7 8

SHORE VISUAL RUNWAY 13L/R

When cleared for Shore Visual to Runway 13L/R maintain 2000' (Mandatory)
until abeam Rockaway Point. Remain west of Rockaway Point, thence east of
Kingsborough Community College. Remain east of the Shore Parkway. Descend
so as to maintain 1500' (Mandatory) until passing the Brooklyn Coast Guard
Air Station. Remain east of the Shore Parkway until the Canarsie Pier.

Runway 13R continue descent between the Canarsie Pier and Twin Stacks.
Runway 13L continue descent after passing the Twin Stacks.

SHORE VISUAL RWY 13L/R

NEW YORK, NEW YORK
NEW YORK/JOHN F. KENNEDY INTL (JFK)

Orig 98337

240

(BETTE2.BETTE) 9719B
BETTE TWO DEPARTURE (VECTOR)
SL-610 (FAA)

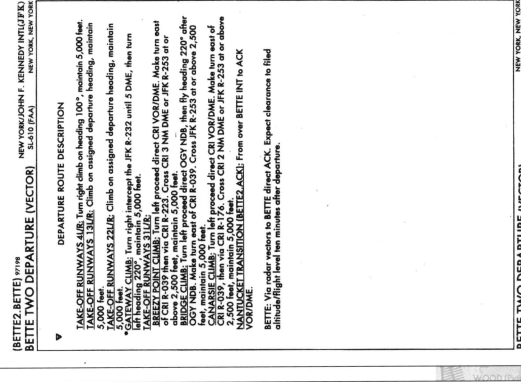

DEPARTURE ROUTE DESCRIPTION

TAKE-OFF RUNWAYS 4L/R: Turn right climb on heading 100°, maintain 5,000 feet.

TAKE-OFF RUNWAYS 13L/R: Climb on assigned departure heading, maintain 5,000 feet.

TAKE-OFF RUNWAYS 22L/R: Climb on assigned departure heading, maintain 5,000 feet.

*GATEWAY CLIMB: Turn right intercept the JFK R-232 until 5 DME, then turn left heading 220°, maintain 5,000 feet.

TAKE-OFF RUNWAYS 31L/R:

BREEZY POINT CLIMB: Turn left proceed direct CRI VOR/DME. Make turn east of CRI R-039 then via CRI R-223. Cross CRI 3 NM DME or JFK R-253 at or above 2,500 feet, maintain 5,000 feet.

BRIDGE CLIMB: Turn left proceed direct OGY NDB, then fly heading 220° after OGY NDB. Make turn east of CRI R-039. Cross JFK R-253 at or above 2,500 feet, maintain 5,000 feet.

CANARSIE CLIMB: Turn left proceed direct CRI VOR/DME. Make turn east of CRI R-039, then via CRI R-176. Cross CRI 2 NM DME or JFK R-253 at or above 2,500 feet, maintain 5,000 feet.

NANTUCKET TRANSITION (BETTE2.ACK): From over BETTE INT to ACK VOR/DME.

BETTE: Via radar vectors to BETTE direct ACK. Expect clearance to filed altitude/flight level ten minutes after departure.

BETTE TWO DEPARTURE (VECTOR)
(BETTE2.BETTE) 9719B
243
NEW YORK, NEW YORK
NEW YORK/JOHN F. KENNEDY INTL (JFK)
NE-2, 15 JUL 1999

(BETTE2.BETTE) 97142
BETTE TWO DEPARTURE (VECTOR)
SL-610 (FAA)

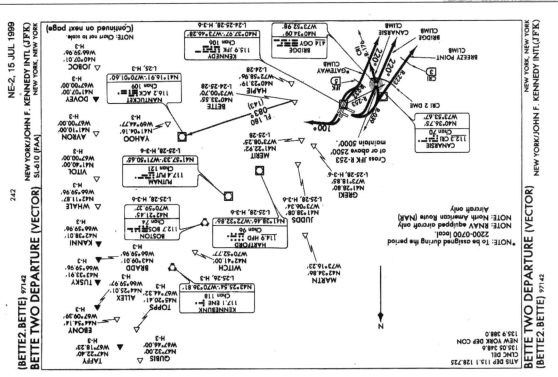

NOTE: Chart not to scale.
(Continued on next page.)

*NOTE: To be assigned during the period 2200-0700 local.
NOTE: RNAV equipped aircraft only
NOTE: North American Route (NAR) Aircraft only

ATIS DEP 115.1 128.725
CLNC DEL 135.05 348.6
135.05 348.6
NEW YORK DEP CON 135.9 388.0

JFK

(GREKI2.GREKI) 97198
GREKI TWO DEPARTURE (VECTOR) — NEW YORK/JOHN F. KENNEDY INTL (JFK)
SL-610 (FAA) — NEW YORK, NEW YORK

DEPARTURE ROUTE DESCRIPTION

TAKE-OFF RUNWAYS 4L/R: Turn right climb on heading 100°, maintain 5,000 feet.

TAKE-OFF RUNWAYS 13L/R: Climb on assigned departure heading, maintain 5,000 feet.

TAKE-OFF RUNWAYS 22L/R: Climb on assigned departure heading, maintain 5,000 feet.

*GATEWAY CLIMB: Turn right intercept the JFK R-232 until 5 DME, then turn left heading 220°, maintain 5,000 feet.

TAKE-OFF RUNWAYS 31L/R:

BREEZY POINT CLIMB: Turn left proceed direct CRI VOR/DME. Make turn east of CRI R-039 then via CRI R-223. Cross CRI 3 NM DME or JFK R-253 at or above 2,500 feet, maintain 5,000 feet.

BRIDGE CLIMB: Turn left proceed direct OGY NDB, then fly heading 220° after OGY NDB. Make turn east of CRI R-039. Cross JFK R-253 at or above 2,500 feet, maintain 5,000 feet.

CANARSIE CLIMB: Turn left proceed direct CRI VOR/DME. Make turn east of CRI R-039, then via CRI R-176. Cross CRI 2 NM DME or JFK R-253 at or above 2,500 feet, maintain 5,000 feet.

MARTN TRANSITION (GREKI2.MARTN): From over GREKI INT to JUDDS INT, then to MARTN INT.

GREKI: Via radar vectors to GREKI direct JUDDS direct MARTN. Expect clearance to filed altitude/flight level ten minutes after departure.

(Continued on next page)

NOTE: Chart not to scale.

ATIS DEP 115.1 128.725
CINC DEL 135.05 348.6
NEW YORK DEP CON 135.9 388.0

*NOTE: To be assigned during the period 2200-0700 local.
NOTE: RNAV equipped aircraft only
NOTE: North American Route (NAR) Aircraft only

GREKI TWO DEPARTURE (VECTOR) — NEW YORK, NEW YORK — NEW YORK/JOHN F. KENNEDY INTL (JFK)
(GREKI2.GREKI) 97142

DEPARTURE ROUTE DESCRIPTION

TAKE-OFF RUNWAYS 4L/R: Turn right climb on heading 100°, maintain 5,000 feet.

TAKE-OFF RUNWAYS 13L/R: Climb on assigned departure heading, maintain 5,000 feet.

TAKE-OFF RUNWAYS 22L/R: Climb on assigned departure heading, maintain 5,000 feet.

*GATEWAY CLIMB: Turn right intercept the JFK R-232 until 5 DME, then turn left heading 220°, maintain 5,000 feet.

TAKE-OFF RUNWAYS 31L/R:

BREEZY POINT CLIMB: Turn left proceed direct CRI VOR/DME. Make turn east of CRI R-039 then via CRI R-223. Cross CRI 3 NM DME or JFK R-253 at or above 2,500 feet, maintain 5,000 feet.

BRIDGE CLIMB: Turn left proceed direct OGY NDB, then fly heading 220° after OGY NDB. Make turn east of CRI R-039. Cross JFK R-253 at or above 2,500 feet, maintain 5,000 feet.

CANARSIE CLIMB: Turn left proceed direct CRI VOR/DME. Make turn east of CRI R-039, then via CRI R-176. Cross CRI 2 NM DME or JFK R-253 at or above 2,500 feet, maintain 5,000 feet.

YAHOO TRANSITION (HAPIE2.YAHOO): From over HAPIE INT to YAHOO INT.

HAPIE: Via radar vectors to HAPIE direct YAHOO INT. Expect clearance to filed altitude/flight level ten minutes after departure.

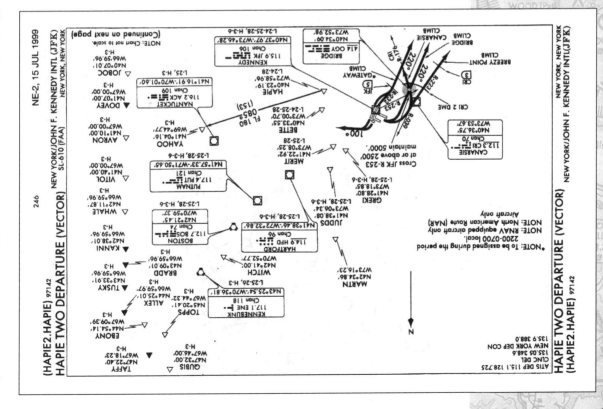

KENNEDY SEVEN DEPARTURE (VECTOR)

96228

NEW YORK/JOHN F. KENNEDY INTL (JFK)   SL-610 (FAA)   NEW YORK, NEW YORK

DEPARTURE ROUTE DESCRIPTION

TAKE-OFF RUNWAYS 4L/R: Turn right climb on heading 100°, maintain 5,000 feet. Thence. . . .

TAKE-OFF RUNWAYS 13L/R: Climb on assigned departure heading, maintain 5,000 feet. Thence. . . .

TAKE-OFF RUNWAYS 22L/R: Climb on assigned departure heading, maintain 5,000 feet. Thence. . . .

GATEWAY CLIMB: *Turn right intercept the JFK R-232 until 5 DME, then turn left heading 220°, maintain 5,000 feet. Thence. . . .

TAKE-OFF RUNWAYS 31L/R:

BREEZY POINT CLIMB: Turn left proceed direct CRI VOR/DME. Make turn east of CRI R-039, then via CRI R-223. Cross CRI 3 DME or JFK R-253 at or above 2,500 feet, maintain 5,000 feet. Thence. . . .

BRIDGE CLIMB: Turn left proceed direct OGY NDB, then fly heading 220° after OGY NDB. Make turn east of CRI R-039, cross JFK R-253 at or above 2,500 feet, maintain 5,000 feet. Thence. . . .

CANARSIE CLIMB: Turn left proceed direct CRI VOR/DME. Make turn east of CRI R-039, then via CRI R-176. Cross CRI 2 DME or JFK R-253 at or above 2,500 feet, maintain 5,000 feet. Thence. . . .

IDLEWILD CLIMB: **Turn right climb on heading 090°, remain within 2.5 DME of JFK ***, maintain 2,000 feet. Thence. . . .

. . . . Via vectors to assigned route/fix. Expect clearance to filed altitude/flight level ten minutes after departure.

* To be assigned during the period 2200 - 0700 local.
** To be assigned by ATC to NON-TURBOJET AIRCRAFT.
*** If unable to remain within 2.5 DME of JFK advise ATC.

NOTE: BAYYS departures expect vectors to BDR VOR or R-054.
NOTE: BETTE departures expect vectors to JFK R-109.
NOTE: COATE departures expect vectors to SAX VORTAC or R-311.
NOTE: DIXIE departures expect vectors to JFK R-221.
NOTE: HAPIE departures expect vectors to JFK R-124.
NOTE: SHIPP departures expect vectors to JFK R-139.
NOTE: WAVEY departures expect vectors to JFK 156.

NEW YORK, NEW YORK
NEW YORK/JOHN F. KENNEDY INTL (JFK)

KENNEDY SEVEN DEPARTURE (VECTOR)

NEW YORK/JOHN F. KENNEDY INTL (JFK)

96228   249   NE-2, 15 JUL 1999

97254   248   NE-2, 15 JUL 1999

KENNEDY SEVEN DEPARTURE (VECTOR)

NEW YORK/JOHN F. KENNEDY INTL (JFK)   SL-610 (FAA)   NEW YORK, NEW YORK

ATIS DEP 115.1 128.725
CLNC DEL 135.05 348.6
NEW YORK DEP CON 135.9 388.0

(Continued on next page)

NOTE: Chart not to scale.

NEW YORK, NEW YORK
NEW YORK/JOHN F. KENNEDY INTL (JFK)

KENNEDY SEVEN DEPARTURE (VECTOR)

NEW YORK/JOHN F. KENNEDY INTL (JFK)

97254

(MERIT2.MERIT) 97198
MERIT TWO DEPARTURE (VECTOR)
NEW YORK/JOHN F. KENNEDY INTL (JFK)
SL-610 (FAA)
NEW YORK, NEW YORK

DEPARTURE ROUTE DESCRIPTION

TAKE-OFF RUNWAYS 4L/R: Turn right climb on heading 100°, maintain 5,000 feet.

TAKE-OFF RUNWAYS 13L/R: Climb on assigned departure heading, maintain 5,000 feet.

TAKE-OFF RUNWAYS 22L/R: Climb on assigned departure heading, maintain 5,000 feet.

TAKE-OFF RUNWAYS 31L/R:

*GATEWAY CLIMB: Turn right intercept the JFK R-232 until 5 DME, then turn left heading 220°, maintain 5,000 feet.

BREEZY POINT CLIMB: Turn left proceed direct CRI VOR/DME. Make turn east of CRI R-039 then via CRI R-223. Cross CRI 3 NM DME or JFK R-253 at or above 2,500 feet, maintain 5,000 feet.

BRIDGE CLIMB: Turn left proceed direct OGY NDB, then fly heading 220° after OGY NDB. Make turn east of CRI R-039. Cross JFK R-253 at or above 2,500 feet, maintain 5,000 feet.

CANARSIE CLIMB: Turn left proceed direct CRI VOR/DME. Make turn east of CRI R-039, then via CRI R-176. Cross CRI 2 NM DME or JFK R-253 at or above 2,500 feet, maintain 5,000 feet.

PUTNAM TRANSITION (MERIT2.PUT): From over MERIT INT to HFD VOR/DME, then to PUT VOR/DME.

MERIT: Via radar vectors to MERIT direct HFD direct PUT. Expect clearance to filed altitude/flight level ten minutes after departure.

MERIT TWO: After PUT expect the following routes; aircraft proceeding:
1. TOPPS/EBONY – Expect direct.
2. ALLEX – Expect direct WITCH direct.
3. TUSKY and South – Expect direct BOS direct.

MERIT TWO DEPARTURE (VECTOR)
(MERIT2.MERIT) 97198
NEW YORK, NEW YORK
NEW YORK/JOHN F. KENNEDY INTL(JFK)
NE-2, 15 JUL 1999
251

(MERIT2.MERIT) 97142
MERIT TWO DEPARTURE (VECTOR)
NEW YORK/JOHN F. KENNEDY INTL (JFK)
SL-610 (FAA)
NEW YORK, NEW YORK
NE-2, 15 JUL 1999
250

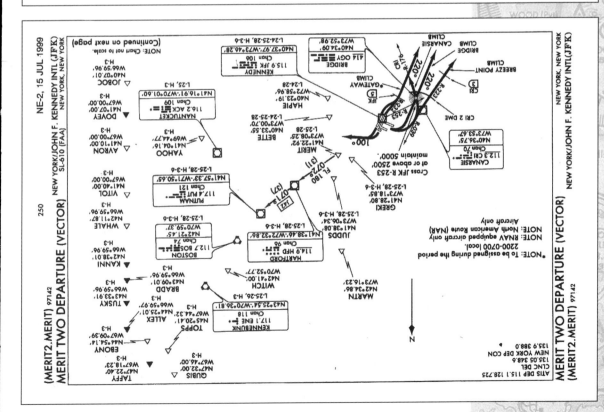

MERIT TWO DEPARTURE (VECTOR)
(MERIT2.MERIT) 97142
NEW YORK, NEW YORK
NEW YORK/JOHN F. KENNEDY INTL(JFK)

ATIS DEP 115.1 128.725
CLNC DEL 135.05 348.6
NEW YORK DEP CON 135.9 388.0

*NOTE: To be assigned during the period 2200-0700 local.

NOTE: RNAV equipped aircraft only
NOTE: North American Route (NAR)
Aircraft only

(Continued on next page)
NOTE: Chart not to scale.

97086
SL-610 (FAA)   NEW YORK/JOHN F. KENNEDY INTL (JFK)
NEW YORK, NEW YORK
SEAVIEW ONE DEPARTURE (VECTOR)

DEPARTURE ROUTE DESCRIPTION

TAKE-OFF RUNWAYS 4L/R: Turn right climb on heading 100°, maintain 5,000 feet. Thence. . . .

TAKE-OFF RUNWAYS 13L/R: Climb on assigned departure heading, maintain 5,000 feet. Thence. . . .

TAKE-OFF RUNWAYS 22L/R: Climb on assigned departure heading, maintain 5,000 feet. Thence. . . .

GATEWAY CLIMB: *Turn right intercept the JFK R-232 until 5 DME, then turn left heading 220°, maintain 5,000 feet. Thence. . . .

TAKE-OFF RUNWAYS 31L/R:

BREEZY POINT CLIMB: Turn left proceed direct CRI VOR/DME. Make turn east of CRI R-039, then via CRI R-223. Cross CRI 3 DME or JFK R-253 at or above 2,500 feet, maintain 5,000 feet. Thence. . . .

BRIDGE CLIMB: Turn left proceed direct OGY NDB, then fly heading 220° after OGY NDB. Make turn east of CRI R-039, cross JFK R-253 at or above 2,500 feet, maintain 5,000 feet. Thence. . . .

CANARSIE CLIMB: Turn left proceed direct CRI VOR/DME. Make turn east of CRI R-039, then via CRI R-176. Cross CRI 2 DME or JFK R-253 at or above 2,500 feet, maintain 5,000 feet. Thence. . . .

. . . . Via vectors to the JFK R-139 to SEIFF DME fix, then turn right proceed direct to the JFK VOR/DME. Expect vectors to assigned route/fix. Expect clearance to filed altitude/flight level ten minutes after departure.

*To be assigned during the period 2200 - 0700 local.

NOTE: RNAV aircraft only.
NOTE: SID to be used when assigned by ATC only.
NOTE: COATE departures expect vectors to SAX VORTAC or R-311.

98057
SL-610 (FAA)   NEW YORK/JOHN F. KENNEDY INTL (JFK)
NE-2, 15 JUL 1999
NEW YORK, NEW YORK
SEAVIEW ONE DEPARTURE (VECTOR)

ATIS DEP 115.1 128.725
CLNC DEL 135.05 348.6
NEW YORK DEP CON
135.9 388.0

(Continued on next page)

NOTE: Chart not to scale.

ALTERNATE MINS

 ALTERNATE MINIMUMS

INSTRUMENT APPROACH PROCEDURE CHARTS

 IFR ALTERNATE MINIMUMS
(NOT APPLICABLE TO USA/USN/USAF)

Standard alternate minimums for non precision approaches are 800-2 (NDB, VOR, LOC, TACAN, LDA, VORTAC, VOR/DME or ASR); for precision approaches 600-2 (ILS or PAR). Airports within this geographical area that require alternate minimums other than standard or alternate minimums with restrictions are listed below. NA - means alternate minimums are not authorized due to unmonitored facility or absence of weather reporting service. Civil pilots see FAR 91. USA/USN/USAF pilots refer to appropriate regulations.

NAME	ALTERNATE MINIMUMS
CAHOKIA/ST. LOUIS, IL	
ST. LOUIS DOWNTOWN-	
PARKS	ILS Rwy 30L¹
	NDB Rwy 30L²

¹NA when control tower closed.
¹ILS, Category D, 700-2.
²Category D, 800-2½; Category D, 800-2½.

CARBONDALE-MURPHYSBORO, IL
SOUTHERN ILLINOIS ...... ILS Rwy 18L
NDB or GPS Rwy 18L

NA when control tower closed.

CHAMPAIGN-URBANA, IL
UNIVERSITY OF ILLINOIS-
WILLARD .... ILS Rwy 32L¹
LOC BC Rwy 14R²
RADAR-1²
VOR/DME or GPS Rwy 22R³
VOR or GPS Rwy 4L²

¹NA when control tower closed. LOC, NA when control tower open, except standard for operators with DME.
²NA when control tower closed.
³NA when control tower closed except for operators with approved weather reporting service.

CHICAGO, IL
CHICAGO MIDWAY .... ILS Rwy 13C
LOC, NA.

CHICAGO O'HARE INTL .... ILS Rwy 9L
Categories A,B, 900-2; Category C, 900-2½;
Category D, 900-2¾.

CHICAGO/AURORA, IL
AURORA MUNI .... VOR or GPS Rwy 36
NA when control tower closed.

NAME	ALTERNATE MINIMUMS
ALTON/ST.LOUIS, IL	
ST. LOUIS REGIONAL	ILS Rwy 29
	LOC BC Rwy 11
	NDB or GPS Rwy 17¹
	ILS Rwy 29
	VOR or GPS-A

NA when control tower closed.
¹Categories A,B, 900-2; Category C, 900-2½;
Category D, 900-2¾.

APPLETON, WI
OUTAGAMIE COUNTY
REGIONAL .... ILS Rwy 3¹²
ILS Rwy 29¹²

¹LOC, NA.
²NA when control tower closed.

BELLEVILLE, IL
SCOTT AFB/
MIDAMERICA .... ILS/DME Rwy 14L¹
ILS Rwy 32R²

¹ILS, Category D, 700-2; Category E, 800-2¾.
LOC, Category E, 800-2¾.
²ILS,Category C,D, 700-2; Category E,800-2¾.
LOC, Category E, 800-2¾.

BLOOMINGTON, IL
CENTRAL IL REGL ARPT AT
BLOOMINGTON-NORMAL .... ILS Rwy 20¹
ILS Rwy 29²
LOC BC Rwy 11³
VOR Rwy 11³

¹ILS, NA when control tower closed. Category D, 700-2. LOC, NA.
²NA when control tower closed.
³NA when control zone not in effect, except for operators with approved weather reporting service.

 ALTERNATE MINS
99196

EC-3, 15 JUL 1999

E1

EC-3, 15 JUL 1999

 TAKE-OFF MINIMUMS AND (OBSTACLE) DEPARTURE PROCEDURES
99140

C2

EC-3, 15 JUL 1999

CAHOKIA/ST. LOUIS, IL
ST. LOUIS DOWNTOWN-PARKS
TAKE-OFF MINIMUMS: Rwy 4, 400-1 or std. with min. climb of 225' per NM to 900. Rwys 30, 30R, 400-1 or std. with min. climb of 225' per NM to 900.
DEPARTURE PROCEDURE: Rwys 30L,30R, west or southwest departures, climb runway heading to 1700 before turning on course, or left turn to 160°, climb to 2000 before turning on course. When weather is below 700-1, north or eastbound departures, climb runway heading to 1100 before turning on course, or left turn after takeoff on course. Rwy 22, west or southwest departures, left turn to 160°, climb to 1700 before turning on course, northbound departure, climb runway heading to 1100 before turning on course. Rwy 4, when weather is below 700-1, westbound departures climb runway heading to 1100 before turning on course. Rwys 12L,12R, climb runway heading to 1000 before turning.

CARMI, IL
CARMI MUNI
DEPARTURE PROCEDURE: Rwy 36, climb runway heading to 1000 before turning westbound.

CASEY, IL
CASEY MUNI
DEPARTURE PROCEDURE: Rwys 4, 22, 36, climb runway heading to 1900 before turning southbound. Rwy 18, climb runway heading to 1900 before turning left.

CENTRALIA, IL
CENTRALIA MUNI
TAKE-OFF MINIMUMS: Rwy 18, 300-1.

CHICAGO, IL
CHICAGO MIDWAY
TAKE-OFF MINIMUMS: Rwy 13L, 300-1 or std with min. climb of 270' per NM to 900. Rwy 22L, 300-1 or std. with min. climb of 340' per NM to 900. Rwy 22R, 300-1 or std. with min. climb of 420' per NM to 900. Rwy 31C, 300-1 or std. with min. climb of 320' per NM to 900. Rwy 31L, 300-1, Rwy 31R, 300-1 or std. with min. climb of 260' per NM to 900. Rwy 36, NA. Rwy 4L,4R, northbound Departures (360° CW 060°), climbing right turn to 2400 heading 100° before proceeding on course. Rwys 13C,13L,13R,22L,22R,31C,31L,31R, climb runway heading to 1000 before turning.

CHICAGO-O'HARE INTL
TAKE-OFF MINIMUMS: Rwy 22R, 300-1, Rwy 32L, straight out or right turn, std., left turn 1000-3 or std. with a min. climb of 240' per NM to 1600. Rwy 18, NA. Rwy 36, 500-1.

LANSING MUNI
DEPARTURE PROCEDURE: Rwy 9, 300-1. Rwy 36, 400-1.

CHICAGO, IL (CONT)
MERRILL C. MEIGS
TAKE-OFF MINIMUMS: Rwy 18, 300-1 or std. with a min. climb of 240' per NM to 3000. Rwy 36, 1500-2.
DEPARTURE PROCEDURE: Comply with radar vectors or Rwy 18, climb to 3000 direct CGT VORTAC. Rwy 36, climbing right turn to 3000 heading 140° to intercept the CGT R-011, then via CGT R-011 to CGT VORTAC.

CHICAGO/PROSPECT HEIGHTS/
WHEELING, IL
PALWAUKEE MUNI
TAKE-OFF MINIMUMS: Rwys 16, 300-1 or std. with a min. climb of 266' per NM to 800.

CHICAGO/WAUKEGAN, IL
WAUKEGAN REGIONAL
TAKE-OFF MINIMUMS: Rwy 14, 300-1.

CLINTONVILLE, WI
CLINTONVILLE MUNI
TAKE-OFF MINIMUMS: Rwy 27, 300-1.
DEPARTURE PROCEDURE: Rwy 9, climb runway heading to 1400 before proceeding on course.

DE KALB, IL
DE KALB TAYLOR MUNI
TAKE-OFF MINIMUMS: Rwy 27, 300-1.
DEPARTURE PROCEDURE: Rwy 9, climb runway heading to 1400 before proceeding on course.

DECATUR, IL
DECATUR
DEPARTURE PROCEDURE: Northbound departures: Rwy 36, left turn, climb to 3000 via DEC R-340 before proceeding north. Rwy 30, right turn, climb to 3000 via DEC R-340 before proceeding north. Rwy 18, climb runway heading to 1200 before turning north. Rwys 6,12,24, climb runway heading to 1600 before turning north.

DELAVAN, WI
LAKE LAWN
TAKE-OFF MINIMUMS: Rwys 18, 36, 300-1.

DIXON, IL
DIXON MUNI-CHARLES R. WALGREEN FIELD
TAKE-OFF MINIMUMS: Rwys 26, 30, 300-1.

EAU CLAIRE, WI
CHIPPEWA VALLEY REGIONAL
TAKE-OFF MINIMUMS: Rwy 14, 500-1.
DEPARTURE PROCEDURE: Rwys 14, 22, climb runway heading to 2500 before turning southbound.

EFFINGHAM, IL
EFFINGHAM COUNTY MEMORIAL
TAKE-OFF MINIMUMS: Rwy 1, 600-1.
DEPARTURE PROCEDURE: Rwy 28, climb runway heading to 2100 before proceeding on course.

 TAKE-OFF MINIMUMS AND (OBSTACLE) DEPARTURE PROCEDURES
99140

EC-3

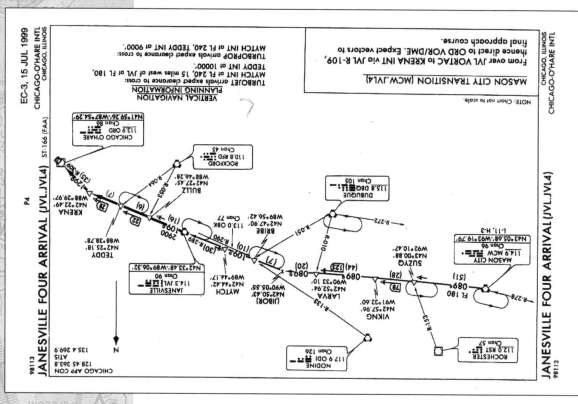

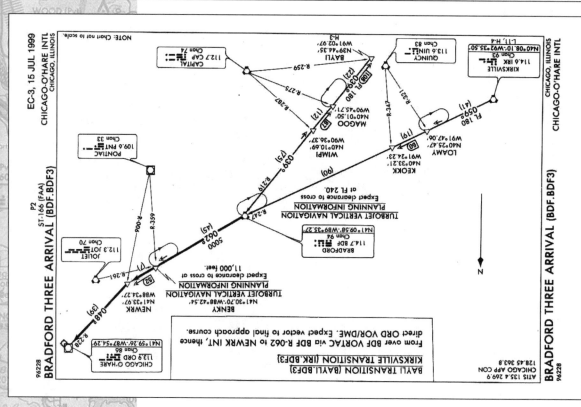

ARRIVAL DESCRIPTION

BRIGGS TRANSITION (BSV.OXI3): From over BSV VORTAC via BSV R-286 and OXI R-095 to OXI VOR/DME. Thence. . . .

DRYER TRANSITION (DJB.OXI3): From over DJB VORTAC via DJB R-270 and OXI R-095 to OXI VOR/DME. Thence. . . .

FORT WAYNE TRANSITION (FWA.OXI3): From over FWA VORTAC via FWA R-311 and OXI R-095 to OXI VOR/DME. Thence. . . .

WATERVILLE TRANSITION (VWV.OXI3): From over VWV VOR/DME via VWV R-248 and OXI R-095 to OXI VOR/DME. Thence. . . .

. . . From over OXI VOR/DME via OXI R-297 to BEARZ INT, thence direct ORD VOR/DME. Expect vectors to final approach course.

KNOX THREE ARRIVAL (OXI.OXI3)
CHICAGO O'HARE INTL
CHICAGO, ILLINOIS
97198

CHICAGO APP CON 119.0 393.1
ATIS 135.4 269.9

(NARRATIVE ON FOLLOWING PAGE)

NOTE: Chart not to scale

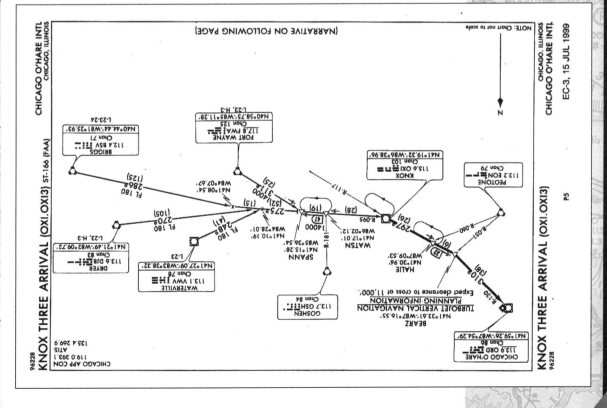

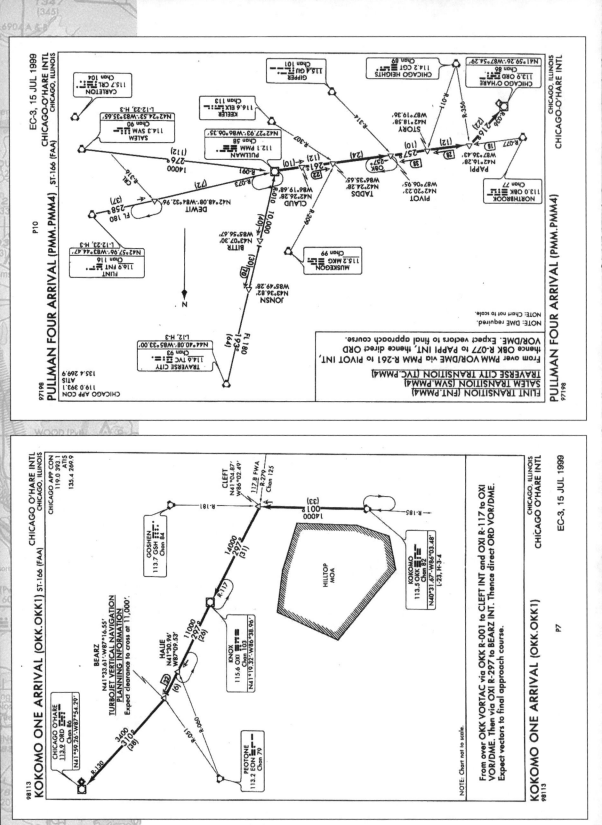

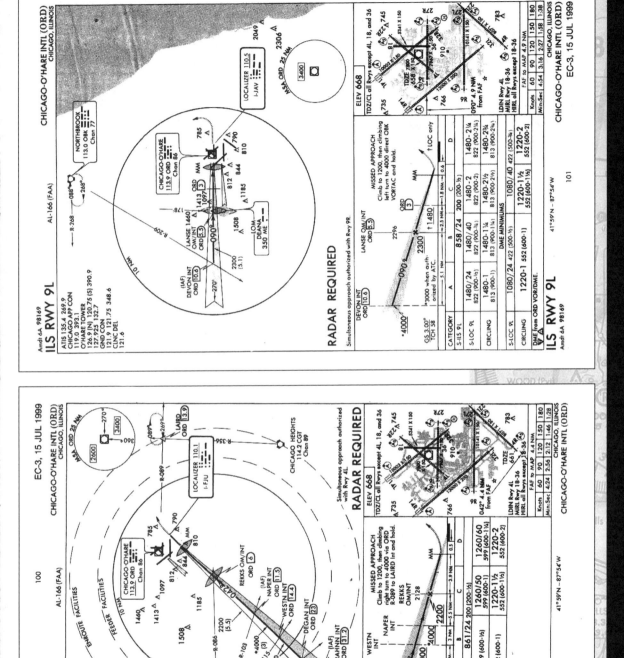

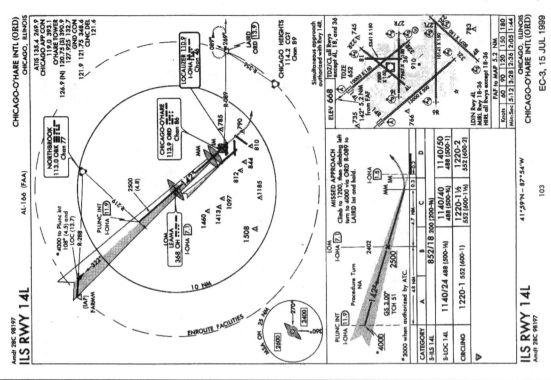

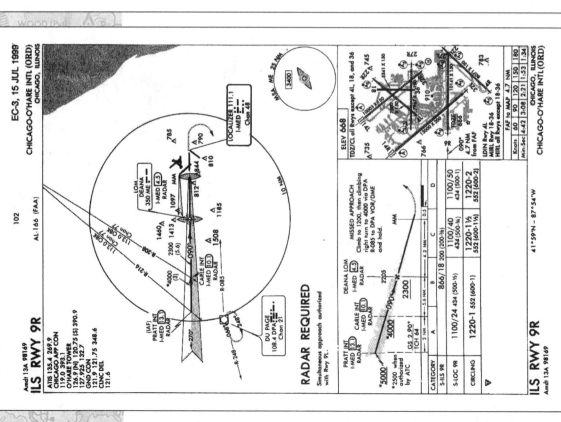

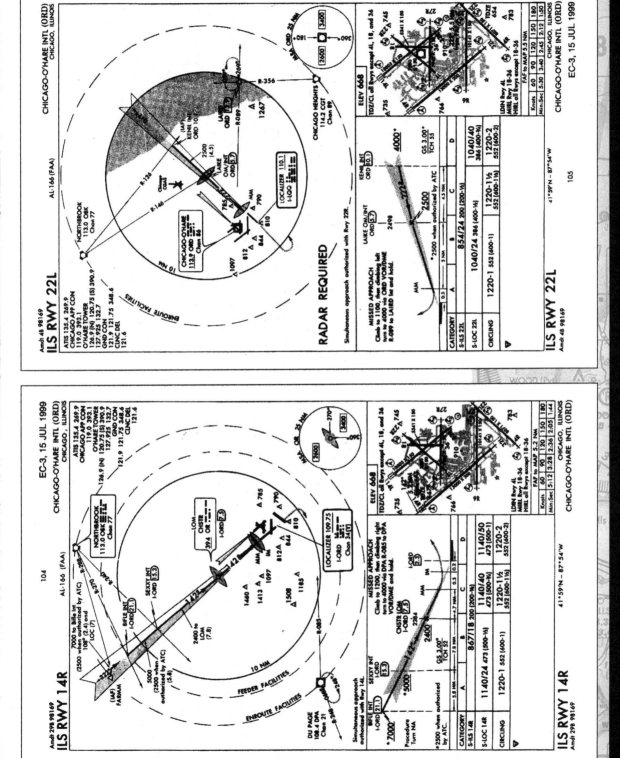

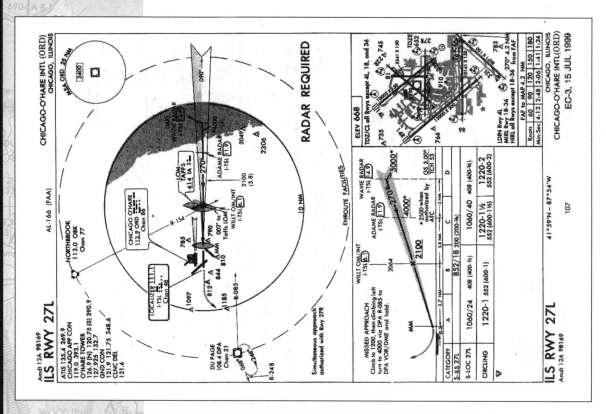

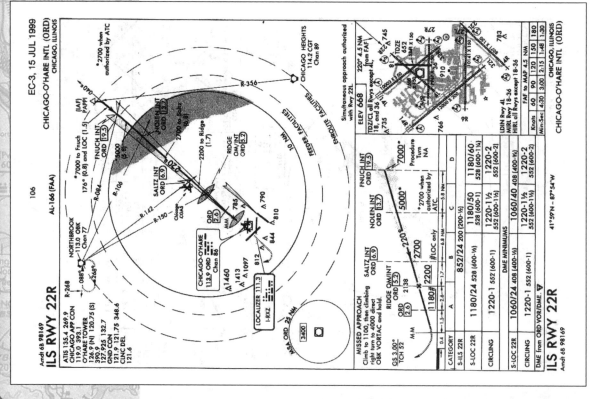

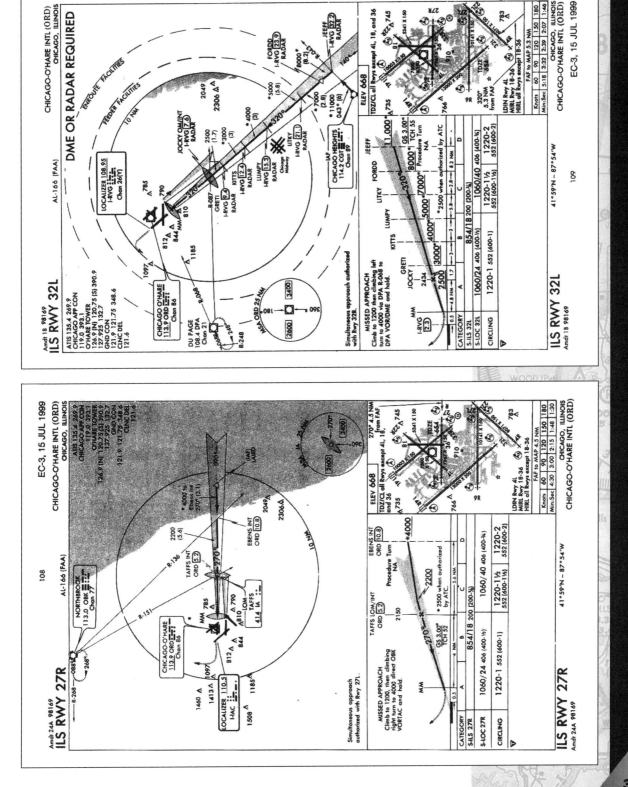

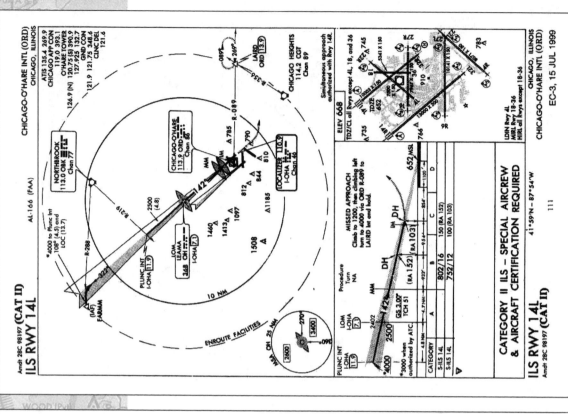

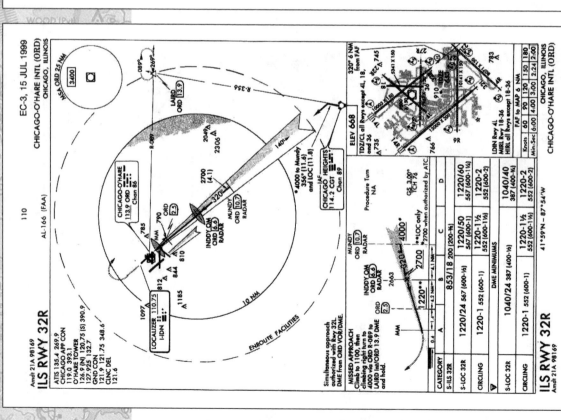

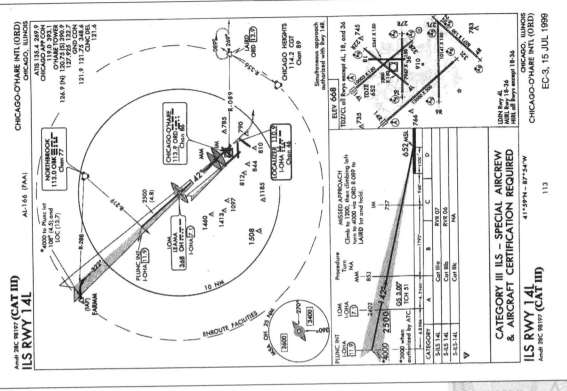

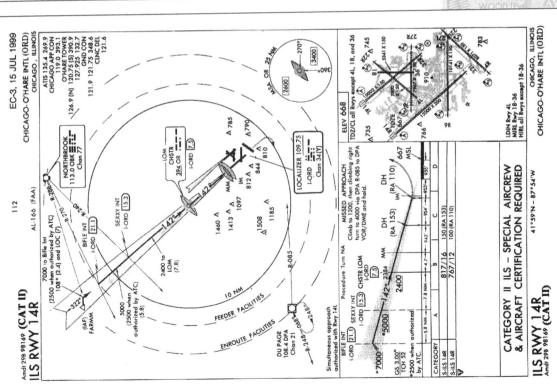

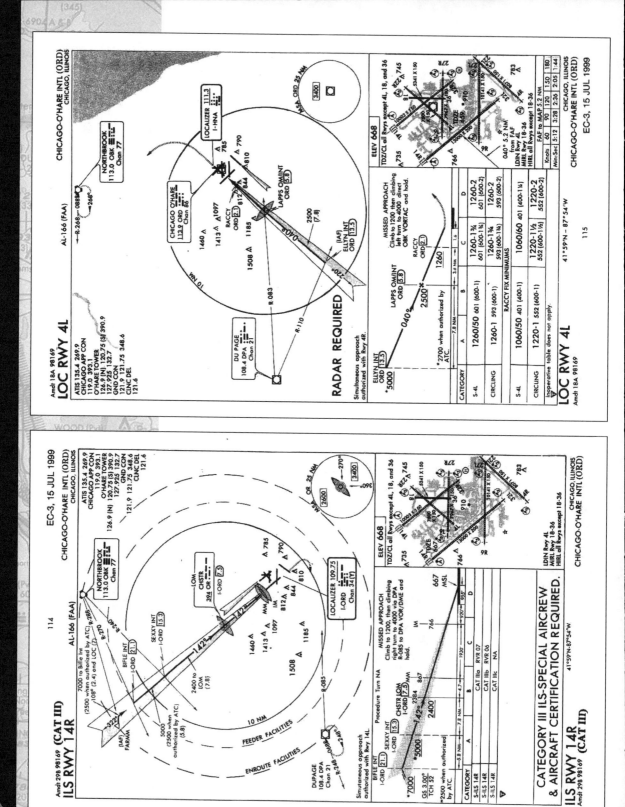

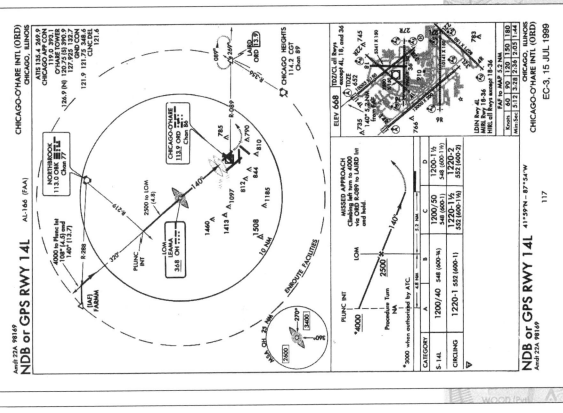

Amdt 22A 98169

ATIS 135.4 269.9
CHICAGO APP CON
119.0 393.1
O'HARE TOWER
126.9 (N) 120.75 (S) 390.9
127.925 132.7
GND CON
121.9 121.75 348.6
CLNC DEL
121.6

NORTHBROOK
113.0 OBK Chan 77

CHICAGO-O'HARE
113.9 ORD Chan 86

LOM
LEAMA
368 OH · ─ ─

LAIRD
ORD [13.9]

CHICAGO HEIGHTS
114.2 CGT
Chan 89

4000 to Plunc Int
108° (4.5) and
140° (13.7)

2500 to LOM
(4.8)

[IAF]
FARMM

ENROUTE FACILITIES

MISSED APPROACH
Climbing left turn to 4000
via ORD R-089 to LAIRD Int
and hold.

PLUNC INT
*4000
*3000 when authorized by ATC.

Procedure Turn
NA

LOM
2500

CATEGORY	A	B	C	D
S-14L	1200/40 548 (600-¾)		1200-1½ 548 (600-1½)	1200-1½ 548 (600-1½)
CIRCLING	1220-1 552 (600-1)		1220-1½ 552 (600-1½)	1220-2 552 (600-2)

ELEV 668 | TDZ/CL all Rwys except 4L, 18, and 36

LDIN Rwy 4L
MIRL Rwy 18-36
HIRL all Rwys except 18-36

	FAF to MAP 5.2 NM				
Knots	60	90	120	150	180
Min:Sec	5:12	3:28	2:36	2:05	1:44

CHICAGO, ILLINOIS
41°59'N – 87°54'W

NDB or GPS RWY 14L
Amdt 22A 98169

CHICAGO-O'HARE INTL (ORD)
EC-3, 15 JUL 1999

117

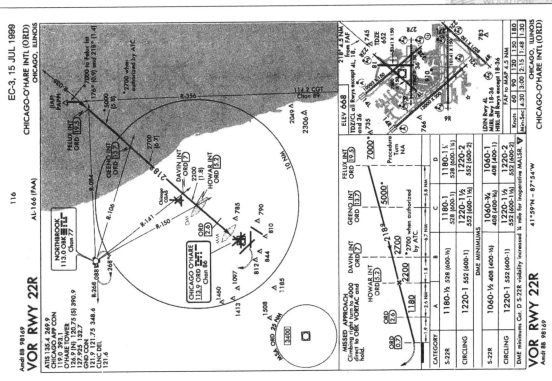

EC-3, 15 JUL 1999

116

Amdt 8B 98169

ATIS 135.4 269.9
CHICAGO APP CON
119.0 393.1
O'HARE TOWER
126.9 (N) 120.75 (S) 390.9
127.925 132.7
GND CON
121.9 121.75 348.6
CLNC DEL
121.6

NORTHBROOK
113.0 OBK Chan 77

CHICAGO O'HARE
113.9 ORD Chan 86

CHICAGO HEIGHTS
114.2 CGT
Chan 89

[IAF]
PAPPI

FELUX INT
ORD [19.3]

GEENO INT
ORD [13.7]

DAVIN INT
ORD [7]

HOWAR INT
ORD [5.2]

ORD [2.6]

7000 to Felux Int
176° (0.9) and 218° (1.4)

*2700 when authorized by ATC.

*5000
(5.8)

2700
(6.7)

MISSED APPROACH
Climbing right turn to 4000
direct to OBK VORTAC and
hold.

FELUX INT
ORD [19.3]
7000*

Procedure
Turn
NA

GEENO INT
ORD [13.7]
5000*

DAVIN INT
ORD [7]
2700

HOWAR INT
ORD [5.2]
2200

ORD [2.6]
1180

ORD [0.7]

CATEGORY	A	B	C	D
S-22R	1180-½ 528 (600-½)		1180-1 528 (600-1)	1180-1¼ 528 (600-1¼)
CIRCLING	1220-1 552 (600-1)		1220-1½ 552 (600-1½)	1220-2 552 (600-2)

DME MINIMUMS

	A	B	C	D
S-22R	1060-½ 408 (400-½)		1060-¾ 408 (400-¾)	1060-1 408 (400-1)
CIRCLING	1220-1 552 (600-1)		1220-1½ 552 (600-1½)	1220-2 552 (600-2)

DME minimums Cat. D S-22R visibility increased ¼ mile for inoperative MALSR.

ELEV 668 | TDZ/CL all Rwys except 4L, 18,
and 36

LDIN Rwy 4L
MIRL Rwy 18-36
HIRL all Rwys except 18-36

218° 4.5 NM
from FAF

	FAF to MAP 4.5 NM				
Knots	60	90	120	150	180
Min:Sec	4:30	3:00	2:15	1:48	1:30

CHICAGO, ILLINOIS
41°59'N – 87°54'W

VOR RWY 22R
Amdt 8B 98169

CHICAGO-O'HARE INTL (ORD)

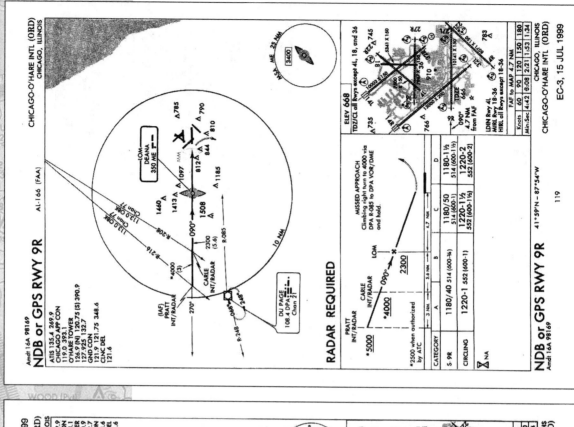

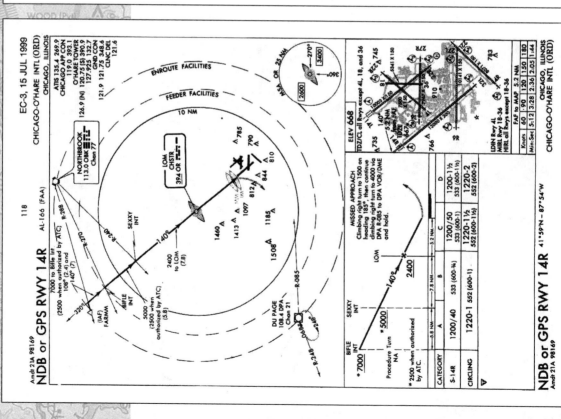

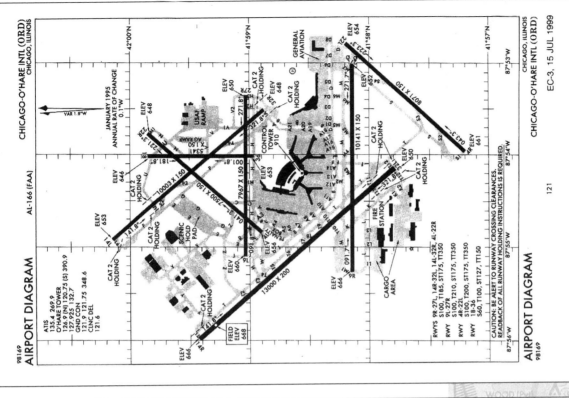

AIRPORT DIAGRAM

CHICAGO-O'HARE INTL (ORD)
CHICAGO, ILLINOIS

AL-166 (FAA)

98169

ATIS
135.4 269.9
O'HARE TOWER
126.9 (N) 120.75 (S) 390.9
GND CON
127.925 132.7
121.9 121.75 348.6
CLNC DEL
121.6

FIELD ELEV 668

CONTROL TOWER 910

USAF RAMP

GENERAL AVIATION

FIRE STATION

CARGO AREA

RWYS 9R-27L, 14R-32L, 14L-32R, 4L-22R
RWY 9R-27R
S100, T185, ST175, TT350
RWY 4R-22L
S100, T210, ST175, TT350
RWY 18-36
S100, T200, ST175, TT350
S60, T100, ST127, TT150

CAUTION: BE ALERT TO RUNWAY CROSSING CLEARANCES.
READBACK OF ALL RUNWAY HOLDING INSTRUCTIONS IS REQUIRED.

AIRPORT DIAGRAM
98169

CHICAGO, ILLINOIS
EC-3, 15 JUL 1999
CHICAGO-O'HARE INTL (ORD)

121

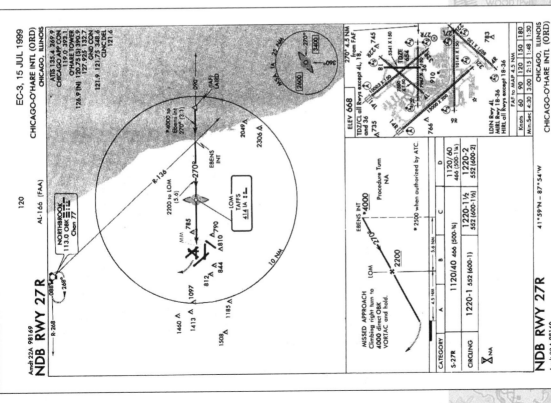

Amdt 22A 98169
NDB RWY 27R

120

AL-166 (FAA)

EC-3, 15 JUL 1999
CHICAGO-O'HARE INTL (ORD)
CHICAGO, ILLINOIS

ATIS 135.4 269.9
CHICAGO APP CON
119.0 393.1
O'HARE TOWER
126.9 (N) 120.75 (S) 390.9
GND CON 127.925 132.7
121.9 121.75 348.6
CLNC DEL 121.6

NORTHBROOK
113.0 OBK Chan 77

LOM TAFFS

ELEV 668

TDZ/CL all Rwys except 4L, 18, and 36
HIRL Rwy 18-36
HIRL all Rwys except 18-36

LDIN Rwy 4L

270° to 4.5 NM from FAF

MISSED APPROACH
Climbing right turn to 4000 direct OBK VORTAC and hold.

CATEGORY	A	B	C	D
S-27R	1120/40 466 (500-¾)			1120/60 466 (500-1¼)
CIRCLING	1220-1 552 (600-1)	1220-1½ 552 (600-1½)	1220-2 552 (600-2)	

NA

Procedure Turn NA
*2500 when authorized by ATC.

EBENS INT 4000
2200
4.5 NM
5.6 NM

FAF-to-MAP 4.5 NM

Knots	60	90	120	150	180
Min:Sec	4:30	3:00	2:15	1:48	1:30

NDB RWY 27R
Amdt 22 A 98169

41°59'N – 87°54'W

CHICAGO, ILLINOIS
CHICAGO-O'HARE INTL (ORD)

343

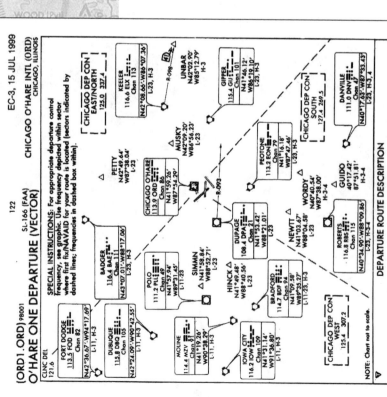

Keyboard
Command
Reference

Appendix C

*K*eyboard commands can be accessed from the kneeboard, but many sim'ers feel it's less intrusive (and more realistic) to have such documents lying in front of them. For your convenience, here are Flight Simulator 2000's default keyboard commands. They're categorized into Simulator Commands, Control Surface Commands, Engine Commands, General Aircraft Commands, Light Commands, Radio Commands, Autopilot Commands, Instrument Commands, View Commands, Slew Commands, and Multiplayer Commands.

▶ *Note*

Make sure Num Lock is OFF before using numpad commands.

SIMULATOR COMMANDS	KEYSTROKE
Pause	P
Sound on/off	Q
Reset current flight	CTRL+ ; (Semicolon)
Save flight	; (Semicolon)
Exit Flight Simulator	CTRL+C
Exit Flight Simulator immediately	CTRL+BREAK
Stop video (replay or recording)	ESC
Stop analysis	\ (Backslash)
Send ATC text message	Numpad + (Plus Sign)
Add text to video	, (Comma)
Repeat last message (lessons/adv.)	CTRL+M
End lesson/adventure	ESC or CTRL+U
Reset lesson/adventure	CTRL+R
Closed captioning on (lessons /adv.)	CTRL+Y
Closed captioning off (lessons/adv.)	CTRL+W
Mouse-as-Yoke mode on/off	CTRL+Numpad DEL
Joystick on/off	K
Select item 1	1
Select item 2	2
Select item 3	3
Select item 4	4
Select time compression	R
Increase selection	= (Equals Sign)
Increase selection slightly	SHIFT+ = (Equals Sign)
Decrease selection slightly	SHIFT+ - (Hyphen)
Decrease selection	- (Hyphen)

CONTROL SURFACE COMMANDS	KEYSTROKE
Bank left (ailerons)	Numpad 4
Bank right (ailerons)	Numpad 6
Aileron trim left	CTRL+Numpad 4
Aileron trim right	CTRL+Numpad 6
Yaw left (rudder)	Numpad 0
Yaw right (rudder)	Numpad ENTER
Center ailerons and rudder	Numpad 5
Pitch down (elevator)	Numpad 8
Pitch up (elevator)	Numpad 2
Elevator trim up	Numpad 1
Elevator trim down	Numpad 7
Retract flaps fully	F5
Retract flaps (in increments)	F6
Extend flaps (in increments)	F7
Extend flaps fully	F8
Extend/Retract spoilers/airbrakes	/ (Forward Slash)
Arm auto-spoilers	SHIFT+/ (Forward Slash)

ENGINE COMMANDS	KEYSTROKE
Engine auto start	CTRL+E
Cut throttle	F1
Decrease throttle	F2 or Numpad 3
Increase throttle	F3 or Numpad 9
Full throttle	F4
Reheat/Afterburner on/off	SHIFT+F4
Arm auto-throttle	SHIFT+R
Engage takeoff/go-around (TOGA) mode	CTRL+SHIFT+R
Set prop RPM to low	CTRL+F1
Decrease prop RPM	CTRL+F2
Increase prop RPM	CTRL+F3
Set prop RPM to high	CTRL+F4
Set mixture to idle cutoff	CTRL+SHIFT+F1
Lean mixture	CTRL+SHIFT+F2
Enrich mixture	CTRL+SHIFT+F3

continued on next page

ENGINE COMMANDS	KEYSTROKE
Set mixture to rich	CTRL+SHIFT+F4
Carb heat/De-ice on/off	H
Select engine	E
Select magnetos	M
Select jet starter	J
Increase selection	= (Equals Sign)
Increase selection slightly	SHIFT+ = (Equals Sign)
Decrease selection slightly	SHIFT+ - (Hyphen)
Decrease selection	- (Hyphen)

GENERAL AIRCRAFT COMMANDS	KEYSTROKE
Set parking brake	CTRL+ . (Period)
Apply/Release brakes	. (Period)
Apply left brakes	F11
Apply right brakes	F12
Landing gear up/down	G
Manually pump landing gear	CTRL+G
Fully lower Concorde nose/visor	F8
Lower Concorde nose/visor (steps)	F7
Raise Concorde nose/visor (steps)	F6
Fully raise Concorde nose/visor	F5
Master battery/alternator switches on/off	SHIFT+M
Smoke system on/off	I

LIGHT COMMANDS	KEYSTROKES
All lights on/off	L
Strobe lights on/off	O
Panel lights on/off	SHIFT+L
Landing lights on/off	CTRL+L

RADIO COMMANDS	KEYSTROKE
VOR1 ident on/off	CTRL+1
VOR2 ident on/off	CTRL+2
DME1 ident on/off	CTRL+3
DME2 ident on/off	CTRL+4
ADF ident on/off	CTRL+5
Select transponder	T
Select ADF	A
Select DME	F
Select COM radio	C
Select OBS	V
Select NAV radio	N
Increase selection	= (Equal Sign)
Increase selection slightly	SHIFT+ = (Equal Sign)
Decrease selection slightly	SHIFT+ - (Hyphen)
Decrease selection	- (Hyphen)

AUTOPILOT COMMANDS	KEYSTROKE
Autopilot master switch on/off	Z
Attitude hold on/off	CTRL+T
Localizer hold on/off	CTRL+O
Approach mode on/off	CTRL+A
Heading hold on/off	CTRL+H
Altitude hold on/off	CTRL+Z
Wing leveler on/off	CTRL+V
Back course mode on/off	CTRL+B
NAV1 hold on/off	CTRL+N
Airspeed hold on/off	CTRL+R
Mach hold on/off	CTRL+M
Yaw damper on/off	CTRL+D

INSTRUMENT COMMANDS	KEYSTROKE
Reset directional gyro	D
Reset altimeter	B
Pitot heat on/off	SHIFT+H
Select EGT	U
Increase selection	= (Equal Sign)
Increase selection slightly	SHIFT+ = (Equal Sign)
Decrease selection slightly	SHIFT+ - (Hyphen)
Decrease selection	- (Hyphen)

VIEW COMMANDS	KEYSTROKE
Full screen mode (no menus or taskbar)	ALT+ENTER
Display menus (in full screen mode)	ALT
Maximize view	W
Cycle views (cockpit, tower, track, spot)	S
Cycle views backwards	SHIFT+S
Display/Hide additional panel windows (radios, engine controls, GPS, etc.)	SHIFT+1 through 9
Display/Hide kneeboard	F10
Cycle coordinates/frame rate	SHIFT+Z
Create new view window	[(Left Bracket)
Create new top-down view window	SHIFT+] (Right Bracket)
Close view window	] (Right Bracket)
Bring window to front	' (Apostrophe)
Zoom in	= (Equal Sign)
Zoom out	- (Hyphen)
Set zoom to 1x	BACKSPACE
Instrument panels on/off	SHIFT+[(Left Bracket)
Switch to top-down view	CTRL+S
Switch to next view	CTRL+TAB
Switch to previous view	CTRL+SHIFT+TAB
Select view direction	Numpad / (Forward Slash)
Look ahead	SHIFT+Numpad 8
Look ahead/right	SHIFT+Numpad 9
Look right	SHIFT+Numpad 6
Look back/right	SHIFT+Numpad 3

VIEW COMMANDS	KEYSTROKE
Look back	SHIFT+Numpad 2
Look back/left	SHIFT+Numpad 1
Look left	SHIFT+Numpad 4
Look ahead/left	SHIFT+Numpad 7
Look up	SHIFT+Numpad 5
Look ahead/up	CTRL+Numpad 8
Look ahead/right/up	CTRL+Numpad 9
Look back/right/up	CTRL+Numpad 3
Look back/up	CTRL+Numpad 2
Look back/left/up	CTRL+Numpad 1
Look ahead/left/up	CTRL+Numpad 7
Look down	CTRL+Numpad 5
Pan view left	CTRL+SHIFT+ BACKSPACE
Pan view right	CTRL+SHIFT+ENTER
Pan view up	SHIFT+BACKSPACE
Pan view down	SHIFT+ENTER
Pan view reset	CTRL+Spacebar

▶ *Note*

Slewing repositions your aircraft without flying.

SLEW COMMANDS	KEYSTROKE
Slew mode on/off	Y
Set heading north/attitude straight-and-level	Spacebar
Toggle coordinates/frame rate	SHIFT+Z
Move forward	Numpad 8
Move backward	Numpad 2
Move left	Numpad 4
Move right	Numpad 6
Freeze horizontal movement	Numpad 5
Move up slowly	Q
Move up quickly	F4
Move down slowly	A
Move down quickly	F1
Freeze vertical movement	F2
Rotate left	Numpad 1

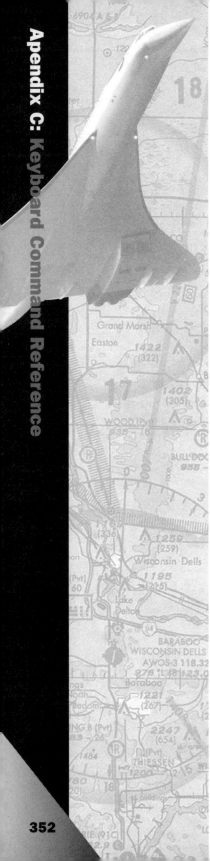

SLEW COMMANDS	KEYSTROKE
Rotate right	Numpad 3
Freeze rotation	Numpad 5
Move nose up	F3 or 9
Move nose up quickly	F5
Move nose down	F7
Move nose down quickly	F8
Freeze pitch	F6
Bank left	Numpad 7
Bank right	Numpad 9
Freeze banking	Numpad 5
Pan view up	SHIFT+BACKSPACE
Pan view down	SHIFT+ENTER
Pan view left	CTRL+SHIFT+BACKSPACE
Pan view right	CTRL+SHIFT+ENTER

MULTIPLAYER COMMANDS	KEYSTROKE
Track mode on/off	CTRL+SHIFT+D
Cycle through other players	CTRL+SHIFT+T
Follow other player	CTRL+SHIFT+F
Switch to observer mode	CTRL+SHIFT+O
Chat window on/off	CTRL+ENTER
Switch focus to chat window	ENTER